JOE BOB GOES
TO THE
DRIVE-IN

How Sick Is
Your Local Newspaper?

Do you live in a wholesome American community?
Can the people in your community read?
Can they read a newspaper?
If the answer to any of the above is yes, you may never have heard of
"Joe Bob Goes to the Drive-In," the only newspaper column ever to be

• banned in Fort Smith, Arkansas; Dallas, Texas; Cleveland, Ohio;
and Raleigh, North Carolina

• picketed by feminists in San Francisco

• condemned from the pulpit in Tyler, Texas

• endorsed by *Hustler* magazine

• excluded from the finest homes in America and laughed at by
millions

So what have you missed? You missed a brilliant review of *Bloodsucking
Freaks,* an analysis of *Gas Pump Girls* and *Invasion of the Blood Farm-
ers* that could stop your heart, and the official breast count in *I Spit on
Your Grave.*

Joe Bob Briggs is the world's only drive-in movie columnist. Accept no
substitutes.

JOE BOB GOES TO THE DRIVE-IN

Joe Bob Briggs

Introduction by Stephen King

Delacorte Press/New York

A DELACORTE TRADE PAPERBACK
Published by
Delacorte Press
1 Dag Hammarskjold Plaza
New York, New York 10017

Manufactured in the United States of America

First printing
Library of Congress Cataloging in Publication Data

Briggs, Joe Bob.
   Joe Bob goes to the drive-in.

   1. Drive-in theaters—Anecdotes, facetiae, satire, etc. 2. Moving-pictures—Anecdotes, facetiae, satire, etc. I. Title.
PN6231.D73B7   1986   791.43'0207   85-20654
ISBN 0-385-29442-5 (pbk.)

JOE BOB GOES
TO THE
DRIVE-IN

This Guy Is *Really* Scary!

By Stephen King

anned in Boston: You've heard of that one, right? But banned in *Dallas?* Dallas, *Texas?* You know, down there where they call that black stuff you put in your car awl, like the carpenter's tool? Where they drink Lone Star beer and eat chili so hot it comes with its own fire extinguisher (only what you say down there is *far* extinguisher)? Where men are still men and women aren't? Banned in *Dallas?*

Say *what,* boy?

Only one time it's been done, so far as I know. Only one man who could do it. You are holding that man's first book in your hand; it was a little too much Powder River for even Big D to handle, and what that means is we must be talking the one and only Joe Bob Briggs, sometime squire of the memorable and mammacious Cherry Dilday, frequent driver of the only Toronado in the United States that runs on beer-cooled suspension, and drive-in movie critic to those millions whose thoughts turn to window speakers, slowly burning bug coils, sleazy films, and torrid backseat embraces as soon as the temperature warms up past, say, fifty degrees or so.

In his hotly controversial career, Joe Bob himself is the only one who has remained constantly cool and above the fray, rating pictures according to kung fu, breast count, how many heads roll, and other criteria that really matter to the hardcore drive-in patrons across the United States. The "high sheriffs" (as he calls the newspaper editors, syndicate managers, and pressure groups that have frequently tried to slip a muzzle over his yapping jaw) finally tarred him, feathered him, and ran him out of Dallas on a word processor, but not before he had gotten in some pretty good licks at Steven Spielberg ("indoor bullstuff," Joe Bob sniffed at *E.T.),* the anti-drunk-driving movement (it was Joe Bob who started an organization called D.A.M.M.—Drunks Against Mad Mothers), the Republican Convention in Dallas (not a drive-in movie, but almost as good), and a hundred others. In his time, Joe Bob Briggs has turned a fair number of sacred cows into cheeseburgers.

Is he gone? From the Dallas *Times-Herald,* yes. From a good many other papers, no . . . and then, of course, there is this book, in which you can sample Joe Bob's unique brand of critique-by-flamethrower for yourself. I think that Jonathan Swift, the Irish essayist and satirist who once suggested that the English could take care of the Irish problem once and for all by developing both a taste and some really good recipes for cooking Irish babies, would have liked Joe Bob's work. As with Joe Bob, the high sheriffs tried to muzzle Swift . . . not to mention George Orwell, Ambrose Bierce, Oscar Wilde, Robert Crumb, and a half a hundred other literary gadflies. Bad satirists are left alone; it only hurts when it's good. And when the rowel bites deep, the horse frequently bucks. When that happens sometimes even the most experienced riders are thrown. But tough guys rarely stay in the dirt for long, and when it comes to satire, that is just as well for all of us; if there wasn't someone around to yell "The emperor has no clothes on!" from time to time, Sears Roebuck would be selling birthday suits . . . and what's more, folks would be buying them. It might be good for business, but it would be bad for our souls.

Well, that's enough indoor bullstuff from this kid. You women step into your frillies, your shortest skirt, your tightest tank top, and your penny loafers; you

guys, throw a case of beer in the trunk and grab your Case hat out of the closet. None of that wearing it backward either—that's strictly for wimpolas. I think Joe Bob just pulled up out front; I can hear the big 442 rumbling under the dented hood of that Toronado with the Texas plates. I have never exactly seen the guy's face, but I can see his hands right now, big ones with a lot of black hair growing between the knuckles, one caressing the head of that Hearst shifter and the other caressing the peach-smooth thigh of the delicious Ms. Dilday. By God! I think it's time to go to the drive-in! Heads are going to roll, kung is gonna fu, and Joe Bob is gonna strut his stuff. This is pretty fine stuff, friends and neighbors; we're talking dusk to dawn here; we're talking all-American here; most of all, we're talking some of the funniest, most perceptive film and social criticism that you will ever read. If you know Joe Bob, you know what I mean. If you don't, brothers and sisters, I envy you the experience you're about to have.

Big Steve King says check it out. ∎

How Joe Bob Briggs Became a Film Critic, or, As He Said, "What?"

By John Bloom

Joe Bob Briggs once told me that he had seen 6,800 drive-in movies, but I told him that was impossible because nobody nineteen years old could possibly have seen 6,800 drive-in movies, but Joe Bob said, no, I was wrong, because he was counting triple features. Then Joe Bob launched into this long story about how once he'd driven up to Chillicothe, Oklahoma, just to go to this one drive-in where they start at dusk and show twelve movies every night. And I said there aren't enough hours in the nighttime to see twelve movies in Chillicothe, Oklahoma, in one night, and Joe Bob said, "You han't seen these movies."

Joe Bob Briggs is the kind of guy who can make "haven't" into a one-syllable word, but except for that, I like him fine. He has seen more drive-in movies than anyone in history, most of them from the comfort of his 68 baby-blue Dodge Dart, which actually he didn't buy until 76, because before that he had a Packard. Joe Bob can't remember what year the Packard was, because of that night in Texarkana at the Ark-La-Tex Twin when a dough-head in a Barracuda crunched his rear door and scared Dede Wilks half out of her halter top. (I forgot to tell you that Dede Wilks was in the backseat. Dede was Joe Bob's third wife, or at least he says she was, but I think Joe Bob has forgotten a couple before her. That's why I seriously doubt that Joe Bob is really nineteen years old. I know this because one night Joe Bob was trying to impress me with a description of his latest girlfriend, and he dropped a reference to Mamie Van Doren that I can't repeat here.)

Anyway, I got to know Joe Bob Briggs one night at the Century in Grand Prairie when Joe Bob went up to the man behind the concession stand and started complaining because Joe Bob had asked for a Tub o' Corn and he'd gotten all the way back to the car before he realized he had a Barrel o' Corn with Butter. (Joe Bob never gets butter because he says it messes up his upholstery.) I remember this one particular evening because we were in the middle of an all-night Bela Lugosi marathon and I was anxious to get back for *Mother Riley Meets the Vampire*. So to make a long story short, I said, "Here, mine's unbuttered. Take it." And Joe Bob thought that was about the nicest thing anyone ever said to him.

For the rest of that night, Joe Bob and I sat in the lawn chair section, and Joe Bob told me all the scenes of *Zombies on Broadway* before they happened. (May Ellen Masters didn't care much for Joe Bob after that, though, and I can't really blame her, since she waited four hours for a Tub o' Corn and finally got so mad that she drove off in Joe Bob's car with the speaker still hanging on the window. I always wondered what happens when you do that. The speaker was fine. But May Ellen ripped the plate glass right out of the frame, and ever since then Joe Bob has had to jab the window roller with an ice pick before it will come loose and work right. I forget what happened to May Ellen.)

So after that I started going to the drive-in with Joe Bob Briggs on a more or less regular basis. I say "more or less" because I think May Ellen went with him one time after that, but Joe Bob was so mad about the plate glass that he took her to see *Kung-Fu Waitresses*, which was rated X and had a lot of breather scenes, and May Ellen's father was a preacher. That's the kind of guy Joe Bob is.

One night after Joe Bob got rid of May Ellen, I said, "Joe Bob, you need to get a job."

Joe Bob didn't say anything because he was prying off his radiator cap with a Boy Scout knife.

"Joe Bob, I mean it," I said. "You're the world's foremost authority on drive-in movies and what good has it done you? All you've got to show for your life is a mouth full of those little slivers that get between your teeth and gum when you eat popcorn."

Joe Bob raised up from his radiator. "I know how to get those out of your mouth," he said.

"That's what I mean. Joe Bob, you know *everything.*"

Joe Bob lifted his Caterpillar Tractor cap, ran his hand through his hair, and bent back over the engine so he could spit into the air filter.

"I've got the answer, Joe Bob," I persisted. "I know the one job you're qualified for."

Joe Bob started banging on the carburetor with the wrong end of a Phillips screwdriver, so I had to yell over the commotion.

"YOU'RE A FILM CRITIC!"

For a long time Joe Bob didn't answer. Finally he straightened up and said, "I don't know from film but I know movies. I don't know from critic but I know what I like."

"Precisely," I said. "You are the avatar of popular culture, the personification of the Drive-In Everyman, a connoisseur and a prince of a fellow. You must write. You must transform the mass consciousness into a critical art form."

Joe Bob said, "What?"

So I explained it to him again, and he gave me his characteristic expression of perplexed contentment. "Think about it," I said.

Joe Bob never said yes or no after that, and I guess I would have forgotten about him altogether—until last week something extraordinary happened. I came to work one day and there on my desk was Joe Bob's first critical essay; it had obviously been left sometime during the night. (Joe Bob rarely stirs during daylight hours, which is why he always gets to Bill King's Brake-O at 6:05.) I read the manuscript with growing amazement. All my assumptions were correct. Joe Bob not only had style; he had the authentic and noble honesty of the American midwestern yeoman. It took me awhile to find Joe Bob again, but a few nights later I finally saw him at the Astro on Loop 12, and without even saying hello, he said, "What was that you said again about being a critical?"

I hired Joe Bob on the spot, as the first *Times Herald* Drive-In Movie Critic. I told him he was going to be as famous as Vincent Canby or Pauline Kael or John Simon.

Joe Bob said, "What?"

I told Joe Bob that he would start reviewing movies on Friday, January 15, 1982. Joe Bob said okay. ∎

Why God Created Drive-Ins

When God created the drive-in, back in 1932, He had to go all the way to Jersey to find a guy who would build the altar. That's how sick this country was in those days. In fact, the Big Guy was a little p.o.ed. So you know what His Largeship did? Do you?

He said, "Let there be Camden, New Jersey."

And Camden, New Jersey, was formed out of the void.

And then He said, "Let there be a bunch of sleazy guys hanging around Camden, New Jersey, trying to hustle up enough jack so they can move to Atlantic City."

And suddenly, a prophet was born. Richard Hollingshead Jr., Little Dicky Hollingshead, the King of Industrial Solvents and Cleaning Liquids for all of southwestern New Jersey. They called him Mr. Clean, and the Lord told him it was time to vacuum America with all the Hoovers he could muster.

Course, the Prophet Dicky was already famous throughout a two-square-block area of Camden. There's where he put up his deluxe gas station, with palm trees all around the pumps that he had to ship up from Lauderdale, and it was *right there,* while Dicky was pumping one day, that he got his first vision. He looked at all the cars lined up, waiting to get hosed, and he said to hisself, "Why can't people have some form of entertainment while waiting to be served?"

(I might need to point out right here I'm not making any of this bullstuff up. Dicky was one of those guys that talked to hisself in quotation marks. The Lord might work in mysterious ways, but Little Dicky wrote all his part of it down before he died.)

Anyhow, Dicky puts up a screen on his driveway and starts throwing flicks up there for the people waiting in line.

El Bombola. Wrongo. No way, José. That idea lasted about five minutes.

Then Dicky tried it again. And in 1932, the universe as we know it was changed forever.

You probly already know what happened next.

Little Dicky applied for the most famous patent in history. United States Patent No. 1,909,537: "The Park-In Theatre."

At this point God said something to Dicky like "I said *drive-in,* you ignorant turkey. Not *park-in.* Drive-in."

So when Little Dicky and his partner, Willis Warren Smith the insurance broker, opened for binness on Admiral Wilson Boulevard in 1933, they called it the "Drive-In Theatre." A quarter a person, a quarter a car, or a buck a carload, whichever's cheaper. Little Dicky rigged up a canvas screen on the roof of his machine-parts shop, bulldozed his gravel lot into semicircles that could hold 400 cars, set up a teensy-weensy little projector at the back, and bought him the biggest goldurn speakers he could find in the greater Camden metropolitan area. The man had taste too. The first drive-in flick in the history of the world was *Wife Beware.* It was about how people get nookie on the side. If you rolled down your windows and listened real hard, it sounded approximately like this:

"Hmmmmmmmmmmmm."

Now, I wanna make one thing perfectly clear. The drive-in movie was the first drive-in *anything.* You can keep your wimpola drive-in Burger Kings, your drive-in Fotomats, your drive-in Seven-Elevens, your drive-in banks. When I say drive-in, I'm talking one thing and one thing only. I'm talking a place where people can go watch flicks in their natural state, like God intended, in the privacy of their own personal automobiles.

Okay, so far ever schoolboy in America knows the story I been telling. Christopher Columbus, George Washington, Abraham

Lincoln, and Little Dicky Hollingshead. But let's see just how good your drive-in IQ is. Listen up now.

What was the *second* drive-in in the United States?

If you said the one on Pico Boulevard in El Lay, built in 1934, you are correcto-matic. And it could hold up to five hundred cars. Then Dicky and Willis got *really* busy, and they started franchising these suckers like Bic lighters. They put one up in Weymouth, Massachusetts, then in Burbank, Santa Ana, San Bernardino, and Union City, New Jersey. Then, course, you probly know what's coming. God looked down on His work and He said, "You little jerk, you thought you could keep everything for your ownself, didn't you?"

And Little Dicky said, "Who you talking to?"

And God instructed the Supreme Court to declare Dicky Hollingshead's drive-in patent null and void. They said, what the hey, you can't slap a patent on a drive-in any more than you can take out a patent on blowing your nose. Ever American citizen is *born* with the right to open up a drive-in. And in 1945, the year when there were exactly one hundred drive-ins on the face of the known globe, the drive-in was snatched out of Dicky's greedy little paws and handed over to the rest of the nation.

Okay, Dicky, that's it for you. You're history. I'm tired of writing down your name. Get the heck out of this story.

After World War Numero Two-o, people started throwing up drive-ins like they were Babtist churches. And the place that built more of 'em than anywhere else was Texas. Texas took the lead in 1948, when we had seventy-nine drive-ins spread out from Pecos to Texarkana, and it's been that way ever since. Texas has got more drive-ins than any country in the world, with California and Ohio right behind, and North Carolina and Florida right behind them, and Jersey knocking all theirs down but still pretty high up there, and Colorado and Arizona hanging in there, and New Mexico the only state in the union that's got more drive-ins than Negroes.

But back in the forties, when we were just getting started, we had *problemas*.

Problem numero uno: You couldn't hear the dang movie. Now, this never has bothered me personally, but some people were upset when they couldn't hear the words the actors were saying. So we solved this one right away, when the miniature in-car speaker and speaker-pole combo was invented in 1946. So now you could hear what they were saying even when your windows were rolled up. But it still took till 1948 to put that little knob on there, so you could turn it off when you *didn't* want to hear what the heck they were saying.

Problem numero two-o: The big Hollywood studios hated the drive-ins and wouldn't let em have any movies until they were older than horse manure. You may recall there was a reason for this. Hollywood went Communist around this time, and Senator Joe McCarthy had to clean things up out there, and as you well know, anywhere there's Commies they go after the drive-ins before anything else. You realize there's not a single drive-in in Communist Russia? See what I mean?

Course, there was another reason they wouldn't give us any decent flicks at the drive-in. It's cause the big studios thought the drive-ins were owned by a bunch of farmers and barbers and feed-store cowboys that didn't know diddly about the movie binness. You know why they thought this?

Cause the drive-ins were owned by a bunch of farmers and barbers and feed-store cowboys that didn't know diddly about the movie binness.

Problem numero three-o: A lot of the people that went to the drive-in were dumber than dirt. Actually, this problem solved the *other* problem, cause these turkeys didn't have any idea they were watching *last year's* movie.

We licked this one too, though, along about 1949, when we finally threatened to beat the bejabbers out of Warner Brothers if they didn't give us a decent movie to premiere at the drive-in. So they held the world premiere of *Colorado Territory,* with Joel McCrea and Virginia Mayo, at a drive-in in Denver, and that was the biggest event in drive-in history up till 1969, when we packed ten thousand raving maniacs into the Gemini Drive-In in Dallas for the world premiere of *True Grit,* and John Wayne, the Duke himself, stood up on top of the concession stand and shot off his gun. It brings a tear to my eye, just thinking about it. I was in the crowd that night. I guess we all were. You didn't do the sixties unless you saw the Duke that night, in his greatest moment, *at the drive-in.*

Problem numero four-o: The drive-in owners of America were these intellectual types that kept giving interviews in the newspaper about how their places were *not* "passion pits." *Last year* they were passion pits, but this year they got all the illegal nookie cleaned up, and so they're "family entertainment centers." I don't know how long this bullstuff went on, but here's a big stupid statistic for you:

In the fifties, half of all drive-in moviegoers went to the movie in their pajamas.

Let's face it, these people were human fog machines.

Once the drive-in got going, there wasn't hardly nothing you could do to stop it. Pretty soon the Rhodes scholars that owned drive-ins were giving away bottle warmers for Mama, putting in playgrounds so the little monsters would get all tuckered out by the time the flick started, offering free auto-mechanic service during the movie, setting up sit-down lounges, pony rides, hotdog sellers that walked up and down the rows, portable in-car heaters, laundromats, those little lights that fry the heads off bugs when they fly into em, picnic areas, dance floors, shuffleboard courts, barbecue pits, motorized bingo games (you played by the numbers on your speedometer), DDT foggings to kill all the skeeters and give everbody permanent lung cancer, fireworks, live animal acts, trapeze artists, swimming pools, midget-car racing, midget racing, dancing midgets, diaper rooms, fishing ponds, driving ranges, miniature railroads, wading pools, Punch and Judy theaters, and electic snack carts. To name just a few. In South Carolina they had these kids that'd do grocery shopping for you while you were at the drive-in. In Texas, in the winter, they'd give you a gallon of gas to keep your motor running during the movie. And at the Starlite Drive-In, on Federal Highway 20 outside Chicago, home of drive-in showman Stanford Kohlberg, the genius who offered the first drive-in charge card ("The Starlite Happiness Book"), they spent $20,000 one night for bands, singers, dancers, acrobats, a first-run triple feature—and when it rained that night, Stanford said, "Hell, I'm gonna do it anyhow," and a *thousand* non-Communist drive-in lovers showed up that night to prove what this country is made of.

That's the kind of people we are. We *never* come in out of the rain.

There is *nothing,* absolutely nothing, that can stop a dedicated drive-in-goer from going to the drive-in. Rain? Piece of cake. What are your durn wipers for?

Snow? So there's a few specks on Jayne Mansfield's cheekbones. Sleet? Turn up the sound. In fact, about the only thing that can *almost* close down a drive-in is heavy ground fog, but there's a new thingamajig they can put on the projector that'll cut through that gunk like Bruce Lee's foot through Velveeta cheese. It's the greatest drive-in invention since the owner of the San Pedro Twin in San Antonio devised the "breakaway post" for speakers. Instead of ripping that sucker off, as soon as you start driving away, the whole thing just springs right out of the ground. You get home, find this pole hanging off your car, and just drop it in any mailbox.

I guess we hit our peak around 1956, the year we passed the five thousand figure on American drive-ins. But then we leveled off, stayed around that number for the next ten, fifteen years, and I'll tell you why.

That's when the Passion Police showed up. I don't know why, I don't know how, but there were people calling theirselves Americans who didn't want the drive-in to survive. The first time it happened was up in Canada, where the Quebec Catholic Church banned all their members from going to the drive-in, in spite of the fact that the drive-in has been the biggest supporter of that great Catholic double feature, *I Drink Your Blood* and *I Eat Your Skin.* Then they started sending out the Gestapo down here. And the first thing they did was ban *Rock Around the Clock,* the first rock-

and-roll flick in movie history, in eight states, cause they said it was nasty.

Hell, it wasn't nasty, it was Bill Haley and the Comets.

There's always been basically three kinds of drive-in movies: Blood, Breasts, and Beasts. (A lot of people would throw in Boots, for kung fu, but ever since Bruce Lee went to the big Tae Kwon Do Academy in the sky, I just can't include it as a separate category. I'm sorry. It's the way I feel. I know it's not a popular opinion, but I've gotta be my own person.)

This is not the place or time to name all the legendary giants of the drive-in movie or, as it is known in Europe, the cinema alfresco. Course, we had Roger Corman, King of the Drive-In, producer of more than 200 drive-in flicks, who came to Dallas in 1982 as the guest of honor at the First Annual Joe Bob Briggs World Drive-In Movie Festival and Custom Car Rally. Back in the fifties, Big Roger was turning out stuff like *Teenage Doll* (who could forget the Vandalettes?), *Rock All Night* (Abby Dalton forced to sing rock-and-roll at gunpoint!), *A Bucket of Blood* (Dick Miller makes sculptures out of dead bodies), *The Monster from the Ocean Floor* (the giant one-eyed octopus is onscreen for a full ten seconds), *Swamp Women* (live gators and live bitches, all trying to eat Mike Connors alive), *The Day the World Ended* (it was a Tuesday), *Sorority Girl* (great hair-pulling sequences by nasty, nasty broads), *Machine Gun Kelly*

(remember when Charles Bronson screws up and Morey Amsterdam gets his arm blown off?), *Teenage Caveman* (Robert Vaughn in a loincloth), *Not of This Earth* (the one about an alien vampire that disguises himself as a vacuum-cleaner salesman in Beverly Hills), *Cry Baby Killer* (Jack Nicholson hides out in the drive-in while the cops surround him), *Attack of the Crab Monsters* (they eat the heads of scientists!), *Ski Troop Attack* (the best film ever made in Deadwood, South Dakota), and, of course, the immortal *Saga of the Viking Women and Their Voyage to the Waters of the Great Sea Serpent.*

We had great drive-in stars in the fifties too. We had Mamie Van Doren, Queen of the Drive-In, who always wore cashmere sweaters two sizes too small and looked like she was shot through the back with a couple of Pathfinder heat-seeking missiles. We had Jayne Mansfield, the girl with a waist so small she looked like a balloon animal. We had great producers like Sam Katzman, who made *The Tingler*. We had Steve McQueen in *The Blob*. We had *Attack of the Fifty-Foot Woman*. We had *The Incredible Shrinking Man*. We had the immortal Herschell Gordon Lewis, the greatest filmmaker in the history of Chicago, who put nekkid garbonzas on the drive-in screen for the first time in 1959 and who made the first explicit-gore flick, the classic *Blood Feast,* which premiered in Peoria in 1962 and set a modern vomit-and-fainting record that still stands today.

We had knives and nookie, we had rock and roll, and we had *cops all over the lot.*

Then, in the sixties, when the drive-in bimbos really started peeling onscreen, when we had Bikers and Beach parties and Beatles, the underground Communist movement went totally nuts. After 1966 they started closing em down. They said that old farts at nursing homes were sitting out on the porch and keeling over dead from what they saw on the drive-in screen across the fence. They were dark days, even when we were putting out some of the greatest drive-in cinema in the history of Western civilization. We had the advent of the Stewardess flick, and its close cousin the Nurse flick (remember *Private Duty Nurses?).* We had women-in-cages. We had Russ Meyer and some of the largest on-screen hooters ever witnessed by human eyes. We had drive-in inventors hard at work, coming up with new stuff like "radio sound" in 1972 where the soundtrack gets piped in over your car radio. We had on-site gas pumps, to fight against the Arab OPECers. We had rear projection. But let's face it, when they're out to get you, they're out to get you.

It was in those darkest days, in the early seventies, that I first wrote the Gospel According to Joe Bob. (First rule: Life is a fern bar, let's get outta here. Second rule: The drive-in will *never* die.) And ever since then I been fighting the Communist drive-in haters wherever they show their ugly faces. They been closing em down in direct proportion to how many Communists live in their city. Like in New York City, which went Communist about 1927, they only got *one* (uno) drive-in. It's only in the healthy places like Phoenix and Albuquerque and Sarasota where the drive-in still thrives. In Houston they put up a new six-screener in 83, and in Union City, California, they just invented radio *stereo* sound, where you stick this little doowopper in your tape player and you get the flick in stereo.

But that don't really do any good for the great Trail Drive-In in San Antonio, which bit the dust last year, or the drive-in in Lubbock that got burned to the ground last year by foreign agitators, or the Greentree Drive-In in Pittsburgh that got knocked over for a wimp hotel, or the Fountain Valley Drive-In in Orange County, California, where Raquel Welch appeared at the world premiere of *One Million Years B.C.* but which is now gonna be Condo City, or the Kit Carson Drive-In in Taos, New Mexico, where the slopeheads are putting up a Wal-Mart, or the deceased Southside Drive-In in Macon, Georgia, which was the last remaining ozoner in Bibb County, the Northfield Star Drive-In in Cleveland, where they burned the s.o.b. up cause the fire inspector said it was "unsafe," the Dogwood Drive-In in Palestine, Texas, where the PLO put up a *walk-in* moviehouse in its place (it took *four* indoor screens to replace one drive-in), or the 177 Drive-In in Stillwater, Oklahoma, the 183 Drive-In in Irving, Texas (which held the world premiere of *Basket Case)*, and the Ascot Drive-In in Cuyahoga Falls, Ohio, which all got tore down for used-car lots.

And it specially don't help the Cairo Drive-In in Fuquay-Varina, North Carolina, where a bunch of vigilantes went and got a state judge named Henry "Hanky Panky" Burnett to close the sucker down after he watched the flicks they were showing there, decided they were obscene, and declared it a "public nuisance." Only one thing about old Hanky Panky: he had to watch all *nine* of the flicks before he decided they were dirty. The owner of the drive-in had heart trouble and his lawyer bailed out on him one hour before the trial.

You see what I mean? A few years back they even tore down Little Dicky's drive-in in Camden, New Jersey, and we all know what happened then.

God said, "Let there be a void where Camden, New Jersey, used to be."

You seen that place lately?

I'm telling you, don't mess around with the Big Guy.

They can burn us up. They can knock us down. But they can't close the drive-in in our heart. ∎

Joe Bob's Rules
to Live By

Numero uno: I will not do anything that violates my personal code of journalistic ethics. However, I will do anything for money.

Numero two-o: The difference between us and Communist Russia is in Communist Russia they make up a bunch of lies to put in the newspaper, but over here we get to make up our own lies.

Numero three-o: I do not believe in slapping women around, unless they beg for it.

Numero four-o: I am opposed to power drills through the ear, machetes through the stomach, decapitations with barbed wire, flamethrower attacks, and mutilation with a ball peen hammer, unless it's necessary to the plot.

Numero five-o: I love the Meskin people, specially the ones that sneak in. I also love the Meskin hat dance.

Numero six-o: Women should never be judged by their personal appearance. They should be judged by the size of their hooters.

Numero seven-o: I believe my Babtist brothers when they say "Once saved, always saved," cause I only wanna go through it once.

Numero eight-o: Life is a fern bar.

Numero nine-o: Bruce Lee is still the king.

Numero ten-o: The drive-in will never dic. ■

Grim Reaper: It's Got Some Teeth to It

The *Grim Reaper* is this movie about a guy who will use a meat cleaver when he has to, but usually he just uses his *mouth.* (I know what you're thinking; you're thinking vampire. So was I. But you're wrong.) I won't tell you the whole deal, but the Grim Reaper is not a monster; he's a believable human bean who likes to kill people and then chew on them for a while.

There are these three guys and three girls who go to a Greek island on vacation. But, boy, do *they* have a surprise coming! The Grim Reaper has already killed off everbody and stashed them in a cave to make meals for the worms. All that's left is this dark, spooky, old lady who roams around through an abandoned city and doesn't even answer when the guys say things like "Excuse me, ma'am, but can you tell us why nobody's here?"

Then one of the guys gets his head hacked off, and we get a good look at the Reaper. Holy *[Editor's note:* word deleted]! The great thing about the Reaper is that he looks like he just crawled out of a Dempster Dumpster. His long white hair is dry and tangled and windblown, and his face is pitted and creased, and he stands about six ten and weighs 260, and he's like all the psychos because he walks real *slow.* Now get this: The Reaper starts having flashbacks, and we find out he's a *cannibal.* He had to be, though, because him and his wife and their baby were lost at sea on this raft, and after several days the baby died, and the Reaper started licking his chops over that toddler meat. The mother tried to save the kid, but the Reaper turned gonzo and knifed her in the stomach. I think that, sociologically speaking, this episode could explain much of the Reaper's later behavior.

There are three really great scenes in this movie: one in a house where the girls (including a blind girl) are left alone, wondering when the Reaper is going to show his molars; another in the Reaper's crypt, where he has a collection of about fifty moldy bodies; and the final scene when the Reaper chases a cute blonde (Tisa Farrow) and the blind girl through a creaky old mansion.

Besides Tisa Farrow, the movie stars Saverio Vallone as the guy who falls in love with her. It was directed by an Italian named Joe D'Amato, who does some great skin flicks starring Laura Gemser, but, sorry, no flesh in this one.

Joe Bob gives *The Grim Reaper* three stars for scary and two and a half stars for story. ∎

This Month's Art Film:
Mad Monkey Kung Fu

Last Friday night I was out at the Astro watching Cheech and Chong when I got jumped by Bobo Rodriguez. There wasn't any reason for it—I didn't moon him or anything—but Bobo don't usually need a reason. Bobo is just a little guy, though, so as soon as he piled into the car, I reached over and jammed his head up inside the glove compartment and then I said, "Bobo, I'm not a violent person, so let's talk." Bobo said something back but I couldn't hear him.

I had already missed the part where Cheech lights up the big joint, so I let Bobo out of the glove compartment and asked him why he jumped me. It turns out Bobo had snuck over to the No. 2 screen after he'd already seen the stuff on the No. 1 screen, and he said I'd *deceived* him with my column last week and he wanted the dollar back he laid out for the ticket. This surprised the heck out of me because, number one, the Astro han't cost a dollar since 1958, and number two, I didn't know Bobo could read.

So I said, "Bobo, where *is* your car anyway?" But Bobo didn't have beans in the way of explanation, so I knew that Bobo had snuck in again, and now he was trying to jack me for a dollar. Then Bobo explained how I'd written up this movie called *The Grim Peeper* and put a picture in the paper of the peeper chewing up his peep-ees and how Bobo started getting turned on by the picture and then . . .

"BOBO, YOU DUMB SNIT!" I said calmly, only I didn't say "snit." "The movie was called *The Grim* Reaper. Reaper.

Not 'peeper.' Reaper. *The Grim Reaper.*"

So Bobo said, "How bout just a quarter then?"

A newspaper in the hands of a man like Bobo Rodriguez is a dangerous thing. So this week I picked a more intellectual picture, one that would be on my personal Ten Best List of 1982 if I had to write it today.

The name of the flick is *Mad Monkey Kung Fu.* We're talking serious chopsocky here. We're talking Hong Kong direct line. Before I tell you about it, though, I have a question:

Why do people of the Chinese persuasion drink out of those little gold thimbles with handles on em?

I ask this question because I think it might explain why there's so many drunks in kung-fu movies. The drunk in this one is named Chan, and he has moves that could stop a fleet of Toyota Liftbacks. The trouble is that Chan gets suckered into sipping thimbles with a guy named Twon, and apparently whatever they put in those things works like moonshine tequila: It tastes like water and then it goes off like the National Guard at a peace rally. Chan starts fighting with everbody in sight and "running around like a crazy monkey," to quote one of the guys in pajamas. So Twon waits until Chan is passed out on the floor, then he puts him in bed with his *wife* (Twon's wife, not Chan's). And when he wakes up, Chan don't know *what* he might of done.

The penalty for jacking with another man's woman is, of course, death by drowning. Personally I was kind of anxious to see this particular kind of capital punishment, but then Chan's sister jumped up and said, "Spare him, Twon, and I'll be your slave and your concubine."

And Twon says, "Well, all right . . . But I'll have to cripple his hands."

So they play the drum solo to "Inna Godda Divida" on Chan's hands, and he ends up selling candy with a trick monkey named Elmo, which in China is about like hustling pencils on Jackson Street. Then these tough guys in felt hats come along and knock over Chan's candy stand and sling his monkey up against a tree and bash the little bugger's brains out. Chan has a funeral for Elmo, but with his hands all taped up, he can't even work his chopsticks right. So Chan's p.o.ed. For a while this new kid steals food and money for Chan, but then Chan looks at the kid jumping around the street and says, "You know, for a minute there I thought you were Elmo."

So the kid becomes "Monkey" and goes to work doing tricks for Chan. Only the tough guys in felt hats come back with this ape-face who looks like Yul Brynner in a Santa Claus suit, and they tie up Monkey like a bull calf and take all Chan's money, and the kid can't take it any more, so he says, "You must teach me to monkey-box." So Chan takes the kid up into the mountains to train for the big ones—Yul Brynner first, then Tequila Twon. Chan teaches the kid everything he knows while we listen to this Chinese "Rocky" music, and then Monkey comes down out of the mountains, and it's Kung Fu City.

Just to give you an idea, before he gets to the big man, Monkey goes into this whorehouse where they're keeping Chan's sister, and he takes on thirty at once, and they've all got whips, ropes, knives, and Chinaman's swords, and all Monkey's got is this little fan, but he still kicks behinds like a crazy gorilla.

Joe Bob says check it out: three stars for kung-fu moves, four stars for story. ∎

The Venomous May Ellen Learns About Snakes

I decided I would tell May Ellen Masters a thing or two about snakes.

(Before I go on, I know what you're gonna ask me. When the heck did May Ellen Masters come back? She's the one that ran off with my blue Dart last year and didn't even bother to hang up the speaker and ripped the plate glass right out of the side window, and as you know I was plenty hot, and so you probly thought I'd never hear from May Ellen again. But last week she came back, and I don't know, I guess I shouldn't of talked to her, but she brought me the knob off my gear shift, which she had unscrewed and run off with after she left the car puffing smoke in front of the Alamo Tourist Courts where we used to occasionally visit. And, shoot, when she looked at me with those big brown eyes and slipped the dress strap off her left shoulder, well, I don't know, something told me I should forgive her.)

(Plus the fact that a gear knob painted like an eight-ball costs $3.98 at Western Auto.)

So anyway, just to square things up with May Ellen, I reached over and squeezed her on the bicep and I said, "May Ellen, let's talk snakes."

May Ellen went off like a smoke alarm in a Lucky Strike factory. She was screaming and shaking so hard that the fringe on her blouse was forming obscene shapes, or maybe that was just my imagination. Anyway, I put the car in gear and then I said, "May Ellen, I want you to see this movie about a black mamba."

May Ellen stopped shaking for a minute and said, "Is that like the Black Panthers?"

May Ellen is from Hooks,

and I don't have nothing against people from Hooks, but sometimes I think May Ellen didn't take full advantage of the Hooks Independent School District curriculum.

So I explained to May Ellen that a black mamba was a snake that stars in a movie called *Venom* and that it comes from Africa and is about the most poisonous snake in the world.

May Ellen said, "Joe Bob, will you take me to a sit-down movie this time?"

I have to admit I started to get steamed again at this point, since May Ellen knows very well that I don't go to hardtops, never have, never will, and she knows very well that indoor movies are just for poor people who can't afford their own cars and that I han't been poor since I started working for Deke, painting scenes on the back windows of pickups.

"May Ellen," I said, "did you know that a black mamba gets its name from the color of the inside of its mouth? It's really kind of gray and brown on the outside, and when it's resting it has this little crooked grin on its pointy head, but do you know why they call it a *black* mamba?"

May Ellen said she didn't know.

"Because that's the last thing you see before it *kills* you by attacking your *face.*"

After May Ellen calmed down, I took her to see *Venom.*

I have to admit, I never have cared a whole hell of a lot about snakes myself, but I never would admit that to May Ellen. I never had really seen a snake picture either, unless you count that scene in *Raiders of the Lost Ark* when Indiana Jones and his girl get tossed into that cobra pit, which I don't count because I knew they weren't gonna die because the movie wasn't near over at that point.

Venom is different. *Venom* was made in London by a guy named Piers Haggard, directing a story made up by Robert Carrington, who is not much of a fun guy. It starts out with this maid and butler (Oliver Reed) trying to kidnap a little rich kid to get some money for a blond German crook (Klaus Kinski). Only just before they run off with the kid, he goes to the pet store and gets this snake he's been waiting for. Only it's not the one he ordered. It's been mixed up with a black mamba that's on its way to a research lab.

I'll just let you consider the possibilities here for a minute. The black mamba is not just the deadliest snake in the world. It's also the fastest. It can strike from fifteen feet away. As soon as it sees movement, it kills. And you know what they tell you at Boy Scout camp, about how if you don't bother the snake, the snake won't bother you? Doesn't wash with the black mamba. The black mamba *likes* to kill. As the scientist in the movie says, it's "paranoid, aggressive, and doesn't like to be confined" (like in a house). It bites first and asks questions later. In fact, it always bites *repeatedly.*

We get a pretty good idea of what a bite is like when the little boy's maid takes the black mamba out of his box. It goes right for the face—again, and again, and again, and again. May Ellen didn't see half of it, since she was down on the floorboard when it jumped out of the box. After the black mamba got through with that girl, she went into convulsions and then her face started turning purple and blotching up around the bite marks and then blood started coming out of her mouth and she started screaming like a hyena and twitching on the floor.

Anyway, what happens is that *nobody can leave the house,* because this policeman comes to the door to tell them about the black mamba and Oliver Reed panics and blows him away with a shotgun, and then Oliver Reed and Klaus Kinski have to hold the boy and his grandpa (Sterling Hayden) hostage until this policeman (Nicol Williamson) will let them get out of there. Which is worse, leaving by the front door and facing the S.W.A.T. team outside, or waiting to see where the mamba turns up?

Just to give you an idea of what happens, first the mamba gets into the ventilator shaft, which means he could be *anywhere* in that house. Once he does show his fangs, Oliver Reed has been wounded and so he has to just lie there while the mamba *crawls up his pants leg.* And, finally, that's not the worst thing

the snake does: The last scene has some *slow motion.*

Check it out, even though it drags in the parts when the snake is just slinking around eating pet rabbits and stuff. Three stars for story, four stars for the snake camera.

Okay, May Ellen, you can open your eyes now. ∎

Editor's Note:

Sometimes Joe Bob Didn't Quite Meet His Deadlines

Joe Bob Briggs called this week from a pay phone somewhere in East Texas to say that his car was up on blocks because it threw a rod on I-20 and Gus Simpson didn't have all the parts to fix it. Joe Bob said that he knows for a fact that he can get to the drive-in next week, even if Gus flakes out on him again, because May Ellen Masters says she can borrow a car from Junior who works at the Gulf station. Joe Bob said he knows his name is Junior because "Junior" is written on the flap of his pocket.

Joe Bob also said Gus Simpson is a turkey "and you can print that."

The Beast Within:
When Were You Last
Raped by a Cicada?

Any movie that starts off with a woman being diddled by a giant katydid can't be all bad.

"Cicada."

That was Horace Busby disagreeing with me. Horace works at TI so he thinks that entitles him to use words like "cicada." I can't say "cicada," so I ignored Horace. Horace drives a Mercedes; I guess it makes him think he has the right to say something.

As I was saying, it was a giant katydid. It came lurching out of the trees and ripped this woman's clothes off and had insect sex with her.

This reminds me of this guy I used to know named Burl who kept tarantulas in a glass box on top of his microwave. Burl used to say that tarantulas had sex through those little hairs that stand up on their kneecaps. I told him that tarantulas don't have kneecaps. He said that they have little hairs where their kneecaps should be. Burl wasn't a very intelligent individual when it came to insect sex.

So when I went to see this movie called *The Beast Within,* I took Horace Busby with me because Horace works at TI, and I figured that's a place where they would know about ladies who have katydid babies. Actually we went to the movies in Horace's Mercedes because my car is up on blocks and Gus Simpson took out the motor last week and lost part of it. Plus the fact that Horace refuses to ride in my car anyway.

The first thing Horace asked me was what I meant by diddled.

I know that Horace has a Ph.D. from the University of Arkansas at Jasper so I ignored the question. So Horace piped up like a jerk.

"What happened is that the protagonist was raped by a cicada which appears to be one of the larger species."

I said, "What?"

So after that . . . Wait a minute, I forgot to tell you: The woman got diddled on her wedding night. But the guy she marries, he *understands.* He doesn't *care* that she went into the woods and got poked by an insect. And so he says—get this—this will just be *our little secret.*

Forget it, though, because

seventeen years later this same woman has to take herself to the hospital where this doctor that is played by one of my favorite actors, R. G. Armstrong, says the kid has this "occult malignancy." (The kid is sixteen years old—get it?) And he's gonna die, and there's nothing R. G. can do "unless, of course, there's something we don't know."

She got diddled by a grasshopper, R.G.

"The premise of this film," said Horace, "is that science has no known way to deal with impregnation of one human being by another who has transmogrified into a cicadalike creature and transferred the seventeen-year cycle of death and rebirth *inter genus.*"

I told Horace that that's what R. G. would have said, but the biggest word R. G. can say is "rooster."

So instead of telling R. G., the parents go back to that little piddling Mississippi town where she got katydiddled, and they go snooping around in the newspaper office and the courthouse to see if there are any reported insect rapes in there.

Meanwhile, this kid is turning into a you-know-what. So he climbs out of his hospital bed, goes crawling around through an empty house, and then he kills a fat old guy by chewing clean

through his spaghetti-strap T shirt and making hamburger meat out of his stomach. The guy is making a hamburger at the time, so it all gets mixed up together on the floor of his kitchen.

Horace said, "Carnivorous behavior."

After that the kid turns weirdo. He keeps jumping out of that bed and loosening his jaw and sucking up blood. Only one thing: He only goes after guys named *Kerwin.* This is fine with me because I used to know a guy named Kerwin. He was one of those guys that, when he walked, both of his arms would swing in the same direction.

I think the kid does about three more necks before he turns *completely* into a katydid, which happens right before your eyes, and which was so much of a grossout that Horace almost lost his voice. And then after that happens, the kid, who is now a *katy*kid, has *one more guy* named Kerwin that he wants to get and then this *girl* named Kerwin. But this lamebrain girl named Kerwin runs into the *same* forest.

When she did that, I just turned to Horace and I said, "Are they gonna let that katydid rape that little girl?"

And Horace said, "She may very well get diddled."

Joe Bob says check it out. Indoors and out. ■

Shrimps and Wimps: *Time Bandits* Has It All, Including Gimps

L ast week I thumbed out Highway 80 to find Gus Simpson and tell him to put my motor back in so I could go to a midget movie called *Time Bandits,* only Gus had spread metal across his gravel lot like marmalade on a Ritz cracker. Gus has a sign in front of his Sani-Can that says "USED PARTS SOLD HEAR," which made me suspicious, so I said "Just where *is* my motor anyway?" And Gus made this little limp wiggle with his finger at a pile of scrap that had foreign writing on it, and I told Gus where he could put his Toyota flushings cause I didn't just get off the boat from Yokohama. And so finally, I just said to forget it, cause you can't reason with a french-fry head like Gus, and I wasn't going another week without wheels, and then I called up Rhett Beavers and told him I needed a ride to the flicks.

Rhett said, "A what movie?"

"Midget movie."

"How short is it?"

"You don't understand. It has shrimps in it."

"I don't wanna see no wimp movie."

"It han't got wimps, just shrimps."

And that's when Rhett Beavers asked me to explain the difference between shrimps and wimps.

Rhett was staring me in the belt buckle at the time he asked, so I said, "Sure, Rhett, whatever you say, old buddy."

A shrimp don't have to be a wimp, but a wimp is always a shrimp, that's what I always say. You take the six shrimps in *Time Bandits.* They're so shrimpy that they're actual midgets, name of Randall, Fidgit, Wally, Og, Strutter, and Vermin. Average height three foot ten. I know what you're thinking. Wimp City.

Nope. We're talking shrimp but no wimp. What we have here in the first scene is a kid named Kevin, living in a future time, lying in bed trying to go to sleep, and these six shrimps fall out of the sky and land in Kevin's room. (Kevin is not a wimp. Since all kids are shrimps, the only way to tell a wimp from a shrimp in this case is to hang around the playground and wait until somebody yells "Dogpile." For example, if somebody were to say "Dogpile on Kevin" and then thirty guys sat on Kevin, then Kevin would be the wimp. This is because life in the fourth grade is not fair.)

Now what happens in *Time Bandits* is that these six shrimps just stole this secret map from the Supreme Being, and they're running around through the universe breaking into time zones and making off with valuables—like if they landed in my room, they'd probly take the marble burro bookends that Dede Wilks brought back from Matamoros. But they don't land in my room, they land in Kevin's room, and right away you know they're not wimps because they've got more blue metal than you can find on Industrial Boulevard at 2 in the A.M. We're talking knives and *pistolas.* We're talking heavy wimp-removal machinery.

I should mention that Rhett Beavers has a diploma that he got from a preacher named Biff Wooley who used to carry a foldup neon cross in the back of his Eldorado, and ever since the Reverend Wooley gave it to him, Rhett has professed an interest in the theological nature of life. That's why, at this particular point, Rhett said, "What about the Supreme Being? Shrimp or wimp?"

Rhett was obviously not into this movie yet.

So I explained that some people are *neither* shrimp *nor* wimp. For example, once the seven shrimps leave Kevin's room, they start flying through space and time and meeting people like Na-

poleon and Robin Hood and this ogre and King Agamemnon and various shrimps, wimps, and pimps. But then there's this one part of the movie where they're on the deck of the *Titanic* but it sinks, and then they get fished up out of the water by this ogre and his wife, and then the boat rises up out of the ocean and they're on top of the head of this giant who's walking through the water. The giant is the *opposite* of a shrimp.

"What's that?" asked Rhett Beavers.

"Blimp."

I could tell Rhett was about to have an actual thought, so I moved on. Another guy the shrimps meet on their travels is Robin Hood, only the actor they got to play him is John Cleese. I asked Rhett if he knew who John Cleese was.

"Shrimp?" he asked.

"Nope. Limp wimp."

When I first saw this guy, my wimp detector went off the scale. He's one of those guys who shakes hands with three fingers and says words like "beastly." He's a tall guy, though, which just goes to prove that wimpery is a state of mind.

Then there's King Agamemnon, who is swinging this caveman club at a half man half horse out on the desert when Kevin falls out of the sky and lands on the monster and the king kills him. Agamemnon is Sean Connery. Let's talk wimp meter for a minute. This guy registers in the negative digits. When Kevin saves his A, he's all crippled up and exhausted, and so he walks funny when he starts heading over to his horse to go home.

"Which proves what?" said Rhett Beavers.

"That he might limp."

"Okay."

"And his leg might be gimp."

"Right."

"But he's not a wimp."

Just to sum this thing up, I told Rhett Beavers that, to get a true idea of the difference between a shrimp and a wimp, he had to see this Löwenbräu commercial they show during football season. Rhett said he thought he'd seen it.

"You know the one where the four guys get together for a weekend on the beach with their wives?" I asked

"Yeah."

"And then they sit around in this restaurant and say stuff like 'Steak and Löwenbräu, why didn't I think of that'?"

"Yeah."

"And then one of them proposes a toast and says, 'Here's to good friends'?"

"Yeah."

"Wimp City."

Rhett Beavers said he got the idea. ■

Wanted: Joe Bob

Last week the drive-in owners of Dallas County put out an APB on Joe Bob Briggs. Ticket-takers were given a description of Joe Bob's car—which don't mean doodly, since Gus Simpson has Joe Bob's car anyway—and told to refuse him admission on the grounds that he "is not representative of the typical drive-in patron."

Joe Bob said, "What?"

Then Joe Bob said he was going to Caddo Lake to think this thing over, which is why "Joe Bob Goes to the Drive-In" does not appear this week.

Joe Bob's last words before he hiked out to I-20 were "There han't been a drive-in built strong enough to keep *me* out."

Joe Bob will be back.

Editor's note: ▬

About this time, things got so complicated that I've invited John Bloom, Joe Bob's mentor (well, he did get him the job), to try to explain what was going on.

Why They Put Out an APB on Joe Bob and What He Did About It

Joe Bob Briggs was making a noise that sounded like "crush her" or "bust her" or something else that's not very printable, and so I started getting p.o.ed. All I could see was the top of Joe Bob's head, which looked like the inside of a Big Mac after it's been left on the dashboard three or four days. I kept repeating my question to the back of Joe Bob's head, but I couldn't be sure he even knew who he was, so finally I pressed my face up against the bars and I told Joe Bob he'd better have a pretty damn good excuse about why he's been diddling around Bossier City, Louisiana, instead of talking drive-ins which is what he gets paid $3.20 an hour to do.

"PUSSER!"

Finally Joe Bob got the Milk Dud residue off his molars and spit out a word I could understand. He started raving about Buford Pusser (may he R.I.P.) and about how there's no law and order anymore and how Bossier City doesn't have a single man who can Walk Tall. And I told Joe Bob I didn't drive three hours to Bossier City to listen to him talk about Buford Pusser, and then Joe Bob got this kind of quizzical look on his face like his gray matter was starting to clear and he was beginning to recognize my face, and so I said, "Okay, J. B., you wanta tell me what you're doing in the Bossier City Jail?"

And that's when Joe Bob explained where he's been the past month.

"It started with the Have-A-Ball Tourist Courts in Uncertain, Texas."

That sounded logical, so I told Joe Bob to go on.

Well, to make a long story short, since Joe Bob can't tell anything in less than eighty-six minutes running time, what happened is that after the Dallas County drive-ins put out an APB on Joe Bob, he got sort of depressed. It didn't have anything to do with May Ellen Masters, even though she'd run off with his eight-ball gear shift knob, and it didn't have anything to do with Gus Simpson, who had apparently taken Joe Bob's '68 baby-blue Dart and broke it down for parts and sold 'em to Junior Stebbens in Mineral Wells. And it didn't even have anything to do with Joe Bob being asked to be the movie critic of Rockwall, Texas, which can be pretty depressing when you realize Rockwall doesn't have a moviehouse, and if you've seen Rockwall, you know why.

No, the thing that got to Joe Bob was what the ticket-taker at the Century said to him one night after *Terror of Tiny Town,* which is one of Joe Bob's favorite all-midget movies. What the guy said was "Joe Bob, there ain't a gravel drive-up entrance from Loop 12 to the Grapevine Highway that ain't being watched. You're finished in this state." And then the ticket-taker—his name was Stu—went and got this letter that the drive-in owners had sent out about Joe Bob. And it said Joe Bob wasn't welcome any more because he was "not representative of the typical drive-in movie patron."

Joe Bob said, "What?"

So Stu explained and Joe Bob took it pretty hard, since Joe Bob has seen 6,848 drive-in movies (counting triple features) dating back to he won't say when, and the last time Joe Bob set foot in a hardtop moviehouse was 1968, and that was only to get change for a five.

But that was the night Joe Bob disappeared. He said to Stu, "There han't been a drive-in built that can keep Joe Bob out," and then he hitched around Loop 12 until he hit I-20, and then he kept moving west until he hit the Caddo Lake cutoff, and then he figured he'd keep going until he found a catfish place to eat, only it was about that time Joe Bob realized you can't get catfish after 2 A.M. in Uncertain because of the local Blue Fish Laws, and so he went over to check in at the Have-A-Ball Tourist Courts.

I interrupted Joe Bob to ask whether that didn't bring back some pretty disgusting memories. But Joe Bob said no, because Dede Wilks was the only woman he ever took there and Dede was pretty disgusting anyway.

Anyway, Joe Bob never checked in to the Have-A-Ball that night, because just when he got even with the cigarette machine there by the first row of Tee-pee Cabins, he froze in his tracks. There, under the filmy yellow light of a mosquito-repellent porch light that had mosquitoes swarming around it, Joe Bob saw *a 1968 baby-blue Dodge Dart with a missing antenna and an ice pick jammed into the front driver's window.*

"I guess you were pretty happy to find it," I said to Joe Bob.

But then he told me the rest of it. On the left door, written in white fingernail polish so it stood out strong and clear against the new paint job Deke had done last year, were the words "GUS SIMPSON AUTO PARTS."

"Oh, my God," I said, or something to that effect.

But Joe Bob said there was one *more* thing about it. Hanging from the rearview mirror, reflecting that yellow mosquito light like the chrome on a trailer hitch, was the personalized ankle bracelet of May Ellen Masters. Joe Bob moved up close to make sure. Sure enough, on the back where he'd had it engraved by that guy at Fair Park, it said "JBB & MM," which had always ticked off May Ellen because Joe Bob wouldn't spring for the "E" in May Ellen Masters.

Well, as soon as Joe Bob saw that, it was all over. When old Dr. Shinners found him the next morning, Gus Simpson looked like a side of Swift's Premium on its way to Denny's. Joe Bob had gone through that wigwam like a commercial Osterizer, and the only reason he didn't slap May Ellen around too was that she was buck nekkid on top of the sheets when he busted in, and it made Joe Bob sick to look at her. After it was all over, Joe Bob took Gus's keys and tore out around the lake and hit Oil City, Louisiana, before they spotted him, and would have got clean away if he hadn't

stopped in Bossier City to hose off "GUS SIMPSON AUTO PARTS" at the U-Wash-Em. Apparently Dr. Shinners was plenty ticked off about that wigwam.

As they arrested him, they told him he never could've hit Vicksburg because they had an APB all the way to the big river. And Joe Bob said, "Yeah, I know. I'm not representative of the typical drive-in movie patron." And that's how Joe Bob ended up in the Bossier City Jail.

After I heard Joe Bob's explanation, I said, "Joe Bob, don't you think that story strains credulity?"

Joe Bob said, "What?"

So I told Joe Bob just to write his column, but, by God, the money I paid to a bail bondsman named Luther was coming out of his $3.20 an hour, not to mention the towing fees I paid to a guy named Buster to get Joe Bob's car back.

Joe Bob said okay. ∎

This Is *The First Time?* Where Were These Girls When JB Needed Them?

After I got back from Bossier City last week, I hung up a No-Pest Strip on the rearview mirror to get rid of those bugs that are attracted to the Gus Simpson hair-oil smell that was still lingering on the upholstery. (Gus must have done something pretty disgusting on the backseat.) Then I got Deke to loan me some money for some Lysol and a new eight-ball gear-shift knob, and pretty soon the '68 Dart was looking like it was no older than a '69. Deke was only willing to give me the money after I explained I gave a hundred bucks to a lawyer named Butch who is going to defend me on the breaking-and-entering, vandalism, public nuisance, DWI, and drunk-and-disorderly, but not on the crossing state lines in the commission of a felony or the attempted rape, which would require an extra hundred. Deke asked me if I was guilty, and I told him no, I didn't have more than four beers that night, so he gave me the money and told me I could paint some rear-window hunting scenes on pickups to make up the difference.

After that I thought a long time about May Ellen Masters and how I'll probly never see her again, which reminded me of the first time I saw her, which reminded me of this movie called *The First Time,* which reminded me of the question: How come when you're nineteen you can't get any? [Note from Joe Bob: I just went to ask the editor if I can explain what "get any" means and he said no sirree, Joe Bob.]

Anyway, the star of *The First Time* is this guy from Dallas named Tim Choate who can't get any. He goes to this place called Blossom College that has eight girls to every guy and he still can't get any. He has this jive dude roommate (Raymond Patterson) who gets all he wants and tries to help Tim get some, but he still doesn't get any. He has this faculty advisor who's fat with a funny little mustache (Marshall Efron), and he starts telling Tim how he should be happy because he's looking for true love and not just cheap sex, and this just makes him more depressed, and he's still not getting any. Then Tim sees this knockout girl (Krista Errickson) and he thinks he's going to get some, only what happens is that she sees this actor on campus (Bill Randolph), and he's one of those guys that has a big pile of blond hair on his forehead and silver mirror glasses, and he has the best line in the film. He says, "Yeah, I'm always being typecast in these Warren Beatty roles, it's a real drag." And so, of course, the knockout girl goes off with him, and Tim doesn't get any.

There's only one girl who wants Tim to get any. Her name is Eileen (Wendie Jo Sperber), and her thighs alone weigh more than my car, and Eileen could break Tim's nose off with the weight of her chest if she wanted to, and she pretty much jumps him and sneaks up on him and makes a nuisance of herself. This is the girl, by the way, that reminds me of May Ellen Masters. May Ellen has had her feet up in the air so much that she has risen arches. But anyway, after a few experiences with Eileen, Tim doesn't *want* any.

The only other guy in this movie I should mention is Wallace Shawn, who is the wild-haired one in *My Dinner With Andre* and plays a crazy film professor in this flick and who keeps giving Tim a hard time. Shawn goes on the nomination list for the Joe Bob Briggs Best Gonzo Supporting Performance of 1982, along with Linden Chiles, nominated last week for *Forbidden World*.

The director of this movie is Charlie Loventhal, and he was twenty-two when he made it. Pretty disgusting, isn't it?

Tim finally gets some.

Joe Bob says check it out. No breasts. No moaning. Three stars. ∎

Joe Bob's Mailbag ——

Dear Briggs:
You owe me $640 for the custom trim job on the car you stole from the lot of the Have-A-Ball Tourist Courts in Uncertain. If you don't pay up, I'm going to start talking about that little incident at the Ark-La-Tex Twin when Dede Wilks got her dress all messed up.

Gus Simpson

Dear Simpson:
You're still a turkey.

To the Entertainment Editor:
Hey, Bubba, what happened to Joe Bob?

Ever since the guru of the drive-in scene disappeared off the pages of the Times Herald, us B-movie junkies have been going through withdrawal.

Who can we look to for guidance? Where can we turn to for help? . . .

Look, man, I don't want to waste $1.95 on some cheap flick that doesn't deliver on the goods. Only J. B. would tell about the missing impaled eyeball scene! You see, when Joe Bob says "heads will roll," then I know "Heads Will Roll!" . . . .

Geeeez, how am I going to know if the movie is going to gross my date out or not? Shoot, I mean if you guys aren't going to use J. B., send him north to Sherman and Denison. We need a bona-fide drive-in movie critic. We even have two drive-ins.

I don't want to get nasty, but if you don't bring Joe Bob back, I'm going to quit borrowing the Times Herald from my neighbor's yard. . . .

Signed,
You Won't Kick Me
Around Anymore

Dear Kicker:

I'm already the official film critic of Rockwall, Tex., which will be a big enough job whenever they get their moviehouse back, and besides, I can't go to Denison without smelling Oklahoma.

Intimate Moments, or, Will Joe Bob Be Able to Keep This Review Clean?

The ladies to my right here [photo censored by New York high sheriffs] were not my dates at Texas Stadium Drive-In last weekend, although I understand why you might make that mistake. Before I drove out there, I went by the Big Boy on Highway 80 in Grand Prairie and talked to Slim and he told me that May Ellen Masters was sniffing around town and that I should watch out because she was plenty miffed about "having her figure held up to public ridicule," which Slim reckoned was a reference to what happened when I caught her pointing her toenails at the moon in the tourist courts at Caddo.

So anyway I thought I'd make it plain that nobody jacks with Joe Bob like that, so I paid Junior Bodine's sister $2.50 to get me five girls from Thomas Jefferson High School who would go to the movies with me, which turned out to be a hell of a lot of money for appearances since all they did all night was feed their faces and talk during the heavy breathing and say stuff like "What's he doing with his hands?" and—after I would tell them—"Gross-out City." Sometimes they would say,

"What are you doing with *your* hands?" and squeal like stuck pigs, but that was only four of the five. Junior Bodine's sister didn't say a thing.

No, the ladies to my right here aren't members of T. J. Pep. They're the meat in *Intimate Moments,* which is a pretty good movie if you'll just imagine what might happen if you were to get under one of those dresses. I am speaking exclusively to the male reader at this point, although there's this one scene where two of these skirts get down on an airplane seat and start . . . [If you've been keeping up, you might have noticed that every week the *Times Herald* keeps monkeying around with Joe Bob's copy in order to keep it "family-oriented" and "tasteful," which is about as easy as making May Ellen Masters a virgin again, but Joe Bob had to make a solemn promise this week not to be so "explicit."]

Anyway, these two skirts have lunch on an airplane.

Now, the point of *Intimate Moments* is that all these ladies work for Madame Claude, who is played by Alexandra Stewart and who is the woman with the biggest cathouse in Paris. Madame Claude is so big that she sends the hired help all over the world, going wherever the four winds blow. Jobs like that are hard to find, but they pay so much that pretty soon she'll have $2 million to buy a bowling alley and retire. There's a story to this movie too, about how the French government is using Madame Claude to help with foreign policy, but to tell you the truth I wasn't paying much attention because of Junior Bodine's sister.

Okay, let's get down to the nitty.

Not much in the first twenty minutes: The only thing is the opening credits when Lise Thoresen whips off her clothes and sits on one of those white bedspreads that looks like it's made out of llama hair. Nothing happens, though. She puts on a fur coat and goes out on a date.

Next there's this woman named Kim Harlow who spreads out on a shrink's couch and starts talking about this man she met in an elevator and saying things like "Warm, erect, velvet smooth, it offered itself to my . . ." which was such a beautiful line of dialogue I damn near cried. So the shrink gets off on what Kim is saying, but that's about it. She's a talker. No flesh.

The next porkchop is Dirke Altevogt. Her gig is to go to London and stay in an English mansion with this lord. Only on the first night he has to play cards, so she makes it by herself on the *mirror.* Only it's a two-way mirror with a videotape recorder attached to it, which she doesn't know, so the next day the lord rolls that tape and while he's watching the tape she bends over his desk and we're on the verge of getting scissored here, but the bottom line is:

Good scene. Plenty of breasts. Moaning. Thighs. Long

camera shots. The movie's getting down to business.

Then there's a lot of plot before the next one.

Next we have some jailbait. Lena Karisson is another blonde who looks about fourteen, and she's kinkier than a Brillo pad. She flies off to Hong Kong and starts playing the cello while Beatrice Philippe (the one with the legs who looks like a Chinawoman) strokes her groceries. There's also this other Chinawoman who lies on a couch and watches. Making it with a cello is too damn weird for me.

I'm not into pain, but Johanna Perkins does a pretty good job of taking it on the buns with a riding crop. This is the one on the airplane. After getting beat on for a while, she makes it with a stewardess while this guy watches, then she does it with him. Final score: five on a ten scale. She's na-

ked for a long time. Johanna is the one on the front of the couch, leaning on her elbow.

Last but not least, Lise, the one who whipped off her clothes in the opening credits, comes back for the climax. She gets sent to the Bahamas and does it in the surf with an Arab. This is supposed to be a big turn-on, but the director, a guy named Francois A. Mimet, just has a lot of slow-motion shots of the water dripping off her breasts, and it just seemed like a lot of that California surfer stuff to me, so in my opinion it ended on a downer.

So I'd sum it up as a pretty decent breast flick. They all get nekkid. Good moaning. Not too kinky. Three and a half stars. I'm tentatively making this No. 3 on the Joe Bob Briggs Best of '82 Drive-In Movie list, right behind *Mad Monkey Kung Fu.*

Check it out. ∎

Come On, You Guys, Only Twenty-one Murders and One Beheading?

'm sorry, but you people have *filthy* minds, and I think it's pretty disgusting, the letters I got this week about *Intimate Moments,* the breasts-and-nookie movie I didn't take May Ellen Masters to see last week. If this

keeps up, I'm going to cancel *my* subscription to the *Times Herald.* You turkeys are *sick!* [Note: I would like to send a private thank you to Angus for the Magic-Marker drawings.]

Before getting down to the

nitty this week—and we're going back to harmless stuff like mass murder and beheadings and forget this R-rated sex before the perverts in my audience get too crazy —I know what you'd all like to know: Where does Joe Bob stand on the Ann Landers question?

First I'd like to go on record here to say that every letter in Joe Bob's Mailbag is checked out by this girl named Brenda who works at the Pitt Grill in Buffalo. [Special note to Dede: This is not the same Brenda you saw at the White Sands Motel and Restaurant on I-45, and you are mistaken about that entire incident, and we can discuss this further at the It'll Do at the usual time.] Brenda can verify that we use each letter one time and one time only, except the weirdo letters, which I used to keep in my glove compartment but they kept getting stolen, so now if you want to look at them you'll just have to ask. The world is full of *twisted* people, I'm telling you. Also Brenda says that Gus Simpson can't be in Joe Bob's Mailbag any more because he writes a letter every week and it's always boring stuff about money.

But listen, Ann baby, I know the problem, so hang in there.

I didn't have much time for the flicks this week because Butch called me from Bossier City about my trial date. [Butch is the lawyer I gave $100 to—or really Deke gave him that money but I'm working it off by painting rear-window hunting scenes on pickups. Butch said it takes that kind of money when you've got raps like mine, even though out of the seven charges, only two of them are felonies, and one of those is May Ellen Masters's imagination. How could I rape her? That night at the tourist courts I couldn't even look at her.]

Anyway, Butch called and kept saying, "Joe Bob, plead *nolo.*"

I said, "What?"

So Butch said, "I think I can get you two hundred twenty years probation if you send another C-note and plead *nolo.*"

"What?"

"These police officers in Louisiana seem like nice people."

"Two-twenty is the best you can do?"

"Yeah, they've added a charge of sexual deviancy with an animal."

"I didn't touch May Ellen."

"Gus Simpson says different."

So Butch said he could keep me out of the Crossbar Hotel for a while if I would send him another hundred, so I got Deke to paint some more green on my palm and I went to the drive-in.

I had to sneak in over the chain-link fence to see *Kill Squad* because last week five drive-ins put out another APB on me. As you know, I am *not representative of the typical drive-in patron.* But I didn't worry much about it, because there han't been a drive-in built that can keep me out.

Kill Squad is, of course, a light comedy. It's about these six vets from Nam who get a little ticked off when their platoon leader's wife is raped and murdered by a guy named Dutch and his six-man gang of burglars. After Joe gets out of the hospital—Joe is the leader—he calls up his black buddy who's a business executive and says, "Larry, assemble The Squad."

Chopsocky time.

First Larry kung-fus this guy who won't build a tool right in Larry's shop. The guy tries to kill Larry with a gun, but he blows his foot off instead and it's pretty hilarious.

Then this big muscleman white guy kung-fus some punks.

Then this black pimp kung-fus this other black pimp and two white pimps.

Then this Japanese gardener kung-fus his boss and a bunch of other people around the pool.

Then this construction worker kung-fus all the other construction workers because they're lazy.

Then this businessman kung-fus three other guys in monkey suits.

These six guys are The Squad. They're trying to find the fat slob Dutch. (Cameron Mitchell is Dutch.) So they have to go kung-fu a lot of people who won't tell them where Dutch is. Every time they start making chicken-fried steak out of some goon's brain and he starts to tell where Dutch is, this sniper in a black hood kills the stoolie with a single shot fired from a water tower. (They always stand next to water towers to kung-fu these guys.)

As you all know, any kung-fu or splatter film with at least thirty violent killings (or five beheadings, if they are all *shown* and not just *implied*) goes automatically on the Joe Bob Best of '82 Drive-In Movie List. *Kill Squad* didn't make it—just twenty-one dead men and one pretty good beheading (double-edged ax)—but I'm giving extra points this week for the orange blood on Cameron Mitchell when he buys the farm.

Joe Bob says check it out. Average kung-fu. One great car crash scene thrown in for no reason. One great mob kung-fu fight with some dude kickers in a corral. One breast (about five seconds on screen). Two stars. ■

Joe Bob's Mailbag ——

Dear Joe Bob:

Us women would like to know a little more about the men in all these movies. It's understandable that you should notice breasts and such right off the bat, you being a red-blooded male with a hot car and all, but how about a little equal time? We're talking buns, thighs, muscular chests, etc. If you can't focus on more than two objects (breasts) at the same time, why not ask May Ellen Masters to help you out? From what you say, she has the experience it takes.

Sincerely,
An Unidentified Group of
Devoted Admirers
Somewhere in North Texas

Dear Skirts:
I know a Denton postmark when I see it. I've seen enough of May Ellen to know her experience is severely limited. However, I have submitted a request in writing to the Dallas Times Herald for a full-time personal secretary to deal with correspondence and "other matters."

Joe Bob Briggs:
You should fall head first in a bucket of Hog Slop and drown and the world would be better off—

I'm cancelling my Times-Herald subscription after reading Your *slimy* article in "WeekEnd" titled Joe Bob Goes to the Drive-In and letting the Times Herald know why, too.
You are really a degenerate.

[unsigned, Dallas postmark]

Dear Prose Artist:
We've had several requests recently for hog-slop snuff film reviews, which I will be happy to provide in the future.
Which slimy and degenerate article?

The Devil Made Her Do It, But Why Does Joe Bob Want to Go to France?

I told Wanda Bodine it was time to trade cars at Hoss on Ross because I was gonna drive to France, but Wanda wasn't listening. Wanda Bodine han't listened to a single word I've said since 1971, and the only reason she listened to me then was I had to tell her I might have a social disease.

Anyway, Wanda is Junior Bodine's sister, and the only reason I wanted to tell her about the France thing is she's the only person I know that speaks French—the only person in Rockwall County anyway. Wanda runs the Le Coiffure on the old Greenville highway, which, if you've seen it, you'll know is a trailer house with the back of Wanda's head painted

by the front door. I know it's
Wanda's hair on the trailer house
because Wanda has the whitest
hair between Mount Pleasant and
Lake Ray Hubbard. Wanda claims
it's blond, but the truth is she's
got more chemicals in that nest
than Mamie Van Doren and that's
the reason it hangs straight down
off her head like a football helmet.
She says that's the way they wear
it in France.

You're probly wondering
what I was doing with Wanda Bodine in the first place, and I have
to admit I was starting to have my
own doubts about calling her up,
since I hadn't seen hide nor hair
of her since that time in the parking lot outside Club Gigi's at the
Holiday Inn Dallas-Fort Worth
Airport North when Junior Stebbens poured a Schlitz down her
dress. Anyway, it was there at
Club Gigi's that Wanda let it drop
about the French, and I figured if
I was gonna drive to France I
might need somebody like Wanda
along. So I asked her to come
down to the Hoss on Ross, Making Deals on Wheels, so we could
trade in the Dart on something
that could haul all the way to
France.

"You can't drive to France,
Joe Bob."

That's the first thing that
dropped out of her mouth, kind of
sarcastic, like she'd tried it or
something.

"How do you know?" I said.
"You tried it?"

"You can't drive to France
because of the ocean between here

and there." She fluttered her eyelashes. "The Pacific Ocean."

I had to admit I'd clean forgot about the Pacific Ocean, but
something in the way Wanda said
that kind of gave me some doubts
about her experiences in France.

So I said, "Wanda, if you
wanna go to France you can start
by making yourself helpful. So
what does Le Coiffure mean anyway?"

But Wanda wasn't listening
again. She was just staring at the
white line and mumbling stuff like
"Mavis came in for a rinse and set
today, and I'm telling you, that
face job stuck to her like ugly on a
pit bulldog."

I pulled onto Ross and
started looking for a sign that said
"Se habla Espanol," which is the
way I can tell whether it's a place
I wanna trade cars or not. I can't
tell a "habla" from a mud flap,
but I've always said that any man
smart enough to sell cars in a foreign language is a man who knows
how to deal. My personal favorite
lot on Ross is run by José
Liebowitz, who can speak three or
four different languages including
some that don't exist anymore.

Thank goodness José had a
72 Toronado. At first José wanted
$500 for it, but I pointed out that
somebody had ripped off the curb
feelers and so he said, "What the
hell, okay, a hundred dollars."

That's when Wanda said, "It
don't matter, José, cause he's just
gonna drive it into the Pacific
Ocean anyway."

So I told Wanda to shut her
mouth if she wanted to go to

France, and then I forked over $75 and the keys to the Dart, and then we got out of there because José was heading for his trailer house to get some stuff about flood insurance. (José also runs Liebowitz Loan, Insurance and Bail Bond Co.)

You should have seen the Toronado that first night after I sponged it down to the original paint job: metallic maroon, white vinyl roof, three mag wheels, squeaky plastic upholstery covers so slick that Wanda darn near slipped down under the dashboard, six and a half miles to the gallon. Lean, mean racing machine, with enough horsepower to take us all the way to El Paso, much less France.

But before we left I told Wanda Bodine I wanted to try it out one time, so we slipped out Central to the Gemini last Saturday night and went to see *Fury of the Succubus,* which is this movie starring Britt Ekland and Lana Wood, who is the sister of Natalie Wood.

The idea of *Fury of the Succubus* is that Lana Wood is real lonely even though she lives on the beach in California with her husband and daughter, and so when she's there in the house by herself this purple spirit comes in and has sex with her. (In case you're wondering how that happens, the camera moves in real close and Lana slips off her top and starts to moan and slither around in the bed while the demon is having his fun.) This goes on for quite a while. Sometimes

we see this demon standing around the house getting jealous when Lana talks to her husband. He looks like one of those foreign students at UTA, getting ready to burn a flag or something.

Then one day Lana's husband comes down and hears Lana making whoopee with the succubus. (Wanda says the foreign student is a succubus. I don't know a succubus from a Greyhound bus.) So he busts in and says, "Okay, where is he?" And she says, "Who?" and he gets real upset and goes to talk to Britt Ekland about it.

Britt Ekland is a psychic. She decides to come talk to Lana Wood in the hot tub. But while they're talking, the succubus comes and starts messing with Britt underwater, and Lana's husband has to save her. I think after that Lana goes back in the house and moans some more with the succubus, but I can't be sure because these hippies came and parked their van in front of the Toronado and I had to go up and make it plain I was ready to rearrange their acne if they didn't move that piece of scrap to the back row so that decent people could watch the movie.

Then Lana turns gonzo and starts painting weird pictures all the time. Then Britt explains what's going on: This succubus is a spirit walking the Earth between lives who latches onto lonely people because they're weak and that's how he gets his kicks. Anyway, the long and the short of it is that the succubus wants Lana's family out of the picture, so he starts making noises in the basement, so they'll come down there where he can get at em.

Joe Bob says check it out,

even though Britt Ekland keeps all her clothes on. Two violent deaths. One beheading. Lots of moaning. Breasts (Lana only). Two stars. ■

How Joe Bob Drove to France and What He Saw When He Got There

CANNES, which is in France—Wanda Bodine couldn't keep her mouth shut all the way to France. First she wanted to know why I had to go to France at all, so I told her again how they had an APB out for me in Dallas County at all the drive-ins and we had to go to where the movies came from.

Wanda Bodine said, "I didn't know they make drive-in movies in France."

"There's a lot of things you don't know, Wanda," I told her.

"I thought they made em in El Paso."

So I had to explain how they only sell drive-in movies to guys in El Paso, after they make em in France and show em at Cannes.

"What's Cannes?" Wanda Bodine said.

Wanda doesn't have any more sense than a stump-leg rooster.

"That's where the drive-ins in France are."

So Wanda finally agreed to shut down Le Coiffure for a week, even though it would mean giving up that $60 beehive permanent that Mavis was due for, and we set off for France. I told Wanda I wanted to take the interstate all the way, so I tuned up the Toronado and we headed over to I-45 and turned down toward Corsicana and started looking for signs to France.

Anyway, I don't have time to explain just why this is, but driving to France is not easy business, and we got all the way to Houston before I figured out how to do it after talking to this Turkish guy in the Harbor Lights Bar on the Houston ship channel. His name was Kamal. Kamal said it would cost me $400 to drive to France, and that's how much I had to give him to put the Toronado in a container that was going on this Liberian freighter. Four hundred dollars was more money than the whole car cost, but Kamal kept saying "good Turkish price, good Turkish price," and I didn't know what else to do, so I gave him the cash.

After we'd been out on the Pacific Ocean three or four days, Kamal said he'd only charge me $200 for a container to put Wanda in, but I was running low on money at the time, so I just locked her down there in the engine room where the guys were used to noises like that.

We finally got to a town called Marseilles, and that's when I found out the real truth: Wanda speaks about as much French as a French poodle. I don't know how she figured out "Le Coiffure," the sign on her trailer house beauty salon, unless someone just told those words to her. I was so steamed I was ready to hand her over to six or eight of those greasy Turkish sailors, but they wouldn't take her, so I told her to shut up and sit in the backseat.

I have to say the Toronado was fairly impressive on the highways of France, and it wasn't just the new curb feelers I bought in Houston. The Frenchmen all drive these midget cars like Peugeots and Renaults, but you'd be surprised how they think those little two-cylinder go-karts are real machines, hauling around corners like drunk women. Just to show em what a car can do, I had to bump a couple off the highway on the way to Cannes. Actually I didn't mean to. I was just trying to pass on those midget roads, and a few of the wimps got in the way.

There were a bunch of people walking around who looked like they were from California—pink hair and stuff—so I figured that must be Cannes. I eased the Toronado along the ocean until I saw this big palace with a bunch of flags on the top and little wimps in Cub Scout uniforms and Inspector Clouseau hats standing in front of it. I didn't have time for a lot of nonsense after driving all the way to France, so I just knocked over a couple of those Cub Scouts—they kept waving their arms like they were doing semaphore or something—and ran the car right up the steps of that palace. Then I stopped, and one of the Cub Scouts started acting like he was p.o.ed about the whole thing.

"Monsieur . . . Monsieur . . ." he said.

Wanda didn't know what that meant either.

"Monsieur, you cannot drive into La Palais des Festivals. You must turn around."

"Nothing doing," I told the guy, who was getting on my nerves. "I'm Joe Bob Briggs, and I'm the movie critic of Rockwall, Texas, and I'm here to go to the drive-in."

"But, Monsieur," the guy said, "Rockwall has no cinema."

Wanda said "cinema" meant moviehouse, but I think it was just a lucky guess.

He was right about that, though, so I told him I was just doing it till the job in Grapevine opened up, and he said, "Incroyable," which I figured must mean I could go in.

Since we got there in the middle of the night, we just went in and started watching the first thing that came along, and it was this flick called *Parsifal* by a guy named Hans-Jurgen Syberberg, and as you all know, Joe Bob will watch anything, but this was ridiculous . . . this Parsifal was one screwed-up guy. It takes him a couple hours just to figure out his own name, which is not my idea of a good plot, and so I told one of the Cub Scouts I'd already seen all this stuff in *Conan the Barbarian,* and Hans could can it. And he said "Incroyable" again, and he was really starting to get on my nerves.

Well, to sum up all that happened over there, the long and the short of it is that they don't have drive-ins at Cannes at all, which made me get pretty hacked off until I found out that they do have this one place called the Olympia Theatre that is almost as good. I watched drive-in movies at the Olympia just about all week, even though it was a little uncomfortable not having a steering wheel in my hands, and I saw some pretty decent ones.

The best one they have is not even in the competition this year, which is pretty amazing since it means the Cannes Film Festival prize won't mean much when *Basket Case* is not even entered. The day they showed *Basket Case* at the Olympia there were only two movie critics there: Joe Bob Briggs and a funny guy from New York named Rex Reed. Rex and I agreed on pretty much everything except women, which is too bad because I was planning to unload Wanda Bodine on him if I could. But anyway, Rex was there, and I was there, and you can ask him if you don't believe me, because as soon as it gets to Dallas *Basket Case* is going to No. 1 on the Joe Bob Briggs Best of '82 Drive-In Movie list. (Briggs's rules make it eligible only after its Texas outdoor premiere.)

Basket Case is about this kid named Duane who carries a picnic basket around with him everywhere he goes, and when other people open the basket they get their faces chewed off. We get to watch two or three people get their complexions turned into pepperoni pizzas before we actually see what's in the basket. And this is the good part: It's the kid's brother.

The kid's brother is about ten inches high and looks like a squashed octopus with enormous hands and these big teeth, which would make him one of the best slime creatures since the mutant in *Forbidden World* if it weren't for the fact that he's really not a creature but a deformed human who was growing out of the side of Duane's waist when they were born as Siamese twins. They lived together like that for twelve or thirteen years and then these quack doctors came and cut em apart, and they thought the creature brother was dead but he "only got stronger," as Duane says in the movie.

Anyway, the kid checks into this 42nd Street walkup hotel with his picnic basket and makes friends with some hookers and weirdos, and then every day the kid and his pet brother go out together—to bars, restaurants, and "appointments" with the doctors who did the cutting. In one scene, the creature brother saws his father in half—pretty hilarious.

The kid is played by Keven Van Hentenryck in a great performance, but the only guy to make the Joe Bob Briggs Best Drive-In Actors Awards of '82 list is Robert Vogel, as the hotel clerk who suspects the kid of keeping pets in his room.

Joe Bob has seen about thirty movies here this week in an attempt to scout talent for the World Drive-In Movie Festival and Custom Car Rally to be held on Labor Day, and hopes to secure three world premieres—one in each of the categories of "Blood," "Breasts," and "Beasts" —for the event. Joe Bob would also like to report that there is a movie disguised under the title of *Anthropophagous* being shown at Cannes, which would be instantly recognized by all Joe Bob followers as *The Grim Reaper,* an Italian blood flick reviewed in January.

Note to Wanda Bodine's mother: Wanda says she's not going back on a boat, and that's all right by me. ■

Joe Bob's Back from France After Stopping to See *Senior Snatch*

You're probly wondering why I'm back already and where Wanda Bodine is, and I have to admit I thought there'd be more going on in France to keep me busy, but I can tell you right now if you've never been there: There ain't nothing in France you can't find at Big Town Mall. I didn't even see a single drive-in the whole time, and after a while I got the woolies and decided to come home, Wanda or no Wanda. The last time I saw her, she was prancing off with one of the Frogs and telling him how she invented the beehive hairdo at Le Coiffure. The only thing Wanda Bodine ever invented at Le Coiffure was her sex life. (If she's not back by next week, I'm gonna drive out to Mineral Wells and tell Junior Stebbens he can have his trailer house back, because Wanda let it slip that she never had forked over the downpayment of $50 when she opened Le Coiffure.)

Anyway, I'd just as soon forget about France if that's okay with you and get right down to the nitty. I'm damned proud to announce that I got a message this week from a film company in New York letting me know that *Basket Case* is being rushed to Dallas so that it can become, as promised, No. 1 on the Joe Bob Briggs Best of 82 Drive-In Movie list, replacing Roger Corman's blockbuster science-fiction epic *Forbidden World* (formerly *Mutant),* and the art film of the year, *Mad Monkey Kung Fu. Basket Case* was the only thing at the Cannes Film Festival worth a dang, even though I had to watch it indoors. This fellow in New York said to give him a couple weeks, maybe three, and I told him Joe Bob's fans were already damn near starting a riot cause he showed it in France before he showed it in Dallas, and he said he'd get his behind in gear.

Second thing is the First Annual World Drive-In Movie Festival and Custom Car Rally, Joe Bob Briggs, Founder and Chairman, and the nominations that keep on rolling in. While I was in France, I lined up a major, major world premiere of a major, major drive-in movie, to be announced publicly in August to Joe Bob's readers right here in this column. That's all I can say right now, except for one hint: If the Dallas Motion Picture Classification Board thought *Poltergeist* was rough, they have no idea what a camera in the hands of a truly diseased person can do.

Anyway, a lot of you turkeys wrote in to say, "Why didn't Joe Bob Briggs go to *Senior Snatch* last week?"

Good question. Such a good question that I'm going to chuck my usual policy and review last week's movie instead of this week's, because some films are just timeless. Don't get me wrong now. I'm not saying don't check out *Funeral Home,* which starts today, but I couldn't get Cherry Dilday to go to *Funeral Home* with me because her dog just died. It didn't bother me much—it was one of those weenie dogs that's always sniffin around people in embarrassin places—but she got all choked up when I said *Funeral Home* and so I took her to see *Senior Snatch* and *Eager Beavers* instead. I told her, "If there's two things I like, it's kidnapping stories and animal movies." Cherry Dilday is not the smartest girl ever to lose her shoes in a cornfield, so I got away with it.

One thing I can't stand is a bunch of wimpola surfers in a movie. The only people who do that surfing stuff are people who can't drive cars. I guess that's why I was a little peeved at *Senior Snatch* when it started out with all these nymphomaniacs rippin off their graduation gowns and jumpin into the ocean. The only reason I know they're nymphomaniacs is that they go off to Hawaii and start making it with this holy man who looks like Moses after a three-day drunk and who lives up on top of a volcano because he never has to wear a shirt up there. The guy's name is Kahuna. The reason he's been turned out to stud up on the volcano is that he caused this woman to get killed 150 years ago and then he became immortal. The way she got killed is that she was sent over on a ship to be the wife of this Puritan preacher, and on the way over she got horny and opened the hatch for ever guy on the crew. But this preacher didn't know, and so he married her anyway, and then on her wedding night the Kahuna slipped into her room while the preacher was off being holy, and then the preacher came back and shot her through the head, and they gave the Kahuna a hundred lashes and ever since then he's been sitting up on this volcano waiting for some surfer girls to come. Frank Fillman is the name of the guy who made this movie, and he can really think up the plots. Frank likes a lot of closeups of surfers, but he's kind of a Puritan himself: minimum breast action. No moaning. All teasing and no pleasing. Only two stars on this one—for most original plot of the year.

Eager Beavers will be remembered by drive-in regulars as last year's *Swinging Barmaids.* New title, same movie. Still starring William Smith, "The Biller," as a cop tryin to find the sex maniac who keeps murderin cocktail waitresses because they don't bring him the right napkin and they keep calling him "Sonny." A three-star classic, holding steady the second time around. Joe Bob says, if you get the chance, check it out.

Cherry Dilday said to mention that the Biller is a hunk. ■

Joe Bob's Mailbag ——

Dear Joe Bob,

Just finished reading your latest fly & I'll tell you . . . Your pnash & splondder are in my alley!

I don't by many papers & movies are a scarce commodity, but keep it up howevertheless.

A NEW FAN
Fort Worth

Dear ANF:

I like your style. Would you please keep it in Fort Worth?

Visiting Hours, or, Where Was This Fellow When Wanda Was Here?

I felt like some light entertainment after I ran into May Ellen Masters at the Unique Steakhouse on Commerce, so I went to see this flick called *Visiting Hours* about a psycho who likes to torture women.

I guess I oughta explain about May Ellen Masters first. You probly thought you'd never hear another word from May Ellen after I caught her under a sheet at the Have-A-Ball Tourist Courts with Gus Simpson. I know I did. Last weekend all I wanted was a Rib-eye Special with fries at the Unique, so I called up Cherry Dilday again and told her to start teasin her do and I'd get her some red meat. I normally don't go to restaurants where you can't eat in your car, because you never can be too careful about sanitary conditions, but I made an exception for Cherry in view of the fact that she's always wanted to see that hole in the ground which the phone company is puttin on Commerce.

I'd already gone to look in the hole with Rhett Beavers, who's a peculiar guy anyway, and I've always suspected he han't been the same since he was employed by the phone company. Rhett just stared in the hole for a long time and said, "Do you realize that this earthen cavity is a perfect metaphor for the voracious maw the telecommunications industry has become?"

I said, "What?"

So anyway, last week I parked the Toronado at Commerce Street Newsstand (I would have parked it at the Adolphus but those guys in Cub Scout uniforms got a funny look on their faces when I pulled in), and then I took Cherry Dilday over to look in the hole, which she enjoyed very much, and then we went on inside the Unique.

Now, I have to admit that Cherry was lappin up all the attention from the time we got inside. Cherry has hair so red it looks like a Buick chassis that's been left upside down in the rain for two months, and she mixes this sparkly stuff in it that was reflectin the blinkin bulbs on the "STEAK" sign outside, and I have to say the result was a few tongues hanging out of a few heads when we stepped into the Unique.

Cherry acted like she didn't notice, which you may have noticed is what all foxes do when they're sure they're being noticed, and by the time we sat down she was so full of it that she expected me to buy *two* Rib-eye Specials, one for me and one for her, and I had to tell her not to press her luck because she was damned fortunate that I brought her downtown to eat in the first place. I did allow her to order one additional vegetable.

I don't recall exactly when it happened, but I believe it was after Shirley brought my lemon-rang pie but before Cherry Dilday asked for a cinnamon toothpick. What happened was this woman poked her head over the railing on the mezzanine level and looked directly down at us and said something that sounded a little like "witch" or "stitch" or maybe "Mitch." At first I didn't know who it was, because I han't seen May Ellen wearing actual clothes in a good six months. But then she stood up and raised her eyebrows into teepees and let out that old familiar screech, and I said something like, "Cherry babe, I know you're waitin on a toothpick, but we'd best make for the door before that woman swan-dives onto this table."

And Cherry said, "What?" and then she started pattin the back of her hair, just in case we were on TV or something.

I grabbed Cherry by the wrist and started haulin her out toward the Commerce door, but by that time May Ellen Masters was yellin like a crazy woman and threatenin to throw herself into the phone company hole. The only things I could make out were "I'll see you in court" (referring to May Ellen's hysterical, trumped-up version of what actually happened at Caddo Lake), "two-timing s.o.b." (referring to her twisted imagination's guess about what Cherry Dilday and I were planning to do that night), and "you crook" (referring, of course, to the grand-theft-auto charge resulting from my taking my '68 Dart back from Gus Simpson after he got hair-oil smell all over the upholstery).

So I shoved Cherry Dilday in through the driver's door, pushed her across the hump, and fired up that Toronado. As we pulled past the Lasso Bar and that sign that says "AMUSEMENTS UPSTAIRS," I tried to explain to Cherry what happened.

"You remember what I told you about May Ellen Masters?"

"Yeah."

"And about Gus Simpson?"

"Yeah."

"And about, you know, Bossier City?"

"Uh-huh."

"May Ellen's back in town."

Cherry said something that sounded like "witch" or "stitch" or maybe "Mitch."

Visiting Hours may sound like a good old-fashioned splatter movie, but it's really full of what Rhett Beavers says are psychological subtleties. In other words, killer-creep snuff movie. The creep in question is this guy named Colt Hawker—I call him the Hawk—who is actually played by Michael Ironside, this guy who weighs about 220 and who's been working out on the Nautilus for a while. The Hawk could pretty much snuff your breath with the strength of his thumbs alone, but he prefers to use a six-inch stiletto.

Jean Claude Lord, this Canadian guy who directed *Visiting Hours,* obviously doesn't know much about stilettos, or he'd know that it's not enough just to shove that knife into the chest cavity. You need to *twist* that sucker once you get it in. (The Hawk does do this once, when he's snuffin this nurse who sleeps around a lot, but mostly he just *plunges repeatedly,* as we say in the business.)

Anyway, the Hawk has plenty of reasons to be p.o.ed, but the main one is this: Even though he writes letters to important people all the time, expressing his opinions about Negroes, Jews, females, and people of the Meskin persuasion, *nobody* answers his letters. This makes the Hawk a little miffed.

So one day the Hawk is watching the tube and he sees this *woman* reporter (Lee Grant) who's got a mouth on her like May Ellen Masters, and she's talkin about how this battered wife had a right to *kill* her husband.

The Hawk is peeved.

So the Hawk goes to Lee Grant's house and *waits.* Unfortunately, he blows it the first time and Lee Grant gets took to the hospital with a bunch of stiletto wounds to her chest cavity. (Remember, this guy doesn't know how to *twist* that sucker.) So the Hawk is forced to go down to the hospital disguised as a flower delivery man so he can shut Lee Grant up.

From there on out, the Hawk spends most of his time in that hospital, making a bunch of foolish mistakes that causes him to keep killin the *wrong* people. This is understandable if you've ever tried to find your way around one of those places; all the doors look alike. Then, sometime during the movie, the Hawk goes and picks up this blond nympho (Lenore Zann) and takes her to his apartment and starts running that stiletto up and down her nekkid body like he's gonna *do* something with it—only he just marks her up a little and lets her go.

Anyway, the Hawk eventually gets back to tryin to find Lee Grant and snuff her in the hospital, and it takes a long time and to tell you the truth I was beginning to think the Hawk would *never* get his act together and get her cornered in a hospital room, because they have all these flashbacks about what happened to the Hawk when he was a little boy. (His mother threw hot oil all over his daddy's face and made him look like the Elephant Man.) After that I could understand why the Hawk was so perturbed.

Only about five snuffs. One partial breast. No kung fu.

Joe Bob says check it out. Two stars. ■

Going All the Way: A Lesson May Ellen Never Had to Take

The star of this movie called *Going All the Way* is a wimp. Now, I've talked about wimps before, and you all know my position on wimpery in general. But in this case we're talking Total Wimp. We're talking Wimp City. We're talking . . . to give you an idea of what we're talking, this guy tries to make out with this girl while his car is *up on blocks.*

In other words, Wimpola.

The guy's name is Artie, which is a wimp name, and the whole idea is that he has the hots for this girl named Monica but he doesn't know how to get from point A to point P. It kind of reminds me of the time I took Dede Wilks to see *Voyage to the Planet of the Prehistoric Women,* and she made me agree to let her little brother Shep come with us. Shep was not only a wimp; he was a kid wimp, or a shrimp wimp, which is the worst kind. (Shep reminds me of this guy in *Going All the Way* who keeps standing up in class and saying stuff like "Well, *I* was wondering about, you know, the meaning of life." The guy's name is Howard. We spell that W-I-M-P.) So anyway, we put Shep in the backseat of the 66 Mustang, which at that time was one of your better drive-in cars because third-gear position got that shift knob almost plumb to the ashtray, and Shep immediately starts askin questions like "What are you doing with your hand, Joe Bob?" or, "Why is my sister doing noises like Mr. Greenjeans, Joe Bob?" (I have to admit that Dede knew her barnyard sounds.) And I didn't give a diddly what Shep was pipin up about in the backseat, but you have to understand that Dede was the kind of girl who lost her concentration fairly easily and she—oh, what the heck, Dede was dumber than a box of rocks. So the only way I ever got out of that one is that I had to bag Shep. Burlap.

But that was *my* problem. Artie's problem is that he's a wimp. Artie doesn't know what this chick is talkin about when she stands up in Senior Problems class and starts in about pocket rockets. Come to think of it, neither did Cherry Dilday, but while we were watchin this one Cherry was preoccupied.

My point is that *Going All the Way* is one of those flicks that takes all night to go all the way. First Artie goes to Reggie and asks him how he can go all the way with Monica. And Reggie says that they'll get a motel room, only when Artie gets Monica to the motel room she's p.o.ed. So then Artie and Reggie go cruisin for some physical relief, and they get picked up by these two blondes who start shuckin their tunics on a public parking lot, and for a while it looks like Touch-down City, but—well, I don't like to give away the plots of these suckers.

But Artie still han't got all the way.

Then there's a lot of stuff in there about female mud wrestling, which is some weirdo California routine, and then Artie lucks out when this box-of-rocks special named Candy calls him up and asks him to come over. Unfortu-nately, Candy's boyfriend Bronk is present when Artie arrives. Bronk is the kind of guy who likes to do can-openers when everbody is sleeping around the pool. Bronk offers Artie a fist sandwich.

Then Artie goes to this party wearing a baby-blue wimp wind-breaker, and he dances with Candy, so Monica dances with this creep named Roger, and then Bronk tries to rearrange Artie's face, only by that time Roger's al-ready put the moves on Monica. (Roger, by the way, is the kind of guy who says things like "Have you ever been to a music record-ing session?" Roger looks like ev-ery guy in Cafe Dallas.) But then Artie gets saved from Bronk by this female weightlifter named Boom-Boom, who I forgot to tell you about, but she's a big mama who had the hots for Bronk but he treated her like a one-night stand, and so she gets her weightlifter girlfriends together and they pretty much clean and jerk Bronk right there on the spot.

Artie finally goes all the way.

Joe Bob says check it out. It goes to No. 5 on the 1982 Best Drive-In Movie list, on the strength of breasts alone (at least fifty breasts). Josh Cadman goes onto the Best Supporting Actor nominees' list for doing Bronk so well, and Robert Freeman gets a tentative nomination for Best Nookie Director.

Three and a half stars. ■

Joe Bob's Mailbag ——

Dear Joe Bob Briggs,

Sadly, I live in Manhattan and won't be able to attend the drive-in film festival. (A Texas friend told me about it.) But I do have a couple of recommendations. (list of seventy disgusting movies at-tached)

Thanks,
Jim Poling

Dear Jimbo:

It's okay if you live in Manhattan. We let people from Kansas in.

Joe Bob's Best of '82: *Basket Case* Makes Its World Drive-In Premiere

I drove the Toronado out Mineral Wells way and had Junior Stebbens do a complete overhaul, and it's been in the shop ever since because Junior Stebbens, I recently realized, don't know jack about brakes. (I wouldn't have Junior messing with such an important component as brakes except I always get to Bill King's Brake-O at 6:05.) I just assumed Junior knew cars because he has a little patch on the pocket of his bib overalls that says "Junior," plus he *claims* he used to do lube jobs for Clete Tankersley at the Cities Service in Clyde, which is a claim I now seriously doubt after discovering a noise that sounds like tin foil rubbed up against a dead cat whenever I turn left. Sometimes this noise is indistinguishable from a noise that Cherry Dilday makes—but I'm gettin off the subject here. Junior apparently overhauled the Toronado's ability to *move,* and I'm a little worried now because I need it purring for the world premiere tomorrow night.

I know. A lot of you turkeys didn't expect me to show. I'm not what you call a *public* kind of guy.

But this is different. This is premiere night. This is one of the top ten movies of the decade. This is sick and grotesque and hilarious. This will totally gross out Cherry Dilday if I can con her into going. We're talking classic cinema here. We're talking No. 1 on the Joe Bob Briggs Best of 82 Drive-In Movie list.

We're talking *Basket Case.*

Two weeks ago these guys from New York called down here and asked Joe Bob where, in his opinion, the world drive-in premiere of *Basket Case* should be held. I told them there was only one possible place.

Highway 183 Drive-In, Irving, Texas.

[One thing you should know about drive-in standards: Never trust any drive-in that's not named after a road. If the name doesn't tell you where it is, then they've forgotten their roots.]

So I started tellin them how the 183 was right off the Airport Freeway, down a piece from Texas Stadium, behind a big stack of cartop carriers, and how there was a lot of *character* to the place, thanks to it being in Irving, and how you could see one of the screens from the freeway, and—well, I couldn't even finish before they said "Perfect" and started makin the plans for the world premiere.

As a lot of you know, I discovered *Basket Case* at Cannes, which is in France, although I must admit I didn't get the complete effect because I was forced to watch it indoors. Saturday night will be a different matter. Out there under the stars we're going to watch something small, pliable, deformed, and *disgusting* crawl up out of a basket and start *squeezing* people to death. I'm sorry, but I can't say anything more about what's in the basket. But you'll know after the first five minutes the kind of stuff the thing in the basket is capable of.

The first time we see the actual basket, it's being carried around Times Square by this guy named Duane (Kevin Van Hentenryck), who checks into this walk-up hotel full of hookers and geeks and then goes out for junk food. Then he throws the junk food into the basket and we can hear *whatever it is* having dinner. The next morning Duane takes the basket to see an old friend, and pretty soon *whatever it is* doesn't need so much junk food because he's biting into other things.

It turns out that *the thing in the basket* is not so bad after all, once you get to know it. You see, there's a *reason* that thing lives in a basket. There's a *reason* it wants to squeeze people to death.

There's even a reason that the monster is sexually kinky. And it all has to do with a very unhappy childhood when the thing was *separated* from his brother Duane.

That's all I'm saying. This film was made by Frank Henenlotter, who I don't know from Adam, but who uses *excellent* blood, specially in this one scene where a lady doctor gets about six scalpels plunged into various parts of her face, and who had the good taste to dedicate this movie to Herschell Gordon Lewis, the master of gore.

Basket Case also receives five Joe Bob Briggs Up the Academy Awards nominations:

Kevin Van Hentenryck, as the spooky kid with the basket, Best Actor;

Terri Susan Smith, as a blond receptionist with a big mouth and big garbonzas, who falls in love with the kid but finds out his friend likes her better, Best Actress;

Beverly Bonner, as the nastiest hooker on 42nd Street, Best Supporting Actress;

Robert Vogel, as the walk-up hotel clerk, Best Supporting Actor; and

Belial, the thing in the basket, Best Monster.

Basket Case goes to No. 1, followed by *Forbidden World* (formerly *Mutant*), *Mad Monkey Kung Fu, Intimate Moments,* and *Eager Beavers* (formerly *Swinging Barmaids*).

Joe Bob says check it out.

Heads roll. One-half bare top. Some kung fu. Four stars. ∎

Nostalgia Weekend: When Tobe Hooper Worked Outdoors

"There's a lot of violent, antisocial, demeaning trash on the movie screens of America today."

As you can see, Wanda Bodine is back from France. Somebody obviously told her to say that. Probly somebody in Cannes, which is in France, which is where Wanda was last seen plying her wares, so to speak. When she said that last weekend, what I really wanted to say was that she was startin to sound pretty durn tacky for somebody born in a trailer house. But it was her first day back and everything, so I just said, "There's a lot of *violent, antisocial, demeaning trash looking* at the movie screens too." I should have added that most of the trash was indoors, but I didn't think of it at the time.

It turns out that Wanda Bodine pretty much crashed and burned in France after I took the Toronado and came home. There was some guy who said he was going to invest in Wanda's "chain of Texas personal grooming salons" —by which she meant Le Coiffure, her retrofitted trailer house on the Grapevine Highway—but

the only thing he ended up investing in was a hotel room in Genoa, Italy. Wanda came home feeling pretty exhausted, but the first thing she said was that she had discovered "new dimensions" in her personality and wanted to enroll in aerobics dancing class. I asked her where she intended to find the money for *that,* and she said she was planning to pry the boards off Le Coiffure and open it under a new name: Le Bodine.

Since Wanda was not feeling too great, I didn't even tell her about Cherry Dilday, who was mad at me anyway ever since the world premiere of *Basket Case* last Saturday at the Highway 183 Drive-In in Irving. As most of you turkeys know, we got there at midnight just like the ads said, but we had to wait an hour and thirty minutes before those geniuses could get *Basket Case* up on the screen. (I discovered that it was not their fault. There were some *domestic* problems involved, which is one thing I can identify with.) When Cherry Dilday found out we were gonna watch something called *Beach House* first—or that *I* was gonna watch it, because she was makin lewd and inappropriate suggestions for a world premiere night—I had to explain to her what a classic *Beach House* was. It's about all these obnoxious people from Philadelphia who go to the beach in New Jersey and mumble things nobody can understand, including several songs; it's a classic in view of the fact it's the only movie in motion picture history that has absolutely no plot. (I take that back. It's the *second*, after *The Terror*, starring Jack Nicholson and Boris Karloff.) I told Cherry Dilday that it was a supreme compliment that people would sit through *Beach House* in order to be at the world premiere of *Basket Case* at one-thirty in the morning. I didn't know it at the time, but *Basket Case* set the house record that night (212 cars), and now it's going into second run beginning tonight at midnight at the Inwood Theater (sorry, it's a hardtop).

Anyway, no matter what I said, Cherry Dilday wasn't buying it. She wanted to leave right after the first dismembered body in *Basket Case*. So I told her to take a hike, and although she *didn't* take a hike because she's never walked more than three feet in her life, she *did* imitate a Buddha for the rest of the night and made some remark about Bruce Lee that almost made it necessary for me to use force on a female.

So I was a little depressed, and Wanda Bodine was a little depressed, and so I knew it was time for that heart-warming classic.

Time for *The Texas Chainsaw Massacre*.

A lot of people come up to me and say, "Joe Bob, when are you gonna do *Chainsaw?*" And I have to tell *them* that I'm not a person who lives in the past and 1974 is a long time ago and a lot of cars have run up and down that gravel drive since old Leatherface started Black-and-Deckering people to death. It's what you call a seventies theme, and this is the eighties, so let's get with it.

But I feel I have a duty to speak up this week, because some *brilliant* mind is bringing out *Chainsaw* again for one reason and one reason only: Tobe Hooper made some kind of indoor trash film called *Poltergeist*. I haven't seen it, of course, because I don't watch movies indoors, and I specially don't watch any *so-called* horror films that are suitable for family viewing. Let's face it—Tobe Hooper has been slummin ever since he made *Chainsaw*, and he's probably lost to us as a drive-in director.

We all have our favorite scenes in *Saw*. I guess mine is the one where Leatherface puts Pam on a meat-hook so he can continue his Homelite work on Kirk. I also rather enjoy the armchair in Leatherface's house. When Leatherface says armchair, he means *arm*chair. But, of course, the most brilliant thing about *Chainsaw* is that it can scare the bejabbers out of you to the point where you think it was *made* by a cannibal. A lot of people say *Psycho* is the scariest movie ever made. Bullstuff. *Chainsaw* is the only movie ever made in which *any*body can die at *any* moment. It's also the only movie with *three* psychos who are buddies workin shifts, so as soon as Sally and Franklyn veer off that main highway, they're potential meals. Think about *that* the next time you stop for gas in a strange place.

Joe Bob says check it out. Again.

A classic. Four stars. ∎

Joe Bob's Mailbag

Dear Joe Bob,

I know you probably won't print this, but I'm writing anyhow. I read & enjoy your column regularly (though I'm a couple of weeks behind at the moment & trying to catch up).

This is in reference to your review of *Visiting Hours* & the story preceding it regarding your escapade with May Ellen Masters & Cherry Dilday *(CHERRY DILDAY?!?)*. You mentioned that in your efforts to escape May Ellen, you had pushed Cherry through the drivers door & across the hump in your Toronado. Hence my curiosity.

I would like to know if you would be interested in selling this one-of-a-kind car? (a '72, if I remember correctly). I say it must be one-of-a-kind because Oldsmobile Toronado has never been manufactured with a hump. Since it's introduction, it has been hailed as a revolutionary concept in luxury cars because it has FRONT WHEEL DRIVE. It thereby offers greater legroom & passenger comfort (not to mention the other benefits of FWD).

If you still have this unique vehicle when I am released from prison in '84, I would be very interested in purchasing it as its value as a one-of-a-kind vehicle is going to make me rich.

Your Devoted Fan,
Bruce W. Harper #319709
Beto Unit
Tennessee Colony

Dear Bruce:

You probly think I don't have a perfectly logical explanation for this.

The "hump" I referred to is an arm rest that comes down out of the middle of the front seat. I had it custom-ordered. May Ellen hurt herself trying to get across it.

However, I would like to do business on the occasion of your release in '84. They don't call Joe Bob the walking man's friend for nothing. (If you'd like me to put you in contact with Butch, my personal lawyer, I'd be happy to. Most of Butch's clients are in Ellis Unit, so you can ask anybody around there about him. He specializes in early-release temporary insanity work programs.)

You also might want to check with Bobo Rodriguez (formerly Walls Unit, now at Rusk). Bobo has been trying to get the TDC to put in prison drive-ins for all prisoners with cars. Bobo says the

authorities don't look kindly on this idea due to his habitual-offender grand theft auto conviction.

I'll see what I can do about that two-week lag time on your drive-in reviews. Take my advice, though, Bruce, and don't check it out. I'll see you in '84.

Nominations Are In: Joe Bob Says Vote or You're a Turkey

Time to get down to the nitty. The Joe Bob Briggs First Annual World Drive-In Movie Festival and Custom Car Rally is accepting your ballots this week and this week only, so if you turkeys think you know drive-in movies, put your Crayolas to work and decorate this form and send it in to Joe Bob.

Now, I know that a lot of you people don't vote. You don't have to tell me who you are; I *know*. And in most elections I'd have to admit that I don't either. I'm ashamed of myself, because that's exactly what the Russians want.

But this week we're not just talking mayor, or president, or even cable TV referendum. This week we're talking movies. And we're not only talking movies,

we're talking *drive-in* movies. We are talking the Twenty-seven *Greatest* Drive-In Movies in the History of the World. (I'm just asking you to vote for ten, though, because I realize that many of you can't do numbers in excess of your fingers.)

Now after you turkeys vote, that's *it*. It's all over. No second chances. These *will be* the twenty-seven greatest drive-in movies of all time. Period. They will be enshrined forever as the movies shown at the very first annual World Drive-In Movie Festival and Custom Car Rally, Dallas, Texas, 1982. So what I'm trying to tell you is I don't want to hear any *whining* if you don't vote. If you don't vote, I don't want to hear from you. Understand?

As a special added incentive, I plan to do a personality analysis of everyone who votes, based on their choices, which will include your personal wimp-meter rating. Cherry Dilday is gonna operate the wimp meter and type up the ratings if you send in a self-addressed, stamped envelope. This is assuming that Cherry Dilday can type, which I don't doubt since she usually knows what she's doing with her fingers.

And finally here's four more rules:

1. If you turkeys really blow it, I'm gonna *rearrange* the ballot box, if you get what I mean.

2. Gus Simpson cannot vote under any circumstances. Anyone caught casting a ballot for Gus Simpson will be disqualified and *barred* from the drive-in on the night of the festival.

3. Write-ins are okay even though they're a royal hassle.

4. The Era of the Drive-In begins in 1946 because I say so. No movies before that accepted.

And the nominees are:

Detour (1946): Tom Neal, Ann Savage in the first road picture, made in five days, a mad, perverted tragedy; meaningless death, mistaken identities, gloomy as all get out.

The Beast with Five Fingers (1947): Andrea King in the story about the hand of a concert pianist that takes on a life of its own after its owner dies, starts crawling around strangling people.

Black Gold (1947): Anthony Quinn's first starring role and the first western with Indians as good guys.

Nightmare Alley (1947): Tyrone Power as a carnival con man who becomes an evangelist; thirteen years before *Elmer Gantry;* the Babtists didn't like this one; also Joan Blondell, Coleen Gray, Helen Walker.

They Live by Night (1947): Very first version of the Bonnie and Clyde story; *Thieves Like Us* is a remake of this.

Cheyenne Takes Over (1948): Lash LaRue, ex-hairdresser turned King of the Bullwhip, in his debut.

Force of Evil (1948): John Garfield's best movie, dark, seedy, depressing movie made by a Marxist, Abraham Polonsky, that Joe McCarthy had to get rid of; also Beatrice Pearson.

Naked City (1948): "Police procedure" movie shot on location in the Big Apple.

Criss Cross (1949): Burt Lancaster in a fatalistic caper film, set in the Bunker Hill area of LA; also Yvonne De Carlo, Dan Duryea, Percy Helton.

D.O.A. (1949): Edmund O'Brien as the victim of a slow-acting poison, searching for his killers before he dies; Neville Brand as the trigger-happy hood.

Down Memory Lane (1949): Steve Allen's first movie (made in two days), with W.C. Fields, Bing Crosby and the Keystone Kops doing gags.

Follow Me Quietly (1949): William Lundigan and Paul Bryer in the story of a newspaper reporter trying to track down a killer who strikes only on rainy nights.

Francis (1949): Donald O'Connor's first movie, starring a talking mule; Arthur Lubin never would tell how he did that, so they hired him for *Mr. Ed.*

Gun Crazy (1949): John Dall and Peggy Cummins in another version of the Bonnie and Clyde legend, which critics call "an existential masterpiece," whatever that is.

I Shot Jesse James (1949): They don't make B westerns like Sam Fuller made em.

The Locket (1949): Laraine Day is a psycho kleptomaniac who destroys everyone and herself in this movie that has flashbacks within flashbacks within flashbacks; pretty weird; also Robert Mitchum, Brian Aherne.

Pirates of Capri (1949): Louis Hayward buckles his swash in this costume drama full of duels, battles, moonlight balls, and all the usual pirate stuff; also Rudolph Serato.

Wild Weed (1949): Came right out after Big Bob Mitchum was arrested for narcotics; Arrested with him was a girl named Lila Leeds; she stars in this as the woman who takes one puff of grass, gets hooked, drives her brother to suicide, gets reformed, and helps Lyle Talbot track down the Pusher, Alan Baxter.

Lady Without a Passport (1950): George Macready, Hedy Lamarr, John Hodiak in a story about smuggling Cubans to Florida; sort of the drive-in *Casablanca.*

Bedtime for Bonzo (1951): Ronald Reagan, Diana Lynn and Bonzo, back when they were still working.

The Steel Helmet (1951): Gene Evans as the battle-hardened sergeant who leads a lost patrol to a Buddhist temple; one of the best Korean War drive-in movies.

Invasion U.S.A. (1952): An all-out nuclear war with the Russians turns out to be the result of mass hypnosis; it grossed a million.

Kansas City Confidential (1952): John Payne in one of his gangster flicks, "based on a true story."

Red Planet Mars (1952): Hard to explain, but Peter Graves discovers this superior civilization on Mars, see, only then he gets these messages from outer space that tell him the Martians have landed and an Ayatollah Martian has taken over Russia, but then he finds out that Herbert Berghof who used to be a Nazi is now a Communist and he's been sending all those messages himself, and so Peter has to blow him up before the Russians take over.

Devil's Canyon (1953): Virginia Mayo as an outlaw in 3-D.

Glen or Glenda? (1953): Also known as *I Led Two Lives,* released right after Christine Jorgensen changed closets; a documentary on transvestites, with Lyle Talbot as a cop, Timothy

Farrell as a shrink, Bela Lugosi as a crazy narrator, and a bunch of transvestites.

Invaders from Mars (1953): The flying saucer people start turning normal Americans into automatons; some people like it better than *Body Snatchers;* with Jimmy Hunt, Leif Erickson, Helen Carter.

99 River Street (1953): John Payne and Jack Lambert in a crime story that got people upset because it was a little long on violence.

Robot Monster (1953): George Barrows is the Ro-man, who looks like a gorilla wearing a diving helmet, and he wipes out all but six people on earth with his Calcinator Death Ray; when the critics reviewed this, the director had a nervous breakdown.

Wicked Woman (1953): Beverly Michaels and Percy Helton; very naughty.

Johnny Guitar (1954): The first wild-youth movie, with Joan Crawford, Sterling Hayden, Mercedes McCambridge in a western with kid gangs in it; Joe McCarthy didn't like it.

Jubilee Trail (1954): Vera Ralston, Buddy Baer in a Republic western that did not make Vera famous.

Monster from the Ocean Floor (1954): First movie of Roger Corman, the King of the Drive-In Movie, bar none.

The Wild One (1954): Marlon Brando, Lee Marvin raising hell in a small town.

The Big Combo (1955): Jean Wallace, Cornel Wilde, Richard Conte in one of Joe Lewis's best gangster movies.

The Blackboard Jungle (1955): Glenn Ford, Anne Francis, Sidney Poitier, Rafael Campos in the first film about JDs (juvenile delinquents).

The Delinquents (1955 or 1957): Teen-torment film, a cheapie by Robert Altman, starring Tom ("Billy Jack") Laughlin as the troubled boy, Richard Bakalyan as the greasy punk, and Peter Miller.

Francis in the Navy (1955): The mule is back for Clint Eastwood's first movie, which got him fired from the studio.

Kiss Me Deadly (1955): Ralph Meeker, Albert Dekker in the movie that got a lot of abuse for being too brutal, full of torture and pain, based on the Mickey Spillane book.

The Naked Dawn (1955): Semi-western by Edgar Ulmer, shot in ten days in lurid color.

The Phenix City Story (1955): Edward Andrews, Kathryn Grant in an "expose" movie about the most corrupt town in America, Sin City, U.S.A.—Phenix City, Alabama.

Rebel Without a Cause (1955): James Dean, Natalie Wood, Sal Mineo in the popular messed-up teenager picture.

Bigger Than Life (1956): James Mason, Barbara Rush, Walter Matthau about a guy who gets hooked on cortisone and starts turning gonzo; by the master, Nicholas Ray.

Crime in the Streets (1956):

John Cassavetes, James Whitmore, Sal Mineo as bad JDs.

Don't Knock the Rock (1956): Sequel to *Rock Around the Clock* (see below).

The First Traveling Saleslady (1956): Ginger Rogers and Carol Channing (her first movie) gawking at Clint Eastwood's physique.

The Girl Can't Help It (1956): Tom Ewell, Jayne Mansfield (her first film), Edmund O'Brien in a seedy showbiz story featuring the famous milk-bottle scene; music by Little Richard, Fats Domino, The Platters.

Invasion of the Body Snatchers (1956): Kevin McCarthy, Dana Wynter in the best aliens-infiltrating-human-bodies movie.

The Killing (1956): Cheapie thriller by Stanley Kubrick, lots of gunplay and violence, with Sterling Hayden, Coleen Gray, Vince Edwards.

Love Me Tender (1956): First Elvis film, a Civil War western; boffo.

Plan 9 from Outer Space (1956 or 1959): The flying saucers look like paper plates (because they are), and Bela Lugosi, Vampira, Tor Johnson, and Criswell are all wonderfully bad.

Rock Around the Clock (1956): Made by Sam Katzman, who invented the word "beatnik," this is the first rock musical, with Bill Haley and His Comets doing nine songs; banned in several cities.

Rock, Pretty Baby (1956): Fay Wray, Sal Mineo in the first mild (as opposed to wild) youth movie; clean All-American kids having a good time with their guitars.

Rock, Rock, Rock (1956): With thirteen-year-old Tuesday Weld (Connie Francis dubbing her singing voice) and teen heartthrob Teddy Randazzo; Cirino and the Bowties, Frankie Lymon singing "I'm Not a Juvenile Delinquent."

Swamp Women (1956): Marie Windsor, Michael Connors; made by Roger Corman long before swamp movies were in.

Amazing Colossal Man (1957): Glenn Langan is irradiated in an atom test and starts growing ten feet a day; they call in the Army for *large* special effects.

Baby-Face Nelson (1957): Mickey Rooney, of course.

Forty Guns (1957): Barbara Stanwyck as the queen of Tombstone Territory.

I Was a Teenage Werewolf (1957): Whit Bissell as the scientist, Michael Landon as the teen with fangs; there were imitators, but this was the first.

Jailhouse Rock (1957): The best Elvis movie, with Judy Tyler, Dean Jones.

The James Dean Story (1957): Documentary by Robert Altman, including Dean's screen test.

Not of This Earth (1957): Paul Birch as a vampire from outer space who rents a Beverly Hills mansion; featuring Dick Miller.

Teenage Doll (1957): Fay Spain, June Kenney in the story about wars between all-girl gangs, predating punk by twenty years.

Untamed Youth (1957): Lori

Nelson, Mamie Van Doren as girls sent to a prison farm for vagrancy; John Russell as the psycho who runs it; Mamie wiggles through several numbers, finishes with a Carmen Miranda imitation.

The Attack of the Fifty Foot Woman (1958): Nancy Archer, kidnapped by a monster in a flying saucer, returns to earth, where she shoots up to fifty feet, bursts through her roof, becomes a female King Kong.

Big Boat (1958): Musical with the Del-Vikings, the Diamonds, Fats Domino, the Four Aces, Harry James, the Mills Brothers, and George Shearing.

The Blob (1958): Steve McQueen and his hot-rod gang against a giant red protoplasmic substance that keeps getting larger (an Amoeba from outer space); the grownups won't listen.

The Cool and the Crazy (1958): Scott Marlowe, Gigi Perreau in an evil-weed classic, shot on location in Kansas City, with plenty of ducktails and JDs.

High School Confidential (1958): The hottest of all Mamie Van Doren's movies, as she tests the fibers on several cashmere sweaters, with John Drew Barrymore as the cool cat, Jackie Coogan as the school narc, Jerry Lee Lewis pounding out a couple of songs including the real gone opener.

I Married a Monster from Outer Space (1958): Tom Tryon, Gloria Talbott, in the story about aliens taking over bodies; neglected masterpiece.

Machine Gun Kelly (1958):

Charles Bronson, Susan Cabot in Roger Corman's attempt at history.

Terror in a Texas Town (1958): Big Oil trying to take over a town, with the final showdown between Sterling Hayden, as a harpoon-wielding Swedish sailor, and Nedrick Young as a laid-back black-hatted hired gun.

Three in the Attic (1958): Chris Jones in an attic with three girls.

Thunder Road (1958): Robert Mitchum starred, wrote, composed music, sang, produced, fathered the second male lead; moonshine-plot road picture, always big at drive-ins, with Keely Smith, Gene Barry.

Touch of Evil (1958): Albert Zugsmith, the king of exploitation pictures of the fifties, collaborating with the destitute Orson Welles.

War of the Satellites (1958): Roger Corman got this onto the screen within eight weeks of the launching of Sputnik.

A Bucket of Blood (1959): Dick Miller, Barboura Morris, in what may be Corman's best picture, a mystery/horror story set in his favorite place, the Long Beach beatnik scene.

Gidget (1959): Sandra Dee, James Darren, Cliff Robertson, Doug McClure, the Four Preps; first of its kind.

Go, Johnny, Go (1959): King of the rock-and-roll exploiters, with black novelty groups like the Cadillacs and the Pink Flamingoes; Ritchie Valens singing "Ooh, My Head," Eddie Cochrane doing

"Teenage Heaven," Chuck Berry on "Little Queenie"; starring Jimmy Clanton.

Hercules (1959): First of the Steve Reeves muscleman movies made in Italy.

The Immoral Mr. Teas (1959): Russ Meyer's first movie, and the first American nudie film.

Ride Lonesome (1959): Randolph Scott revenge western (yes, his wife is dead again); drifters and outlaws include Henry Silva, Richard Boone, Lee Marvin.

The Tingler (1959): A crablike parasite is growing at the base of Judity Evelyn's spine; weird scientist Vincent Price removes it, but it remains alive and escapes— into a movie theater.

The Amazing Transparent Man (1960): Sci-fi movie shot at Fair Park by the B master, Edgar Ulmer, along with *Beyond the Time Barrier,* both shot in 11 days.

Beyond the Time Barrier (1960): See above.

Black Sunday (1960): The first explicit horror film, pretty tame today, by the Italian Mario Bava; Barbara Steele in her first starring role; witchcraft, ancient curses, spikes and maggots, etc., with John Richardson.

Hell to Eternity (1960): War movie featuring 10,000 extras, shot in Okinawa.

Hercules Unchained (1960): Steve Reeves, Sylvia Koscina in the sequel; erotic and sadist.

Key Witness (1960): First movie about Central Park muggers.

The Little Shop of Horrors (1960): Jonathan Haze, Jackie Joseph in Corman horror classic about man-eating plant, set in shop on Lower East Side of New York.

Peeping Tom (1960): Carl Boehm, Moira Shearer in the movie considered so perverted, destructive, trashy, and amoral that for years it could *only* play drive-ins; nightmare about a movie director who murders his subjects as he films them; recently made "respectable" by Martin Scorsese; Martin who?

The Colossus of Rhodes (1961): A Sergio Leone muscleman/gladiator movie with Rory Calhoun as the pec-flexer.

Living Venus (1961): First film of gore king Herschel Gordon Lewis, about a sex magazine publisher's rise and fall.

Lucky Pierre (1962): The first comedy nudie, made in Chicago in four days with *very* ugly girls.

Twist Around the Clock (1961): The maker of "Rock Around the Clock" strikes again, getting Chubby Checker onscreen within sixty days of "Let's Do the Twist" hitting No. 1; also Dion and the Marcels.

Wild Youth (1961): Robert Hutton, John Goddard as drug crazies.

The Young Savages (1961): Burt Lancaster, Dina Merrill, Shelley Winters in the gang-fighting movie.

Don't Knock the Twist (1962): Sequel.

The Intruder (1962): First Roger Corman film to get good reviews, and the first one to fail at the box office; about integration in the South, too socially redeeming for the drive-in.

Naked Gals of the Golden West (1962): Russ Meyer's personal favorite, which failed due to overpastying the girls.

State Fair (1962): Pat Boone, Ann-Margret, Tom Ewell, Big Tex, a pig, living in a trailer house at Fair Park.

Wild Guitar (1962): Very funny super-cheapie wild youth movie with Arch Hall, William Walters.

Beach Party (1963): It all started here, with Annette Funicello, Frankie Avalon, Robert Cummings, Dorothy Malone.

Blood Feast (1963): Featuring the famous scene in which a girl gets her tongue ripped out by a maniac.

The Brain That Wouldn't Die (1963): Joseph Evers' girlfriend is decapitated in a car wreck, but he leaves her marinating in a lab tray and cruises the bars, looking for a body to screw her head onto; she has other ideas.

The Nutty Professor (1963): Jerry Lewis as Jekyll/Hyde; his best, with Stella Stevens.

Shock Corridor (1963): Reporter Peter Breck gets himself committed to an asylum to expose the abuses there, but then he starts going insane; with Constance Towers.

The Terror (1963): Boris Karloff, Jack Nicholson in a movie shot in two days; the first movie ever made with absolutely no plot.

A Hard Day's Night (1964): The first, the best, the only.

Lorna (1964): Russ Meyer's first offering of sex, violence, and nudity for a general audience.

Santa Claus Conquers the Martians (1964): Joseph E. Levine's masterpiece.

Strait-Jacket (1964): Joan Crawford, who by this time was a queen of the drive-in circuits.

Two Thousand Maniacs! (1964): An entire town in the South goes crazy, featuring effects Sam Peckinpah never dreamed of.

I Saw What You Did (1965): John Ireland and Joan Crawford (again) in an exploitation thriller.

Mudhoney (1965): Considered Russ Meyer's best movie by some people.

Swinging Summer (1965): The last beach movie, featuring elderly teenagers, a lot of bottom wiggling, music by the Righteous Brothers, Gary Lewis and the Playboys, "Mr. Personality" Donny Brooks, and a conclusion featuring Raquel Welch leaping onstage to belt out "Ready to Groove!"

The T.A.M.I. Show (1965): Some believe it's the best rock musical in history, featuring the Rolling Stones in their movie debut, Chuck Berry, James Brown, the Beach Boys, and Marvin Gaye.

Your Cheatin' Heart (1965): Quickie biography of Hank Williams.

Mondo Topless (1966): Russ Meyer's version of a documentary on the topless club explosion; featuring thousands of . . .

The Wild Angels (1966):

Granddaddy of the biker movies, with Peter Fonda, Nancy Sinatra, Bruce Dern being nasty and rotten.

Hell's Angels on Wheels (1967): Some say it's the best of the bikers.

Riot on Sunset Strip (1967): Based on a true story, with Aldo Ray, Mimsy Farmer, rushed out to capitalize on the headlines.

The Shooting (1967): Warren Oates, Jack Nicholson, Millie Perkins, Will Hutchins, being ugly and cruel to one another on the godforsaken Utah desert.

The Conqueror Worm (1968): Vincent Price, Ian Ogilvy in a 1645 witch-hunt, with Price as the hunter, evil incarnate about to take over the world.

Greetings (1968): Jonathan Warden, Robert DeNiro, in 28-year-old Brian De Palma's anti-establishment picture, dealing with draft evasion, computer dating, porn movies, the Kennedy assassination, random violence, and, of course, Nam.

Maryjane (1968): Fabian, Diane McBain smoking grass.

Night of the Living Dead (1968): George Romero's crude classic about an army of walking zombies that close in on a town in Pennsylvania; banned in several cities because it's *sick.*

She-Devils on Wheels (1968): Herschel Gordon Lewis' all-time best grosser.

Targets (1968): Charles Whitman-type psycho starts picking off moviegoers from his perch inside a drive-in movie screen; last film of Boris Karloff; first film of Peter

Bogdanovich; produced by Roger Corman.

The Trip (1968): Peter Fonda in Roger Corman's only LSD movie.

Vixen (1968): First Russ Meyer film that people took dates to.

Wild in the Streets (1968): Rock-and-roll star takes over the country.

Evel Knievel (1969): Quickie, with George Hamilton as the biker jumper.

Once Upon A Time in the West (1969): Sergio Leone's best spaghetti western, with Claudia Cardinale, Henry Fonda, Jason Robards, Charles Bronson.

Beyond the Valley of the Dolls (1970): Russ Meyer hits the bigtime, loses his drive-in touch.

The Honeymoon Killers (1970): Shirley Stoler, Tony Lo Bianco in a sleazy, violent, crude story based on the Lonely Hearts murders of the forties; she's a 200-pound nurse, he's a stupid Spanish gigolo; they're in love and on a murder spree.

The Student Nurses (1970): First of its kind.

Billy Jack (1971): About a bigoted town that has to have some peace and love kicked into it by Tom Laughlin.

Two-Lane Blacktop (1971): James Taylor, Warren Oates in a 60s-type road movie, better than "Easy Rider."

The Velvet Vampire (1971): First to combine vampires with sexy women.

Behind the Green Door (1972): Best of the extremely

naughty, with Marilyn Chambers, the Ivory Snow girl.

Beware! The Blob (1972): Directed by Larry Hagman (yes, the same), starring Robert Walker in this continuation of the saga.

Blue Sunshine (1972): People go bald and turn into raving maniacs as a result of using LSD in the sixties.

The Gore-Gore Girls (1972): Also known as "Blood Orgy," about women who like to mix business with pleasure.

The Hot Box (1972): First movie to combine two genres, nurse and women-in-prison.

It's Alive! (1972): Including the legendary birth-of-a-monster scene.

Enter the Dragon (1973): Next-to-last, and best, of the four Bruce Lees.

The Harder They Come (1973): First Jamaican reggae movie, with Jimmy Cliff as the Rastafarian, Rude Boy Ivan.

Student Teachers (1973): First of the sexy-teacher movies.

Walking Tall (1973): Buford Pusser vs. an evil town, one of the drive-in classics.

Big Bad Mama (1974): Angie Dickinson as a woman gang leader, with Tom Skerritt, William Shatner, Robbie Lee, Susan Sennett.

Caged Heat (1974): Best of the women-in-prison pictures, with Barbara Steele, Juanita Brown, Erica Gavin, Roberta Collins.

Emmanuelle (1974): Sylvia Kristel, not as naughty as Marilyn Chambers, in her first American movie.

The Texas Chainsaw Massacre (1974): The most famous family of cannibals in the history of movies.

Bug (1975): Giant firebreathing insects thrown up out of a volcano; first of the new eco-disaster movies.

Death Race 2000 (1975): Futuristic car-stunt movie, one of the best crash and burns.

Shivers (1975): Parasites attack the residents of an apartment block, turning them all into raving maniacs; fairly disgusting monsters.

Hollywood Boulevard (1976): Roger Corman's in-house joke movie.

Jackson County Jail (1976): Yvette Mimieux in the kind of small-town story you don't want to think about.

Piranha (1977): Killer fish.

Halloween (1978): First of the psycho/knife/teenager movies, and the most profitable independent movie in history; with Jamie Lee Curtis, Donald Pleasance.

Up in Smoke (1978): Best of the Cheech and Chong, a movie class of its own.

The Brood (1979): Hospital horror, child monsters, bodies in revolt, grisly diseases; with Oliver Reed, Samantha Eggar.

The Lady in Red (1979): Pamela Sue Martin turns gangster.

Mad Max (1979): Our only foreign entry, the violent Australian car-motorcycle movie, a contemporary stunt western, with

Mel Gibson as the only gunslinger left after the oil wars.

Rock 'n' Roll High School (1979): Mix of all the teen exploitation movies of the past, with the Ramones providing the music, P.J. Soles as the school troublemaker, Mary Woronov as the principal, Paul Bartel as the music appreciation teacher, Vince Van Patten as the football star, Clint Howard as the devil.

The Warriors (1979): Michael Beck, James Remar; gang violence in New York.

Friday the 13th (1980): Knife-wielding psychos vs. high school girls, in an attempt to go "Halloween" one better.

Humanoids from the Deep (1980): Sci-fi monster picture, about creatures that upset the ecology.

Basket Case (1982): About a guy who carries a basket around with him all the time; when he opens it, people die.

Forbidden World (1982): Sci-fi, sex, monsters, and genetic engineering all in one movie.

Joe Bob Was Busy, So Chubb Fricke Has Been Checking It Out

Some of you people gave the wimp meter such a workout in last week's voting for the Twenty-seven Greatest Drive-In Movies in the History of the World that I'm gonna have to give you one more week to vote. Cherry Dilday hired the entire drill team at a Mesquite high school to help slice open those ballots, and they're still processin the Yankee entries and eliminating all the people who couldn't resist being turkeys and voting for Gus Simpson. There han't been so much commotion at the *Times Herald* mailroom since "Ask Mr. Brock" debuted in 1957. (Those of you requesting the Joe Bob Briggs/Dallas Cowboys betting lines or the Joe Bob Briggs romantic advisory service will have to wait until those two subsidiaries have been officially established. To the guy in Forney who sent the pix: Shame on you, and thank you.)

Since I was so busy this week, what with the ballots and the wimp meter breaking down and the negotiations for the World Drive-In Movie Festival and Custom Car Rally, I was tied up on official business and didn't get out to see *Forced Vengeance,* which is a white-boy chopsocky flick. Actually I *did* go out to Texas Stadium on what you might call a site-selection visit, along with a guy named Sam Frogg who claims he knows drive-in movies and is bidding on the Joe Bob Briggs World Drive-In Movie Management contract. But mostly Frogg and I just hung around the concession stand and talked to Chubb Fricke.

I usually try to avoid Chubb because of his shirts alone. Chubb wears those Meskin shirts with the square bottoms and the flaps on the pockets and the pink peacocks on the back, only Chubb's peacocks aren't pink anymore. They're kind of a putrid pea color because Chubb don't ever wash em. Chubb is what you might call a big man, and so he wears his trousers way up on his rib cage and hooks em in back with a safety pin. Now that I think of it, Chubb is pretty disgusting.

Anyway, Chubb claims he's been going to drive-in movies since 1933, and I don't doubt it because Chubb is what's known as —well, I can't say what he's known as because of the new rules of the Big Boss at the *Times Herald*, but Chubb is *old*. You can tell he's old because he's a chewer. He don't talk much anymore; he just *chews* a lot. He was chewing when me and Frogg caught him buying a super-dog last week.

"Chubb, you're gonna bust the safety pin off those pants and get mustard all over your flamingos if you keep chewin them super-dogs."

Chubb chewed on that for a minute. Then he said, "It's for Aileen."

Aileen is Chubb's wife, and he generally don't bring her to the drive-in because she don't hear too well, and he has to turn up the speaker so loud that Chubb has to sit in the backseat so he can stand the sound. So I considered this a highly unlikely story. Ordinarily I would of told Chubb he was fat and a liar, but under the circumstances I needed a favor and so I asked Chubb to wait a minute while I told him how I was all tied up with the festival and all and needed to get some information from him on a chopsocky called *Forced Vengeance*. I knew Chubb had seen it because he considers himself a master of the martial arts ever since he drove his foot through a board in his front porch. Now, the precise circumstances of how Chubb happened to do that are, in my opinion, highly suspect, and don't have a whole lot to do with his *proficiency* in the Oriental fighting arts, but I have never actually asked Chubb to demonstrate any kicks or body moves because I don't think it would be a pretty sight.

So I told Chubb I needed some fast-and-dirty info on *Forced Vengeance* because my public was counting on me to check it out. Chubb chewed for a while. Then here's what he allowed (after each sentence he paused for a chew):

"It has Chuck Norris in it."

"He goes to Hong Kong and gets a job as a private cop in a casino."

"There's this other casino that the mob owns, and they're tryin to take over the good-guy casino where Chuck works."

"Chuck's bosses don't wanna sell, so the syndicate starts wastin people."

"The only ones left are the boss's daughter, Chuck's girlfriend, and Chuck."

"The mob sends out some gorillas to take care of all three of em."

Chubb chewed for a long time after that sentence, so I kind of nudged him. "What finally happens?" I asked.

Chubb jerked his pants up under his armpits and started walkin out of the concession stand. When he got to the door, he looked over his shoulder, chewed once or twice, and said, "Kung Fu City."

Now, Joe Bob is not saying check it out, because I never advocate any particular flick unless I've personally witnessed said movie under the stars. But since this'll be Chuck's ninth film and he han't failed us yet, I'd say it's a pretty decent bet that I *would* be saying check it out if I wasn't so busy. I understand that the blond old lady in this movie is not bad. ■

Joe Bob's Mailbag ──

HAVE-U-COUNTED THE COST?
Someday you will stand before GOD
Life is Short
Death is Sure
Sin the Cause
Christ the Cure
Northside Baptist Church
Mesquite

Dear fellow Babtists:
OK.

Dear Joe Bob:
Your Drive-In reviews are truly filthy, perverted, demented trash, designed solely for the purpose of titillating the reader. Your mind must truly be demented on some sort of left-over sixties drug. Keep up the good work!

signed
John Lennon, former Beatle
Dallas

Dear John:
I am the walrus.

Basket Case Beset by Wimps; Joe Bob Vows to Retaliate

As most of you turkeys know by now, I'm not a violent kind of guy. I don't go looking for jerks who need their skulls cracked open. I wouldn't kung-fu anybody who didn't threaten my immediate person first. I've never laid a hand on Cherry Dilday, even though, as most of you know, she's tougher than a 50-cent steak. When the farmboys start spraying their RCs in the concession area, I'm the first person to toss my Grapevine letter jacket over Cherry's nekkid shoulders and move her on out of the way. What I'm trying to say is I'm just an easygoing kind of individual . . .

Until somebody *ticks me off.*

I don't know how to break this to you, so I'll just get right down to the nitty:

Some mushmouth, french-fry-head writer in San Francisco says that you and me and Cherry Dilday and everybody like us are "disgusting" and "kooks." His name is Peter Stack. He writes movie reviews for a slime sheet called the San Francisco *Chronicle.*

I want to thank a Joe Bob reader named Jeff Vetter for going out to San Francisco and investi-gating this matter for me. Jeff is staying down in Sacramento so he won't have to associate with the drive-in haters in San Francisco, which, we all know, is the Wimp Capital of the World. He wrote the following letter to Joe Bob's Mailbag:

Mr. Briggs,

Before you throw away the return envelope because it is addressed to California, I don't live there, I'm just staying there for a little while. I just thought you'd like to know that here in California Basket Case *is playing in walk-in theaters in the early evening, and furthermore they had to cut it up so all the fruits out here in California won't get grossed out. I'm enclosing an article . . . etc., etc.*

Inside was a review of *Basket Case,* the No. 1 Movie on the Joe Bob Briggs Best of '82 Drive-In Movie list, which I personally discovered at the Cannes Film Festival even though Rex Reed tried to take credit for it, and which set a world drive-in box office record at its world outdoor premiere last month at the Highway 183 Drive-In in Irving. This city has taken this movie to its heart, and so I want you to *hear* what this creep Stack has to say:

If you thought horror movies could sink low, you haven't seen Basket Case, *currently one of the hottest films on the cheap-thrills midnight movie circuit.*

Basket Case—*too ugly to be serious—sneaked into San Francisco's Roxie Theater recently, where audiences have been rolling in the aisles. . . .*

You have to like horror movies, and black humor, and chintzy production values, to appreciate why Basket Case *is so bad. It leaps logic's concrete wall into unsavory goodness—a romp of macabre confections. . . .*

I won't go into details, except to say that the premise is amusingly executed with many nasty executions. The ugly twin is played by a truly unconvincing rubber monster who can eat thirty Big Macs in one sitting, as well as assorted human beings. . . .

All things considered, first-time director/writer Frank Henenlotter has done a decent job of pacing this seedy sucker.

By now I assume you can tell this guy Stack is a royal jerkola, but wait until you hear the last two graphs:

It's interesting to note that the Basket Case *playing here is a greatly watered-down version. A full-tilt, truly disgusting "splatter" version is raking in tons of cash on the midnight drive-in circuit in the deep South and Texas, where horror-film cultists like their meat real rare.*

So, maybe we're not the kook capital we thought we were. Have a nice daycapitation!

Let's just review a few of the words here now: "low" . . . "cheap" . . . "ugly" . . . "bad" . . . "unsavory" . . . "nasty" . . . "unconvincing" . . . "seedy sucker" . . . "truly disgusting" . . . "kook capital" (referring to *us).* Now, I don't know how that sounds to you, but I'd have to say it's not the kind of thing we can ignore. It might be time to mash in a few wimp noses. It may be time for those three magic words: Kung Fu City.

But since their mothers apparently won't let em watch the whole movie out there in the city of geeks and weirdos, and since I personally wouldn't go to Texarkana just to beat up a wimp, much less to California to beat up an entire *city* of wimps, I suppose I'm just going to have to settle this in my own way.

First, I think we should all agree that Peter Stack is a wimp. But this isn't Russia, so I want to make sure I'm doing this in the democratic way, and so I want you to fill out the ballot at the bottom of the page and send it in to me, marked either "yes" or "no" after the question "In your opinion, is the french-fry-head San Francisco writer named Peter Stack a wimp or not?" Answer yes if he is a wimp, no in the unlikely event that you believe he isn't. I will personally tabulate the results and then send a letter to Mr. Stack that reads as follows:

Dear Mr. Stack:

The combined drive-in-going population of North Texas, East Texas, and a few people from New Jersey and Kansas who get the paper in the mail have determined that you are a wimp and your newspaper is a wimp front, but since this isn't Russia, we're inviting you to the First Annual World Drive-In Movie Festival and Custom Car Rally anyway. Then maybe you'll get to see the man's version of Basket Case, *and you can tell all your wimp friends about it, and maybe it will do the wimp city of San Francisco some good.*

Now, I know some of you turkeys have just finished voting for the Twenty-seven Greatest Drive-In Movies of All Time, and you don't have your wimp-meter ratings back yet, because I'm still counting those mothers up and I had to go to L.A. this week to talk to the King of the Drive-In Movies about coming to Dallas for the fest. But I want you to vote in the "Peter Stack Is A Wimp" campaign anyway so that we can restore *Basket Case* to its place as the unquestioned 1982 drive-in champion (six Drive-In Academy Award nominations, including Best Monster). I consider this a declaration of war: You're not just voting against one wimp, you're voting against the wimp capital of America, and so I say it's time for a special election. Do it for Joe Bob. Do it for your country. ■

Joe Bob's Mailbag ——

Dear Joe Bob,

Trash, litter, lies and scandal thrive in the media today. Questions of untruth are forced into our minds. Who can we believe today? Joe Bob Briggs, *WE BELIEVE IN YOU!!!* We knew that we had to turn to you after belching over these enclosed lies [*Newsweek* article entitled "The Disappearing Drive-In"]. It hurts us to read such material, knowing that the authors obviously have not attended the 183 Drive-In in a '63 Fairlane. Joe Bob, please tell us that we're not wrong!

The Rock 'n Roll Mailroom
Irving

Dear boys in the mailroom:

Do you know where Newsweek *is published? Well, do you?*

New York City.

Have you ever seen a drive-in in New York City? Well, have you?

Of course you haven't. They don't go to the drive-in in New York City. They don't even know what you're talking about when you say drive-in.

I rest my case.

Joe Bob's Survey of California Cities: Frisco, No, L.A. Okay

I know, I know, I know. You're thinking, "Joe Bob has been out *screwing around* again, and he didn't count up those ballots like he said he would, and the twenty-seven greatest drive-in movies in the history of the world are *not in the paper again this week.*"

I have two excellent excuses.

No. 1: You turkeys went *overboard* on this thing. Cherry Dilday got so p.o.ed that she refuses to open any more ballots on the principle that she was misinformed about the precise number of voters. Her exact words were "I ain't no Santa Claus helper." So there's this big pile of priceless drive-in history stacked up on the rear floorboard of the Toronado. Last weekend Chubb Fricke was eatin a tub of nachos back there, and he dripped cheese sauce all over some of the ballots, and now it's pretty disgusting just to put your *hand* back there because you don't know what's gonna stick to it.

No. 2: I've been doing the official business of the First Annual World Drive-In Movie Festival and Custom Car Rally. And this week I have an important announcement to make:

The Master is coming.

Roger Corman, undisputed King of the Drive-In Movie, director, writer, and/or producer of 170 films since 1954 including such outdoor classics as *The Little Shop of Horrors,* all the Edgar Allen Poe movies with Vincent Price, all of Jack Nicholson's early movies, the very first biker movies including *The Wild Angels* (Peter Fonda, Nancy Sinatra, and Bruce Dern), *Machine Gun Kelly* (Charles Bronson's first starring role), *Teenage Caveman* (starring Robert Vaughan in a loincloth in one of *his* first roles), *The Man With the X-Ray Eyes, The Trip* (best of the LSD movies), Francis Coppola's first film *(Dementia 13),* Peter Bogdanovich's first film *(Targets),* Martin Scorsese's first film *(Boxcar Bertha),* the first nurse picture *(The Student Nurses),* the best women-in-cages picture *(Big Doll House),* and some of the best titles in history, like *Attack of the Crab Monster, She Gods of Shark Reef, A Bucket of Blood, Gas-s-s-s, I Escaped from Devil's Island, Night of the Cobra Woman,* and *The Great Texas Dynamite Chase*—the man who did all this will be the guest of honor at the First Annual World Drive-In Movie Festival and Custom

Car Rally. Roger gave Joe Bob his personal assurance that he's going to check it out. [Details later about where you can go to meet the Master.]

Now, I want you to know that I put about three thousand miles on the Toronado just gettin out to L.A., where Roger was unfortunate enough to locate his company, New World Pictures. I was a little leery about venturing out there where they make all that surfing bullstuff, especially since I had just started my get-tough-with-Frisco-we'll-see-you-turkeys-in-the-NFL-playoffs campaign. (By the way, the results of the "Peter Stack Is A Wimp" balloting were overwhelmingly in favor of *Basket Case* and opposed to the yellow journalism of the San Francisco *Chronicle* drive-in hater's crusade. Said movie critic will be receiving his official letter of disapproval this week.)

Anyway, I was a little leery about going to California this time of year when all the surfers are on the loose.

But I didn't have to worry about it because I decided L.A. is okay. L.A. is the only place outside of Texas where people know how to relate to their cars. They know how to drive in that town. They have drive-ins in that town. But the clincher came when I took the studio tour.

I'm not talking about the Universal Tour; I've been on that sucker, and it's overrated.

I'm not talking about the Twentieth Century-Fox Tour; not what it's cracked up to be.

I'm talking New World Pictures, where the drive-in movie is king.

The New World studio is on a street that looks roughly like Lemmon Avenue, or maybe Industrial Boulevard down by the Trinity, only twice as wide and nine times as crowded, and it's in the neighborhood of Venice, which is where a lot of quiche-eaters and roller-skate jerks live. That's why New World is *disguised* as a lumberyard. Actually, it used to *be* a lumberyard, but now it's the place where Roger Corman makes drive-in classics like *Forbidden World* (formerly *Mutant*), still No. 2 on the Best of '82 Drive-In Movie list. As I was walking through the lumberyard, a tear came to my eye when I saw the actual Mutant, a piece of movie history, mutilated and water-soaked, left out in the open air to rot away right next to the computer control panels of *Battle Beyond the Stars*, and just a few yards from the school bus where some of the New World crew members live, no doubt to be close to their art.

My tour of New World was conducted by a guy named Paul, who *claims* to be a Joe Bob reader even though I try to keep foreign circulation to a minimum, and Paul said that the studio had just finished shooting *Android* (starring Klaus Kinski) and that it took *three* weeks to make. (You have to understand the lack of self-control in Southern California; we could have made it here in five days.) And then we went past some buzz saws and lumber stacks into the New World special effects department, and watched some people playing around with a giant bat-monster that's gonna star in *Sorceress,* and then we went out to have dinner and look at some quiche-eaters, who look pretty much like the quiche-eaters on Greenville Avenue except they don't spend as much money on threads. The reason the quiche-eaters go to this one place in Venice is that this congressman's daughter was murdered there, and so Paul thought that would be a *swell* place to eat. Normally I would have said "No way, José," on the assumption that some dope-head surfer jerk had turned maniac and started picking off quiche-eaters with a razor-sharp Frisbee or something. But Roger likes Paul, and so I decided to humor him, and we got out alive so that I could go back to my hotel, which was the place where they found John Belushi dead one night.

That's what I mean about California; even though L.A. is basically okay, I had to get out of there, and so I told everbody at New World to come check out the festival, and they said okay, and so the bottom line here is that the Master will be present. ■

Joe Bob's Mailbag ——

Dear Joe Bob,

We just *love* you and your delightful column. It really spices up our Fridays. We are so terribly sorry that we haven't met anyone like you because real men, who appreciate fine trash, are hard to find. Wanda Bodine and Cherry Dilday and that nasty May Ellen Masters simply are undeserving of your company and we hope that someday we will meet you at the Route 183 Drive-In in Irving when you surface for popcorn.

If you publish this ever so eloquent fan letter, please don't use our real names because Billy Joe and Johnny Mack and our mothers read your witty remarks and we have enough trouble handling them.

Your devoted admirers
Lisa Alcazar-Pesante
Tana Torclan
Members: Man Spotters of
America
Denton

Dear Lisa and Tana:

Whoops!

Look for the Toronado with the personalized plates, but please remember one thing: Count heads in the car BEFORE you open the door. I don't know how many times I'm going to have to tell you girls this. Count the heads, and if the numbers are right, THEN open the door.

The Beastmaster:
No, It Isn't a Kinky
Kitchen Appliance

Wanda Bodine promised she'd stop putting stuff in her hair that made it smell like rattlesnake repellent, and she said her brother Junior Bodine would let me use his grease rack this weekend for some chassis work I need to do on the Toronado, and so, all things considered, I agreed to take Wanda to the drive-in last week under the condition that I didn't have to listen to her talk. One word from her, and I would put a bag over her head. That was our deal. Silence got her a free movie; one peep and she would be looking at the screen through eye-holes cut out of the word "Safeway."

Chubb Fricke told me I was a grade-A jerkola for making what he called *unreasonable* demands, but Chubb is too old to take seriously, specially if you've had a chance to see his wife, Aileen. Aileen is the only woman in North Texas with teeth that look like wood-handled steak knives. Chubb didn't understand that Wanda Bodine is a motor-mouth of the first order. If Wanda was told she was gonna *die* if she uttered a single word, her first sound would be "Would you please repeat the question and instruc-

tions?" We're talking IQ 23. We're talking, as most of you turkeys know by now, box of rocks.

I knew Wanda Bodine wouldn't last the night, so I stopped off at Red Coleman's for some Bud and some brown paper bags. (By the way, if I catch any of you people with Löwenbräu or any of that other foreign bullstuff at any of the area drive-ins, I may not be responsible for my actions. I made my views on Löwenbräu known several months ago, when I posed the question "Have you ever seen *anyone* in a Löwenbräu commercial who was not a wimp?" You know—the guys who sit around in their corduroy jackets, saying "Here's to good friends." Vomit City. Nevertheless, some of you continue to bring Löwenbräu to the drive-in theater, which is *okay as long as you drink it in the privacy of your own car and conceal the label from public view.* Because, hey, this is a free country and you can drink Löwenbräu if you want to. But let's not make a public spectacle of it. Let's not be lewd. There's nothin more obnoxious than a wimp who advertises.)

Anyway, since I was doing all the talking, I said, "Wanda,

we're going to *The Beastmaster,* and you're gonna *like* it." (I should explain, for the benefit of those who didn't read about what happened in France, that ever since Wanda and I got back into the country we han't been *really* dating, if you get what I mean and I think you do. Wanda has been mostly supervising the remodeling work on Le Bodine, which is going along so well that she just hired a new girl named Vida to help on the manicure work. I'd tell you more about Vida, but I don't have room and I'm pretty bored with Wanda Bodine anyway. I'll just say this about Vida: She fills out a white uniform.)

Wanda didn't say anything, but I knew she would later. I stuffed my paper bags up under the seats.

I don't know what you think about this Conan-the-Barbarian bullstuff, but I can usually take it or leave it. I never can remember the names of the movies, so I call all of em Conan-the-Barbarian movies. This one is about a guy who dresses up like a barbarian, wearing those little loincloth pants and those thongs on his arms, because he's been working out on the Nautilus and he wants you to know it. His name is Marc Singer, which I know because he was in *If You Could Only Hear What I Saw,* or something similar to that, since I don't exactly remember that one either. But I remember Marc Singer because he was the blind guy in that movie who drives a car. In this movie he's not exactly blind, but he can only see right when he talks to the animals and turns on his ESP so he can see

through the animals' eyes. This makes sense when we're talking eagle or panther. It don't much matter when we're talking weasel, because they don't see shinola. But you get the idea. He *communicates.*

I forget most of the plot, because I was waitin for a chance to bag Wanda Bodine, but I remember Singer gets his whole race wiped out by a tribe called the Juns who stick a bunch of corpses up on poles and burn down the cities and kill his father. So Singer goes off to kill him some Juns, only on the way he meets some animals and starts talking to them, and then after a while he meets Tanya Roberts, the Charlie's Angel, who just *happens* to be taking a bath, and so she drops her top and we get a look at a couple of . . . actually, I didn't see much of anything because Wanda grabbed me at just that instant and managed to distract me sufficiently, but I'm going to guess *four* female appendages since there were two women in the scene. (I won't be responsible for the precise number in this case, and I apologize for not getting all the facts straight before now, and I'll do better next week.)

Then later on Singer and Tanya Roberts meet up with Gordy from *The Mary Tyler Moore Show*—the guy who did sports and replaced Ted when he was on vacation—only Gordy has also been working out on the Nautilus, and he has his own tribe that hates the Juns, and so he joins up with Singer and they decide to kill Juns together. The only guy in their way is Rip Torn, the evil priest who is guarding Tanya Roberts, who I forgot to mention is his slave. So how does Singer get the slave girl out of the evil castle where the evil priest is gonna kill her. *He gets the animals to help him.*

I can't say anything else about the ending, but I'll say this: I never got to bag Wanda. I was pretty disappointed too, because I figured there was no *way* she could get through this one without just a *little* scream. Wrongola. There must have been three hundred guys die in this one movie, most of them by getting swords shoved through their bodies, but there was *no blood.* Not a single drop. I just don't understand it. A bunch of guys die violently. Nobody bleeds. Wanda remains unbagged.

Not realistic. Only two stars. No kung fu. Some martial-arts sword work. Unofficially, four female appendages. Heads do not roll.

Check it out anyway. ■

Joe Bob's Mailbag ——

Dear Joe Bob,

I believe in you, too. But I have to reply to your aspersions about Peter Stack. You picked the wrong guy for a wimp.

First of all, this IS the Wimp Capital of the U.S. Any woman could tell you. Furthermore, there are generally more wimps per square inch in this newspaper (not all of them readers) than in your average insurance agency, for chrissakes.

But I'm here to tell you, as a long time associate and fellow drive-in movie goer of Peter Stack, he's not a wimp. He's actually a pretty sexy little sucker. So blood doesn't turn him on, so what? There's still sex, drugs and rock n roll. So I vote NO.

Meanwhile, every woman at the Chronicle is hungry for your body. But you're right, stay out of SF, it's full of wimps and crazy women.

Cordially,
Kate Regan
San Francisco Chronicle
San Francisco, Calif.

(I'm not going to bother telling you what *I* review, you'd freak out)

Dear Kate:
Ballet, huh?
OK, I get the picture. You've got the hots for a wimp. It's OK. It's lonely out there. But don't try to tell me that alleged movie critic Peter Stack's recent attack on a) "Basket Case," b) drive-ins, c) Texas drive-ins that show "Basket Case," and d) Texas, was not the work of a jerk.
We're talking jerkola at the minimum. We're probly talking wimp.

J.B. Gives In, Reviews
Friday the 13th, Part 3, 3-D
by Popular Demand

Wanda Bodine, Chubb Fricke, Cherry Dilday, Rhett Beavers, May Ellen Masters, and my ownself all went down to the Bronco Bowl Saturday night for dinner. We *were* going to the Apollo to see *Baby Dolls* ("There's Nothing These Girls Can't Handle!"), but at the last minute Wanda said she wanted to go to the Texas Stadium to see *The Pirate Movie*, and I said "No way, José," and by the time we finished scrappin about it, Wanda was threatening to scissor off my gazebos with her beautician's shears. So I gunned it out the Grapevine Highway and was gonna dump Wanda in front of Le Bodine, but when we got there I saw Rhett Beavers standing out on the gravel lot having a smoke and waitin for Vida Stegall to come out.

Vida Stegall has hair like the mane on Trigger and eyes that can burrow right through you like laser beams through a scarecrow and she has to lean a little forward when she walks, if you know what I mean and I think you do. Vida's been working as a cutter for Wanda for about four weeks now,

and everbody knows she belongs to Lute Fenwick and she never would leave him because Lute owns a Western Auto in Cleburne, but ever time Vida sticks her grillwork out the front door of that trailer house Rhett Beavers gets the shakes and starts trying to tell her that he's a personal friend of David McDavid, the famous Pontiac dealer. Rhett is gonna get his elbows sawed off his arms if Lute Fenwick ever finds out about it, so when I saw him out there, I asked Wanda if she would *distract* him for me, for his own good, of course. But Wanda flat refused.

Anyway, to make a long story short, I ended up making a deal with Wanda: She agreed to be Rhett's date to the Bronco Bowl, in exchange for me buying two beers and paying shoe rental. But now I had to get a date myself, so I went in Le Bodine and used the pay phone by the back chair and called up Cherry Dilday and told her to hustle over and meet us at the Bronc. What I didn't know is that Chubb Fricke was hanging around Cherry's when the phone rang, and Chubb can smell a bowling lane from ninety miles distance. That part of it didn't bother me. It was the May Ellen Masters part that turned my stomach into Rice-a-Roni.

I han't seen May Ellen Masters since she did that swan dive onto my table from the mezzanine of the Steakhouse Unique and made a fool out of me and Cherry Dilday and all the other people who were just minding their own business that night. I heard that Gus Simpson dumped May Ellen just as soon as he was finished doing whatever it was that they were doing in the Have-A-Ball Tourist Courts in Uncertain where I found em last March. But that was ancient history as far as I was concerned, and I'd been to France with Wanda Bodine since then until she ran away, and then I'd been hangin around with Cherry Dilday until she got diarrhea of the mouth and refused to do my necessary secretarial duties, and so even though I'm not what you call a guy with a good track record woman-wise, May Ellen I didn't need. As soon as she showed up at the Bronc with Cherry and Chubb, she started rubbin up against me like a cat on a sofa leg, and so I had to tell her what trash she was, which caused her to say something that I'm embarrassed to say in this newspaper because there might be ladies reading it.

Now, normally I would've been enjoying myself, because there is no finer place in the world, in my opinion, than the Bronco Bowl. I'm not a political kind of guy, but there's a lot of people who say that Bunker Hunt is just a rich guy who don't do diddly for anybody, and whenever I hear that kind of talk, I have to say, "Hey, turkey, Mr. Hunt built the Bronc and don't you forget it." That's the kind of achievement that still stands after a man passes on. Now, I don't necessarily agree with everthing he did, like putting in archery ranges when he could've had space for four more batting cages or about fifteen more pool tables. But, hey, this is not Communist Russia and so he can do what he wants to. Bunker Hunt may have a lot of money, but he's still an American.

So the only reasons I couldn't enjoy myself last Saturday were (a) May Ellen, (b) Wanda Bodine, who started whining like she always does when she sees Collier's Coiffures and can't understand why Le Bodine can't get a concession in the Bronc like that, and (c) Cherry Dilday, who is the only person in the world with the ability to screw up *automatic* scorekeeping. When May Ellen started dropping her ball *behind* her, so it rolled *sideways* and started bothering these Brothers from South Dallas, I said, "Okay, that's it, we're gettin out of here," and the kind of state I was in I was ready to stuff May Ellen into the ball return chute. Chubb Fricke wasn't too happy either, cause Chubb is a rather large man and so he was rolling his usual fatman 200 game in which the pins get splintered into about 17,000 pieces. Rhett Beavers didn't care diddly, cause he was still thinking about Vida.

I herded that flock of turkeys into the Toronado and turned around in the seat so I could look at the back of May Ellen's neck and I said, "All right, heads are gonna roll." I knew May Ellen couldn't stand the sight of blood. I knew the one movie that would get to her. It's a movie that everybody keeps writing to Joe Bob's Mailbag about because they want me to see it. Up until now I'd been thinking it was indoor bullstuff. But I was royally ticked and so I said it so May Ellen could hear me: *"Friday the 13th, Part 3."*

She raised up her head and looked at me like a deer on the first day of season.

"We're talking Splatter City."

Now I'm sure all you people already know what happens in *Part 3*—the same thing that happened in *Part 1* and *Part 2*. All these teen-age kids who are dumb as a box of rocks go to a lakehouse and start messing around until a geek in a hockey mask starts using them for shishkebob meat. The first guy is named Harold. Harold, for example, gets a meat cleaver imbedded in his chest. Harold's wife is named Edna. Edna gets a knitting needle pushed through her noggin. In both cases they show you the blood and the actual *penetration*, so to speak, but I was a little disappointed with the way they cut away from the main event so quick. May Ellen wasn't. She started to relax—until I told her there were *eleven more to come.*

They're pretty good ones too.

I won't go into all of em here, except to say that one guy gets it with a pitchfork, one guy with a plumber's wrench, one especially stupid girl gets it through the eye with a speargun, one guy gets cut in half *lengthwise* (startin at the bottom), one girl gets a knife through the neck—well, anyway, as you can see, you could watch a lot of this movie with the mistaken impression that heads do not roll.

But I'm saying it here and now: Heads *do* roll in *Friday the 13th, Part 3*. I'm not gonna tell you when, where, or how, but I'll say this: It's okay because the guy who gets it looks like a wimp quiche-eater. He gets his eyeball popped out first, a pretty nice effect in 3-D. When it happened, May Ellen got completely hysterical and barfed all over Rhett Beavers's yellow blazer, and I threatened to dump her there on the spot but of course I didn't because I'm a *nice guy* and so I took her back to Cherry's and dumped her there.

Friday the 13th, Part 3 is okay, though, even though I thought it was indoor bullstuff. No kung fu. Approximately two bare tops. Thirteen corpses. Heads roll. Three stars.

Joe Bob says check it out.

One of you turkeys sent me an article out of the *Ladies Home Journal* about drive-ins. It was written by a wimp named Gene Shalit. Here's what he has to say: "You need a warm outdoor society. That's why there are more drive-ins in California than anywhere else: 269."

Now, this is what happens when amateurs mess around in a subject they don't know anything about. As we all know, Texas has had more drive-ins than any other state since 1945. This Shalit jerkola is talking about drive-in *screens*. The correct figures, according to my own personal research in the *International Motion Picture Almanac*, are 194 drive-ins in California (but 269 drive-in screens).

Texas has 223 drive-ins. This *is* the drive-in capital of the world.

Shalit is from the drive-in-hating city of New York, New York. When Joe Bob talks drive-ins, Joe Bob gets the true facts. ∎

Heads Don't Roll, but *Last Virgin* Makes J.B.'s Best of '82 List

I ended up in a car with May Ellen Masters for the second straight weekend, and I'll tell you what, I'm getting a little sick of that girl, but for once it wasn't her fault, so I guess I'll drop it. I took her and Rhett Beavers and Cherry Dilday to a flick called *The Last American Virgin*, which meant I had to explain the title to everyone in the car, since nobody but Rhett knew what it meant. Especially not May Ellen.

It was actually all Rhett Beavers's fault. He called me from a pay phone in Weatherford last Friday night, and when I picked it up I didn't half recognize his voice, he sounded so pitiful. He just kept saying "Peter Pan, Peter Pan," like that was supposed to mean something to me, and then making a whimpering noise like a dog that's had its paw mashed by a pickup. It turns out the man wanted me to come get him—at the Peter Pan statue in Weatherford.

As soon as I got out there to see what was wrong, I could tell Rhett had been into some bad bullstuff. His face looked like a Cheese Whopper, his eyes were clamped shut like he'd just got the double whammy from the snake lady, and he had a bunch of crusty, dried red stuff all over his blazer. I thought it was blood until I found out later, it was left over from where May Ellen barfed on him the week before at *Friday the 13th, Part 3*. I would like to point out, however, that this had nothing to do with the fine dinner we all had at the Bronco Bowl earlier that evening.

Naturally I said to Rhett Beavers, "What in [censored]?"

Rhett said something but I couldn't understand it, because his mouth was all puffed up like a tire bubble. I didn't find out till later what happened.

It turns out that Rhett was just minding his own business, sitting in his apartment in Euless, having dinner and watching *Family Feud*. Rhett can prove this because he han't touched the big old round grease spot on his Panasonic where the Church's box was. When Richard Dawson started French-kissing this fat woman, Rhett reached over to grab him a piece of dark meat—and that's when the three gorillas in overalls kicked in the storm door and started making kung-fu noises and doing lines out of old episodes of *Hawaii Five-O*. The last thing they said was "Hey, Beaver, Lute Fenwick wants to see ya," and when they said that, Rhett just about went through the fiberboard room divider.

He didn't have much time to think, though, because they grabbed him and stuffed him into the back seat of an El Dorado and headed for Cleburne before Rhett could make a phone call or put down his drumstick. When they got to Cleburne, they pulled up in back of the Western Auto and took Rhett over to the grease rack and chained him up like a trained monkey and then they all had to wait because Lute was inside taking Weed Eater inventory.

Lute Fenwick walked on out to the grease rack, wiped some of the oil off his neck, ran his hand through his hair, and said, "I hear you been botherin Vida."

Rhett's quick and brave reply was "No sir, Mr. Fenwick, sir, I wouldn't do that, sir."

Lute Fenwick stood there for about two minutes thinking about that and wondering what to say, then he said, "I hear different."

"No sir, Mr. Fenwick, I never laid a hand on her, sir."

"Well, let's make sure you don't."

And that's when Lute Fenwick bashed in Rhett Beavers's nose with a right cross. Actually, it wasn't the right cross that did it, it was the garnet class ring that Lute Fenwick was wearing at the time. Not that Lute Fenwick ever had a *class*. He bought that ring at a garage sale even though he won't admit it. It says "Hockaday '79" on it. Lute claims he played football there.

Anyway, that's how Rhett Beavers's face came to look like a Cheese Whopper. After Lute finished making pancake batter out of Rhett's skin with that Hockaday ring, he told his gang of Ph.D. candidates to take Rhett over to Weatherford and dump him in front of the Peter Pan statue so somebody'd find him.

If I told Rhett once, I told him a hundred times, to stay away from Vida Stegall, Lute's girl that works at Le Bodine as a cutter and fills out that white uniform and drives Rhett crazy even though she won't talk to him. I knew that Rhett never laid a hand on her, though, because she was the kind of girl that would've kung-fued him right through the throat if he'd even tried it. But even after I got him cleaned up, Rhett still had the shakes—I don't know if it was from thinking about Lute or thinking about Vida —and so I knew I couldn't leave him alone, and there was only one person I knew who wouldn't have a date that late on Friday night, and so I called her: May Ellen Masters.

That's how I ended up at *The Last American Virgin* with that same flock of turkeys. It was a waste too, because it turned out to be a highly decent flick. In fact, it turned out to be such a decent flick that it's going to No. 3 on the Joe Bob Briggs Best of '82 Drive-In Movie list, taking the place of *Intimate Moments* and pushing *Mad Monkey Kung Fu* down to No. 5.

That basic idea here is that we got three teen-age guys as horny as Rhett Beavers, trying to get from point A to point P with a number of girls who are more or less hot to trot, except one who is hot to not trot. One guy is named Rick, and he pretty much gets whatever he wants because he's blond and macho and with it. Another one is this fatso named David, who has a lot of money and so he gets some slack when he needs it. And the title role is played by a pizza delivery boy named Gary, who's on the verge of being a wimp because he has the hots for a foxy woman named Caren but he doesn't do jack about it.

Anyway, these three guys hang around together, doing stuff like making extra pizza deliveries to this blond Mexican woman named Carmela who likes to get nekkid in the afternoon, making fun of the school nurd Victor, and chippin in on a group rate for hookers. Of course, what happens is that Rick goes for Caren and so Gary gets p.o.ed about that, and the Three Musketeers start to fall apart, and I won't give it away, except I'll say that the action never stops.

This flick also has some of the best tunes of the year, including stuff by Blondie, the Cars, the Commodores, Devo, Quincy Jones, Journey, K.C. and the Sunshine Band, Oingo Boingo, the Police, REO Speedwagon, and about ten more bands. Diane Franklin gets a drive-in Academy Award nomination in the foxy flesh category for her portrayal of Caren. Boaz Davidson gets a Best Director nomination. And Louisa Moritz, as Carmela the Mexican lady, gets a big Supporting Actress nod for being so sexy she reduced Rhett Beavers to tears.

A few bare tops. No kung fu. Good music. Heads do not roll. Three and a half stars.

Joe Bob says definitely check it out. ■

Why *Parasite* Leads This Year's Glopola Hit Parade

*P*arasite is not only a description of Chubb Fricke but a flick that I can highly recommend with the following words: Glopola City. Now, the *alert* reader—if any of you turkeys know a shin from Shinola—will remember that glopola is the technical term for the drive-in monster of the eighties. We're not talking mechanical monsters and gorillas (thirties). We're not talking werewolf bullstuff (forties). We're not talking outer-space green-cheese eaters (fifties). We're definitely not talking geeks and psychos like Bette Davis (sixties). And we're not talking sickola sex maniacs that go around slashing nekkid girls into chicken fricassee (seventies).

No, we're talking biology here. We're talking *DNA.* We're talking serious diseases.

We're talking Glopola City.

Just to give you a recap of the year—you saw it in *The Boogens,* you saw it in *Forbidden World,* and now, in the best glopola face-eating performance yet, you're gonna see it in *Parasite.*

Just to give you an idea of what we're dealing with here, I'd like to quote Cherry Dilday: "This is *sick.* This is *stupid.* This is *disgusting.*"

In other words, this monster is a candidate for the Joe Bob Briggs Best of '82 Drive-In Movie list. When this thing gets through with the cast, they all look like Rhett Beavers after that night when Lute Fenwick turned his face into a Cheese Whopper by grinding a Super Bowl ring into his nostrils. (For those who sent sympathy cards, Rhett is much better now but has to be tied to his wheelchair so he won't start fantasizing about Vida Stegall and end up hurting himself.)

I took Cherry Dilday to the drive-in last week because I decided it was time to kiss and make up—well, at least make up, anyway. Cherry went on TV last week and made a fool of herself on the cable, so I thought the least I could do was forgive her for the 917 ways she's already screwed up the First Annual World Drive-In Movie Festival and Custom Car Rally.

It didn't exactly work out that we made up, though, because on the way out to the Gemini I told Cherry I was giving her another job to do, and it was to run the Miss Custom Body Contest at the FAWDIMF&CCR, since a lot of lovely young ladies were getting a little surly from all the *delays.* And Cherry said several things, and one of em was "No way, José." So I said drop it, just drop it, she was the most miserable unpatriotic excuse for a human being since the guy who invented motor vehicle emission control equipment. And finally Cherry said she *might* do it, but only if she could ride in a 1971 T-Top 'Vette with the optional LS-5 454 cubes rated at 365 ponies with 465 pounds of torque muscle. I said, "Cherry, you're so sixties it's pathetic. Watch the movie."

"Metallic blue," she said. "It has to be metallic blue."

"Watch the flick!"

So the first thing we saw was this doctor in a laboratory monkeying around with some minnows in a tube. Only he screws up and the tube breaks, and the minnow jumps out and gloms onto his stomach and starts *burrowing* into him while he screams, and then it starts growing inside him and getting bigger and bigger and his stomach turns purple and starts to look like a pizza with Canadian bacon and Italian sausage (thick crust, no anchovies), until it breaks open and this glopola monster jumps out in a shower of blood and eats the doctor's head.

Cherry Dilday had already barfed by the time I could tell her it was *only a dream.* The doctor

wakes up in his van on the side of the road; he's been having a nightmare. He *does* have a glopola parasite inside his stomach, but it's under control so far. He's heading out into the countryside, trying to find a place where he can work on a cure. It turns out it's 1992 and—you guessed it—everything's wasted. This turkey has to pay $40 a gallon for gas and it's not even unleaded. They won't take his paper money. He goes into this deserted town and finds these two cretins who have this ugly woman chained up and they're ripping off her clothes and trying to do something *nasty.* He saves her with his ray gun, but once he cuts her loose, she goes nuts and *turns* on him and tries to kill *him.* She *liked* it, whatever it was they were doing. She musta been from France or something.

So the world's gone nuts, and this doctor has a parasite eating up his stomach, and the only way he ends up getting away is that he's wrestlin with this fat goon, and they get too close to a rattlesnake, and so the rattler goes directly for the goon's throat, and then the doctor has time to ram a pipe through the man's stomach while the snake is still glommed onto his throat. Blood drips out of that pipe like a faucet, which, I have to hand it to these people, is pretty original stuff.

There's really too much to go into everthing here, but I'll just say that the gist of the matter is that the doctor ends up in this town called Joshua, and he checks into a hotel and starts settin up his lab equipment, but then he goes downtown to the grill for some soup, and these teen-age punkola kids start hasslin him. They cut his arm and steal his money, and then—*real* smart—they grab this big old Thermos that he keeps his experimental parasite in. We know this because it springs out of that Thermos like a flying leech as soon as a dumb kid named Zeke unscrews it, and it gloms onto his shoulder and starts eatin and burrowin and turnin his skin into thirteen shades of designer fabric.

We finally find out what's going down here when a guy shows up wearing a suit that looks like he's stayin at the Fairmont Hotel or something, and the punkola gang leader named Ricus recognizes him. He's a Merchant. The Merchants are the guys who have taken over America and got the doctor working on inventing those parasites—and this particular Merchant is cruisin through town in his muscle machine so he can get rid of the doctor and save the parasite. What he don't know, though, is that a fairly foxy lady named Patricia is takin care of the doctor out at her place. When Patricia came on, Cherry Dilday said Patricia was really Jackie Templeton on *General Hospital,* which is some of that trash indoor small-screen bullstuff she watches ever day, but anyway the girl's name is Demi Moore and, like I say, she's fairly foxy even though she keeps all her clothes on.

So what we got here is the glopola parasite on the one side and the Merchant with his laser-ray pencil on the other, and they're both going for the doctor. What we got, actually, is a whole lot of death by glopola. The glopola grows teeth after a while, for example, and starts turnin up in a lot of weird places—once it goes for this girl under the sheets of her bed, another time it dive-bombs this painted lady (remember Vivian Blaine from the fifties) who runs the hotel, and it goes to work on her *head.* What I'm saying is that I don't have the words to describe, but the end of this thing is Glopola City.

This time of year is just drive-in heaven, the hits come so fast, so I'm afraid I'm gonna have to move *Parasite* to No. 3 on the Joe Bob Briggs Best of '82 Drive-In Movie list even though *The Last American Virgin* has just been there a week. I'm also going to have to nominate the slime glopola monster for a Drive-In Academy Award and to enter for consideration the supporting performances of Luca Bercovici as Ricus, one of the most disgusting, perverted performances I've ever seen; James Davidson as the sleaze Merchant; and Al Fann as an easygoing black guy who runs the cafe and helps chase down the glopola.

Everything in this one. One kung-fu scene. Two bare tops. Eight corpses. Excellent slime monster. Hands roll. Heads roll.

Three and a half stars.

Joe Bob says check it out. ∎

Joe Bob's Mailbag —————

Mr. Briggs
I don't know it you are for real. I can't believe anybody would write such *TRASH* as your reviews of movies are . . . The Times Herald was a pretty fair newspaper until they included Joe Bob Briggs in the Friday section. I think this is a *SICK MIND* coming from someone if you are for real. I feel sorry that the Herald has to include such mess in their paper.

David E. Hill
Park Heights Baptist
Church
Tyler

Friend, I shall pray you will clean up your act.

Dear friend and fellow Babtist:

I want to remind you of the good work of our brother Roger Williams, the Babtist who founded Rhode Island as a place where men could speak their minds and pray in the manner of their choosing. Pastor Williams liberated New England from narrowmindedness, and I have set out, in my small way, to make Texas as big a place as Rhode Island.

Dear Joe Bob,
What a wimp *you* are! In your column of September 10, 1982 you mention driving by the Albuquerque 6 Drive-In on I-27, and comment that "they still know their drive-ins in New Mexico—six screens!" It's a shame you don't know your geography as well as they know their drive-in movies! I-27 happens to extend from Amarillo to Lubbock—both of which are in Texas in case you hadn't noticed. Anyone who can't tell the difference between Albuquerque and Amarillo and/or Lubbock must be a moron or, at best, a certifiable wimp!

Sincerely yours,
Steve Sundgaard
Dallas

Dear Steve:

I'm gonna have to jump on those people at the Times Herald *for all these printer mistakes showing up in my column.*

The Albuquerque 6 is in Albuquerque.

Kung-fu Killers
Defeated; World
Festival a Success

For you guys I promised it to, Wanda Bodine's phone number is (censored by the New York high sheriffs). I don't know where Cherry Dilday is hanging out now, but you can find her at Billy Bob's tomorrow night. Now if I could only get one of you turkeys to take May Ellen Masters off my hands and out of my life, I'd consider the First Annual World Drive-In Movie Festival and Custom Car Rally a complete and total success. While all you animals were out there in front of the concession stand yellin "Where's Joe Bob?" and startin riots last weekend, I was making some serious progress toward *relieving* myself of all outstanding romantic involvements. Cherry got picked up twice, and Wanda got picked up almost as many times as she *wanted* to get picked up, and the long and the short of it is I can now get down to serious movie reviewing again and forget all this female bullstuff. Anyway, I can't stand people who let their personal life interfere with their jobs. (Even though I picked that Kat woman as my personal favorite for Miss Custom Body, I swear

I didn't lay a hand on her. She had more class than Wanda, Cherry, and May Ellen all put together.)

• *Beach Party* got booed and hooted on opening day, and I can't say that I blame you people, because it's basically California wimpola surfer bullstuff. Why were you turkeys watching that screen anyway, when *Rock Around the Clock* was on?

• The contestant in the Miss Custom Body Contest who started describing her upcoming layout in *Hustler* magazine durn near got us all arrested.

• And, of course, the highlight of the entire weekend was the appearance of the King on Saturday night on top of the concession stand. Roger Corman, creator of more than two hundred flicks, the man who made *The Wild Angels* and *Pit and the Pendulum* and *Little Shop of Horrors* and *Teenage Doll* and *The Trip* and has done more for the American drive-in than any living being, accepted the Joe Bob Briggs Life Achievement Award of 1982. The engraved Chevy hubcap read simply "ROGER CORMAN: KING OF THE DRIVE-IN," and I don't know about you, but when he made that stirring speech to the multitudes ("You're the true movie lovers of America, not those critics back East!"), I saw a tear roll down out of the corner of his eye. Let's face it, the man was *moved*.

And, for all of you who missed the greatest drive-in weekend in history, here's the film festival line-up—the thirty-two Greatest Drive-In Flicks in the History of the World.

BEACH PARTY *(1963), Frankie Avalon, Annette Funicello, Robert Cummings, Dorothy Malone.*

ROCK AROUND THE CLOCK *(1956), Bill Haley and His Comets, The Platters, Freddie Bell and the Bellhops.*

HIGH SCHOOL CONFIDENTIAL *(1958), Mamie Van Doren, Russ Tamblyn, Jackie Coogan, Jan Sterling, Jerry Lee Lewis, John Drew Barrymore.*

ROCK 'N' ROLL HIGH SCHOOL *(1979), The Ramones, P. J. Soles, Vincent Van Patten, Clint Howard, Dey Young, Mary Woronov, Dick Miller, Paul Bartel.*

JOHNNY GUITAR *(1954), Joan Crawford, Sterling Hayden, Scott Brady, Mercedes McCambridge.*

A HARD DAY'S NIGHT *(1964), The Beatles, Wilfrid Brambell, Norman Rossington.*

HERCULES *(1959), Steve Reeves.*

A FISTFUL OF DOLLARS *(1966), Clint Eastwood, Gian Marie Volonte, Marianne Koch.*

FIVE GUNS WEST *(1955), John Lund, Dorothy Malone, Touch Connors, Paul Birch, James Stone.*

ROCK ALL NIGHT *(1956), The Platters, Dick Miller, Abby Dalton, Robin Morse, Russell Johnson, Jonathan Haze, The Block Busters.*

MACHINE GUN KELLY *(1958), Charles Bronson, Susan Cabot, Morey Amsterdam, Jack Lambert, Wally Campo, Bob Griffin, Barboura Morris.*

A BUCKET OF BLOOD *(1959), Dick Miller, Barboura Morris, Anthony Carbone, Julian Burton, Ed Nelson, John Brinkley.*

THE INTRUDER *(1962), William Shatner, Frank Maxwell, Beverly Lunsford, Robert Emhardt.*

KISS ME, DEADLY *(1955), Ralph Meeker, Albert Dekker, Paul Stewart, Maxine Cooper, Cloris Leachman, Juano Hernandez, Jack Elam, Marian Carr.*

BAD DAY AT BLACK ROCK *(1954), Spencer Tracy, Robert Ryan, Anne Francis, Ernest Borgnine, Lee Marvin, John Ericson, Walter Brennan.*

X—THE MAN WITH THE X-RAY EYES *(1963), Ray Milland, Diana Van Der Vlis, Harold J. Stone, John Hoyt, Don Rickles.*

WALKING TALL *(1973), Joe Don Baker, Elizabeth Hartman.*

ENTER THE DRAGON *(1973),* *Bruce Lee, John Saxon, Jim Kelly, Ahna Capri.*

THE TRIP *(1967), Peter Fonda, Bruce Dern, Susan Strasberg, Dennis Hopper, Salli Sachse, Katherine Walsh, Barboura Morris.*

THE BLACKBOARD JUNGLE *(1955), Sidney Poitier, Vic Morrow, Glenn Ford, Anne Francis, Richard Kiley, Rafael Campos.*

REBEL WITHOUT A CAUSE *(1955), James Dean, Natalie Wood, Sal Mineo, Corey Allen, Jim Backus, Dennis Hopper.*

BLOODY MAMA *(1970), Shelley Winters, Pat Hingle, Don Stroud, Diane Varsi, Bruce Dern, Clint Kimbrough, Robert De Niro, Scatman Crothers.*

DEATH RACE 2000 *(1975), David Carradine, Sylvester Stallone, Louisa Moritz, Mary Woronov, Simone Griffith.*

THE WILD ANGELS *(1966), Peter Fonda, Nancy Sinatra, Bruce Dern, members of the Hell's Angels.*

HOUSE OF USHER *(1960), Vincent Price, Mark Damon, Myrna Fahey, Harry Ellerbe.*

THE LITTLE SHOP OF HORRORS *(1960), Jonathan Haze, Jackie Joseph, Mel Welles, Myrtle Vail, Leola Wendorff, Dick Miller, Jack Nicholson.*

I MARRIED A MONSTER FROM OUTER SPACE *(1958), Tom Tryon, Gloria Talbott, Ken Lynch, John Eldredge.*

THE BLOB *(1958), Steve McQueen, Aneta Corseaut.*

THE BROOD *(1979), Oliver Reed, Samantha Eggar, Art Hindle, Cindy Hinds.*

TARGETS *(1968), Tim O'Kelly, Boris Karloff, Peter Bogdanovich.*

NIGHT OF THE LIVING DEAD *(1968), Judith O'Dea, Russell Streinger, Duane Jones, Karl Hardman.*

THE TEXAS CHAINSAW MASSACRE *(1974), Marilyn Burns, Allen Danziger, Paul A. Partain, Willian Vall, Teri McMinn, Edwin Neal, Jim Sledow, Gunnar Hansen, John Dugan.* ■

Spare Body Parts in *Halloween III*

Okay, let's talk bionic eyeballs.

First of all, Vida Stegall looks like she *has* bionic eyeballs, which is why Rhett Beavers has always had the hots for her. But that's beside the point. The reason I took Vida Stegall to the Gemini last week has nothing to do with her eyeballs. It was because she was on the run from Lute Fenwick. (If you're reading this, Lute, and you probly can't, *nothing happened.* Nothing. Got that? Straight home from the D.I. Well, actually we went by Don Carter's to bowl a couple lines, but they had some new girl workin the beer cart who was so slow that I checked in early. But straight home after Don Carter's, except for one quickie stop for a Lumberjack Breakfast at the Jojo's on Stemmons. Then straight to Grapevine.)

Vida never would say anything about how it happened, but I could tell it was Lute who scarred up her nose and tore off her manicure apron, because of where he dumped her. That's right: Peter Pan statue in Weatherford. Same place he dumped Rhett Beavers last month. I'm gettin sick of driving out there, to tell you the truth, and since when

did I become a United Way Agency? I don't know why she would call me except Wanda Bodine probly put her up to it, since Wanda has been p.o.ed ever since I put her phone number in the paper last week and she got fired from her day job. Not that it matters, since Wanda can go on back to Le Bodine now that Vida is bringing in the business again. Vida can cut hair faster than a hundred-dollar Weed Eater, but her main value to Le Bodine is the "executive management training" course she took at Tarleton State when she was gettin her home ec degree. Vida was the one that told Wanda to put in video games so she could take quarters from wimps.

Yes, Vida is a college girl. That's why she asks a lot of questions. Gets on my nerves, but that's okay cause she was scared half out of her D-cups when I took her to the D.I.

She wanted to know about the bionic eyeballs in *Halloween III*, and whether they count like regular eyeballs.

To tell you the truth, I got real problems with *Halloween III*, which is why I been thinking about it three weeks now and tryin to decide whether you should check it out. I don't know about you, but when I see the word "Halloween" on the big screen, I start thinkin Splatter City. When we're talking *Halloween*, we're talking all-time classic of the drive-in screen. We're talking the original Jamie Lee Curtis, creepola - with - a - butcher - knife, hypodermic-in-the-eyeball, barf-on-the-floor-mats show-stopper. We're talking a movie where *anybody* can die at *any time*.

So, okay, I have the following questions about this so-called *Halloween III*.

Numero uno: Where the hell is Donald Pleasence? How can we have believable corpses in a Halloween flick unless Donald shows up thirty seconds after they die and says, "You don't know what you're dealing with here. Only *I* can stop him."

Numero duo: Where the hell is Jamie Lee Curtis? And, if we can't have Jamie Lee Curtis because she's off making indoor bull-stuff somewhere, then where are the little nymphos who provide the raw meat for the slasher?

Numero trio: WHERE IS THE SLASHER???!!! I'm talking about the guy with white stuff smeared on his face who walks around breathin like a Hemi 'Cuda and picking up spear guns that people have left laying out in their yard. If this guy is not in the movie, I'm sorry but this is *not Halloween III*. No way, José. This is something else.

Now, the people who made *Friday the 13th, Part 3*, those turkeys had *integrity*. They made the exact same movie three times, which is not easy. These *Halloween* jerkolas have Gone Hollywood. They obviously got stoked up on cocaine and forgot their roots and, get this, *the flick is not even in Haddonfield, Illinois, anymore, where it belongs, but in some wimp jerkola town in California.*

Okay, so what *have* we got here? What we got is a direct rip-off of *Invasion of the Body Snatchers*, another all-time D.I. classic, only instead of a town full of outer-space Communist zombies, the town in this flick is full of motorized bionic dead people that this Irish maniac makes in his Halloween mask factory. But instead of Kevin McCarthy and Dana Wynter, we got two immortal turkeys named Tom Atkins and Stacey Nelkin. For the head Communist, we got a guy named Dan O'Herlihy. He's riggin all the Halloween masks with detonators and—this is the only good part of the movie—ever kid in America is gonna get his head squashed into Jell-O on Halloween night because the masks are gonna be detonated by a TV signal. There's a test kid who gets it first. His eyes get lasered out of their sockets, and then bugs start crawling out of his mouth, and then finally rattlesnakes start crawling out of the insides of his body and eating his parents. This was actually one of the better dramatic scenes in the movie; the kid can really act.

But the rest of this so-called Halloween movie is not so hot. The reason: bionic gore. If all these people in the factory aren't really *people,* what difference does it make when they get parts of their bodies ripped off? It's just a bunch of springs and wires and stuff. There *is* one fairly decent scene where this zombie puts a power drill through a nurse's ear, but there's not even any gurgles or gasps or anything. In other words, totally unrealistic. If you think about what would happen if somebody drilled you through the ear, it would probly be a kind of squishy sound after the steel popped through the skull, and then if he twisted it around inside like the zombie in the movie does, it would probly gush blood like one of those instant modern art twirling painter machines at the state fair.

Okay, so what we got here is a rip-off plot, but it's ripped off from one of the classics of our day, so what the hey. We got zombies. We got fingers stuck through eyeballs. We got exploding automobiles. We got a drunk who gets his head ripped off by two bionic people. We got two breasts on this Stacey Nelkin person. We got a fat woman who gets lasered to death. We got a big mass death scene for the zombies and the Head Communist.

In other words, we got all the elements for a great movie. But I got an idea what went wrong. The first words that come up on the screen of this thing are "Moustapha Akkad Presents." Are you kidding me? Some turkey named *Moustapha Akkad* tried to make a Halloween movie? He sounds like a Communist-speaking person if you ask me. And I'd say it's no coincidence that Leonid Brezhnev died exactly *thirteen* days after this movie came out. We're talking conspiracy.

You can go see it anyway because this is not Communist Russia. Body count nine. Zombie body count fifteen. Two breasts. Not much kung fu, unless you count a little zombie kick-boxing. Hands rolls, arms roll, and, yes, heads roll. Only two stars because it was made by Arabs.

Joe Bob says check it out. ∎

Ten Violent Women
Not a Description
of Joe Bob's Dates

I was telling Chubb Fricke last week that it's about time we had a good women-in-cages movie come through town.

"Cain't," Chubb said. Chubb never has been the kind to memorize the Gettysburg Address, so that's about all he said at first. Chubb was p.o.ed anyway, because I interrupted him while he was telling me about how Pete Weber blew it in the finals of the Detroit Open last weekend. Chubb was in his usual position at the Apollo Drive-In concession stand, in the booth on the south screen side where all the stuffing is coming out because of Chubb's *excessive* size, if you know what I mean and I think you do. Chubb was explaining how Pete Weber lost his cool in the seventh frame, skyhooked his pickup ball high against the three pin, and left the seven-ten stranded on the boards. Chubb said this is because Pete is just a kid and he han't learned to straight-arrow that sucker from the left side. Pete's daddy would've gone home with the check, because Chubb never saw Dick blow a three-seven-ten in thirty years on the PBA tour.

"Choke City," I told Chubb. That's all it was. It wasn't like Pete Weber got beat by three pins or something. It was *forty-one pins,* and Chubb knew it. Chubb is irrational on the matter, though. He's countin on Pete to keep his daddy's streak going. Chubb is what's known as a *seasoned* bowler, which is a way of saying he's older than the paint job on Rhett Beavers's 63 Chrysler. I wanted to get Chubb off the subject entirely, so I brought up the thing about women-in-cages flicks. It's true. It's been one heck of a long time since the last one came through.

"Cain't make em anymore," Chubb said. "Cain't make women-in-cages because of the feminine movement."

"Who says?"

"Jane Fonda got a law passed —or somebody. I don't know."

"Chubb, normally I wouldn't say this because you're *old,"* I told him, "but I would like to point out that this is not Communist Russia and so what Jane Fonda does outside of the big screen is probly illegal. Not only can we put women in cages on screen, but we can be proud of the fact that America *invented* the women-in-cages movie. Censorship is a disgusting thing, Chubb, especially when it affects the pursuit of *leisure* in this country."

And to prove it I took Chubb out to the Toronado and had him check out *Ten Violent Women*. (If Lute Fenwick is reading this, I would like to state at this point that Vida Stegall *was* in my car at the Apollo, but she slept through the entire double feature, including *Chain Gang Women*, because she needed a place to crash that night and Wanda Bodine locked up the trailer house early. This is the complete truth.)

Ten Violent Women is the kind of movie that can make your eyes all teary, it brings back so many memories. I was there in 1971, when it all started out at the Linda Kay D.I., with *The Big Doll House*, and I was there in 1974, when *Caged Heat* came along at the Cherry Lane D.I. in Fort Worth and we all realized for the first time that movies would never be the same. There's something about a woman in a bikini with a machine gun strapped across her chest that says, "Hey, women are people too." It took women in cages to make America see that.

One thing I admired about *Ten Violent Women* was that, as far as I could tell, there never were ten of em. As I have said before and I'll say again, they don't call em exploitation movies for nothing. But once we get past the title, I must admit this flick leaves somethin to be desired in the inspiration department. That's not saying I didn't like it. There's one scene in *Ten Violent Women* that in my opinion can rank with anything done on the big screen this year. It happens after this gang of skirts has just ripped off a jewelry store for a million in diamonds, and so they go to Vegas to meet a fence. He turns out to be a fat turkey with a goatee and a hot tub who tries to sell em some cocaine in a bean bag, so, believe me, he deserves what he gets. What he gets, to be exact, is a spiked high heel through the heart. The girl who tap dances into his chest cavity is an excellent actress. She stabs *repeatedly* with the sharp end of the heel, until it gets slippery with blood and she has to go. Then she rips off the guy's wimpola shark's tooth, which is hanging on a chain around his neck. The man was obviously from San Francisco and deserved everything that happened to him.

To make a long story short, these girls aren't nuclear physicists. They try to sell exactly $1.5 million in coke to two strangers in a bar. Next scene: Crossbar Hotel.

The best performance in the whole movie is by the lady warden, whose name is Miz Terry but who oughta be named Butch, if you know what I mean and I think you do. Miz Terry looks like this sixth-grade teacher I had named Miz Agronsky who had a red moustache. Miz Terry's idea of a good time is to invite women prisoners to her room in the middle of the night and then get nekkid. Miz Terry's idea of a good opening line is "You're begging for it, aren't you?" Miz Terry is supposed to be responsible for the "unusual bruises" on some of the inmates. Miz Terry likes to use a riding crop, and she don't have a horse. Miz Terry also likes to use that lethal weapon, the rolled-up wet towel.

In other words, we're talking Gonzo City.

Anyway, you know the usual routine for women-in-cages. This one has the usual shower fights, with one big difference: Some of these ladies wear their bras and panties *in the shower.* Not only totally unrealistic but kind of kinky and disgusting, if you ask me. The escape scene is pretty good, especially when they kung-fu the warden and strip her down to her pantyhose so they can get her uniform. *Ten Violent Women* is really not a bad effort, considering all the competition it's had over the years.

Fourteen and a half breasts. (I'm giving them the benefit of the doubt, since two of these girls wear flesh-colored bras.) Seven corpses. Two kung-fu scenes. One nekkid-woman brawl. One car chase, but no stunts. No creatures or beasts. Heads do not roll. Two stars. Joe Bob says check it out. ∎

Chopsocky Weekend:
Dragon on Fire

I took Wanda Bodine out to Caddo last weekend even though I always regret decisions like that after about the first ten minutes in the car listening to her yammer about the trailer house beauty-parlor binness. The main reason I took her along is that I needed somebody dumber than a box of rocks to send out for catfish while I was practicing my kick-boxing.

Now, I know what *some people* out there are thinking. *Some people* are thinking that I drove all the way to Caddo to get away from Ishmael Robles, the so-called No. 1 ranked contender for the PKA Full Contact Karate Super Welter Weight Championship of the World. This is a completely false rumor. Let me tell you turkeys, though. I *got the message* from Ishmael. I got the message right after I wrote the following sentence in my November 19 column: "Tommy Williams is defending against Ishmael Robles, only in my opinion anybody named Ishmael couldn't kick his way out of a Glad Bag." Evidently Ishmael was training in Dallas at the time, somebody showed him the column, and he issued a challenge to meet Joe Bob Briggs any-time, anyplace, any *style* of mar-tial arts.

Am I right, Ishmael? Did I hear right? If so, I want your "X" on the dotted line, buddy. I want a contract for the Sportatorium, no later than six months from today, five rounds, $50,000 minimum, and my style is mad-monkey kick-boxing, the martial arts technique immortalized in the drive-in clas-sic *Mad Monkey Kung Fu.* So ei-ther put your name on the paper or go back to Albania. My agent is Chubb Fricke, and he'll be waiting for your lawyers at the Bronco Bowl, where he spends most of his waking hours.

To get into the chopsocky spirit, I brought Wanda back early from Caddo and dumped her over by SMU and told her I was head-ing for the Highway 183 Drive-In with Chubb and Rhett Beavers to see a kung-fu flick called *Dragon on Fire.* Wanda saw through this ruse immediately and *assumed* that I was going by to pick up Miss Custom Body of 1982, other-wise known as the Kat Woman.

Anyway, I really did go to the 183 with Chubb and Rhett be-cause I didn't want Wanda or Cherry to start barfing on the up-holstery like they have the last *three* times I took em anywhere. *Dragon on Fire* stars Philip Ku and Dragon Lee, even though anybody who knows their chop-socky will instantly recognize Dragon Lee as Bruce Lee. (Some-times these American turkeys who do the dubbing don't know their shin from Shinola.) As we all know, first off we need a goonhead drug pusher who beats up little boys and takes everybody's money, so that at the end of the movie Philip and Bruce can mash his head into a Chinese pancake. And we got a *great* one: The guy looks exactly like Peter O'Toole, only he has white stuff smeared all over his face and a Fu Manchu and he only eats live cockroaches and frogs and he sits in a wheelchair all the time.

Now, I'm sorry to say that we're at one of those places in the movie review where the *Times Herald* editors are gonna start sharpening up their scissors if I tell you *why* this Peter O'Toole Quasimodo guy is in a wheelchair. I'll just put it this way. When he was a young man, he tried to rape this girl, but while he was doing it, the girl's rabid dog got loose and chased him down and bit him. Where did he bite him, you want to know? As you know, at various times in the past, Joe Bob has talked about heads rolling, arms rolling, legs rolling, hands, ears, fingers, and a lot of other severed body parts that were necessary to the story. This *particular* body part is none of the above, and it does roll because the dog bites it plumb off. It's not a pretty pic-ture. Take my word for it, you'd want a wheelchair too.

Okay, so next thing is here's the goonhead sittin in his wheel-chair tossing out coins to these kung-fu masters who journey to his place so they can try to kill each other for the money. He keeps the best ones and teaches them the "iron fist" technique so they can guard his drug-smuggling setup. Only he doesn't count on Philip and Bruce wanting revenge on his most invincible creepola, because *his* daddy killed *their* daddy. Meanwhile, the geek in the wheelchair has *rabies* by now, and so he's startin to slobber like a German shepherd and swallow his frogs without properly chewing first. He knows some hands-only kung fu too, which he calls the "mad dog" technique. Bruce has to use the "eagle's claw" technique to go after him. Philip uses the "invisible hand" technique on Wheelchair Billy's No. 1 creepola.

Anyway, what we got here is nonstop Hong Kong chopsocky. The flick runs about one hour thirty-five, and I would say a good solid hour is kung-fu action, including some decent three-on-one bouts, excellent hand action, and a few astounding overhead leaps. Comedy chopsocky includes Philip dusting these two punks with his *toes* only and Bruce catching sailing plates on his hands, feet, and the back of his neck. Acting is okay. The mad-dog parts are terrific, specially when Mr. Wheelchair is slathering around like a cocker spaniel, trying to sink his molars into Bruce's deltoids. Final fight scene goes on about fifteen minutes and has some great kung-fu spread-eagle leaps.

No motor vehicles. One breast. No creatures. Can't tell you what rolls. Three stars.

Joe Bob says check it out. ∎

Malibu Hot Summer:
It's Better Than *E.T.*
in the Garbonza Department

It's not exactly my idea of a good time to fork over $4 for a cardboard bowl with seven Doritos in it and a scoop of Cheez Whiz dumped in the middle like leftovers at a Salvation Army dinner for illegal aliens. Don't get me wrong—I don't have anything against Meskin food. But what we're talking here is Sports Arena Food. We're talking Grade A Purina Wimp Chow. To get down to the real nitty, what we're talking is Tarrant County Convention Center Nachos.

Now I have to admit that TCCC Nachos are slightly better than Arlington Stadium Billy Martin-Breath Nachos, but that's pretty much one of your academic questions since nobody's bought any Arlington Stadium Nachos since 1974, except for the people who move here from New Jersey and think they're ordering soup. They never know the difference, because you can drink those suckers through a straw anyway. No, I'm talking about a different kind of animal. I'm talking about the new flavor they have over in Fort Worth, the kind of nacho that smells roughly like Rhett Beavers's socks after he's bowled nine lines in a pair of rental shoes.

I mention Rhett because he witnessed what happened over in Cowtown last Saturday night. I *told* Vida not to touch those Tarrant County Nachos. I *told* her they looked like the insides of a Brahma bull after he's been fed a duffel bag full of Big Macs. But she couldn't just settle for a super dog like any ordinary person; she had to sink her teeth into that orange glopola and get us all in deep stuff, if you know what I mean and I think you do.

First off, I'd like to say that the Welter Weight Kick-boxing Championships came up pretty near the end of Chopsocky Weekend, and so I was durn near exhausted by the time we got over to Convention Arena to see Alvin "Million Dollar Baby" Prouder defend his title against my personal friend, Billy "Jack" Jackson. After I dumped Wanda Bodine last week, I took Vida to see *Dragon on Fire,* and then we went out to the kung-fu demonstrations at Red Bird Mall.

That's why, after all that ac-tion, I wasn't entirely prepared to *argue* with Vida when she demanded that I buy her some orange No. 3 motor oil to pour down her throat. Not that it mattered to me, since I didn't intend to get my face near hers anyway, at least not for a few hours, and I could always put a bag over her head. So we went on into the arena to watch the prelims—and that's when the bullstuff started.

First this turkey-faced Ishmael Robles, the Super Welter contender who thinks he wants to fight me, got up in the middle of the ring with a microphone and started talking about how "Joe Bob *Biggs"* won't meet him man to man. (See what I'm talking about? The jerkola can't even spell.) As everyone knows, I have accepted this challenge in spite of the man's name, and have selected the martial arts form of first choice: mad-monkey kick-boxing, with eight-inch Nunchaku sticks. I didn't even want to dignify the wimp's remarks with a response, since, *numero uno,* I'm not a violent kind of guy, and, *numero two-o,* the King of Kung Fu, Chuck Norris, was in the audience and I didn't want him to have to step in and force us apart. It would be embarrassing for everone involved.

But what I didn't count on was Wanda Bodine. There she was, *sitting on the front row ringside with Rhett Beavers.* And as soon as Ishmael went into his rap about "Joe Bob Goes to the D.I.," she flung herself up out of that chair, scattering eyelashes all over the ring mat, hiked up her velveteen Spandex aerobic-dancing pants, and started running up one row of chairs and down the other like Jamie Lee Curtis. Then she started screaming "I know you're out there," and I guess I knew at that moment that it had been a bad idea to tell her I wasn't going to the Kick-boxing Finals because I wanted to read *War and Peace* that night.

I had no idea what she would do if she found me, so I started making for the door, but just as I was prying Vida's fingers out of her nacho bowl, Wanda spotted us from about four rows away, clamped her hand over her bouffant so it wouldn't get dirty, and jumped over those chairs so fast that one guy thought she was part of the show and asked her if she was into aerial Tae Kwon Do. By this time her eyes were bulged out like Bette Davis, and she was so mad that she just stood there a minute, looking at both of us like she couldn't decide whose eyes to poke out first. I saw her leg muscles get tense for a minute, and I remembered that scene in *Ten Violent Women* where the guy gets a spiked high heel through the chest, and I thought, *Oh, my God, not THAT.* But then she jumped at me real quick and grabbed my Nunchaku sticks out of my hip pocket where they were sticking out. They're the laminated hardwood kind, Speed-Chuck model, with the octagon handles, studded grips, and a ten-link steel chain. When I thought about what she could do to my neck with those

mothers, I could hardly stand it. *Oh, my God, not THAT.* But compared to what she *did* do, a few Nunchakus to the kidneys would have been lettin me off easy. Because, before anybody could stop her, she went for the nastiest weapon of them all.

"Oh, my God!" I screamed at her. *"Not the nachos!"*

But she was too quick for us both. She grabbed that cardboard mushbowl so fast that Vida had her eyes sealed shut with glopola before she even knew what hit her. As for me, I'm still tryin to get the nacho smell off of my skin where it ran down both sides of my face and got my Speed-Chuck handles so sticky that they'll probly never be the same again. What I'm sayin is that what Wanda Bodine did to us is not a pretty sight. We were Cheez Whizzed within an inch of our lives.

Vida was so disgusted that she resigned from Le Bodine on the spot, said she wasn't going to work for any *so-called* beauty expert who could do such a thing to a woman's looks, and then Vida suggested—real loud, so that Wanda could hear ever word—that the two of us go and "shower off." I won't go into the rest of the evening because I'm not a public kind of guy, but just let me say that we topped off the festivities with a visit to a fine flick about true love called *Malibu Hot Summer.*

Now, you turkeys may or may not know that this is the first day of the Christmas movie season, and the theaters have been saving up all their best stuff for to-night. I'm proud to say that the drive-ins of Dallas County and the greater Metroplex area haven't let us down and, once again, we have a blockbuster holiday flick, exclusively playing on the outdoor screen. Now, I know what you're thinking. You're thinking *Malibu Hot Summer* sounds like California wimpola surfer bullstuff. But what you don't realize is that not only do we have *thirty-nine* garbonzas in this film (and let me point out, we're talking real garbonzas, not those rip-off flesh-colored bras like in *Ten Violent Women*)—not *only* do we have garbonzas, but we have a crippled midget who drives a Stingray, we have the kind of female high school gym teacher that every boy would love to play volleyball with, we have women who will do *anything* to advance their careers (and they have to, since they're all dumb as a box of rocks), and we have a lot of messing around in couches and beds and on the beach.

To get down to the nitty. Thirty-nine complete breasts. One motor vehicle crash. No kung fu. No creatures. Heads do not roll. Best of all, *absolutely no plot* to make you forget the movie. It's too bad *Malibu Hot Summer* didn't have five more breasts, in which case it could have gone to No. 1 on the 1982 Frontal Exposure List. But *Beach Girls* is still the champ, and *Malibu* has to settle for . . . two and a half stars.

Joe Bob says check it out. ∎

Briggs's Guide to Impeccable Drive-In Etiquette

There are some people in Massachusetts who don't understand why God created drive-ins. There are even some people in New York who don't know what the word "drive-in" *means*. If you know any of these people—or any of the unfortunate people behind the Iron Curtain who are denied the right to attend movies in automobiles—I urge you to clip this article out and send it to them immediately. This is for the poor turkeys who don't have the advantages that you and me have. This is for the suckers who never got the chance to watch flicks in the outdoors the way they were meant to be seen.

RULE #1: *Decide immediately whether you are interested in public or private entertainment.*

The beautiful thing about the drive-in is that the flick is public but your car is not. So if you have something more interesting going on *in* your car than *on* the screen, you should take advantage of the situation by purchasing certain options. One is the retractable steering wheel (to avoid hip injury). Another is the fold-back seat (to avoid the direct imprint of upholstery patterns on the skin). And a final, very important one, is various sundries and toiletry items to be deposited in the glove compartment (consult your pharmacist). If the screen *is* more interesting, as it usually is, all you need is one ice chest and anywhere from four to sixteen six-packs. (Löwenbräu specifically forbidden in Texas drive-ins, but permissible in wimp states like Vermont.)

RULE #2: *No matter who or what you see at the drive-in, DO NOT bring lawn chairs.* The worst you can do is take up space somebody could've used to park in. The best you can do is look like a jerk, sittin in a lawn chair with a speaker hooked on the back. This defeats the entire purpose— namely, to go out for an evening's entertainment while still enjoying all the comforts of your car.

RULE #3: *When approaching another car, ALWAYS count the heads before opening the door.* I think this one is fairly self-explanatory and falls under the heading of Class C misdemeanors.

RULE #4: *Keep your lights off at all times.* Not only does this muck up the picture for people who are trying to watch. It can be damned embarrassing.

RULE #5: *Do not own a van.* If you do own a van, do not bring it to the drive-in because it does not belong there. If you do bring it to the drive-in, please park next to me so that I can shout loud remarks about your virility to the greasers in charge of keeping hippies in line.

RULE #6: *Never order Mexican food at a drive-in.* This includes nachos.

RULE #7: *When the sound goes bad or the picture goes blank, ride that horn like your life depends on it.* There is nothing more terrifying than, oh, about 1000 car horns all blasting at once. The only place you can hear this on a regular basis is at the drive-in, the last place in America where the people can make more noise than the bureaucracy. Problems don't last long at the drive-in. This is why.

RULE #8: *Never remove any article of clothing after the second feature.* You think you're taking off your socks, but after three six-packs, you're actually taking off your pants.

RULE #9: *Never say anything to the ticket booth operator like, "Hey, fatso, we're from Sigma Nu and we're ready to party."* Ticket booth operators at drive-ins tend to weight 240 pounds and carry weapons.

RULE #10: *Never go alone to a drive-in.* The ice chest can't hold that much beer. ■

Fighting Back Is a Great Flick, But No *Death Wish II*

One of the true mysteries of modern times is how you can knock everything down except the five pin. Now, I've mentioned this to Chubb Fricke many times, but he never listens to me. Chubb is retired, and retired people don't have to listen to you. I've never seen Chubb leave a solid five pin, because Chubb is what you would call a big man, if you know what I mean and I believe you do, and being a big man he can throw that sucker so hard it breaks more pins than it knocks over. The five pin don't have a chance.

But last weekend I brought this up again because of Vida Stegall's peculiar bowling. We were at the Bronco Bowl about 1 in the A.M., and Chubb was there as usual and so he witnessed it himself. You ever seen the one-four-five-seven-eight split? I han't either till I went bowling with Vida Stegall. But that's a subject for another column. Mostly she just kept knocking down all the pins *except* the five.

"That's impossible," I told her.

"What do you mean?" she said. "I just did it."

"The five pin is in the exact middle of all the pins. You can't knock the others over without knocking *it* over."

"I just did it."

Vida has a way of looking like she's about to drive a three-inch fingernail through you when you contradict her. I didn't contradict her.

"Let's ask Chubb," I said.

Chubb Fricke later claimed that I destroyed his concentration by going over to Lane 72 and giving him a hard time until he agreed to come and look at Vida's form. But since Chubb is the only ex-member of the PBA tour who hangs out at the Bronc, I told him he had to do it for the scientific value if nothin else. He was about to witness a miracle of modern bowling. (Okay, I know what some of you turkeys are wondering. Just *when* was Chubb Fricke a member of the PBA tour? The following info comes direct from the PBA Almanac. The date: October 22, 1938. The place: Paradise Lanes, Waukegan, Illinois. The opponent: Bucko Swenson. The result: Chubb 208, Bucko 116. Bucko was seven years old at the time. Chubb was not fat at the time.)

Chubb grumbled a little bit and stuck a toothpick in his mouth and spit in his paper coffee cup, but finally he said he'd come on over. Vida was gettin a little irritated by the time I got back, specially since she'd decided it was *me* who caused her to lose her job the week before when she got Cheese Whizzed by Wanda Bodine in the Tarrant County Convention Center Arena. (I'm not telling that story again. You turkeys who didn't read it last week —*tough,* I'm sick of repeatin this stuff.) So Vida was a little ticked, and when Chubb got there she was a little more ticked because she don't like Chubb worth a damn because she claims he smells like the Le Bodine Hairstyling Salon on the second Wednesday of the month, which is the day the Daughters of the Texas Revolution come in for their perms. Sometimes Wanda gets ten, fifteen perms going at once, and I'm telling you, I been there and Vida knows whereof she speaks.

"Let's bowl," said Chubb. Chubb is a man of few words.

You have to understand, first of all, that Vida uses a nine-step approach to the line. Okay, so it's a little unusual, but what the hey, this is not Communist Russia and so she can use any approach she wants. So Vida took her nine steps and let that mother go and sure

enough it happened—hit the head pin and everthing else, but no five.

"Show me again," said Chubb. People were startin to gather around us now that Chubb was giving her so much attention.

Vida hit the reset button and bowled that sucker again. Chubb had to turn away and spit into the ashtray, but when he turned back he had the answer.

"Right English on a right-hand ball," said Chubb.

"What's that?" I asked him.

"Bad news."

We all looked at Chubb. "The thing is," he said, real thoughtful now, "I don't know *how* she gets that spin on the ball. I must've seen a hundred thousand bowlers in my day, and I've never seen spin like that."

I never heard Chubb speak that many words in a row in my life, so I was truly impressed. After that speech, I turned to Wanda and said, "Okay, hon, I want you to do it *one more time, very slowly.*"

"So Egg-Nog Face can watch my rear again?" As I say, Vida don't care a whole lot for Chubb.

"No, really, do it for me." I was pleading a little bit now, because I had to know what was going on here.

Finally she agreed to do it one more time, and this time every eye in the place was on Vida. We watched all nine steps. We watched her legs and her feet and the position of her hand on the ball and her stomach and her hair and her lips and her thighs and . . . oh well, we watched *ever-*

thing this woman did till the moment when she let go of that ball.

I guess I was the first one to notice it. I guess I noticed it even before she let fly with it. I guess I also noticed that everbody else in the Bronc saw it at the same time I did.

"Vida," I said, just when the ball dropped onto the hardwood, "are you wearing a brassiere?"

Her ball sailed over the fourth arrow, popped the one pin full, cleared the decks, and left a solid five. Chubb opened his mouth so fast you couldn't even hear Vida's answer.

"That's it!" he said. "That explains the reverse English . . ." And then he went into this number about gyroscope action in the upper body and how that skews the skeletal frame off the perpendicular and causes the active elbow to rotate slightly outward and, well, I can't remember all of it, except what it comes down to is Vida's garbonzas. You just can't let those things swing free and expect the ball to act normal.

We would of continued this scientific experiment, except word spreads pretty fast at the Bronc, and as I have often said, Vida does fill out a white uniform, and so by the time we got to the fourth frame we had a bigger cheerin section than they had last year at the PBA Tournament of Champions. That's a real shame too, because we were startin to learn a lot about Vida's potential as a bowler, if you know what I mean and I think you do.

Instead of that, though, Vida badgered me to take her to a Christmas movie and even said I owed it to her after *exposing* her to Chubb Fricke. (She didn't mind the cheering section. It was Chubb that got to her.) And since we'd already been to *Malibu Hot Summer,* I took her to the other big drive-in Christmas flick of the year, at the Gemini, of course—*Fighting Back.*

As we all know, I'm not a violent kind of guy. I don't use my Nunchaku sticks unless I have to. But I do know that when the veins start sticking out on Chuck Bronson's neck and he starts blowin people away and getting their blood all over his clothes, he usually has a very good reason. He's generally fed up with all the pinko liberal cop-haters and bureaucrats who won't do anything to keep America safe anymore. He does what any reasonable not-a-violent-kind-of-guy would do: He blows them from here to Communist Russia, where they belong. A lot of people say *Death Wish* was the greatest you'll-get-yours movie ever made but I have to say my personal favorite is *Death Wish II,* mainly because Chuck seems to enjoy himself more in that one and he uses a much greater variety of death weapons.

What I'm leading up to is that this flick, *Fighting Back,* tries to follow in the footsteps of *Death Wish II* and *Walking Tall,* but I'm sorry, man, it just don't wash. I'm not saying don't see it. It's a pure-dee American movie, and the star of it is Tom Skerritt, one of the most macho guys of our time. I remember Tom when he used to run through an abandoned warehouse every week of the TV season so that Mike Connors could put on a $400 suit and chase him to his death in *Mannix*. I know what you're thinking; when Tom played Shirley MacLaine's husband in *The Turning Point*, he was trying to go *indoors* on us. Not true. Tom did it for the bread.

Okay, so Tom Skerritt is this Italian dude in South Philadelphia named John D'Angelo, and his life is all screwed up because, *in one day*, his best friend who owns a drugstore gets sent to the hospital by a bunch of creeps with shotguns; his wife has a miscarriage because she's trying to help this hooker who's gettin the bejeezus beat out of her by a pimp; and Big Tom's mother gets her finger cut off by some punks who want her wedding ring. Pretty disgusting. Let me tell you: Tom's steamed. He starts *organizing*. He goes after the geeks and weirdos and junkies and winos and pimps and punks and royal jerkolas who are screwing up his neighborhood. He goes into *action*.

All the usual *Death Wish* stuff after that: Tom becomes a hero, other people join up with him, the cops get scared, the politicians try to stop him, and the gangsters start killing off his friends *and* (I thought this was a real original twist) the man's *dog*. I damn near cried. Anyway, it takes Tom a little while to get his act entirely together, but finally he Walks Tall and, to get down to the nitty, Fights Back. It's time for revenge. It's time for a little justice. It's time, in other words, to Kick A. We're talkin Kung Fu City.

We've got seven corpses. We've got one fairly decent motor vehicle stunt. We've got kung fu. No creatures. Two breasts. Heads do not roll, but fingers roll. Two stars.

Joe Bob says check it out. ∎

How JB Spent His Christmas Vacation, Part I

I'd like to take a minute to explain the difference between barbecue and B-B-Q. Now, I know that most of you don't *need* this lesson, and I'd actually be ashamed of most people who didn't know the difference unless they were either from New Jersey or they played the accordion for a living. Cherry Dilday is dumber than a box of rocks, and she can't even *spell* B-B-Q, but she does know the difference. The reason I bring this up is that last week I was coming back from Caddo Lake with Vida Stegall, and we were passin through Mineola in the Toronado, and I made a remark about stoppin for some red meat at this place called Bobo's next to a DX Station, but then at the last minute I noticed the sign said "Fresh Barbecue," and so I gunned it on out of there.

"I thought we been looking for barbecue for a half hour," is what Vida said. She don't speak a whole lot, and actually that's one of the main reasons I like her, but I couldn't let a remark like that just pass by.

"B-B-Q," I told her, as friendly as I could manage, "we are *looking* for B-B-Q."

"What's the difference?"

I'm afraid we're talking Rock City, U.S.A.

But I'm not gonna judge other people, except when they deserve it. So I'm prepared to give Vida the benefit of the doubt. Vida is only nineteen years old, and her family didn't move into their first trailer house till she was eleven. In other words, Vida's what you might call your head case. I realize this now because of our week at Caddo, which got cut short because I found out about the PCBs they were finding out by the old pier. It was really a relief to find out, because I'd been tryin to think of a way to tell Wendell Nibbs that the catfish he's been servin had a taste like toasted sweet potatoes. But now we know that Wendell han't lost his touch and his Catfish Surprise is just pickin up a little chemical seasoning.

Anyhow, as I say, we were past Mineola when Vida started to remind me of May Ellen Masters without the runny mascara.

"Vida," I said, "I'm gonna tell you this one time and one time only. Barbecue and B-B-Q are two entirely differnt things."

Vida didn't say anything because she knew I was p.o.ed. I will now repeat for you turkeys the ways to tell the difference.

Numero uno: You can buy barbecue anywhere, even in Red China and Milwaukee. You can only buy B-B-Q in Texas.

Numero two-o: There are some sleazeball liars in other parts of the South who *advertise* B-B-Q. These people are sellin Sloppy Joes and calling em B-B-Q so that people from Texas won't know that they're swallowin that brown glopola that they forced you to eat ever Tuesday in elementary school along with your Halloween cupcake. Genuine B-B-Q is *not* available anywhere east of the Louisiana state line or north of the Red River or in Mexico. In fact, that stuff down in Mexico is goat meat, which I don't know about you but I think that's Puke City.

Numero three-o: The best B-B-Q is sold at restaurants where there is only one word on the sign outside: "B-B-Q." None of this personal editorializing bullstuff, like "B-B-Q Heaven." A single name is okay, like "Joe's B-B-Q." But *never* "Joe's *Bar*-B-Q." That's the sign of a man who can't make up his mind what he's selling.

Numero four-o: B-B-Q is served on a bun, with red sauce and one jalapeno, potato salad and baked beans on the side. No substitutions. If they serve slaw, I'm sorry, but they're serving barbecue.

Numero five-o: There is no B-B-Q served on Greenville Avenue, in any place located in a shopping center, or in any place that sells stuff *besides* B-B-Q.

Numero six-o: B-B-Q is never served by a waitress. You get in line and get it yourself.

Numero seven-o: B-B-Q is always served on a paper plate.

Numero eight-o: Most experts prefer sawdust on the floor. Concrete is optional.

Numero nine-o: Anything else is wimp barbecue.

I do have to report that finally Vida apologized for her box-of-rocks remark, and by the time we rolled into Pleasant Grove I was cooled down enough to let her tag along to the Astro D.I. to catch *One Down Two to Go,* which is the first black chopsocky to come along since my man Leon Isaac Kennedy made *Body and Soul* in 81. We're talking return of Shaft, Superfly of the eighties. We're talkin a lot of cool mean blacks blowing away the white wimps for having the *incorrect attitude.* I love these flicks, because all the black dudes carry .44s and .357 Magnum cannons longer than their arms, and all the white guys carry these little pea-shooters that sound like cap guns, and the object is to make the white guy die before he can even *fire* the sucker.

We got four headliners here. We got Fred Williamson, we got Richard Roundtree, we got Jim Kelly, and we got my main man, Jim Brown. We start off with some serious chopsocky, where all the dudes from California have gone to New Jersey for a full-contact karate match where the winner gets $400,000. Only the white guys are puttin lead weights in their gloves so they don't have to pay up. Only Jim Kelly knocks the guy out *anyway* and the white guys don't wanna pay. I think we all know what that means. We're talking action. We're talking shoeleather to the groin. We're talking Kung Fu City.

First Kelly kung-fus three Mafia guys who are tryin to keep him away from the fight. Then two more honkies follow Kelly and one of em shoots him through the elbow. Then Jim Brown goes to collect the money from a pizza face who's tryin to impress this bimbo in a restaurant. This is where the good stuff starts. Jim Brown is the best Mr. Mean on the screen. All he has to do is push his face up to about one inch this side of a man's nose and whisper to him, "I don't like violence either, Mr. White Boy," and you get the general idea of what's coming next.

What's coming next is the white guys decide to kill all the blacks in the cast. This is not a good idea.

To give you some idea of what we're talking here, we have a total of fourteen white corpses, all wimps. We got Kelly doing some serious chopsocky despite his wrecked elbow. And we got Jim Brown sayin to a banker who won't tell him where the money is "I may not know kung fu, but I'm an expert in gun fu." We got a hotel room shootout. We got a parking-garage shootout. We got two blown-up motor vehicles. We got a shootout inside the house of the Mr. Big Mafia guy. And we got a lot of lovely ladies hanging around but not doing much to help.

No breasts, even in Williamson's big shower scene. No creatures. Minimum blood. Fourteen bodies. One motor vehicle crash. Two explosions. *Mucho* chopsocky. Porno-movie music. Not up to the high standards of *Shaft,* the all-time champion, but a kind of laid-back eighties version of the same stuff.

Two and a half stars. Joe Bob says check it out. ∎

Joe Bob's Mailbag ⸺

Joe Bob:
Ever thought of changing your first names to Bob Seth? Then the initials would explain what you write of the best.

Well, happy holidays Joe Bob and I must say the notoriety you've sent my way is quite intriguing.

Enough of the nicities. It's time to put your money where your pen is. The Dallas Bronco full-contact team will be at the Bronco Bowl January 29th and I'll be there. Will you?

Although it will be one

week before my schedualed K.I.C.K. world title fight in St Louis, I couldn't think of a nicer warm-up fight than to defeat you on your home turf.

So Joe Bob start looking over your health-care insurance and to be on the safe side check your funeral insurance and will.

Until you and I meet face to face take care Joe Bob.

Your sworn adversary
Ishmael Robles
P.K.A. & W.K.A.
United States Champ
Galveston

Dear Ishmael:
Mad Monkey Kick Boxing, twelve-inch Nunchaku sticks, fifteen rounds, winner take all. Wimps named Ishmael beware.
Galveston.   Should've known.

Dear Joe Bob,

A coupla months back, I was told "Basket Case" made No. 1 on the Joe Bob Briggs Best of '82 Drive-In Movie List and I said "Great! What's that?" Then in September I saw a xerox of your courageous attack on San Francisco (" 'Basket Case' beset by wimps; Joe Bob vows to retaliate") and I said "What's going on here and where do we meet this guy?"

But now someone has sent my partner Edgar Ievins all

your back reviews and suddenly everything's become clear. And just for the record, let me state that being No. 1 on the Joe Bob Briggs Best of '82 Drive-In Movie List is an absolute Honor.

Not only are you the only critic in America decent people can relate to, but your girl friends are more interesting than the films themselves.

Wish I could've been there for the big Festival (even though two of my all-time favorites, "The Undertaker and His Pals" and "Wanda the Wicked Warden," weren't even nominated.)

New York may not have drive-ins but we could sure use Joe Bob up here.

All my love to Cherry,
Frank Henenlotter
Director, "Basket Case"
New York, N.Y.

Dear Frank:
I have to admit that "Basket Case" is the one great thing to come out of New York City in the past fifty years. But let me remind you —it took the non-communist drive-in-going public of America to make you what you are today: the most honored outdoor movie director in the nation. If you need bucks for Basket Case II, *you should think about pokin around down here where you're appreciated.*

Joe Bob Is Back, and He Better Have a Good Explanation

I went to the Woolco in Big Town on going-out-of-business day just like everbody else, and I was just minding my *own* binness in Auto Parts and Supplies, stocking up on some 10-W-40 quart cans and forty-seven sets of vinyl seat covers and twenty-six sets of burlap floor mats because I couldn't resist the prices, and nothing would've happened if it han't been for the turkey with the microphone who kept announcing specials like "For the next three minutes only Atari Space Invaders cassettes will be $8," and even that would've been okay but the wimp went too far.

It all started when he announced the 30-cent brassieres.

I've never seen a 30-cent brassiere and I hope I never do. All I know is, as soon as Mr. Microphone said "Bra Sale," I was a goner. I happened to be standing right next to Bowling Accessories, because the Quaker State Open is coming up at Forum Lanes in Grand Prairie and so I'm a bowling fool this time of year, and I guess that's why I didn't see the first one. She blindsided me with a shopping cart completely filled with Burpee seed packets and easy-glue-on Dixie Cup dispensers, but she didn't have time to say anything because the 30-cent brassiere sale was only for three minutes. Right behind her there was this lady wrestler in an Anne Murray wig who rammed her wire-steel push-up support bra through my neck, and believe me, this woman looked like she'd been shot through the back with a couple Cruise missiles. But the one that got me was carryin a floor-to-ceiling plastic pole lamp under one arm, seven *Magnum P.I.* board games under the other one, and an expression on her face that said "I'd *kill* for a Morgan Fairchild makeover." We're talking bad news here. We're talking, of course, May Ellen Masters.

She decked me with her pole lamp, and I still have a suspicion she did it on purpose and not just because of the 30-cent brassieres. May Ellen has probly been wearing 30-cent brassieres most of her life. And even though she was part of the Bra Stampede, I still hold her entirely responsible for the massive pileup right there in front of the La-Z-boy recliners.

But the bottom line is: Assault and Battery of a Female, bond revoked on two priors, remanded to Bossier City, Louisiana, for judgment. Bubba Barclay, my lawyer, was out of town, and I already owed him 20 bucks for the last time, and besides he probly didn't know what "remanded" meant anyway. I won't go into all the details, but I'll just say this: Forced incarceration is not a pretty sight. First off, the judge tells me I either put up $10,000 bail on the ten previous charges—including grand theft auto, which was impossible, because I was stealing my *own* car back from Gus Simpson—or I go to the Crossbar Hotel. So I tell him that would *seriously impair* my ability to review drive-in movies. And he said, "What?" And I told him if I don't go to the drive-in I don't get jack from the *Times Herald*. And he said, "What?" And fortunately *Lunchwagon Girls* was playing in Bossier City at the time and so I could say to the man, "There are millions of readers in the greater Ark-La-Tex area who won't know Fact One about *Lunchwagon Girls* unless I'm out there serving my country. It's a tough job but *somebody* has to do it." He said, "What?" So I said, *"Don't you understand that there's nobody to do the breast count if I don't do it!"*

I'm telling you, that was mistake-o numero uno, because that little outburst cost me two weeks while the judge checked out my story. And let me say at this time that the unidentified individual at the *Times Herald* newspaper who answered the phone last week deserves the credit for me being back so early, because the scene over there in Bossier City was starting to look like *First Blood*. The only thing that saved me was they couldn't find May Ellen to testify, and so they dropped the new charges and gave me five years pro on the rest of em and it probly would've been more but Bubba Barclay never did get back to town to defend me.

As soon as I hit town again, I knew I blew it for the month of January. As everbody knows, this is the most *outstanding* drive-in season of the year. Last year this time we had *The Grim Reaper* and *Mad Monkey Kung Fu*. This year we have *Lunchwagon Girls, Locker Room Teasers, Sweet Sixteen, Ator the Fighting Eagle* (Miles O'Keefe, the beefcake Tarzan who couldn't talk, turns barbarian), and *Timerider* (the first motocross western). But let's get down to the nitty and talk top January drive-in attraction, a flick so special that it had an *exclusive* outdoor engagement at the Astro on Loop 12. This is the picture that the ladies on the Dallas Censor Board thought was so disgusting they gave it *every* rating allowed by law.

We're talking S for Sex.

Gimme a L for Obscene Language.

Gimme a V for Violence.

Gimme a D for Drugola Abuse.

Gimme a N for Nudie shots.

Best of all, gimme a P for *Perversion.*

Whaddaya got? SLVDNP.

Good work, ladies. First clean sweep of the Dallas Censor Board in my memory. We're talking nasty here. We're talking *They Call Me Bruce?* which some of you turkeys know *used* to be called *A Fistful of Chopsticks* only that didn't work so they decided to go with the art-film title.

Anyway, it's chopsocky comedy. Johnny Yune is this comedian who goes on the *Johnny Carson Show* all the time, and in this flick he plays this turkey who thinks he looks like Bruce Lee, and he comes over to America from China because his grandfather tells him to just before he croaks. The old man is lying on one of those scratchy bamboo mats, and before he dies he says to Yune, "Remember, money is not the most important thing in life." And Yune leans right up to his mouth and says, "What is?" and waits for his last words. And the old man says, "Broads—broads are the most important thing." And then he dies, and Johnny Yune goes to America to be an Italian cook for the Mafia. Only all the Mafia guys keep calling him Bruce because they can't remember his name is Chan. And he wants to be a tough dude like Bruce Lee, but he can't

kung-fu worth a durn and besides he got his black belt in one of the states where they only have a written test. He's had a hard life too. "I was once run over by a Toyota," he tells this guy. "Oh what a feeling."

So the Mafia sends him across the country to deliver his Chinese noodle flour, which is cocaine but he's dumb as a box of rocks so he don't know it, and Margaux Hemingway is trying to grab the stuff from him. You remember Margaux. First she made *Lipstick* in 1975, and now this is her second movie, and I'm afraid that based on this she needs to slow down her career a little bit. No breast action from her or from this foxy federal agent named Pam Huntington who's following Bruce around, but there is this one scene where Bruce gets in a hot tub and a geisha girl starts to get in with him, and he says, "You are a ten," and then she drops her kimono and he says, "You are a ten where you should be a thirty-six," and he's right. Only this movie's *not* a ten.

Some good comedy chopsocky. One motor vehicle chase. About seven halfway funny jokes. Two breasts. Seven or eight corpses. The perversion is mostly this fat guy who likes to get whipped on the back by Margaux Hemingway. Heads do not roll. Two and a half stars.

They call me Joe Bob, and Joe Bob says check it out. ∎

Joe Bob's Mailbag

Dear Joe Bob,

Why the Dan Jenkins clone act? Can't you create your own style? We don't need no "commie-pinko" plagiarist telling us about B-B-Q or about some chick with big garbonzas that could "[censored] start" a Harley. Stick with the D.I. reports and let Jenkins be the historian of Texas colloquialisms. Take your best "original" shot—since you have the last word in print.

Thanks,
"Dead Solid Perfect"
Temple, Tex.
Home of the Wildcats

Dear Dead:

Okay, I've been puttin this off long enough. Let's face it, you people in Temple are BORING. In fact, I'll give 20 bucks to the first person who can tell me ONE thing about Temple that's interesting. Until that day, don't tell me about humor, okay, buddy?

Joe Bob Catches Up: Bikes, Barbarians, and Blond Bimbos

Before Lute Fenwick mashed in the front part of Rhett Beavers's brain and made him look like a Mr. Potato Head, Rhett used to say things to me like "Joe Bob, you dress like you're in the fifties. You need to get hip, trade in your threads for some style. This is the eighties, you know what I mean?"

And I would always say, "What?"

But then I went to the finals of the Quaker State Open last weekend at the Forum in Grand Prairie and Chubb Fricke introduced me to Guppy Troup and I'm telling you I'm a changed man. One reason I'm a changed man is that Chubb didn't *know* Guppy Troup when he introduced me, so that's the last time I'll ever trust Chubb around the PBA tour. But the main reason is that I found *the* man with the look for the eighties. I'm talkin plaid slacks and shades. Did you see this man in the finals? I mean, the other turkey bowls six straight strikes, right, and it looks like Perfect Game City, three hundreds-ville, and what does Guppy do? Plaid-slacks him. Flashes those mothers at the peak of his back-swing, lets the chandelier beams reflect the red down on the lane, and the man chokes to death. Guppy watches him miss two spares. Game over. Big check-arooney goes to Guppy. Listen, the man wears shades for a rea-son. Afterward, Guppy told me he might be moving to the area, since he's down on Jacksonville and he wants a major-league bowling town. I told him he's in the land of bowling fools. I told him the Hunt brothers built the Bronc more than twenty years ago. He said, "What?"

Chubb said, "Gimme some slack."

Guppy flashed those mothers again, just for us. I'm telling you, it was the highlight of my life.

I don't have time to visit this week, though, because I got three flicks for you to check out. (I'm telling you, it's been Drive-In Heaven lately.) We're talking quality stuff too. Nitty follows:

Timerider is a biker western sci-fi comedy, probly the best one of the year. It's about this guy who tries to look like Charles Bronson only it never works; his name's Lyle Swann and he's got a mean bike. One day he's toolin through Baja in a race, and these wimpola scientists from the Rea-gan administration have their equipment out on the course, and they *accidentally* zap him back to 1877. Lyle keeps trucking, until he comes to this campsite and an old Meskin sees that bike and drops dead. Then Peter Coyote sees the bike and he tells these weird-beard outlaws he wants it, and they go after him. But this fox named Claire with frizzed hair scares away the turkeys and pastes one of em on the schnozz with her pistol. Then—here's the good part—Claire holds the gun on Swann until he takes off his clothes and gets in her sack. Next day: fox gone, bike gone. Swann wants em both back, but Peter Coyote has her tied up like a *cabrito* dinner. So Lyle has to go kill some creep-olas if he wants more time with the fox.

One good motor vehicle and horse chase. Eleven corpses. Two breasts. No creatures. Heads do not roll. About three decent jokes and a lot of indecent ones. Some kung fu, non-pro. Two and a half stars.

Numero two-o: Miles O'Keeffe has been doing some del-toid work at the gym and he let his hair grow out like a cocker spaniel and they wrapped these fluffies around his ankles like a Clydesdale and gave him a magic shield to wear over his belly but-ton and so now he's Ator, the Fighting Eagle, which is the name of his first talking movie. He made a silent film called *Tarzan the Ape Man* where Bo Derek does all the talking. The only reason anybody ever sat through that turkey was the part where Bo says "I think I'll take a bath," and everbody wakes up to see her nekkid. I'm here to tell you: Bo Derek's naked is nothing compared to Sabrina Siani, this bleached blond Amazon bimbo that Miles finds on his way to the Temple of the Spider. Miles has to go there to kill this Tarantula Man who wears gold makeup, and after that he'll get his wife back. I don't really want to go into it, because it's that barbarian stuff again.

Highlights: One good village massacre, with a lot of baby-killing. Good scene where the Amazons tie up Miles and fight for the privilege of being his sex object for one night. One mass zombie attack. Tarantula torture scene. Volcanic eruption. Two breasts, *supremo*. Heads roll. Corpse count in the high double digits. No kung fu. Three stars.

Numero three-o, last but not least, the rerelease of the season, you saw it last year but you couldn't wait for more. *The Sword and the Sorcerer*. We're talking rape. We're talking pillage. We're talking Barbarian City. Highlights: This conqueror guy named Cromwell goes to the end of the world to meet this slime glopola man, but when he gets there he says, "How do we know a toad like you even has the power to aid us?" And the slime glopola man calls this girl into the room and concentrates real hard and makes her heart rip out of her chest by ESP. Later this Nautilus guy named Lee Horsley rescues a bimbo who's about to be raped by some drunks. Then she says, "Is your sword for hire?" and he gets this look on his face like "I hope so." Same old story: She wants

him to get her brother out of prison. He says okay, but he gets one night in the sack for that. So the *rest* of the movie is this guy going through dungeons and gettin tortured and being in a rat stampede and gettin knocked in the moat and watching this girl get her tongue cut out and seein a guy get crucified and fightin off some snakes—and for *what?* One night with this bimbo? Not logical. One star off for that.

At least ninety corpses. *Mucho* snakes. Heads roll. Minimal kung fu. One beast. No motor vehicles. Magician guy with orange fingernails. Three stars. ∎

Joe Bob's Mailbag ——

Dear Joe Bob,

A *BIG* 10-4 on Temple, pardner. Some years ago I was going out with this lady who was good looking enough to think about marrying when one night in an obvious moment of weakness, we were doing some heavy window-fogging at the Sunset Drive-In (since shut down) here in Amarillo, she told me she was from Temple. I never saw her again after that but did get a note from her later telling me that although she really loved me and wanted to get married too she just couldn't handle the guilt with me knowing where she was from.

Sincerely,
Leo Wyoming
Amarillo

P.S. Here's an extra $20 to add to your "Say ONE Thing Interesting About Temple" contest. If you put our prize money in an interest account we'll be millionaires before we have to pay any thing out to anybody. They best could keep their mouths shut on this one.

Dear Leo:

Okay, the kitty's up to 40 bucks, and so far all we have is one measly attempt by some guy at the high school.

Even his LETTER was boring. He was so boring that he has to pay ME 20 bucks. I can see that we aren't going to have any entries this way, so I'm changing the rules.

It is now the "Say One Thing Even MILDLY Interesting About Temple Contest" and win 40 bucks.

Your 20-dollar bill has been deposited in a trust account at Caesars Palace National Bank of Las Vegas, Nevada, and will be used only in the event of a winning letter.

Vegas has established the line on this contest at 9 billion to five.

Best Art Film of 1983: *Bloodsucking Freaks* Has It All, Says Joe Bob

I've been wondering about one of the mysteries of modern civilization, and I'd like to share it with you this week because, what the hey, we could use a little *intellectual* material on this page and, besides, it's bugging the royal bejabbers out of me.

What I'm talking about is the ultimate riddle: Why do the people on *Family Feud* always play instead of pass?

I know this bothers you as much as it does me. Because, let's face it, we've all been there. Richard Dawson comes out and does a bad joke. Then two wimps (or wimpettes) walk up to that table in the middle and say, "Hi, Richard, I'm from Saginaw, Michigan, and I don't know a shin from Shinola, but I bounce on my toes like this because I've been a nerd ever since the third grade, and this is my moon-faced family, and they have a collective IQ of thirty-seven."

Okay, then the game starts, and Richard tries to focus on the big board, and he says, "Name something that a dog does in the street." And one of the wimps slaps that buzzer and says, "Hitchhikes."

Richard looks up at the big board and he screams, *"Hitchhikes?"*

And then the bell rings and "Hitchhikes" shows up there as No. 4.

Then the other wimp says, "Rubs his leg up against mailboxes."

Richard looks up at the big board and screams, *"Rubs mailboxes?"*

And the bell rings and "Rubs objects" shows up as No. 5.

Okay, so Wimp No. 4, the Nerd Family from Saginaw, Michigan, now has a choice. They can *play*. If they play they have to get *six more right answers* to win, including the last one on the list, which got two votes from the studio audience. Or they can *pass*. If they pass, then the *other* turkeys have to get six answers, and if the others miss three times, even if they already got *five* of them right, then the Nerd Family only has to get *one* answer to win the game. Besides that, they get to discuss it before they answer.

There's only about $10,000 at stake, so what do they do? They *play*. Every *time* they play. And what *happens* when they play? They get all but one or two an-

swers, and then they miss three times, and then the other family gets *one* answer and wins all the money.

Have any of you turkeys ever seen, even *one time,* somebody say, "Dawson, I've watched this game on TV and I want those other jerks to go first"? Has this ever happened in the entire history of *Family Feud?*

Nosiree, Joe Bob. And why hasn't it happened? I can only think of one reason.

Game's rigged. The only families they put on that show are dropouts from the Industrial Trades Institute. We're talking Rock City U.S.A.

That's why I'm not joinin the *Family Feud* team that Lute Fenwick is getting together over in Cleburne. I stopped by Le Bodine last week, talked to Thedadean Griffin the shampoo lady, and she told me Vida Stegall was back with Lute because he told her she could be on the team. Thedadean said he wanted me to join up too, but I told Thedadean that the only way I'd be in a "family" with Lute Fenwick would be if he married my . . . Well, actually, I can't tell you what I told Thedadean. But anyway, I don't care for small-screen video bullstuff anyway. Drive-ins are my life.

I got so bored going through my mail from Temple that I decided to go out to the VFW Lodge Hall and play some horseshoes, but on the way out there I passed by the Gemini and couldn't resist this golden oldie called *Bloodsucking Freaks.* I know, I know, it's a revival. It's *The Incredible Torture Show* being brought out again. We all saw it in 76 at the Highway 67 when it was called *The House of the Screaming Virgins,* but no sweat, because true art lasts forever.

I got all nostalgic seeing it again. We're talking women in cages, we're talking torture, we're talking bodily mutilation, we're talking large breast quantities, large breast qualities, and large breasts, we're talking midget rape, we're talking bondage, we're talking mad doctors, we're talking nonstop death. This is the kind of picture that really makes you miss the seventies.

It starts out with this stage show at the Theatre of the Macabre, where Master Sardu *amuses* his audience by having a midget named Ralphus take this woman's blouse off, strap her in a chair, and tighten an iron tourniquet around her head until blood drips down her face. Then he sticks this nekkid girl's hand in a vise and hacks it off. Then the midget rips her eye out and eats it. Pretty routine stuff. But after the show's over, the wimp critic from the New York *Times refuses to review the show.* Sardu is a little p.o.ed.

So Sardu, the m.c. played by the late great Seamus O'Brien, who has a voice like Vincent Price, tells Ralphus the Midget to kidnap the *Times* critic, which he does by shooting him with a blow dart at an art gallery opening after this bimbo pops open a raincoat and flashes her groceries. While he's waiting for Ralphus to bag the critic and bring him home, Sardu asks these two leather bunnies to paste him across the backside with a bullwhip. Ever once in a while he sends Ralphus down into a dungeon to feed some raw meat to these moaning nekkid porkchops in a cage. He's just keeping them there until he can send his next shipment to the Middle East. The Arabs pay big bucks for Off-Off-Broadway actress meat.

Okay, back to the main action. Sardu tells Ralphus to electrocute this bimbo by pouring five hundred volts through her breasts. This is so the *Times* critic will be impressed. It doesn't work, so Sardu decides to have another show, but first he tells Ralphus to go blow-dart this blond ballerina named Natasha so he can have some choreography. He wants to brainwash her so she can kick the critic's brains out in his next show. Ralphus hides out in her locker in Lincoln Center, knocks out her lights, drags her back to the theater, puts chains around her neck, hangs her up by her wrists, and starts playing the cymbals until she agrees to dance on opening night. They almost overdo it, though, and they have to call *the doctor* so she won't die. When he gets finished, Sardu says, "How much do I owe you?" and the doctor says, "How bout letting me take it out in trade?"

"Another operation?" says Sardu.

Doc goes to work. First he straps a bimbo in a chair and pulls out all her teeth "so you won't bite." Then he decides to do "a little elective neurosurgery"— power drill through the head while he's hummin "Marriage of Figaro." Once he gets in there pretty deep, he wiggles it around, sticks in a straw, and . . . well, you get the title now. Sardu gets grossed out, though, so he tells Ralphus to *feed the doctor to the nekkid women in the dungeon.* Pretty amazing scene, specially when they rip out his heart and rub it over their flesh. Sardu and Ralphus stay upstairs playing darts on a slave girl's backside.

There are just too many highlights to go into. The rest of the flick includes: a blonde who gets stretched on the rack, a guillotine demonstration where a girl has to hold the rope in her mouth and if she opens it the blade falls, Ralphus making love to a head,

Sardu and Ralphus using human fingers as backgammon chips, another ballerina that gets her feet cut off by Ralphus, and a cop who goes down to Off-Off Broadway to investigate the ballerina's disappearance but gets fed to the starving nekkid women, and a pretty good fried-eyeball scene.

There's also some sick stuff that I can't mention in the newspaper.

We're talking Top Ten list. We're talking Best Rerelease of 1983. We're talking Best Director nomination for Joel Reed. We're also talking all-time exposure champion: seventy-six breasts.

Heads roll (four times). Hands roll. Fingers roll. Feet roll. Excellent midget sadism and dubbed moaning.

Three and a half stars. Joe Bob says check it out. ∎

At Last, Joe Bob Names the Drive-In Oscar Nominees

I wanna know what's the big deal about *Francis?* Last week everbody out at the 183 D.I. was asking me, "Joe Bob, why wasn't *Francis* nominated for the Academy Awards?"

(Vida Stegall said it was the best movie she's ever seen, which don't mean much when you realize Vida Stegall spent the first sixteen years of her life in a trailer house.)

I'm sorry, but I don't know what the commotion's about. I saw *Francis* in 1949 when it first came out, and I liked the talking mule better than Donald O'Connor, but what the hey, it wasn't any *Mr. Ed.*

So I looked up the ad in the paper and it said, *"Francis* is shocking, disturbing, compelling . . . and *true."* Okay, so you see the gimmick now, don't you? Universal Pictures claims the mule can really talk. They're bringin back *Francis* because they found a mule that can say the Gettysburg Address. But I dare those suckers to put *Francis* in the drive-in where ordinary people can take a look at it, because I'm bettin the mule's no better now than it was thirty-three years ago. Unless they got a brand-new mule who can at least dance or play the harp or something, I'm just not buying it.

So anyway, the answer to your question is *The mule is not eligible for the 1982 Drive-In Academy Awards.*

Now a lot of people ask me another question, which is "Joe Bob, just who's a member of this Academy of Drive-In Arts and Sciences anyway?"

Anybody who can prove they saw ever drive-in movie of 1982. This isn't any Hollywood indoor bullstuff deal, where they wheel em in from Palm Springs once a year to cast ballots for people who send out hams in the mail. This is a legit deal. This is for the drive-in-going public of America. And now, may I have the envelope please? The nominees are:

BEST FLICK

• *Basket Case:* Whatever is in the basket is gross, disgusting, small, deformed, and it only comes out when it wants to eat or make love

• *The Beast Within:* about a family of giant vampire katydids

• *Forbidden World:* they have a little accident on another planet, and people are getting *slimed to death*

• *The Last American Virgin:* about a guy who can't get any, and how he overcomes his handicap

• *Nightmare:* about a guy who axes his father's head off, then gets out of the mental hospital and goes to visit some friends

• *Swamp Thing:* about a vegetable monster that chases Adrienne Barbeau through the Everglades

BEST TITLE

• *Goin' All the Way*

• *Mad Monkey Kung Fu*

• *Mutant (former title of Forbidden World)*

• *Satan's Mistress (formerly Fury of the Succubus)*

• *Senior Snatch* (second feature *Eager Beavers)*

• *Ten Violent Women*

BEST ACTOR

• Paul Clemens, *The Beast Within*, the kid who turns into a maniac insect

• Clint Howard, the wimp

who makes a deal with the devil, in *Evilspeak*

• Marc Singer, the barbarian who talks to the animals, in *The Beastmaster*

• William Smith, the cop trying to find a sex maniac who murders cocktail waitresses because they don't bring him the right napkin, in *Swinging Barmaids*

• Kevin Van Hentenryck, the kid with the basket in *Basket Case*

BEST ACTRESS

• Adrienne Barbeau, flopping through the swamp in *Swamp Thing*

• Debra Blee, forty in a T-shirt, *Beach Girls*

• Krista Errickson, the foxy one in *The First Time*

• Diane Franklin, the object of wimp lust, in *The Last American Virgin*

• Terri Susan Smith, who gets raped by *whatever it is* in *Basket Case*

BEST MONSTER

• Belial (he's in the basket) in *Basket Case*

• Black Mamba in *Venom*

• Dick Durock, as the Swamp Thing in *Swamp Thing*

• The Mutant, which looks like Hamburger Helper with teeth, in *Forbidden World*

• The outer-space mummy in *Time Walker*

• The slime glopola in *Parasite*

BEST KUNG FU

• Dragon Lee, using the eagle claw, in *Dragon on Fire*

• Monkey, the monkey boxer in *Mad Monkey Kung Fu*

• Chuck Norris, kicking his way through Hong Kong, in *Forced Vengeance*

• The Squad in *Kill Squad*

BEST SUPPORTING ACTOR

• R. G. Armstrong, the dimwit doctor in *The Beast Within* who diagnoses the "occult malignancy"

• Luca Bercovici, the disgusting, perverted punkola gang leader in *Parasite*

• Josh Cadman, "Bronk" in *Goin' All the Way*, the kind of guy who does can-openers in the pool when everybody's sleeping

• Linden Chiles, the wheezing, bloodstained scientist in *Forbidden World* who says, "We created a little monster, I'm afraid"

• Louis Jourdan, deranged villain in *Swamp Thing*

• Cameron Mitchell, the fat slob in *Kill Squad*

• Wallace Shawn, crazy film professor, *The First Time*

• Robert Vogel, hotel clerk in *Basket Case*

BEST SUPPORTING ACTRESS

• Bibi Besch, the woman who gets raped by a giant katydid in *The Beast Within*

• Beverly Bonner, the happy hooker in *Basket Case*

• June Chadwick, the blond doctor who walks around in a white terry-cloth spacesuit in *Forbidden World* and says, "Wanna see some trouble?"

• Louisa Moritz, the sexy Meskin lady, in *The Last American Virgin*

• Wendie Jo Sperber, the girl with the Cadillac thighs, who threatens to sit on the hero of *The First Time*

BEST SPECIAL EFFECT

• *Basket Case:* when Belial gets his daddy between the legs with the buzzsaw

• *The Beast Within:* when Paul Clemens gets transformed into a giant vampire katydid

• *Evilspeak:* when the guy gets his heart ripped out of his chest while it's still beating

• *Forbidden World:* when Jimmy gets slimed to death by the glopola mutant

• *Intimate Moments:* when Dirke Altevogt makes it with a mirror

• *Nightmare:* closeup of a head rolling

• *Sorceress:* when one girl gets stroked by a warrior and the other one is not there but she gets turned on by ESP

• *Swamp Thing:* Tony Cecere, the stuntman who sets himself on fire and runs fifty yards and jumps into the swamp, all for the sake of art

BEST CHEST

• Adrienne Barbeau, taking a bath in *Swamp Thing*

• Debra Blee, forty in a T-shirt, *Beach Girls*

• Dawn Dunlap, taking a steambath in *Forbidden World*

• Leigh Harris and Lynette Harris, acting with their identical breasts, in *Sorceress*

• Tanya Roberts, taking a bath in *The Beastmaster*

• The entire supporting cast in *Goin' All the Way* (fifty complete breasts)

• Lise Thoresen, the light-blond porkchop who's so anxious she whips everything off during the opening credits in *Intimate Moments*

• Lana Wood (Natalie's sister), taking it off in *Fury of the Succubus*

• Lenore Zann, the blond nympho that gets marked up with a stiletto in *Visiting Hours*

BEST DIRECTOR

- Wes Craven, *Swamp Thing*
- Boaz Davidson, *The Last American Virgin*
- Frank Henenlotter, *Basket Case*
- Allan Holzman, *Forbidden World*
- Philippe Mora, *The Beast Within*
- Eric Weston, *Evilspeak*

BEST PSYCHO

- The ax murderer weirdo bondage S&M psychosexual throat-slitting father-hater in *Nightmare*
- The Grim Reaper (gonzo cannibal), in *The Grim Reaper*
- Clint Howard, the wimp devil worshipper, in *Evilspeak*
- Michael Ironside, a/k/a the Hawk, killer creep hospital-ward psycho snuffer, using his stiletto in *Visiting Hours*

BEST GROSS-OUT SCENE

- *Basket Case:* when the monster rapes the girlfriend while she's asleep
- *The Beast Within:* when the woman gets katydiddled
- *Dragon on Fire:* when the rabid dog bites off Quasimodo's thing
- *Evilspeak:* the ending, when Coopersmith gets his revenge with maniac pigs, twisted heads, torture racks, cracked brains, and sliced bodies
- *Friday the 13th, Part 3:* speargun through the eyeball
- *The Grim Reaper:* when The Grim Reaper has his baby son for dinner
- *Halloween III:* when the zombie puts a power drill through the nurse's ear
- *Nightmare:* last scene, where George goes totally crazy with a four-foot ax and paints the screen red with rolling heads
- *Ten Violent Women:* when the turkey in a goatee gets a spiked high heel through the heart
- *Venom:* when the most poisonous snake in the world crawls up Oliver Reed's pants leg

Academy members should submit their ballots immediately. I'll be at the Auto Rama like everybody else, checking out the six Playboy Playmates, including my personal favorite, Miss January of 82, and the 51 Mercury coupe, chopped and molded, with 427 Vette ponies, that George Barris built. Rick Nagel will also have some of his street muscle on the floor, including the original 65 "R" Competition Mustang. Nothing else to see this week. The flick at the 183 was *Trick or Treats,* and it violates the Joe Bob Briggs Theory of Film Criticism: A movie can be absolutely anything, except *boring.* About a babysitter (Jackelyn Giroux) and a little monster kid (Chris Graver) and the kid's psycho daddy (Peter Jason) who dresses up like a nurse and escapes from the loony bin. It's the old "boy who cried wolf" deal, with the kid playing jokes on the sitter with his toy guillotine and his fake fingers, only when daddy gets home we get some real knife action. Two corpses. No kung fu. No monsters. No car crashes.

Heads do not roll. Spell it b-o-r-i-n-g. One star. Would've got two, but one off for bringing out a Halloween flick in February. ∎

Everybody Gets It:
It Wasn't Knowledge
That Put Em in College

I had to shoot my dog Tuesday morning. What happened is, he was trying to jump the bob wire next to the power station by Lake Ray Hubbard, and got his hind legs tangled up, and then when he broke loose he run smack dab into the little electric fence by the generator. All the little hairs on his neck stuck up like bristles on the doormat. Didn't kill him but it messed up his brainwaves or something because all he did after that was wander around in a circle and try to bite the [censored] off everybody that came up the drive. He was trained to go after May Ellen Masters, of course, but he sank his teeth into Rhett Beavers's backside one day and I knew he was one sick dog. He liked Rhett. Liked his smell. Dr. Flink said we had to do it or there wouldn't be a [censored] left in town. I'm still bummed out by it. Nothing in life as reliable as a dog.

Many of you know that his name was Elmo, and that he was named after the monkey in *Mad Monkey Kung Fu*, and so I got a hubcap and had Junior Bodine carve "Elmo" on it and I used it to mark the place where I buried him out back by the shed. Elmo was only about six dog years. You can come by if you want to. I've got the Toronado up on blocks. I'm puttin in some Delco tube shocks and split wishbones to try and get that sucker to ride closer to the ground, and I may go ahead and hoist the motor and tell Gus Simpson I'm going by to collect that 340 Mopower V-8 with the Holley double-pump fuel mixer that he owes me. If I can't find Gus, I might do some custom acrylic lacquer work—I just feel like staying close to Elmo.

Meantime, this guy who lives in North Dallas is loaning me his 64 Olds, which I'm accepting even though it needs a complete backyard buildup, including new electrical system and probly new brakes. It looks like some punk rockers took a knife to the left rear door too, but that's what happens when you live in a bad part of town like that.

I took the Olds to the Astro to see *Everybody Gets It in the End,* which I decided to check out instead of *Spring Fever* because, let's face it, if Susan Anton is not gonna take her clothes off, why bother? Course, I have to admit that *Everybody Gets It in the End* didn't exactly break the garbonza meter. I don't know what it is about the month of March, but past experience shows the breast exposure average generally goes down this time of year. I didn't expect it in this case, though, because this is a picture that Roger Corman, King of the Drive-In, brought out last year under a different title, *T.A.G.* Then when it went down the toilet, he took it back, put a different title on it, and sent it back out. I hate to give advice to the King like this, because I generally admire his abilities, but here are a *few* titles he could've used:

Sniper
Campus Assassin
The Killing Game
The University of Death
Bimbos in Distress

See what I mean? Wouldn't *you* go see those? I know I would. But I checked out *EGIITE* strictly for professional reasons.

The first thing wrong with it is, it's about wimpola college students. Most of em are dumb as a box of quartz crystals, so they probly couldn't even spell b-o-r-i-n-g. I *know* they can't spell s-e-x. I like Robert Carradine when he's doing kung fu, but in this flick he plays a grade-A homogenized wimp. He smokes a cigar and goes around writing articles for the college newspaper on this game called TAG, which stands for The Assassination Game, which is where the students go around with dart guns trying to rubber-bullet the bejabbers out of one another. The head geek is this guy named Gersh (Bruce Abbott), who walks around like a zombie and gets a little p.o.ed when a fat kid knocks his plastic gun on the floor and it goes off accidentally and nails Gersh with a rubber dart. But Gersh wants to win so bad that he pastes the fat kid with a real .38 to the forehead, and then he keeps on blowing away students like Charles Whitman, only a lot slower, and then stuffing the bodies in a laundry cart so nobody'll find em.

Anyway, the only thing Robert Carradine is trying to do is get something from this fox named Linda Hamilton, if you know what I mean and I think you do. The fox is playing TAG, but mostly she's playing tease. One time she starts to take off her clothes to distract this guy who's after her, only the camera cuts away and then when it comes back she's in a swimsuit. Rip-off City. Shame on the director, a turkey named Nick Castle.

What I'm trying to say is: breast count zero. Coming from the finest garbonza movie studio in L.A., New World Pictures, this is just a little bit disappointing. Body count five, but only about a half pint of fairly thin blood. No motor vehicle action. Heads do not roll. No beasts. No special effects. No moaning. One measly scream. The best actor is Bruce Abbott, the game-freak psycho. A little slow, but at least it's got completely senseless death going for it. Two stars, just barely.

Joe Bob says check it out. ■

Joe Bob's Mailbag ——

Dear Job Bob—

Alright. Heres my attempt at the "Name one thing *Mildly* interesting about Temple." It is:

"The one thing MILDLY interesting about Temple is that it provides us, through your contest, with something to laugh at, being that it is so dull."

How's that? I expect my money within the week.

Dutifully yours,
John Hinckley jr.,
Advisor to the President
a/k/a Jesse Devine
Dallas

Dear John:
Temple is not a laughing matter. I can't even get those turkeys to defend themselves, it's so pathetic.

Dear Joe Bob Briggs,

Sorry, Joe Bob, you slashed your own throat on this one. Anything taken to extremes is interesting. Being a Temple native, I am painfully aware of its vacuous nature. You will be interested and $40 poorer to know that Temple was recently rated by Rand McNally as the third most boring city in the United States, behind Oklahoma City and White Plains, New York.

David Barnes
Dallas

P.S. Please send the money quickly, because I need to pay for my bowling league membership.

Dear David:
Third most boring? See, mediocre in everything.

Dear Joe Bob,

Here I wrote you that wonderfully concise and meaningful letter about "appendages" and "nuclear" and you didn't even ask for my phone number.

No fair complaining about a lack of intellectually stimulating female companionship until you investigate my qualifications.

I even like B.B.Q.

Maybe Waiting Around
J.L. Haas
Dallas

Dear J.L.:
Show me your appendages.

What Happens to Kids Who Go into the Woods? Camp Shish Kebab

A letter to the editor poured in this week. Mrs. Alan Sinz from Richardson is royally hacked off.

Dear Editors,

It is such poor taste it's hard for me to express this but the letter in Joe Bob's Mailbag Friday March 4 was worse than disgusting. The one signed John Hinckley Jr., advisor to the President. Why did you print it? Doesn't our world and our country have enough problems with out emphasizing inane humor, or should I say such SICK humor! I am more convinced than ever Joe Bob is fictitious but his column only appeals to a certain mentality and I'm sure they never read it; so remove this trash and replace it with quality The Times Herald *is famous for—*

Mrs Alan Sinz
Richardson

PS I have subscribed to the TH *for 22 years and am 44 years old, keep me happy*

I'm glad you brought this matter up, Mrs. Sinz, because I think it's about time the decent people of the greater Dallas-Fort Worth-North Texas drive-in-going metropolitan area, and even Richardson, got together, stood up, and said, "Hey, Jerkola-ville, clean up your act!" In fact, this reminds me of that scene in *The Corpse Grinders* when the owner of the cat-food factory gets too greedy and so Sanford Mitchell and Byron Foster have to shove him into the meat grinder and make him into Little Friskies. He was a sick man with a sick mind. He refused to *clean up his act*. And the moral lesson of that movie is that you can't go *too far* or you'll get chopped into Purina wafers.

Okay, Mrs. Sinz, another example. Remember the scene in *The Gore Gore Girls* when one of the bimbos in Henny Youngman's strip joint gets her face french-fried in a pot of boiling oil? Or the scene where Marlene the waitress jumps off the balcony and then a car runs over her head? You might be wondering "Hey, Joe Bob, what's the point?" The point is they wouldn't *clean up their act*, and they paid the price.

I remember about ten years ago when *Nazi Love Camp #27*

came out, and we had a full ninety minutes of every possible atrocity that the Nazis could do to women —again and again and again—and at the time I wasn't the drive-in movie critic yet but I said to Chubb Fricke, "Chubb, every schoolchild in America should be required to see this flick, to see what happens when people can't *clean up their act.*"

Now you're probly thinking "Hey, Joe Bob, what's this have to do with Joe Bob's Mailbag?"

Just one thing. I'm no longer taking responsibility for the filth and degeneracy that comes across my desk. [I would like to say to Neil in Chico, who sent the fourteen photos of Tina: shame on you, and thank you. And to "Dead Solid Perfect" in Temple, who sent the lifesize poster: *yeeeeeowwwwww.*] As I say, some people don't have the decency and respect for human life that make us different from the slopeheads in Communist Russia. They abuse the privilege of writing to Joe Bob's Mailbag.

Speaking of violence, most of you know I'm not a violent kind of guy. I don't use my twelve-inch laminated rosewood Nunchaku sticks with sterling silver chain unless someone is in desperate need of a fractured skull. And of course I don't like hypodermic needles through the eyeball, power drills through the brain cavity, or spearguns shot through the neck *unless the scene is necessary to the story.*

That's why I'm recommending this flick called *Madman,* which reminds me a little bit of *Invasion of the Blood Farmers* except it's about kids at summer camp. Basically, we're talking a killer-creep psycho, snuff-the-young-children-and-make-em-suffer flick. The psycho is this evil farmer named Marz who had his nose bit off while he was chopping his wife into little bitty pieces, and that made him so mad he turned his daughter into shishkebab meat too. After that these ten neighbor men had to make a lynch mob and hang him, only while he was still strung up one of em did some plastic surgery on his face with a four-foot ax.

When they come back the next morning, the geek was gone.

What's on the farm now? A camp for "gifted children." I guess this means they're dumb as a box of dead crabs, because Madman Marz goes around slicing em into Hamburger Helper one by one, and none of them catch on till the end of the movie.

First he jumps out of a closet at the camp and gets this kid across the throat with your standard butcher knife. Wouldn't be anything special, except you get to see the whole inside of the kid's neck. I imagine those of you training to be doctors will especially enjoy this portion of the flick.

Okay, then this frizz-blond fox camp counselor named Betsy gets in the hot tub with a nerd named T.P., and Betsy moans a little bit, but there's not much action, and then Marz sees em hanging ten through the window. We all know what happens when the psycho sees a little nookie, don't we? Splatter City.

Madman Marz is fat, barefoot, and dirty, and he wears these disgusting overalls like he comes from Louisiana or something. What I like about him is that he goes after the wimps right away. I don't want to give this sucker away, but Marz gets one guy with a rope. A turkey named Dave loses his head, and Marz finds a pretty hysterical place to put it: between the carburetor and the fan belt of Betsy's truck, so she has to turn old Dave's cheek into something that looks like a red pizza before she can get the truck to start. One of the bimbos gets it right between the breasts. There's a meathook scene that's the best one since *Texas Chainsaw Massacre*. Then after a while Betsy goes to work with a double-barreled scatter-gun, and from there on out you can paint the woods red.

We're talking nine corpses. We're talking one motor vehicle crash. We're talking four breasts. No kung fu. Heads roll. Two possible Drive-In Academy Award nominations, for Alexis Dubin as Betsy the bimbo and Paul Ehlers as Madman Marz. *Madman* goes to No. 2 on the '82 list, behind *Bloodsucking Freaks*. Call it two and a half stars.

Joe Bob says check it out. ■

Joe Bob's Mailbag

Dear Joe Bob,

Just who do you think you are, some kind of stud or something? Have you ever been to Temple? If the answer is yes, you were just too stupid to know where to go. If the answer is no, you don't have any right to talk bad about Temple until you come check it out for yourself. We have one of the biggest, or the biggest country & western nightclubs between Billy Bobs & Gilley's. That might mean very little to you, since you probably don't even know to dance. So the next time you get the urge to pick on a town, make sure you have your facts straight.

A agravated student
TEMPLE

P.S. That 40 dollars will come in real handy.

Dear A:

Obviously not an aggravated student of spelling.

Drive-In Heaven:
Joe Bob Goes Wild
for Charity Week

'd like to get serious here for a minute. Next week is Breast Awareness Week. I know this because some of the gals at the *Times Herald* found a poster in the ladies bathroom and told me about it. It said "Breast Awareness Week" on it, and I guess it had some phone numbers for the American Cancer Society, so that people can get their breasts looked over free of charge.

Now, as you all know, *every* week is Breast Awareness Week in "Joe Bob Goes to the Drive-In." But this is no laughing matter. I want you ladies to get those garbonzas checked. You can call the ACS at 631-3850 for the location nearest you, or you can come by the trailer park in Sunnyvale and ask for Dr. Briggs, but either way, we wouldn't want *anything* to happen to those appendages.

In honor of Breast Awareness Week, I called up one of the most breast-aware people I know, Vida Stegall, and asked her to go to the Apollo D.I. with me to see *High Test Girls*. It's about these six Swedish bimbos who own the gas pump in this town in France, and when they say service station, they do mean service. This is the flick that gives a whole new meaning to

the words "Fill er up." But, like I say, I took Vida Stegall strictly for educational reasons.

We are definitely talking breast awareness.

Now, I'd like to take a moment out right here to say that I am treading on *very* thin ice. The high sheriffs at the *Times Herald* got out their scissors again last week and made some of "Joe Bob Goes to the Drive-In" disappear, which is why you probly couldn't figure it all out. I think all you turkeys know my views on censorship in America. There's a big difference between us and Communist Russia. In Communist Russia the government uses the paper to tell lies. Over here we get to make up our own lies. But what I'm trying to tell you is that I am *on probation,* and so I am *not* going to describe exactly what the stars of *High Test Girls* do to their customers.

Let's get down to the nitty, though. We have a brand-new breast exposure champion. We have *eighty-three* full exposures. That's seven more than the previous champ, *Bloodsucking Freaks.* But this is more of your art film than that one, because in one scene they have twelve complete bouncing bare breasts in *one shot,* because these bimbos are running nekkid through the woods, and how they found a camera that could handle it I don't know. Finally, we've got a *giant* closeup side-view breast that completely fills the big outdoor screen. We're talking humongous.

I wish I could tell you about the bimbo with the Princess Di haircut who gets diddled by a TV set, but I don't want this column to get put through a Commercial Osterizer blender again.

No motor vehicle chases. No kung fu. No beasts. No plot to get in the way. Excellent dubbed moaning. The names of the bimbos are Lisa Robertson, Nancy Patricks, Polly Quigley, Sherri Richards, and Kathy Close, and they're all great in the support department, if you know what I mean and I think you do. Three stars. Joe Bob says check it out.

After that we drove over to the Metroplex outdoor palace, the 183 in Irving, to catch *The Concrete Jungle.* It's about time we had a women-in-cages flick in town. We went through all of 82 with just one, *Ten Violent Women,* and I was startin to think that bimbos chained up like animals were going out of style. This is no *Caged Heat,* but it's a fairly classy flick, because *it's all true.* It's about this brown-haired ski bunny named Tracy Bregman who gets busted for cocaine because her wimp boyfriend plants illegal snow in her skis. The only thing the cops say to this porkchop is: "Do not pass Go, do not collect 200 dollars."

Next she's checking in at the Crossbar Hotel.

First she meets the warden: Jill St. John, who has her hair all piled up on top of her head so she can make like Shelley Winters. Only there's one queen bee worse than her: This prisoner played by Barbara Luna, the Cat, who looks so mean she could stare laser beams through a Levi vest. Get the idea? Tracy Bregman is the kind of wimpette who says "ma'am" and "excuse me" and tries to make friends with the Black Muslim sisters. She's a total box of rocks. I know this because Barbara Luna tells her from now on her name will be "Cherry," and if she don't like it she can go to The Hole. The warden and the queen bee are in cahoots, and if Tracy Bregman doesn't *clean up her act* and *get with the program,* she's gonna get *humiliated* and *abused* and, of course, *hosed down.* We wouldn't want that, would we?

Course we would.

We got everything here: one lesbo sex scene, two visits to The Hole, one old hag who gets offed with a hypo injection, one bimbo who gets raped by the guard (this creepola hulk played by Peter Brown), one catfight with blades in the bathroom, one hair-pulling brawl in the lunchroom, one scene where a girl gets it in the stomach with a rat-tail comb, another scene where the whole prison gets *hosed down* in the middle of a muddy field, a great electrocution scene, and, well, you can see we're talking classic women-in-cages.

Only twelve and a half breasts. No motor vehicle chases.

Three dead bodies. No beasts. Some kung fu. Approximately one pint of blood. Mucho sexual deviancy, torture, and humiliation. Academy Award nominations for Barbara Luna, as the Cat woman, and Tom de Simone, the director, and June Barrett, this gonzo white-faced hopped-up punk woman who slimes around the prison doing Cat's dirty tricks. Three and a half stars. Joe Bob says check it out.

We're talking two Academy Award-level flicks this week. *The Concrete Jungle* goes to No. 1 on the Best of '83 Drive-In Movie List, which means I have to drop the crowd favorite *Bloodsucking Freaks* to No. 2. (To those of you wrote in about the *censored* versions of *Bloodsucking Freaks* they've been showing at the Aquarius IV, I'm on top of the indoor bullstuff situation.) *High Test Girls* goes straight to No. 3 on the strength of breasts alone. *Madman* drops to No. 4. ∎

It's Miller Time All of the Time in *Spring Break*

All the beach bimbos in *Spring Break* are rich, drunk, and nekkid. This is okay by me, specially since this is the last day of Breast Awareness Week and I'm still trying to do my part for the American Cancer Society.

(Before I go one step further, I'd like to say three things about the mail I got on Breast Awareness Week:

Numero uno: You people are *sick.*

Numero two-o: I have been requested by the U.S. Postal Service to tell you that certain types of photographs are not allowed to be sent through the mails. What this means, ladies, is: *If you're gonna be nasty,* USE HEAVY CARDBOARD. Otherwise, the perverts at the post office will get you every time.

Numero three-o: Let's give the Channel 4 weather girl a break, okay?)

I took Wanda Bodine to *Spring Break,* which was a mistake, because you get that box of craters anywhere near something about college, and she starts in about her "years" at Tarleton State cow college in Stephenville. I happen to know that she went there for about seven minutes, and she spent most of that time testing the old hammock strings, if you know what I mean and I think you do. When she got back she *claimed* to speak French, which is why she called her beauty shop

"Le Coiffure" when she first opened the trailer house on the Grapevine Highway. As everyone knows when they go by there, it is now called "Le Bodine, A Personal Grooming Salon." That's what college does to you.

Anyway, college is not what *Spring Break* is about anyway. What it's about is Miller beer. You may find this hard to believe, but *everybody in the movie drinks Miller.* I got nothing against Miller. It's not a total wimp brew like Löwenbräu. But the people in this flick consume about 17,000 gallons of Miller onscreen and never touch another single brand. They also throw the Miller at each other and shake up the cans so they'll explode. The only thing I saw anybody drink besides a Miller was one nerd who swigged a Co-Cola and one fox who was chugging Taylor out of a bottle. This did tend to make me barf.

Anyway, this is a great movie except for one thing. In the ads they don't tell you this but you need to know: *It don't make sense unless you're drunk on Miller.* I tested it. I watched it the first time while I was sloshed on Bud, my regular brand. Then me and Wanda skipped the second feature and hiked it over to Super Red Coleman's and bought a case of Miller and iced it down in the trunk, and we got back in time for the 11:30.

I'm telling you, we're talking four stars.

I know what you're thinking: Garbonza City. Nope. The garbonza count is only sixteen, and I'm giving em the benefit of the doubt on two side-breast exposures in the middle of a wet T-shirt contest.

What we actually got is an art film. You're thinking, Hey, what the heck does he mean by that?

What I mean by that is we got *absolutely no plot* to get in the way of this movie. One nerd and one wimp go to Fort Lauderdale and check in to a dump on the beach where they hope they can find some action. No way, José. First they drink some Miller. Then two bozos from New York show up and move into the room with em, and all the wimp and the nerd get to do is *watch* and *drink Miller.* The watching scene is pretty good. The bozos bring two foxes to the room, everbody drops their tops, and then the four of em root around on the bed for a while while the nerd and wimp crawl around on the floor.

Next thing they have a Miller beer drinking contest.

Next thing they send the wimp into a van on the beach to buy some dope from a Meskin.

Next thing they play a song so that some bimbos can jump around on the beach and jiggle their equipment.

Next thing everbody has a Miller.

Next thing they get drunk as skunks and have a wet T-shirt contest.

Next thing the nerd plays a video game while he's having a Miller.

Next thing they have a *He-Shirt* Contest and everbody gets sloshed.

Next thing they all go out to the pool and drink some Miller and some freaks do belly-flops off the board.

Next thing the wimp tries to get something from this girl in a Teenie Weenie Bikini Contest, if you know what I mean and I think you do—

Next thing this black-haired fox, who has a band, puts on a jumpsuit and sings "Do It To You" and makes all these guys smash Miller cans on their heads.

Next thing the wimp gets locked up by these goons, and they don't offer him a Miller, and so he's p.o.ed.

In the big final scene everybody has a Miller.

Bottles, cans, cups, but very few jugs. Breast count: sixteen. One motor vehicle chase. No beasts. Minimal kung fu. Heads do not roll. One Drive-In Academy Award nomination, for the brunette fox who wants to do it to everbody. Chick's name is Corinne Alphen, 1982 Penthouse Pet of the Year. (She keeps her top on.) Two stars on Bud. Four stars on Miller.

Joe Bob says check it out. ■

Joe Bob's Mailbag ━━━

Dear Joe Bob—

Ah Ha! I saw you in the Lounge at the Inwood Theater with Cherry the other night—

> Female bartender
> Teri Weisert
> Dallas

Dear Teri:
Don't make me barf.

Dear Joe Bob, Mrs. Sinz, and Republicans everywhere—

I am writing this letter to apologize to Mrs. Sinz and anyone else who might have been offended by the signature of my letter in Joe Bob's mailbag on March 4th. I am truly sorry, as it was not meant to offend anyone. I am not a psycho, sicky, or anything else besides a normal High School student who seems to have overstepped the tolerance of the public. I truly hope you will accept my apology.

> Sincerely,
> Jesse Devine
> Dallas

Dear Jesse:
1) You didn't offend me.
2) I don't care if you offended Mrs. Sinz.
3) If Joe Bob's Mailbag is ever tolerated by the public, I quit.

The Envelope, Please: Best Drive-In Movie of 82 Is . . . You Guessed It

If you don't mind, I'd like to say one or two words in my defense before announcing the 1982 Drive-In Academy Awards.

I didn't plan it this way, and please don't hold it against me, but most of the winners are gonna celebrate tonight in Geek City U.S.A. I'm not only talking New York City. I'm talking Greenwich Village. I don't have a good explanation for this. I guess all you can say is, it's like that guy from Brooklyn who rides out at the Mesquite Rodeo all the time. He knows that a rodeo cowboy is born, not made—and I feel just about the same about the people who make drive-in movies.

What I'm saying, for you turkeys who get the airmail edition in New York, is be at the Waverly Theatre, midnight tonight their time, for the celebration of the 1982 Drive-In Academy Awards and the public reading of a telegram from Joe Bob announcing the results. They don't call em low-budget movies for nothing, and that's as far as these turkeys could come to accept their Hubbies. (The Drive-In Academy Award is in the form of an engraved Chevy hub cap. Junior Bodine of Mineral Wells has the exclusive franchise to issue the Hubby.)

For those of us low-budget movie *watchers,* the celebration will be at the Toronado, back of the concession stand tonight at the 183.

Okay, let's get down to the nitty.

BEST TITLE

And the winner is:
MAD MONKEY KUNG FU, one of the best foreign films of 1982, direct from Hong Kong, with a stop in Burbank for dubbing.

BEST ACTOR

And the winner is:
KEVIN VAN HENTENRYCK, the sensitive human being who rescues his grotesque Siamese twin from a Hefty bag after their evil father has them cut apart: a moving performance.

BEST ACTRESS

And the winner is:
ADRIENNE BARBEAU, who soaks her blouse repeatedly in the swamp in an effort to bring realism and depth to her character.

BEST MONSTER

And the winner is:
BELIAL, the gross, disgusting, lovable *thing* that lives in a basket, eats Big Macs, and looks like a squashed octopus.

BEST KUNG FU

And the winner is:
CHUCK NORRIS, cause he's American.

BEST SUPPORTING ACTOR

And the winner is:
LINDEN CHILES, who feeds himself to the monster so it'll get cancer and die.

BEST SUPPORTING ACTRESS

And the winner is:
JUNE CHADWICK, who shows us some trouble, if you know what I mean and I think you do.

BEST SPECIAL EFFECT

And the winner is:
TONY CECERE, who burned himself up for art.

BEST CHEST

And the winner is:
DEBRA BLEE, because you can't argue with the numbers.

BEST DIRECTOR

And the winner is:
FRANK HENENLOTTER for *Basket Case,* but who cares?

BEST GROSS-OUT SCENE

And the winner is:
BASKET CASE, because when the normal brother pulls the deformed brother off her, it's *messy.*

And finally, what we've all been waiting for:

BEST FLICK

And the winner is:
BASKET CASE. Was it ever in doubt? That's why all the activity at the Waverly in Greenwich Village tonight. I won't be there, because I can't breathe in New York City. But all the cast and crew will be, and so will Belial. The turkeys even made him a tux. ■

Nymphos and Psychos: Something's in the Attic in *The House on Sorority Row*

Could I have a show of hands here please? If you are a bimbo who can sit in a car seat and watch a flick without imitating a box of rocks or demanding your own box of Milk Duds or getting nekkid during the intermission, would you please raise your arm and your arm only?

That's what I thought.

I think it's time to talk about the Female Problem in this city. I think it's time to name names and get down to the nitty. I think it's time to talk bimbos.

A lot of people say to me, "Joe Bob, how come you can't seem to get along with women?" And I have four answers to that question.

Numero uno: May Ellen Masters.

Numero two-o: Cherry Dilday.

Numero three-o: Wanda Bodine.

Numero four-o: Vida Stegall.

Now, you may be thinking, Hey, what do all these bimbos have in common? Or you may be thinking, Hey, why is Joe Bob tell-

ing us this? Or you may not be thinking anything.

But the simple fact of the matter is, all these bimbos got the same problem: They're bimbos, but they don't know they're bimbos. They think they're Real Women. All they are, mostly, is Real Nasty.

The reason I'm bringing this up is that Chubb Fricke got me a date last week to go see *The House on Sorority Row,* and I had to drive plumb to Waxahachie to get her, and the only reason I did it is because Chubb said she was a Real Woman. I asked Chubb if that meant she was part of the feminine movement or something, but he said no, not that he knew of. Now, I can't say that I've ever actually met a Real Woman, even though I've seen some in *Playboy* magazine that come close, and Chubb says that's because my standards are too high. And I said, "Chubb, you go home ever night for four years with May Ellen Masters and come talk to me about high standards. That woman's got parts of her body ain't seen daylight since *Attack of the Mole People.*"

Chubb had to admit I had a point.

That's why I'm gonna state right here a few ways you can tell a Real Woman:

1. RWs are modest. They keep all their clothes on at least till the movie starts.

2. RWs are healthy. They do not barf on the upholstery when the psycho jams a branding iron through the cat woman's eyeball.

3. RWs are mature. At least thirty-six, if you know what I mean and I think you do.

4. RWs have taste. They eat the concession-stand hot dogs like everbody else, and they do not *ever* say "Let's go to Bennigan's." As far as I'm concerned, that's grounds for automatic roadside ejection.

5. RWs are not dumb as a box of rocks. A box of Meskin jewelry, maybe, but at least not Cherry Dilday rock-level.

6. RWs are graceful. They know how to get between the front seat and the backseat without opening the door and making the light come on.

7. RWs know their place. It's in the passenger seat, at the flick chosen by the guy in the driver's seat.

8. RWs are independent. If they don't like the flick, they find some other way to *amuse* themselves, and they bring their own materials.

If you know what I mean.
And I think you do.

The moral of this story is that the RW is a figment of my imagination. The chick in Waxahachie was named June or Jane, I can't remember, and she was kind of a fox when you get right down to it, but the bottom line was: Rock City U.S.A. I knew it before we hit Lancaster, which is where she wanted to stop for a Co-Cola and mix it with Jack Daniels. Rich girl. *Bud* wasn't good enough for the bimbo. She wanted "highballs."

She also talked all through the commercial for Metroplex Bail Bonds, which is my favorite part of going to the Century. ("In trouble? In jail? We're right across from McDonald's in downtown Grand Prairie.") I don't know about you, but I've got that phone number memorized, in case I ever get arrested at McDonald's.

And, oh yeah, I forgot to tell you the worst thing about Jane or June.

9. RWs are normal human beings. They don't wear those furry socks on their ankles that don't have feet in em. Some kind of aerobic dancing bullstuff.

I took the bimbo as far as Duncanville, dumped her at Red Bird Mall, and told her to call her sister to come pick her up. That's only cause I'm a nice guy.

Anyhow, *The House on Sorority Row* is a fairly decent flick about these college-girl porkchops in a sorority house who get turned into nympho-meat salad by *something* that lives in the attic. It starts out with all the seniors planning a party after school lets out, but their house mother is the original Lady Godzilla and she says no way, José. Then one night she catches this blond fox named Vicki (Eileen Davidson) making like a barracuda with some guy on a waterbed. So the old bag sticks her rat-tail cane through the waterbed and makes em look like a soggy cheese sandwich. Vicki wants to get even, so she points a gun at Mother Creepola and panics the old lady, and pretty soon the house mother's at the bottom of the swimming pool, drinking the chlorine, if you know what I mean.

Next scene: Drunks at the party start wandering off and getting their faces turned into stuff that looks like Chef Boy-ar-dee ingredients. The first guy gets a steel pole through his neck. Then a girl gets a ramrod through the eyeball. Then a real box-of-rocks fox gets a pole through the back and stomach and a few other places in her evening gown. The best one, though, is this bimbo who gets it with a two-foot butcher knife in the back of the neck while she's hiding out inside a bathroom stall. The psycho puts her head in the toilet. It's his little joke.

Normally this one would go pretty high on the Best of '83 list because it delivers in the blood department (pint and a half). But get this: only *three* breasts. Who'd believe it? Thirteen corpses. No kung fu. No motor vehicle chases. Academy Award nominations for Kathryn McNeil, in the Jamie Lee Curtis role; Eileen Davidson, as the bombshell; and Mark Rosman, the director. Rosman used to work with Brian De Palma, so he knows whereof he kills. Goes to No. 5 on the Best of '83 list, right after *10 to Midnight* and just ahead of *Madman*. Three stars. Joe Bob says check it out. ∎

Joe Bob's Mailbag ———

Dear Joe Bob,

I'm a little skeptical about the breast counts you give in your movie reviews. I can't quite believe that a guy that is drunk on Budweiser all the time can keep track of that many breasts. In fact, I can't quite believe that a guy who would actually GO OUT with Cherry Dilday can count past about twenty. What gives, Joe Bob? Who's doing the counting here?

Sincerely,
D. Sweetkind
University Park

Dear D.:
I was not drunk on Budweiser.
I was drunk on Miller.
I stand by my breast count.

Dear Joe Bob,
There are breasts in Temple.

Francis Stiff
Dallas

Dear Francis:
Yeah, but most of em are on chickens.

Why Do Teen-age Boys Go to Border Towns? Not for the Guacamole

This flick *Losin' It* reminds me of the time that my own-self and Rhett Beavers and Junior Bodine and Ugh Barclay all went down to Laredo for the weekend. The only reason we took Ugh Barclay is that it's easy to meet people when you have a person named "Ugh" with you, because they want to know if "Ugh" is his real name, and then they want to know if it's spelled the same way as the regular little-u "ugh." Sometimes it passes the time, talking about Ugh's name, even though Ugh don't know how he got it, and sometimes he'll say, "I don't see nothing different about Ugh." But mostly Ugh doesn't say anything, which is another reason why I took him along to Laredo.

Cherry Dilday told us she wanted to go to Laredo too, but I had to tell her, "We're not going down there to get donkey bookends, you bimbo."

"What, then?"

"We're going down there to become *Animals.*"

Cherry Dilday said, "Oh."

I don't think I need to point out who's the Rhodes scholar in this conversation.

Anyhow, when me and Rhett and Junior and Ugh went down to Boys Town in Nuevo Laredo, we had a few of those rip-off Limeaid tequila drinks in the coconut shells and played touchy-touchy with a couple bimbos, and then we decided to give Junior a present, mainly because he didn't know what the heck he was doing, if you know what I mean and I think you do. It was Junior's *first time* in Laredo.

In fact, it was Junior's first time, period.

Well, the nitty is that Junior Bodine was *turned down for service.* I know you don't believe this. I know you're thinking, Lot of things happen in Laredo, but getting refused service is not one of em. I'm telling you, though, the bimbo refused to do anything with a guy in overalls with "Junior" written on his pocket. I even decided to give her an extra two bucks if she'd take Junior upstairs, but no way, José. She even said she'd do Rhett for two bucks *less.* Fortunately, Junior Bodine didn't know what the heck was going on, since he'd been schnozzled ever since his eleventh beer, which he finished about the time we hauled through New Braunfels.

While I'm on the subject of international affairs, I'd like to mention the peso situation. Okay, all you guys know that a dollar goes a *long way* on the border these days, but hey, let's not get ridiculous. Boys Town etiquette: Never *ever* go below five bucks for *anything.* I'm not talking economics. I'm talking hygiene, if you know what I mean and I'm *sure* you do.

Okay, *Losin' It.* About these four high school guys who go down to Tijuana for a while—actually three guys plus Wendell the Wimp. The wimp's idea of a good time is buying a bunch of cherry bombs to take back home. But Dave, this guy who's *organizing* the trip, pretty much sums it all up when he screams out of the convertible, "We're gonna be crude as we want, filthy as we want, and gross as we want." Then they proceed to do it.

First the guys rip off a bunch of junk food in a Stop-and-Go, and they also pick up the owner's wife, this airhead lady who's going to Divorce Junction. Once they get down there, the guys go straight for the strippers—*always* a mistake—but anyway that's what they do and then after that they go upstairs, only you already know what's coming: the switcharoonie. Girls upstairs aren't like the ones downstairs. We're talking zit-flab city. We're talking prefab breasts. We're talking sickola.

Okay, next they split up and go after some more rip-offs. Dave goes looking for some Spanish Fly. The wimp buys a bunch of bottle rockets. Guy named Spider goes to a Meskin bar and gets punched out by a sailor creepola. Guy named Woody goes to the Alamo Motel with the airhead lady from the Stop-and-Go. Only everthing starts falling apart when this Meskin cop puts Spider in jail for fighting, and the only way to get him out is turn over Dave's '57 Chevy convertible.

Not a bad flick at all. Twelve breasts. Two motor vehicle chases. No kung fu. One fistfight. One drunken brawl. One guy beating the bejabbers out of another guy. No creatures of any kind. Possible DIAA nominations for Shelley Long, the Stop-and-Go airhead; Jackie Earle Haley, the Dave guy, who wears a Frank Sinatra hat and tries to be cool; Tom Cruise, as the shy guy; John Stockwell, as Spider the fighter.

Losin' It is the best border town garbonza flick I've ever seen, so it goes to No. 3 on the Joe Bob Briggs Best of '83 list, right after *Bloodsucking Freaks* and right before *High Test Girls.* People like Junior Bodine should see it for educational reasons.

Three and a half stars.

Joe Bob says check it out.

The Joe Bob Briggs weekly report on censorship comes directly from Communist Russia this week:

MOSCOW (UPI)—Muscovites are being shown too many movies geared to box-office receipts at the expense of artistic talent, the Moscow newspaper Pravda *said Tuesday.*

It said there are 120 movie theaters in the Soviet capital and that 75 percent of the audience were in the 15–35 age bracket.

"Therefore, what is shown and to whom it is shown is important now."

The newspaper said theaters must "raise the ideological and artistic level of the films produced and shown and not be on the lookout for films which provide good box-office returns such as westerns."

Instead, the newspaper said, theater operators should show films that "educate the Soviet people in the spirit of communism."

They don't have a single drive-in in Communist Russia.

Those people will never see *Chainsaw.*

Sometimes we have to take a few moments and be thankful for the privileges we have. ■

Joe Bob's Mailbag ———

Joe Bob,

I have no earthly idea why I am wasting my time and paper to write this. I despise your cynical attitude toward women; however, no matter how disgusting I find your filthy humor, I am thoroughly delighted by your weekly column.

Joe Bob, I think you're a real jerk. It's no wonder you don't think there is an "RW" in this world because *we* all have the good sense to stay away from you. Hopefully, one of these days the "bimbos" will get smart, too.

RW
Greenville

Dear RW:

I been waiting all my life for the bimbos to get smart.

We're all jerks, honey.

Joe Bob Gets Up Close and Personal: A Talk with Bootsie Goodhead

Normally I don't do interviews. Not a public kind of guy, and let's face it, who gives a flying frijole anyway? Did you read all that bullstuff about how Dustin Hoffman understands bimbos now because he dressed up like a porkchop himself? Good. Neither did I. Let's keep the box-of-rocks comments out of the paper. If actors and directors and big-shot producers have something to say, they can write to Joe Bob's Mailbag like everybody else.

But this week I'm making an exception. Because we're talking Academy Award–level acting. We're talking a performance so warm and moving and *sincere* that it gets me all choked up just thinking about it. We're talking drive-in heaven. You've probly already guessed it by now, but I'll go ahead and say it.

We're talking Bootsie Goodhead.

Now, I know a lot of you turkeys went out and sneaked into the walk-ins last week to see Bootsie Goodhead in *Screwballs*. I know the feeling and I don't blame you. *Screwballs* is the latest flick produced by Roger Corman,

King of the Drive-In, but for some reason he decided to stick it in the hardtops for the first week. He wanted to get some good word-of-mouth going among the indoor-bullstuff wimpolas, because he knew he had a great artistic film on his hands.

What he's got on his hands, I can tell you, is probly best described by Bootsie Goodhead herself.

"It has a lot of nudity in it, and lot of boys trying to get [a word they won't let Joe Bob put in the newspaper]."

You may be wondering how I met Bootsie Goodhead. I can't remember myself. But New World Pictures called up one day and said, "How would you like to interview the star and writer of *Screwballs?*"

"Don't do interviews."

"Her name is Linda Shayne."

"Never heard of her."

"She has this scene where she puts her breasts . . ."

"You don't mean Bootsie Goodhead!"

Like I say, I made an exception.

As you can see from her

comment above, Bootsie is not just another humongous set of garbonzas. Bootsie is a writer. That's why, when I went to see her on opening night, we had a lot to talk about.

"Bootsie," I started off, "I'm going to ignore the fact that the top four buttons on your blouse are undone and you are obviously not wearing a bra. That will have absolutely no effect on my objectivity, because I want to talk flicks."

Bootsie giggled a little bit and made big craters in her cheeks. This is caused by the fact that she has approximately twelve more teeth than the average human being. She also threw three tons of blond hair over her left shoulder, so that I could see her. However, I didn't notice at the time, if you know what I mean and I think you do.

"Bootsie, last year we had *E.T.* and this year we've got *Screwballs.* Does this represent some kind of trend?"

"What?"

"I had an idea that would be your answer, Bootsie, and let me just say that I speak for several drive-in critics on my street when I say that your performance in *Screwballs* is truly *awesome,* if you know what I mean and I'm sure you don't."

"Thank you."

"I'll even go further. I think that movie history was made in your famous drive-in scene. Especially the part where you get the nerd to jump in the back of your van with you so you can start rooting around in there while the movie is on."

Bootsie fluttered her eyelashes.

"But, of course, the highlight of the entire movie is when the nerd suddenly has to jump out the back door, and when he does, the door catches on part of your clothing, and you have to rub your breasts up against the back window for a full minute."

"That *was* a challenging scene."

"Does that glass get pretty cold?"

"I did have to repeat it several times for the camera."

"I'm sure you did. Now, I understand, Bootsie, that you wrote that scene for yourself?"

"Well, actually, Roger said I should do it."

"Roger Corman, King of the Drive-In?"

"Yes."

"And did you write your famous opening line to the nerd, the sensitive suggestion, 'Wanna play Hide the Salami?' "

"I did."

"And were you allowed to use stunt breasts at all?"

"No, those were mine."

"Amazing in this day and age, to see a performer doing her own stunts. Awesome. Really."

"Thank you."

"I also understand that you had something to do with the famous bowling-alley scene?"

"Yes, it was my idea for the bowling ball to get stuck on that guy's thing. But it was my partner's idea on how to get it off."

"Amazing."

"I like good old fun T&A films."

"And what are you doing later tonight, Bootsie?"

"Going out to the Prestonwood so I can sign autographs and help kids sneak in."

"I was told that you do a lot of work with children. And will you be wearing anything, uh, different?"

"I'll probably change into a minidress."

"I'm sure you will. . . . And, Bootsie?"

"Yes?"

"What ARE those?"

"What?"

Anyhow, I'm recommending that you check out Bootsie tonight on the outdoor screen and tell *me* whether the drive-in scene is not one of the most *moving* performances in history.

Screwballs is this flick about Taft & Adams High School ("T&A High"), where a bunch of guys all get sent to detention hall for minor infractions of the rules —like this one guy who puts on a doctor's coat and does "breast exams," and this other guy who sticks the wrong end of his Eiffel Tower in the face of Purity Busch. Purity Busch is the school virgin, this icy blond airhead homecoming queen type who has parents named Ward and June. Ward and June are having trouble in their bedroom. "I'm worried about the Beaver," says June. Anyway, all these four guys in detention *do* is try to get Purity, if you know what I mean and I think you do.

Along the way we got twenty-five breasts. One faculty orgy. No kung fu. No creatures. Moaning. Rooting around. Bimbos in the water. Drive-In Academy Award nominations for Bootsie, for Lynda Speciale as Purity Busch, for Jason Warren as Melvin Jerkovski the fat kid, for the director Rafal Zielinski, and for Alan Daveau for his *amazing* demonstration in the bowling-ball scene. ∎

Joe Bob's Mailbag ▬▬▬

Dear Sir:

Do you ever read this trash that you print? I could not believe it. Initially, I thought that this Joe Bob person had a real put on going. Then, I read further, and found out that he is for real, and that he is actually writing for a segment of your audience.

You are appealing to subhumanoids. Obviously, I and my teenagers do not go to drive-in movies. They show pure and adulterated garbage, but do you, as editor, have to lower yourself and your newspaper to promote this third grade material. Does a writer like Briggs have to earn a living with junk like this?

Suggestions:

1. To Joe Bob Briggs—

Stop wasting your time with this junk. You have talent. Start using it for people who appreciate it. You are wasting your time and part of your life.

2. To the editor—You are degrading yourself and your paper with this trash. Question—can you show this article to your family and friends, and say, with pride, "This is my work, and my contribution to society"?

Robert K.
Dallas

Dear Big Bob:
This is my work, and my contribution to society.

On a Mission to Find This Year's Creep in a Picnic Basket

CANNES, which is in France—There's still a lot of French people over here driving around in their little wimp French cars with names I can't say, and evidently the country's gone Communist too, because they let some Russian movies in at the Olympia Theatre this year. I swear to God, this is the last year I'm doing this, coming over here to sin in hardtops all day with a bunch of Froggies.

You turkeys know why I'm doing this, don't you? It's because I care about art.

And it's also because I get two hundred cold cash American.

I drove all the way over again, even though the Toronado's just about played out and I was on the verge of goin down to Goss on Ross, Tradin' Hoss—Se Habla Espanol, and puttin in my order for a new GTO, but I figured, what the hey, why blow the whole two hundred before I leave? I might get thirsty over there.

So I planted a fake story in the *Herald,* to make Wanda Bodine think I was in Salt Lake City, and tooled down I-45 to the Harbor Lights Bar in Houston and hung around there for a long time hoping I could find some Frog sailors that would help me get my wheels across the Pacific Ocean.

No way, José. Had to pay a Turkish slopehead 18 bucks to get the thing in one of these crates they haul up on the container ships. Rolled that sucker in there, took a bunch of the Arabs over to the mall so they could buy some

Pia Zadora albums, and they finally said it was okay, only they weren't going to Marseilles this year, they were going to Barcelona, and I said, okay by me. On the way over, one of the Turks said he remembered Wanda. Got fairly steamed about it too.

Anyhow, I was gonna make this one short and sweet—headed straight for the Olympia, this place where they show the drive-in stuff even though they don't have drive-ins in France. Why they bring it over here when we've got perfectly good drive-ins in Texas, I have no idea. Probly something to do with the king of France, I don't know. But anyhow, it's where I discovered *Basket Case* last year, so it can't be all wrong, right?

So far I've only found one I like. Called *Wavelength*. About these bald-headed space babies that come to Earth and get put in sterilized barrels in a secret military laboratory underneath Hollywood. But the space babies start yellin through their brainwaves and they hook up with this blond fox named Cherie Currie who's hanging around with Robert Carradine at his house in the Hollywood Hills. They go and get Keenan Wynn, who's either the last mining prospector in the Hollywood Hills or the only one Hollywood ever had, I'm not sure which. Keenan lives up there in a tent, telling stories around the campfire, and he helps Carradine and the fox to find how to get down into the military base. Of course, they're all dumb as dirt, so they go down there and get bombarded by bald-headed space-baby brainwaves and then get arrested by the army.

Meanwhile, the bald-headed space babies are killin everbody in sight. So the general decides the only way to save the world is to bury everbody down there, even his own men. Only Carradine and the fox break open the space-baby incubators, and the space babies pour out of there and start knockin down doors until everbody gets out. They decide to get in Keenan Wynn's horse truck and go out to the Mojave Desert for a while with two Indians.

But once they get out there, the whole U.S. Air Force takes off from Edwards and it looks it's gonna be bombola time, but then the bald-headed space babies get nekkid and go out in the desert and talk to another planet. . . .

Well, you can see we're talking art film. Great space-baby effects. Gonna rank pretty high on the best of '83 list when it has its Texas outdoor premiere. No *Basket Case* though.

I got to find one quick so I can get out of this place before Wanda Bodine figures out what's going on.

Hang in there. ∎

Mission Accomplished: Joe Bob Says *Hundra* Has Made It All Worthwhile

CANNES, which is in France—I have a question for these people over here. If the French invented the word "brassiere," why can't they keep their garbonzas tied up?

I've been doing a lot of serious thinking about jigglers. Everywhere you look down here, you got flashers on the beach and jigglers on the street. It's pitiful, I'm telling you, and I'll probly have to do something about it, if you know what I mean and I think you do.

(I'd just like to throw in right here that France has gone Communist, and so nothing works right over here. Like the last time I tried to send an article back from France, the lady at Western Union *claimed* she didn't know how to spell garbonza. That's how they get you—some ridiculous little thing like that. You gotta watch those Frogs.)

Okay, so you're probly thinking, "Okay, Joe Bob, what in heck are you still doing over there, lying on the beach or something?" Course not. Beaches are fairly disgusting anywhere you go, even Padre, but over here they're skinny little numbers with rocks on em, and even if there weren't a lot of pitiful little French garbonzas out there, I wouldn't go near the place because you might not know this, but they never learned to shave their armpit hair over here. That's a true by-God fact. Pitiful.

Nope. What I been doing is finding the best durn outdoor flick of 1983. And I wanna tell you, it han't been easy.

I'm kind of proud of myself, because a lot of people say, "Joe Bob, you're a sexist and a jerk, but mostly you're just a sexist." I'd like to disprove that right here and now.

We're talking Amazon women.

We're talking humongous, if you know what I mean.

We're talking so many dead bodies that even Joe Bob couldn't count em.

We're talking *Hundra*.

Hundra is this flick about a blond bimbo who's the only one to get out alive when her nomad Amazon woman camp is raped and pillaged and burned up by a bunch of boys from the next town.

I'm telling you, these bimbos get hacked up until it's Chop Suey City.

You may be wondering why Hundra don't get sliced into a salami sandwich with all the others. It's because she's out "getting meat" for the tribe.

Hundra is played by Laurene Landon, who was a lady wrestler in *All the Marbles* and is quite a fine fox, but when she gets back to the village of pillage she's p.o.ed. These Vikings in horn hats are finishing everything off. Heads are rolling. Paint the forest red. The works.

Then the Viking geeks see Hundra, and they take off on horseback after her, only she stops behind a rock and starts picking them off with a bow and arrow. She has to take on about thirty of them at once.

She goes for knives, pickaxes, regular axes, and those little stars that you spin through the air and hope they land in somebody's throat. But her main weapon is she kicks em in the legs, if you know what I mean and I think you do.

Finishes em all off, doesn't even get her hair dirty. Time to go see the old lady of the tribe, sitting on her throne in a cave. The old lady says, well, Hundra, that's too bad about the village of pillage, but, hey, get with the program, you gotta go get pregnant or there's no more tribe.

Hundra says, "No man will ever penetrate my body, with his sword or himself."

I'm very familiar with this line, and I have to give credit to the old lady, she handled it pretty well. Convinced Hundra she had to head south to the land of the sign of the bull, but before Hundra gets there, she's attacked by a painted midget with a pitchfork. Hundra doesn't kill the little guy but she does take his pitchfork and break it in half. I should have mentioned before—Hundra loves to break spears in half.

Next Hundra decides to take a bath in the ocean while riding on her horse. Good for Hundra.

Anyway, I gotta leave out a bunch of Hundra's adventures, but it finally comes down to Hundra goin to the walled city of the Sign of the Bull, where women are herded up like cattle and fed to the slobbering men in the castle. It's a fairly good place to get pregnant, since that's about all the women do there, but for some reason Hundra don't care for it. There's only one guy Hundra wants to do it to her, but the guy thinks Hundra is one big turnoff. So she has to learn the arts of being a woman before the guy will agree to . . . well, let me just say that Hundra does go back for more.

We're talking outdoor classic. We're talking the kind of stuff you can't say in the paper, specially in Communist countries. We are talking in excess of seventy corpses. Heads roll repeatedly. We're only talking fourteen breasts because I don't count dead ones. No motor vehicle chases, but one orgy makes up for it. Great kung fu. I'm afraid I need an immediate drive-in premiere so I can award this movie the four stars it deserves and start it on the ladder of success.

I've got France checked out now, and I gotta get out of the country anyhow because Wanda Bodine showed up over here despite all my efforts to prevent it. We're talking madwoman. ■

Joe Bob's Mailbag

Dear Joe Bob,

Do you think I should show "Joe Bob Goes to the Drive-In" to Miss Penson, my creative writing teacher?

Is your column descriptive or satirical or what?

Diane
Arlington

Dear Diane:
It's what.

Bimbos Behind Bars: Joe Bob Says It's Good to Be Back in America

Wanda Bodine claims I ruined her Rockabilly Glamourcize tape and I owe her 45 bucks for a new one, but she's lying through her fangs. The only reason I went by Le Bodine last week was to find out how in the name of Frogs she got somebody to take her back to France this year, specially since I told those Turkish sailors in Houston she was gonna try to make a run for it and they put out to sea two days early so they wouldn't get trapped and have to haul her across again.

But when I got out to the Grapevine Highway, I knew things were a lot more serious. Next door to the trailer house Wanda put up a Porta-sign-on-wheels with neon letters hanging off it, and it said:

INSTITUT DE BEAUTE BO-DINE
"Look Like a Hundred Francs"
Vertical Hair-do Training
Aerobic Dancewear

**Exclusive Mid-Cities Franchisee
for "Rockabilly Glamourcize"
Opening July 1983**

There wasn't nothing back of the sign but a big pile of gravel that Lute Fenwick had evidently brought over from Cleburne, because Western Auto managers get a break on rock prices and he's been trying to find some way to get Vida Stegall's attention. I know Vida was there because as soon as I flung open the door to the beauty-parlor side of the trailer, all I could see was about seventeen porkchops stuffed in yellow body stockings that had "Le Bodine" stamped right across the garbonza portion. They had the Rockabilly Glamourcize tape going so loud that it made you part blind, and if you squinted your eyes and looked across the *top* of the room all you saw was these heads popping up and down like jumping jacks. I never saw so many stacks of shellac in my life.

I did the only thing a man in my position *could* do. I yanked "Rockabilly Glamourcize" right out of the Betamax.

The first thing I saw when my head cleared was Cherry Dilday, wearin one of those ribbon scarf doohickeys that you just wrap around three parts of your body and tie behind your neck and everthing else shows, and I have to say the sight was so disgusting that it reminded me of that movie Cherry made in New Orleans, *Mardi Gras Massacre,* where the director had her get buck nekkid on a table so a geek could tie up her arms and legs, slice open her chest, and pull out her heart on camera. Cherry's last words in that movie are "Whatever turns you on."

This particular scene at Le Bodine did not turn me on.

Now, I think my views on aerobic dancing are well known to the general public by this time, and I think my views on the character of Wanda Bodine, Cherry Dilday, and the entire Rockabilly Glamourcize dance team are also well publicized. As you turkeys know, I'm not a violent kind of guy. I could've turned Wanda Bodine's face into a Cheese Whopper, but that's not too cool, is it? I probly could've sliced open Cherry Dilday's upper chest cavity with one of those super-size steak knives they give you at Dunston's. That would have been rash and messy.

So all I did was rip up one little bitty Rockabilly Glamourcize videotape and tell Wanda she's dumb as a box of plastic paper clips and the only sign that place needed was "See Rock City" and then I suggested what she could do with her pink Renault, and soon as I said that she started screamin because that wasn't *her* Renault, it was one that Maurice bought for Ugh Barclay's sister so she could sell Mary Kay cosmetics in it.

I figured it out as soon as she said "Maurice." Remember the guy last year who wanted to show Wanda his hotel room in Italy, and she went with him and showed up a week later with enough jack to change Le Coiffure to Le Bodine and hire Vida to do manicures only? *She found the sucker again this year.* Touched him for another few hundred, got him to spring for a Frog ticket, told her he'd build Institut de Beauté Bodine on the side of the highway. Probly took her back to Italy too, and he'll regret it the rest of his life. I never met Maurice but I imagine he was fairly normal and decent, for a Frog anyway, before all this happened, but he don't have a prayer now.

It was so depressing that I needed a good women-in-cages flick to give me some perspective on real life. Of course, most of you maniac turkeys already know what I'm talking about because you were all acting like gorillas last weekend at the Astro D.I. We're talking lust. We're talking perversion. We're talking male guards in a female prison.

We're talking best Bimbos Behind Bars of 1983.

We're talking *Chained Heat.*

Chained Heat, of course, is Part 2 of the serious documentary study of our nation's prisons that began with *The Concrete Jungle,* currently No. 2 on the Joe Bob Briggs Best of '83 Drive-In Movie rankings. The same turkeys made this one, only instead of Jill St. John as the crooked prison officer, they got Stella Stevens. And instead of Tracy Bregman as the little lambchop that gets put through a commercial Osterizer, they got Ms. "Exorcist" herself, Linda Blair.

You turkeys know how I feel about sequels, and the reason *Halloween III* was a rip-off and *Friday the 13th, Part 3* was such a great flick. If you know what you're doing, the sequel can be *exactly the same movie* as the first one. That's what we got here. It starts out with Linda Blair goin to prison for *no reason at all.* She really wanted to be an interior decorator, but then she killed this guy in a car accident, but it wasn't her fault, but it doesn't matter because they pack her off to the Crossbar Hotel. Okay, then we got the Good Friend (poufy brunette named Sharon Hughes, about a six on a ten scale) and the Evil Friend (Sybil Danning, a blond fox, as the white gang leader). Then we got the black gang leader, Tamara Dobson. In this version she's a graduate of Vassar. We got the warden, John Vernon, who likes to take jailhouse bimbos to his hot tub and entertain, if you know what I mean and I think you do. We got the S&M freak guard, Henry Silva, who does pimp and drug work.

This one has some plot, but it doesn't get in the way. These bimbos-behind-bars people are definitely maturing as artists. *The Concrete Jungle* had less than ten breasts. This time we got thirty-three complete breasts without any body-stocking fakes. One shower scene. Three rapes. One bimbo neck impaled on a wire. Two strippers doing their stuff. One transvestite wrassling scene. Minimum of lesbo stuff. Two brawls, one black-on-white, with plenty of gouging, hair-pulling, knees in embarrassing places. Pretty good hot-tub murder. Nine corpses. No motor vehicle chases. Another death-in-the-john scene. Moderate kung fu. Heads do not roll.

Academy Award nominations for Stella Stevens, Sybil Danning, director Paul Nicolas, Henry Silva as the geek sadist prison guard. I would've ranked this one higher, because I was expecting some pickets from the feminine movement, but I han't heard a peep out of those bimbos. So, three and a half stars, and it goes to No. 7 on the Best of '83 list, right behind *10 to Midnight*, the best Chuck Bronson-sweeps-the-scum-off-the-street flick of the year, and just ahead of *The House on Sorority Row*, about the psycho who makes meat salad out of college girls.

Joe Bob says check it out. ■

Don't Go in the Woods:
Heads Roll and Arms Roll and the Blood Runs Cold

Last week after I almost got my head kicked in by Wanda Bodine's Rockabilly Glamourcize class at the House of Shellac, otherwise known as the Le Bodine beauty parlor, I ran into Stookie McMahay in the parking lot and almost went right by him because I didn't know he had hair again. It turns out he got a transplant by mailing in a coupon to *Fling* magazine. Stookie is district manager for Magnum Power Tongs out of Houston, and he's basically in love with Wanda. I say "basically," because she said she wouldn't marry him for less than $10,000, and he never has realized that's highway robbery even for a bimbo that would actually jump in the sack with Stookie.

"Delivering your check, Stookie?"

"Yeah."

"How much this time?"

"Let's just say the high two digits."

"Stookie, do you realize how many Magnum Power Tongs you got to sell before you can even *talk* marriage?"

"You saying I can't do it?"

"Stookie, no man on this earth would be happier to see Wanda Bodine married and pregnant, specially if you get transferred to the home office. But that woman's charging you 22 percent *interest* on those payments, Stookie."

Stookie got out his payment book and we looked it over. I showed him the fine print that said when he got through paying, he still wasn't through due to interest *and* service charges, if you know what I mean and I'm sure Wanda does. Stookie would have to sell Magnum Power Tongs from here to Communist Russia.

"Stookie, it's not worth it."

"What if I had a Taco Bell franchise on the side?"

"You been talking to Rhett Beavers?"

"What if I got Lute to get us a couple *Love Boat* tickets, just me and Wanda for a week?"

"Stookie, she'd take em but it wouldn't do any good. We're dealing with a woman who made up a payment book that they'd be embarrassed to give out at Walking-Man Pickups on Ross Avenue."

"How about a condo in Oak Cliff?"

I could see that nothing I said was gonna make any difference. Stookie was already a goner. Dying quail. Stookie thought it was his last chance, and so he was puttin out the vibes that said Desperation City. Wanda was gonna play him like a bass fiddle.

"Stookie, go get drunk or something, but don't go in there."

"Huh?"

"Forget it."

I watched Stookie go on in with his checkbook sticking out of his green jacket, and I didn't have the heart to tell him Wanda was just using that money to build the new Institut de Beauté Bodine. We're talking serious gold-digger action. It makes me barf to think about it, but I would guess Stookie's not the only one gettin the $10,000 treatment, especially since she *apparently* brought Maurice back from France again. I'm starting to consider putting together a little deal to actually *buy* Wanda for Stookie, just to see if she'll come across with the groceries, but meantime I'm a working man and so I gotta go count some bodies.

I'm talking about *Don't Go in the Woods,* this teen-age-meat-salad flick starring my buddy Hubcap Carter. Hubcap works at KLIF, but in the flick he's a sheriff who goes running around in the mountains looking for a big hairy hippie in a Viking costume who likes to wear beads on his face and slice skulls open with a machete. He also likes to rip people's arms off, like he does in the first scene.

What we got here is your basic dumb-as-a-cement-truck backpacker party that don't know there's a Viking hippie up there choking the guts out of tourists. Sometimes he just hangs around campsites breathing real loud and waiting for somebody to say "I think I'll go see what the noise is out there." One guy gets out of his van and goes yelling through the woods "Come out of there, you jerk you!" which is one of the finer lines in the script. This turkey gets it from behind, machete across the throat, so that he vomits up some blood on the window just before the psycho-hippie sets the van on fire and burns up his wife.

Now you're probly wondering: Where the heck is Hubcap? Hubcap is the local sheriff, and he's up in a plane, searching for all the "missing persons" that are getting reported. Hubcap han't figured out yet that you can't see the Viking cuttin up babies when you're five thousand feet up in the air, so he turns around and goes home and says, basically, no big deal. Then a couple campers get zipped up in their sleeping bags, hung up on a tree, and run through with a four-foot blade, and then a fisherman gets impaled in a bear trap, and then Attila the Hun gores this guy with a pick-axe, and then our heroes the box-of-rocks campers start to get wise and so they go to the psycho's house to check it out. They find one of their friends there. He's in a Hefty Bag.

Meantime Hubcap is on the case, asking questions like "What's the story on this wild man?"

And Mr. Nice Guy with the buffalo-hide tuxedo is still making sausage out of people out there, including one guy in a wheelchair. That's about all I can say except: Heads do roll, and the big paint-the-woods-red finale is fairly disgusting.

Sixteen corpses. Zero breasts, which makes me seriously doubt the integrity of the people Hubcap is getting mixed up with. One guy gets a whole tree limb run through his body. No motor vehicle chases. Approximately seven buckets of blood. Minimum kung fu. Heads roll. Arms roll. It's no *Chainsaw* but it'll do. Two stars.

Joe Bob says check it out. ■

Stadium Screens Are Gone; Did the Cowboys Do It? Joe Bob Calls for Protest

I been pretty bummed out ever since they ripped out the screens at Texas Stadium, and so I asked Rhett Beavers to go over there and find out what the hey is going on, but Rhett kind of fades in and out and I never know whether he's been purchasing those foreign cigarettes again, if you know what I mean and I think you do, and so I don't completely buy Rhett's version. In fact, I refuse to believe what Rhett told me.

Rhett says the Dallas Cowboys pulled down the screens at Texas Stadium.

I know this is not the case. No way they're gonna do something that unpopular in the year of the USFL. To me those screens *are* Texas Stadium. Give you an idea what I mean: Where do you park at a Cowboys game if you have a Super Gold Card "Personal Friend of Tom Landry" V.I.P. Texas Veteran and Roger Staubach's Mother Sky-Box ticket to the game? Where do you park for the Cowboys games if you're the governor, or the governor's girlfriend?

You park in the drive-in.

Or what used to be the drive-in. Everbody knows that. That's what you're *paying* for when you buy those $490,000 season tickets. Because after the game is over, on Sunday night, you can sit out there and watch *Driller Killer* for no extra charge.

I think we *all know* who's responsible for this. I think we *all know* who tore up a perfectly good trailer park and donated it for Texas Stadium in the first place. I think we *all know* who the Nazis are in this story. It's time to name names. I'm sorry, but I'm getting all choked up thinking about the great flicks I saw at Texas Stadium. Remember *Malibu Beach* in 78, *Maniac* in 81? Remember *Living Nightmare?* ("What is the worst act a woman can be forced to commit . . . again and again and again?") If I keep this up I'm gonna lose control.

So where were the so-called historic preservationists when this was going on? Where was the Texas Historical Society or whoever it is that goes around sticking up plaques on buildings?

Like I say, we *all know* who's behind this.

We're talking City of Irving.

Thank God for the 183 D.I., because these jerkolas are knocking em off one by one. Remember the Park Plaza D.I., double screen and a back row so far away you could get lost out there? It's a *Sesame Place,* for God's sake. It's based on an indoor-bullstuff TV show. It's *G-rated.*

Now, let me get one thing straight. I'm not talking about people who *live* in Irving, which used to be a great city before they let Las Colinas in. David McDavid has the finest line of Toronados in North Texas, and also stars in the second-best commercial on TV. (The first best is the one for P.T.'s Nekkid Dancin Bar.) Many of my close personal friends work at the Frito warehouse over in Irving, and I'm proud to say they voted wet last year so all my Babtist buddies can start drinking in front of each other.

What I'm talkin here is leadership. I'm talkin corruption in high places. I'm writin to the mayor today, and I wanna urge you to do the same thing. I think it's time to say "Hey, we want some answers." Your letter should read as follows:

Dear French-fry Head Mayor of Irving:

We want some answers.

We want the jerkolas who ripped out the screens at Texas Stadium.

We want their heads on a plate.

Anything you could do would be appreciated.

Thank you,
(your name here)
P.S. *Joe Bob says to stuff it.*

Have I made myself clear? I want a full explanation and, like I say, I don't believe the Cowboys did it.

Every true fan of the drive-in felt a big fist in the gut last year when Vic Morrow got killed while making an indoor-bullstuff movie. Remember his great ones? *Deathwatch, Message from Space, Babysitter,* the list goes on and on. And now everybody will be going to see Vic one more time this week, to remember what he could do so well. It's Vic's last summer, maybe Vic's last flick on the big screen.

Of course, I'm talking *1990: The Bronx Warriors.*

I tooled out to the 121 Twin in Lewisville to catch it, mainly because I wanted to get off by myself and drink some Bud's in Vic's honor, and also because Wanda Bodine is trying to find me so she can kick the tar out of me over remarks I made the last two weeks about her Rockabilly Glamourcize class. Anyhow, I folded Rhett up and packed him in the backseat and we motored out to Lake Dallas and picked up three sixes and then we were ready to roll.

The flick turned out to be a definite highlight in Vic's career. It's all about these gangs that kill each other in the Bronx after the cops give up on the place and declare it a war zone and go back to Manhattan. It's the only flick I've ever seen where all the violence is for absolutely no reason, and everybody gets killed *the same way:* They get crowbars rammed through their chest so they come out on the other side. Well, actually that's not completely true, since one guy gets rammed through the back with a wooden stake and another guy gets shishkebobbed with a hockey stick.

We're talking some serious drama. There's this one gang of hippie black-leather Indian punkola bikers, and this other gang of freaks on roller skates, and then all these black dudes who follow around after Fred Williamson in their pimpmobiles. The basic object of the movie is to get all these guys killed off with crowbars and knives and kung fu, only Vic Morrow don't go for that stuff, he just blows people away with a shotgun.

Almost forgot: This one bimbo named Stefania Girolami gets tossed around and kidnapped, and one of the Indian punkolas is trying to get her back, and she's supposed to be a Patty Hearst-type, dumb as a box of Bic lighters, who ran away from her corporation so she could live on a dirtpile in the South Bronx with a guy named Trash. No matter what they do to her she never changes expression. That's because she's the director's daughter.

Here's a few highlights. First these two hockey-puck guys get their knees scissored off by a biker. Then Vic shows up with his double-barrel pump-action and blows away this punkola biker while he's lying on top of his girl-friend, and then he blows away the girlfriend, and then when they chase him, he sets one of em on fire. Next thing all the gangs start a war, which is what Vic wants because Vic is working for the cops. Then the bimbo gets kid-napped by some Zombies, only they don't rip off her blouse or anything because she's the direc-tor's daughter. Then Trash de-cides to rescue the bimbo. Trash is one of those guys with breasts, which he shows off underneath his black leather safety-patrol straps. (Male breasts, even when they are larger than female breasts, do not count in the Joe Bob Briggs fea-ture-film breast inventory. Just so there won't be any misunder-standing.)

Then these guys called the Scavengers start jumping on Trash's friends like those gremlins in the Wicked Witch of the West's castle, and what these guys do is they drive stakes through the heart and then string you up and let you bleed to death. Two guys get shishkebobbed before Trash kung-fus his way out of there.

Then Vic has to crowbar a guy, and waste four others with his pump-action, but then Fred Wil-liamson and Trash join up and get a black leather witch to go along and strangle people with her whip. You've heard of brass knuckles? This fox has brass fingernails that look like they've been shellacked at Le Bodine. I'm talking lethal.

Fred Williamson kung-fus *eight freaks at once* in an out-*standing* scene. Then we got crow-bars against hockey sticks for a while. One guy gets it in the neck with a shoe knife, like the ones in *From Russia with Love*. Then Vic rides in with the cavalry. I'm talk-ing nine hundred guys carrying in-dustrial-strength blowtorch guns, and their basic orders are to burn the eyes out of everbody they see. People start getting blown away left and right until only Vic and Trash are left. Fire against crow-bar. Outstanding.

We're talking thirty-seven dead bodies that I can personally verify. Normally this would auto-matically qualify for Top Ten con-sideration, but we got a problem: zero breasts. (Director's daugh-ter.) We got three motor vehicle chases. Two creatures. Five quarts of blood. Heads roll. Excellent Fred Williamson kung fu. No plot to slow it down. It goes directly to No. 6 on the Joe Bob Briggs Best of '83 Drive-In Movie list, right behind *Losin' It* and just ahead of *High Test Girls*.

Three and a half stars.

Joe Bob says check it out. ■

Joe Bob Briggs Decides to Get Tough with Irving, Channel 4, and *The Incubus*

Maybe I didn't make myself perfectly clear. Maybe you turkeys didn't understand me last week. Let me repeat myself: I'm not a violent kind of guy, and I do *not* want to have to resort to something nasty like a kung-fu exhibition in the main lobby of Irving City Hall. This would not be a pretty sight on the Action News.

I'm just stating the facts.

Numero uno: The drive-in screens at Texas Stadium were ripped down.

Numero two-o: Nobody will confess to the crime.

Numero three-o: The city of Irving owns Texas Stadium.

Numero four-o: Tex Schramm owns Irving.

Numero five-o: Last week I asked you turkeys to get me some answers from the french-fry head mayor of Irving and most of you thought I was making some kind of little *joke,* didn't you?

Now, as you all know by now, when Joe Bob says heads will roll, *heads will roll.* So I'm saying it right now: When I find out who ripped down the screens at Texas Stadium, *heads will roll.*

(Even the *Rams* have a drive-in in their stadium lot. Come on, you guys, gimme a break, the *Rams?)*

Okay. First. If anybody knows the name of the mayor of Irving, please send it in to me so we can make the man sweat blood.

Next thing, since this is not Communist Russia and I don't want anybody to have any doubts about how democratic we're doing this, I want you to fill out the ballot on this page, which says "In your opinion, should the royal jerkola who ripped down the screens at Texas Stadium have his head severed from his worthless body or not?" [Editor's note: Even JB admits that this poor man suffered enough, so you folks are *not* getting a ballot.] If the answer is yes, I will personally supervise the wheelbarrow brigade that will carry all ballots to Irving City Hall and dump them on any desk within chopsocky range. In the unlikely event that the answer is no, I will assume that Tex Schramm did it and you people are covering for him. Obscenities and stray marks on the ballots are optional.

And if *this* doesn't work, I'm sorry but we're talking Kung Fu City.

Last week after the early show at Holiday Inn DFW Airport North, I motored out to the Kaufman Pike with Vida Stegall, who's had Inflated Bimbo Brain ever since they took our picture out in front of the Bronco Bowl and put it in *D Magazine.* I'm not gonna repeat my well-known feelings about the liberal northern media establishment and the way they splash my personal life all over their pages, but let's face it: When we talk *D Magazine,* we're talking Wimp City U.S.A. Vida was so hyper that she got sloshed on Coco Locos at the Club Gigi's lounge at Holiday Inn DFW Airport North and if I hadn't been one heck of a decent guy she would have ended up in Cleveland with a bunch of regional sales managers for Magnum Power Tongs. The 747 was waiting and so was Vida, if you know what I mean and I think you do.

So I packed her in the backseat and headed for the Kaufman Pike D.I. to catch some *Incubus.*

We're talking best invisible-demon-rapist flick since *The Entity.*

I know this may be hard to believe since you probly noticed John Cassavetes is running around in this movie. But all he does is go around explaining the *scientific* evidence after the *whatever it is* rapes and brutalizes all the women in his particular small town. The very first scene, this guy gets it in the forehead with a board that has a nail sticking out of it, but that's only because the guy's hanging around so the demon can't get to the groceries. After they start hauling the bleeding bimbos to Parkland Emergency, the flick goes into how this wimp kid talks to himself every night and has dreams about a torture chamber and—well, what I'm saying is you have to go through quite a bit of plot in the middle. Anyhow, the wimp kid will say something like "I been having this dream, Grandma," and then *wham!* the town librarian gets it by whatever it is. And John Cassavetes is the doctor who keeps saying "The windpipe was smashed, the vertebrae crushed, the insides ripped to smithereens —but I think it was *one man."* How does he know that? Because of the *weird sperm* they find, and I'd tell you more about that except I just danced out on the gangplank and there's a high sheriff watching to make sure I don't go off the end. If you know what I mean.

Then Cassavetes makes a fool of himself over this fox newspaper reporter named Kerrie Keane, because she keeps showing up whenever there's just a *little commotion,* like the scene where the farmer gets a pitchfork rammed through his neck and blows off his feet with his own shotgun and then the whatever-it-is goes into his farmhouse and finishes off two women, including one in a wheelchair. Or the girl who gets it in the bathroom at a moviehouse. (I try to tell those bimbos to stay out of hardtops; it's not safe.) Anyway, it takes Cassavetes *forever* to figure out what's going on.

We're talking ten corpses. Five breasts. No motor vehicle chases. One beast, green frogman variety. Two pints of blood. No kung fu. Heads do not roll. Feet roll. The numbers don't add up to Top Ten status.

Two stars.

Joe Bob says check it out. ∎

Joe Bob's Mailbag ——

Dear Joe Bob:

Just for the record, do your breast tallies refer to singles or pairs?

S.W.M.
Dallas

Dear SWM:

Think about it now—how could you count pairs when you're dealing with stuff like side views and garbonzas mashed up against bodies and your occasional garbonza closeup.

Singles, obviously.

Rhett's in Some Big Trouble; Meanwhile JBB Checks Out the New King of Chopsocky

I was planning on going over to Irving this weekend to kung-fu the mayor, Bobby Joe Raper, who still han't explained to the drive-in-going public of Dallas County *exactly* what happened to the screens at Texas Stadium, but I have to put it off because of Rhett Beavers getting arrested in Garland on the Fourth of July.

Rhett claims the charge is Theft-Under-200 but I seriously doubt that considering that his bail is $90,000 and on a good day Rhett could ordinarily raise about 9 cents. I been trying to get Bubba Barclay, my Bossier City lawyer, to drive over and handle the case and make a quick hundred, but Bubba says, "The Mississippi

Highway Patrol is one thing, but you're talking Garland Police. No way, José."

Bubba you gotta understand, is basically a chickenstuff.

From what I understand, they came and got Rhett right there in the trailer park in front of everbody, and when they got there Rhett was in no condition to understand his Miranda warning because he'd been smoking all morning, if you know what I mean and I think you do, and also because he didn't remember where he'd been from about June 5 to July 3. This made it difficult when the monkey faces started in on him with the first tough question:

"Where'd you get those shoes, Mr. Beavers?"

Rhett answered quick as a cat, as usual. "What?"

"Where did you *acquire the footgear,* sir?"

Rhett kind of bent over a little and stared down at his feet. He had on suede shoes that were red on one side and blue on the other. On the heel of both shoes was a big number "11" in raised white letters.

"Bought em at James K. Wilson," Rhett said.

This is where I understand things started going wrong for Rhett.

"Do you have a receipt?" asked the officer.

"Of course I do," said Rhett. (Bad sign when you start to act like a horse's patoot and you still don't know where you woke up this morning.)

"Could we see it, please?"

"I bought these shoes with my American Express Gold Card." Rhett pulled a mutilated piece of plastic out of his pocket and held it up to the light. In the bottom left corner of the card it said "WANDA BODINE, LE BODINE, INC."

"Mr. Beavers," the cop said, "it appears this credit card does not belong to you."

Now, normally in a case like that the thing to do is just stop talking and call Joe Bob, but Rhett told the Garland Police to wait while he went in his bedroom and rooted around in his duffel bag and came back with a credit card receipt for $337.42.

"As you can see," Rhett said, "I paid for the *alleged* shoes in full."

Rhett thought they would be impressed by the word "alleged."

The cop unfolded the receipt and took it outside so he could read through all the blurry ink, but the paper was all stiff and faded from setting up on Rhett's dashboard for approximately nine years. The policeman finally made out that it was a receipt for six tires, a set of shocks, and a battery from Carco. It was dated October the 12th, 1974, and it was a Bank-Americard charge on the name of Billie Sol Estes. Rhett had signed it "Bruce Lee."

"Mr. Beavers, I'm going to ask you once more. Where did you get the shoes? Might I suggest a bowling alley?"

"Why do you think James K. Wilson would sell shoes to a bowling alley?"

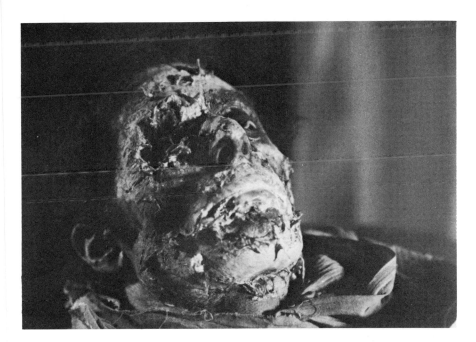

The movie that started it all—
Joe Bob's first review, that
tourist-eating cannibal classic,
The Grim Reaper
*(Photo courtesy of Independent
Network, Inc.)*

THE TENANT IN ROOM 7 IS VERY SMALL,
VERY TWISTED, AND VERY MAD

BASKET CASE

an IEVINS / HENENLOTTER production starring KEVIN VanHENTENRYCK TERRI SUSAN SMITH BEVERLY BONNER
Director of Photography BRUCE TORBET Music GUS RUSSO Executive Producers ARNIE BRUCK TOM KAYE
Production Executive RAY SUNDLIN Produced by EDGAR IEVINS Written and Directed by FRANK HENENLOTTER

FROM SAFIR FILMS LTD.
Townsend House, 22-25 Dean Street, London W1V 5AL.
In Cannes: SIDNEY SAFIR and LAWRENCE SAFIR, Majestic Hotel.

Basket Case **one-sheet**
(Photo courtesy of Edgar Ievins)

One of the nicer guys in *Pieces*
(Photo courtesy of Melrose Associates)

Sweet, innocent little Donna Wilkes, the high school girl who makes her spare change on Hollywood Boulevard in *Angel*
(Photo courtesy of New World Pictures)

The director of *The Power* expressing his views on retakes

(Photo courtesy of Independent Network, Inc.)

Misty Rowe in *Meatballs Part II*, one of her greatest performances since *Hee Haw*

(Photo courtesy of Tri-Star Pictures, Inc.)

Bo Derek, bodacious in *Bolero*, the movie that made her what she is today—the Oral Roberts of the Drive-in

(Photo courtesy of Cannon Films, Inc.)

Betsy Russell, who had a head-on collision with Max Factor right before she made *Avenging Angel*
(Photo courtesy of New World Pictures)

The "Woman Called Horse" scene in *Make Them Die Slowly*
(Photo courtesy of Aquarius Releasing, Inc.)

Mutilations! Intense Pain!

Lucinda Dickey, the Drive-in Queen of 1984, in *Ninja III— The Domination,* **the flick that answers the question, "Wanna see my sword?"**
(Photo courtesy of Cannon Films, Inc.)

"Mr. Beavers, let me review the facts here."

"Uh-huh."

"You are standing before me this moment in a pair of size-eleven blue-and-red bowling shoes."

"If you want to get technical about it."

"Asked where you got them, you first produced a corporate American Express card registered to another individual. You then produced what is apparently a fraudulent receipt for automotive products purchased nine years ago. This same receipt was inscribed with the name of a man who at the time of purchase was serving a federal prison term for fraud. The suspicious instrument is, in addition, signed by an East Asian foreign national who died in the year 1973."

"Seventy-four."

"I beg your pardon?"

"Bruce Lee—he died in 1974. Can't you get your facts straight?"

"Signed by an East Asian foreign national who died in the year 1974. Furthermore, you have produced no evidence which would serve to link the transaction which allegedly occurred on October 12, 1974, with the particular pair of bowling shoes currently affixed to your rather large feet. Is that about it, Mr. Beavers?"

Rhett thought for a minute, looked down at his shoes again, and then looked back at the cop.

"That's my story," he said, "and I'm sticking to it."

Speaking of Bruce Lee, I motored out to the 183 last weekend to see the new King of Chopsocky, direct from Hong Kong, Jacky Chan, making the flesh fly in *Eagle's Shadow*. I wasn't ready to believe all the bullstuff they been putting out on this flick, about how Jacky Chan is breaking Bruce Lee's box-office records all over the map, because everbody knows there'll never be another *Enter the Dragon* so, hey, what's the point? But I gotta say, the kid knows his chopsocky. This is no *Mad Monkey Kung Fu,* and I still want to see *Karate Killers on Wheels* this summer before I start nominating *Eagle's Shadow* for any Drive-In Academy Awards, but we're talking lethal stuff here.

The plot is about a bunch of Yul Brynner lookalikes trying to destroy everbody who knows snake-style kung fu—which is what Jacky Chan does. Snake-style is so fast that the old-man master (Simmon Yuen, the guy who always plays the old-man master) can kung-fu mosquitoes in his sleep. In fact, the old bearded guy with goat hair all over his face is the last living snake-style fighter, so he has to go around dressed like a beggar so nobody can slice him into cat food. Anyhow, Jacky Chan is a nobody; he has to scrub floors at the kung-fu school, except when the dragon-fist master tells him to go out and be a human punching bag for this fat little rich kid who's wasting his time trying to learn how to bust up bricks with his fist. The old goat-hair guy takes pity on Jacky

Chan and leads him out into the wilderness to get tough and "Rocky"-up for the big snake-style paint-the-desert-red fistfest with one preying-mantis-style guy and one guy who dresses up like a priest but actually he's a guy sent over from Communist Russia to murder Goat-Hair. None of these turkeys realize Jacky Chan's secret, which is when he combines snake-style stuff with cat's-claw style, because if you ever noticed, a cat *can* kill a snake due to its claws being so fast. (We know this because Jacky Chan watches a cat kill a snake.) The great thing about the cat's claw is when Jacky Chan grabs his opponent in the place we can't talk about in the newspaper, if you know what I mean and I think you do, and when he does that and yanks up, the guy *dies. Painfully.*

We got *fifteen* complete kung-fu fight scenes, including everthing from one-on-one to four-on-one to eight-on-two. We got three complete kung-fu comedy scenes, including one with a scrub brush that's *almost* as good as Bruce Lee. We got excellent dubbed thwocks and whooshes. We got minimal stickwork, one

guy who karates three layers of bricks, but no Nunchakus. No beasts. No motor vehicle chases. Less than one pint of blood. No breasts. Five corpses. Heads do not roll.

Serious chopsocky. Three and a half stars.

Joe Bob says check it out. ■

Joe Bob's Mailbag

"Message for the Mayor": Raise the Screens!

Nuthin' Personal but if we lose freedom of movie viewing in Texas—The rest of the world is gonna go down fast

Scott Meador
Dallas

Dear Scott:

This is, of course, the well-known drive-in domino theory, proven in Vietnam, where the lack of drive-in screens has already spread to ALL Southeast Asian countries.

Rhett's Still in Trouble; JB and Wanda Check Out Burt and Loni in *Stroker*

I went over to Garland Jail last week to tell Rhett that so far Bubba has raised $28 in the Free Rhett Beavers crusade. I was gonna have this all-night vigil in front of the jail to raise some more jack, but nobody wanted to stay up all night. Anyhow, I told Rhett that we have 28 bucks and we only need $89,972 more to make bail. Rhett was happy to hear it.

But now I got some unpleasant business.

Rhett never told me about the Arkansas Polio Weed.

Rhett never told me that $88,000 of his $90,000 bail was on the charge of possession of Arkansas Polio Weed.

I told Rhett not to touch that stuff. I *told* him I was suspicious of why he had to go visit his mother in Jasper, Arkansas, *every* dang weekend. I *told* him if he kept smoking that stuff they grow up there in the mountains he was gonna end up with the inside of his brain looking like a flashlight battery that's been left out in a field for seventeen years.

You probly know the stuff I'm talking about. Rhett used to light up one of those suckers and

forty-five minutes later we'd have to carry him over to Parkland Emergency for heart massage. Sometimes he'd forget to take it out of his mouth before total paralysis set in, and his arm muscles would start twitching like a frog in biology class and then he'd play the whole drum solo to "Inna Godda Divida" on the end of a Van Camp's Pork and Beans can. There's nothing you can do when he gets like that. After two or three hours he'll start begging you to drive him out to DFW Airport so he can "fly Braniff."

We're talking some wicked weed.

Anyway, the Garland cops found three ounces of Arkansas Polio Weed (estimated street value $9,000) in Rhett's bowling bag, and when I asked him about it Rhett claimed he had it stored in there to *prove* it was for "recreational use."

"Rhett," I told him, "we're talking Garland Police here, and they'll need to request FBI assistance just to *spell* recreational."

Rhett said he didn't think of that, and besides, he was still p.o.ed about the Theft-Under-200 charge they laid on him for "possession of stolen shoes." Rhett swears he didn't swipe those shoes, and he thinks one of the cops just wanted some new dogwarmers and liked Rhett's because they looked like something you couldn't get at True Value Hardware. You probly remember how the alleged shoes were red suede on one side, blue suede on the other, and they had a big number "11" in raised white letters on the heels. Rhett said he bought those shoes specially to wear to Bobo Rodriguez's wedding and he didn't see what was so suspicious about red-and-blue shoes anyway.

"Rhett," I told him, "you're gonna miss Bobo's wedding unless you come up with ninety thou."

"Does that mean you're taking the twenty-eight back?" he said.

I told Rhett the next time he inhaled any Polio Weed, I was taking him straight to Southwestern for a brain scan.

"I think the Texas Association of Geologists might be interested in the rock formations," I said.

"After that will you take me to DFW?" he said.

I was so bummed out after seeing Rhett in that kind of condition that I actually asked Wanda Bodine to ride out to the Astro— in the backseat, of course—so I could see *Stroker Ace* and watch Burt bust up some race cars. I had to go see Wanda anyway to tell her that the Garland Police confis-

cated her American Express Gold Card that they took off Rhett when they arrested him and they were wondering why it had her name on it but when you traced down the numbers it was Lute Fenwick paying the bills. Wanda came along to *Stroker Ace* under *my conditions,* which meant she was forbidden from taking her clothes off at any time, because she *suddenly* didn't want me to mention the Lute Fenwick part to Vida Stegall. I found out Lute came into some money awhile back when he sold his Western Auto franchise in Baird so he could devote full time to the Cleburne store, and I figured he was using it for a little extra service at the beauty shop, if you know what I mean and I'm sure you do. Anyhow, I won't go into that because it's almost as depressing as the Rhett Beavers story.

One thing I like about Burt Reynolds, to get back on the subject, is that ever time he makes a new movie he *matures* as a actor. I mean, he'll never make another *W.W. and the Dixie Dancekings* because, let's face it, that was a once-in-a-career kind of flick. But what I'm talking about is last five, six years, starting with *Smokey and the Bandit* and going on through *Hooper* and *Smokey II* and *Cannonball Run,* and skipping over all the indoor bullstuff like *Paternity* and *Best Friends* because, let's face it, they make him do those films so he can make some bread and get back to the drive-in work he loves and besides

I han't seen those flicks anyway. But what we're talking here is *attitude*. Burt has got it down now. He can do a whole movie without any plot to get it all mucked up.

Like in *Stroker Ace*. I have to admit I expected some Loni Anderson garbonza exposure in this flick, and if you don't have the word yet, I gotta be truthful: no celebrity jugs. Loni Anderson's in it, but she acts like she's not. Gomer Pyle is in it. Here's what happens. Burt drives around in this car with only three wheels on it and then he guns around and totals a race car at Daytona and then he dumps wet cement in his sponsor's car and then Ned Beatty comes in and asks him to sign a contract the size of a phone book and Burt does it cause he needs the jack but after he signs it he finds out he has to promote these fried-chicken outlets and wear a chicken suit while he's racing at Talladega and some other tracks and he tries to get in bed with Loni but it doesn't work and then he punches some guys out with Gomer Pyle and then he goes and finds his daddy, who makes jewelry out of do-do, and his daddy comes watch him win the race at Charlotte, which is where he crashes up some more cars.

Five motor vehicle chases. Eight crashes. No beasts. No breasts, but Loni comes close. One beer-joint brawl. One guy through a plate-glass window and into the swim pool. No kung fu. No plot. Two and a half stars (one off for lack of sufficient Loni anatomy).

Joe Bob says check it out. ∎

Bobby Joe Has a Message for Joe Bob

Bobby Joe Raper came out of the Irving Rose Garden last week and made his first public statement on The Texas Stadium Crisis.

Bobby Joe says he didn't do it.

Do we believe this turkey?

This is not Communist Russia, so I'm gonna let you hear what the ole boy has to say and make your own judgment:

Mr. Joe Bob Briggs
Movie Critic of Rockwall, Texas

RE: Concerning the Drive-in Movie Operation at Texas Stadium

Dear Air Head:

The stadium is owned by the City of Irving and managed by the Texas Stadium Corporation. Texas Stadium Corporation, some years ago, entered into a lease agreement with CEBE Concessionaires whereby CEBE installed the necessary equipment to operate a drive-in movie at Texas Stadium. For the past year the drive-in has been operating at a non-profit level, so, for this reason the concessionaire has chosen not to renew the lease for continuation of the drive-in. I don't believe this necessarily classifies these folks as "jerkolas." We're talkin' bottom line here.

Texas Stadium was built by the issuance of revenue bonds which means that these bonds must be retired by revenue received by various stadium activities. Certainly the City of Irving and Texas Stadium Corporation would be interested in any realistic proposals from solvent operating entities.

No bull-stuff inquiries.

If Fort Worth can have Billy Bob's Texas, why not Joe Bob's Texas Stadium Drive-in in Irving?

I hope this gives you some answers.

Sincerely,

City of Irving
Head French Fry
Bobby Joe Raper
MAYOR

P.S. I was overwhelmed by the response I received from your readers, both of them print very well.

P.P.S. Irving says stuff it!

Yes. Well. Ahem.

Good thing for you, Bobby Joe, that you decided to speak, because the running vote on the question "Should the royal jerkola who ripped down the screens at Texas Stadium have his head severed from his worthless body or not?" is:

Yes—643

No—1

We're talking some angry s.o.b.s out there, Bobby Joe. Listen up. ■

Joe Bob's Mailbag ——

"Message for the Mayor":

HEY! This isn't Communist Russia or someplace like that where somebody can go around and tear down an outdoor movie screen whenever he wants to, am I right or what? This was probably Irving's major cultural attraction.

Ken Ray
Arlington

Dear Ken:

Not counting the Frito factory.

"Message for the Mayor":

If drive-ins fall, can Civilization be far behind?

Jean King
Richardson

Dear Jean:

No, just Irving.

Rhett's Still Behind Bars and Needs Lots of Help; He Wants Don Byrd's Lawyer

"What does it say on Don Byrd's bumper sticker?" Rhett Beavers said he didn't know. "I brake for light poles."

Rhett didn't get it, but this scumbag in the next cell had just been transferred from Dallas County Jail, and so he started screeching like the psycho in *Bury Me Deep*. I ignored the guy and looked at Rhett.

"I hope you're not referring to the sheriff of Dallas County," Rhett mumbled. It didn't sound like Rhett talking.

"Course not," I said. "But how bout this one: Why does Don Byrd arrest twice as many people between four and six o'clock?"

Rhett said he didn't know.

"Happy hour."

I could tell Rhett wasn't in the mood for sheriff jokes, by the way he sort of stared cross-eyed at one of the bars on his cell, but it took me awhile to realize he couldn't focus a tall. I pulled on his arm.

"Rhett," I whispered at him. "Rhett, tough it out now, boy, what the heck's wrong?"

Rhett raised his head up a lit-tle bit and tried to grab me. His face looked like the inside of a Dempster Dumpster, and he was drooling all over his supper bib.

"Rhett, get with the pro-gram. We got thirty-three more bucks this week in the Free Rhett Beavers fund. If we get a full hun-dred it'll be enough to bring in the big legal guns."

"What?"

"I'm talking cream of Bossier City."

Rhett still wasn't focusing.

"I'm talking Bubba Barclay, the man himself."

Rhett roused himself a little bit. "Mad Dog," he said.

"Okay, Rhett, where'd you get the Polio Weed? We're out here trying to hep you and here you are smoking illegal substances in the Garland City Jail."

"Mad Dog," he said. "I gotta have Mad Dog."

"What the *heck* are you talk-ing about?"

"Hire Mad Dog Mulder for me. *Please* do it. I'll do anything."

Mulder! Rhett wanted Don Byrd's lawyer.

"Rhett," I said, "we got money but we ain't Bunker Hunt.

They're puttin street value on that Arkansas Polio Weed at $9,000."

"Personal use," Rhett said.

"I know that. You know that. Nobody *else* is gonna believe you could smoke $9,000 worth of Arkansas Polio Weed and live to tell about it."

"They do it in the Ozarks."

"Rhett, you ever looked at those people up close? *Have you?* You wanna have a skull shaped like a Australian football?"

"*Please!*" Rhett was begging me now.

"Rhett, what do you call three Scotches, seven beers, two margaritas, and a bottle of tequila?"

Rhett didn't answer.

"A minor stroke."

Rhett was a lousy audience.

"That's *it,*" said Rhett. "I had a stroke. I had a stroke just before I brought that Arkansas Polio Weed in the trailer house. That's why I didn't recognize it was illegal under the Texas Controlled Substances Act."

"Rhett, you get a minor stroke ever time you smoke that stuff."

"That's why I want Mad Dog Mulder on my case."

"Rhett, did you hear what Don Byrd's doctor said when they brought him this patient who was paralyzed and couldn't speak?"

"What?"

"Get that drunk out of here."

For a minute I thought Rhett was gonna get the point, but then he looked up at me and had this terrified expression like the Ar-kansas Polio Weed was really kicking in. I feared the worst.

"Rhett, you aren't gonna do your Wayne Newton imitation, are you?"

Rhett's face was frozen.

"Rhett, if you go into that Wayne Newton imitation in the jail, I'm walking out of here. You can just 'Donka Shane' all over the floor and I won't help you."

Rhett still wasn't talking, so I decided to try a little levity.

"Hey, Rhett, what do you call twenty men weaving down Jackson Street and pouring popcorn on each other?"

The scumbag in the next cell said, "I don't know. What?"

"Sheriff's posse."

I could see the Wayne Newton coming, though, and so I headed for the gate. Rhett was going into a seizure. The corners of his lips were startin to curl up over his cheeks. He winked at me and grabbed a piece of metal pipe and shoved it up against his lips like a hand mike.

"I'm leaving, Rhett, and you're not getting the bread till you go cold turkey."

I stopped at the scumbag's cell. He looked at me like he knew something was coming. I decided what the hey.

"Do you know why Dracula passed out on the sidewalk?"

The guy just shook his head and grinned.

"He drank Don Byrd's blood test."

We're talking standing ovation. It was enough to drown out

Rhett when he started in on "Tie A Yellow Ribbon."

The man is sickola.

I almost forgot to tell you about *Krull*. It's about these jerkolas called the Slayers who start out by offing about forty-five guys with swords *and* Darth Vader lasers, only they miss Ken Marshall, which is too bad because it coulda saved us about two hours. Anyway, Ken decides to make like the Beastmaster and avenge all these Slayers, but only after the Old One comes down out of the Granite Mountains and tells him to go kill the Beast in the Black Fortress. The Beast is keepin Lysette Anthony in his eyeball. But before he can fight the beast Ken has to go get this five-edge super-spin-action magic switchblade that's called a Glave, or a Glade, a Blade, a Glabe, I never could tell what the heck they were saying but that may have something to do with Toronado AM static. But even after he gets the Glabe, Ken can't just go kung-fu the Beast. First he has to Seek the Vision of the Blind Emerald Seer. Then he has to make friends with a Cyclops and kill a few scumbags. Then he has to Seek the Emerald Temple, only on the way these Slayers rise up out of a swamp like Darth Vader clone mutants, and while Ken is distracted, there's this Fake Blind Emerald Seer who comes along and replaces the *real* Blind Emerald Seer, but Ken figures out he's dealing with the Changeling and

so he tosses the jerk into a vat of quicksand. But now he doesn't have a Blind Emerald Seer anymore, so Ken asks the Cyclops what the hey, and the Cyc says, "There is one who might help—the Widow of the Web." Where the hell is she? Ken says. In the Iron Desert, the Cyc says. No sweat, Ken says. So he hikes over to the Iron Desert and the Old Man from the Granite Mountains says, Hey, I'll go in and talk to the old lady. But while he's in there, trying to escape from this Giant Spider, the Sands of Time run out for the Old Man and he goes belly up. Before he croaks, he tells em about the Fire Mares. Get on these Fire Mares and fly over to the Black Fortress and get the heck on with it. They have to wait till the Cyc dies, cause it's his turn for the Sands of Time deal, but then they go hellbent for leather till they're all over that Fortress, dying like flies and Ken has to pull out that Glabe, which is a kind of Frisbee with switchblades on the edges of it, and get the Beast in the eyeball so Lysette Anthony can get out.

Heads roll in this one. We're talking seventy-seven corpses. Half a quart of blood. No breasts. Several varieties of beast, but the main Beast is blurry. No motor vehicle chases. Minimum kung fu. Several swords through bodies. Most of the world gets blown up. Excellent torture chamber. I'm calling it three stars. Joe Bob says check it out. ∎

Joe Bob on Rapid Transit

Last week they decided to have a Forney Area Rapid Transit election out my way, cause they realize it's our only chance to get the Pleasant Grove Galleria II when it goes up. I'm studying the issues at this time to decide whether the Forney Area Rapid Transit plan is worth the hind end of a javelina hog, or whether the bus we got now will do the job. Next week I'll be discussing the issues with Forney Area Rapid Transit chairman Bobo Rodriguez. Bobo claims that the Forney Area Rapid Transit system will *"alleviate"* the growing traffic problems of the Greater Forney/Seagoville area by taking my car off the street and letting Bobo drive his. "Alleviate" is the longest word Bobo ever said in his life, so I imagine the Forney Area Rapid Transit plan has something to do with Bobo having a piece of the Pleasant Grove Galleria. Either that or the new trailer courts over on Kaufman Pike. Bobo's been takin out ads in the newspaper with pictures of these cars all gummed up around the Forney water tower, mainly cause that's where Jody McKaskle likes to double-park his Bronco and roll down his window and talk to Zack Strahan about how it han't been the same since they closed the grain elevator. Bobo also says

I been spreadin a lot of lies about the Forney Area Rapid Transit. He says he only gave a hundred to it cause he's patriotic and I'm not and anyway I'm against progress.

San Francisco's got the Bay Area Rapid Transit (BART), Bobo says.

Dallas is votin in Dallas Area Rapid Transit (DART).

Why cain't we have a Forney Area Rapid Transit?

Anyhow, I told Bobo to hold off on the b.s. cause I han't said jack about Forney Area Rapid Transit, and so we'd debate all the issues next week before the election. But whenever somebody says to vote some new taxes for "progress," I smell a Yankee in the area.

Stookie McMahay, you out there?

Judging by Joe Bob's Mailbag last week, some of you turkeys been letting Don Byrd drive again. I'm talking about the bimbos that want some *Staying Alive* reviews in "Joe Bob Goes to the Drive-In," and I'm sorry but I think it's fairly obvious that we're talking indoor bullstuff here. This ain't the Fred MacMurray Dance Studio. Maybe it's my fault, since I been so busy fighting the slopeheads in Irving and trying to get Rhett Beavers out of Garland Jail that I forgot to do the re-release of *Kinky Coaches and the Pom Pom Pussycats.*

So I picked up Vida Stegall after Rockabilly Glamourcize class and we charged over to the Astro for *Private School.* I figured, what the hey, it's the sequel to *Private Lessons* and so it'll have enough in the bare-hooter department to make up for any plot we'd have to sit through. But I was fairly p.o.ed when I found out what was going on here:

Sylvia Kristel is in this flick for about three seconds.

Okay, I know, this bimbo is starting to sag and so she can't do *Emmanuelle* anymore, but *this is ridiculous.*

I've said it once and I'll say it again. If you're gonna make a sequel, *make a sequel.* Make the *exact same* movie. Like *Friday the 13th, Part 3,* which is just *Friday the 13th, Part 2,* with some new rare teen-ager meat, or *Death Wish II,* which is just *Death Wish I* without all the plot. But *don't* pull a *Halloween III* on us and screw everything up.

Okay, good for us this flick has some other stuff going for it. We're talking Cherryvale Academy for Girls, which is full of these bimbos who go around in their underwear all day so the guys from the Freemount Academy for Boys can come over and go for the groceries. That's your basic plot.

Next we got a nice-girl brunette bimbo named Phoebe Cates and a blond witch bimbo named Betsy Russell, and they both wear a lot of aerobic dancing leotards and underwire bras and, whenever this slobola whale named Bubba is around, they take group showers so he'll fall off the ledge of the building and land in the bushes. Then a guy named Jim gets crazy over Phoebe, only Betsy likes to cut in on other people's action and so she makes like Lady Godiva one day in horse-riding class (we're talking cantaloupes verging on pumpkins). The other great scene is when Sylvia Kristel gets knocked in the swim pool on Parents Day and she happens to be wearing one of those white gauze numbers, and one of the old geezers has to administer mouth-to-mouth.

We're talking barely two and a half, and I'm giving these people the benefit of the doubt because of the decent tunes. We're talking twenty-five breasts. One motor vehicle crash. No beasts. No blood. No kung fu. Extra points for *My Favorite Martian* being the horny chauffeur. Betsy Russell gets a Fox of the Year Drive-In Academy Award nomination. Honorable mention for Martin Mull as the drugstore guy who sells rubber goods. If you know what I mean. And I think you do.

Joe Bob says check it out. ∎

Joe Bob's Mailbag ────

Dear Joe Bob,

In the interest of scatology (an "ology" without Federal funding, I might add), I got to tell you that in your July 15 piece you used the word "do-do" when you meant "doo-doo." Any kid worth his weight in Charmin knows how to spell it. You took the name of an extinct bird and hyphenated it.

Hey, don't get me wrong. Out here, we think you're a good old boy.

Regards,
Bill Meals
Richardson

Dear Bill:

You shoulda seen how I spelled it before the high sheriffs got a look at it.

Joe Bob and Wanda Head South and Check Out *Yor*: No Plot and No Garbonzas

Before I tell you about the World Premiere of *Yor,* I think I need to explain how come I wasn't around last week for the Forney Area Rapid Transit debates with Bobo Rodriguez. You probly know by now that Bobo was trying to get us to vote for the rayroads. Bobo even learned how to say "alleviate" so he could talk about how the streets are congested and how he wants us to "relieve our automobiles from the streets" and start riding the train so he can drive his GTO. Bobo also told me I could make a quick twenty if I'd leave town the day before the election.

So I told Bobo that I couldn't be bought for a quick twenty. So he made it a quick twenty-five. I said I could be bought for a quick twenty-five.

I was fixing to go down to Hurricane City anyway. Wanda Bodine was pointing out last week how I don't take her anywhere any more.

"That is correct," I told her.

(One reason I don't is that she went to the Holiday Inn DFW Airport in Bedford about three weeks ago to learn how to sell Mary Kay cosmetics because she wants to win a pink Cadillac and she also thinks she can keep all that face paint back of the counter at Le Bodine and sell it by the bucket right before Rockabilly Glamourcize class every night. Wanda says she's a "cosmetician." This is because she went up to Sanger's one day and learned how to smear cherry juice on her cheeks the way Charlene Tilton does it. Wanda's ambition this month is to look like Charlene Tilton. She's been pouring cough drops down her throat so she can chirp in the proper manner.)

So I took the Toronado down off blocks last week and told Wanda to wear enough clothes so we could get to Houston without getting arrested for being disgusting in public, and we flew down I-45 to the I-45 Drive-In. You may be wondering what the hail we were doing going down there while the hurricane was coming.

Numero uno: No one has ever proved that you can't show drive-in flicks in a hurricane.

Numero two-o: I got this letter from Columbia Pictures.

Dear Joe Bob:

Under separate cover you will be receiving an invitation to an exclusive Joe Bob Briggs Junket in Houston on August 16.

Columbia Pictures will be sending you round trip tickets on the deluxe, 44 passenger, air-conditioned (bathrooms included), Greyhound Buslines. You will be staying at the luxurious and colorful Motel 6. Upon arrival, you will receive a can of Raid, a personalized fly-swatter, and a complimen-tary individual package of Sanka for your morning coffee.

After viewing the Epic YOR, reservations have been made for your dining pleasure at the renowned Denny's Restaurant on I-45.

Have a swell trip and as they say in Hollywood, "Let's have lunch."

Kind regards,
LaVerne Lust
Columbia Pictures
Dallas

These turkeys were trying to buy me. But then I figured, what the hey, I'll check the sucker out anyway, so I chucked the motel room and the bus tickets and took Wanda with me so I wouldn't be reconized. Ever since Columbia was bought by the Co-Cola company, they been putting out indoor bullstuff like *Gandhi,* so I was happy to see the big boys get back into non-Communist movies.

Yor is about this curly-headed blond beefcake with oil all over his skin, a stick in his hand, and some rabbit fur between his legs. He looks like one of those guys who goes to Confetti's and stands around saying "Hey, baby, have you tried the vermouth and diet Fresca?"

We're talking Rock City U.S.A.

This turkey is Reb Brown, who used to be *Captain America* on TV, only now he fights brontosauruses with his stick. His first scene is not bad. After he kills the bronto and kung-fus eight or nine guys in hairy ape-man suits,

Reb starts sucking their blood out of his hand.

"The blood of your enemy makes you stronger," he tells everybody.

But then he starts getting distracted by a bunch of bimbos who won't drop their tops for the camera. Beefcake but no cheesecake.

Yor don't have any plot to slow it down. In fact, it has less plot than any flick of 1983 except *Spring Break* (also made by the Co-Cola company), and so it goes direct to the outdoor Top Ten. Mostly it's about how Yor is trying to go home. Better than *E.T.*, though, because Yor don't live in outer space, he lives in *Turkey*. He lives on this island where he got zapped sort of like the guy in *Timerider*, still the finest motocross western ever made, where Yor don't know if he's in the past or in the future. So he just goes around collecting bimbos and killing a bunch of foreign actors.

In this one scene, he bumps off a giant bat and takes the wings and hang-glides down into a cave where the extras from *Planet of the Apes* have been hiding out for the last fifteen years, and then he knocks a hole in the wall and the inside of that cave turns into Wet 'n' Wild amusement park. Then he goes and fights some fire creatures in the Land of the Diseased, and when he gets there he dumps his original French bimbo, Corinne Clery, for this blonde who's about to get sacrificed by a bunch of hillbillies who want to appease the misty gas gods. Then Yor kung-fus six or seven mummy heads and sets fire to them with a flaming stick, and then he decides to become a Mormon and have two wives, until the bimbos start fighting and almost get raped by a gang of gorillas. Yor saves em but the blond bimbo gets busted in the head with a rock, and she's not gonna make it, but her final vision before she dies is the island where Yor comes from. This is right before the giant lizard attack, where Yor has to plunge his sword in the lizard's eye, and before he goes and makes it with a Tahiti bimbo while her village is exploding, and then after that there's a giant whale attack and then he gets zapped into the future and the rest of the flick is about Yor fighting this creep who dresses like Darth Vader and wants to put Yor in a test tube so he can "cultivate your seed." This sounds promising, but the guy never does it.

We're talking two quarts of blood. Several decent beasts, including the lizard and the brontosaurus. No motor vehicle chases. A little kung fu. About twenty-five corpses. Heads roll. *No breasts* —inexcusable but it probly has something to do with Co-Cola. No talking, except in scenes like the one where Yor is talking to the Android Army and he says, *"Get a move on!"*

We're talking three stars. Not worthy of the I-45 Drive-In that Gordon McLendon built down there last year. (3,000 cars!) But it does go to No. 7 on the Ten Best list, right after *Losin' It* and right before *1990: The Bronx Warriors*.

Joe Bob says check it out. ∎

JB's Steamed: The Bimbos in This Flick Aren't Worth the Effort of *Getting It On!*

I trucked over to the Century last week to see one of the best flicks ever made in Hickory, North Carolina. Piece of business called *Getting It On!* First picture I ever saw where they make you wait for an hour for the itty bittiest little breastolas allowed by law in this country.

If Rhett was here, he'd ask me, "How small are they?"

I'm talking smaller than half-pint cartons. I'm talking *so* small that I missed one completely due to a .22 bullet hole on my front windshield.

If breasts were states, these mothers would get annexed by Rhode Island.

I'm talking little and I'm talking bitty.

You're probly still wondering how small they are.

All I can say is, if this gal went to get measured for a strap-less, they'd have to glue Sno-Cone cups on her.

If Rhett was here, he'd say, "No, how small are they really?"

We're talking bra sizes in the negative numbers.

If they made this movie in Communist Russia, they'd have to put in some subtitles so you'd know what they are: communistic appendages.

They were *so small* that the ladies of the Dallas Censor Board wanted to give this picture a G rating.

I hope I've made my point about the size of these alleged hooters. If not, please write in and I'll tell you how little they were.

Okay. Now somebody out in East Texas sent me a letter last week about "gratuitous nudity" and I believe that individual knows who he or she is so we won't single him out here in the newspaper because I'm feeling like one heck of a nice guy today. Here's my opinion of gratuitous nudity:

I only approve of gratuitous nudity when it's necessary to the story.

Or when it's a real boring movie and you need some nekkid women to liven things up.

Also, I keep getting these letters from bimbos who say, "Hey, Joe Bob, you seem to have this *thing* about garbonzas and female flesh, so why don't you ever talk about *male* nudity, because we like to look at [a male nickname not allowed by the *Times Herald* high sheriffs unless it has a capital letter on it]."

Answer to that one: I am not a United Way agency. This column is not for a bunch of nympho bar bunnies working in a insurance office somewhere, trying to get their jollies out of the paper because they cain't get a drink poured down their dress at Confetti. This is a movie review column. There's still a *few* of us who take our job seriously and don't go around asking people to write kinky bullstuff so they can hide it under the Sealy Posturepedic and get it out after the Letterman show. There's still a few of us who have some ethics.

Okay. I hope I don't have to say that again.

Now let's get back to the number of breasts in this movie.

Technically, we're talking eleven breasts. But two of those belong to this blond bimbo who must remain anonymous because she is waiting at Danny Thomas Hospital in Memphis with a surgical transplant team in case a breast donor becomes available. So I'm not counting those for medical reasons. That means *Getting It On!* gets a pathetic nine.

Basically what we got here is a couple high school punks who go around settin up video cameras

so they can point em through bedroom windows and then go back to their monitor and breathe heavy. The problem is, this flick was made in Hickory, North Carolina, where I didn't know this but it's a damned interesting fact, but the bimbos in that town sleep with their bras on 90, 95 percent of the time. This makes it tough, especially since the star bimbo, Heather Kennedy, won't pop her top, no way, uh-uh. The whole idea is for Alex the wimp to get his hands on Heather, only as close as he gets is slobbering over a bunch of girls on the track team doing bend-over exercises. When Alex and his buddy finally get some decent material on their videotapes, it turns out to be . . . the Attack of the Itty Bitties. They have to go get a hooker named Kim Saunders and have her jump the principal on camera so they can stay out of reform school, but you don't even see the guy go for the groceries.

No blood. No beasts. A little pitiful kung fu. No motor vehicle chases or crashes. Nine official breasts. One decent gonzo performance by this party band called The Late Bronze Age, with a lead singer who looks like Dumbo the Elephant trying to fly drunk. No gross-out scenes.

Two stars.

Joe Bob says check it out. ∎

The Hulk and Hercules Don't Mix

A lot of you turkeys probly went to *Hercules* last week thinking, hey, this is one of the Joe Bob Briggs Twenty-seven Greatest Drive-In Movies in the History of the World, it made the list last year. No way, José. This piece of beef jerky is a *Hercules* rip-off and they didn't even have the decency to name it *Hercules II.*

We all know who the *real* Herc is. I'm talking 1957, Steve Reeves, Muscle City.

So you may be wondering: How can you tell this *Hercules* from the other one?

Numero uno: Lou Ferrigno is the *alleged* Herc. Lou has a face like a cinder block and the veins on his arms stand out like a road map of Louisiana. I'm sorry. I don't mean to be a jerk. But let's just say it: We're talking winner of the 1983 Ugly-Rama. Lou's dubbing is superb, though.

Numero two-o: You can't make a Herc movie without man-acle-whirling. Herc breaks out of his irons in prison and he starts spinning those suckers like a hammer-throw until you see em disappear into the skull of a Roman wimp cadet who's standing there waxing his spear. No manacle-whirling in the new Herc. Just a bunch of arrows in the back and spears through the stomach.

Numero three-o: Steve Reeves always wrestled a rubber crocodile. The Hulk roots around for a while with a stuffed bear, so I guess that counts for a decent try, but you don't get the wet-head look. They do pour some oil all over the Hulk's bod so they can get some *additional* audience, if you know what I mean and I think you do.

Numero four-o: Steve Reeves always pole-axed some bald wrestlers, or tossed em up in the air like Frisbees. All the Hulk can do is pin eight skinny guys up against a wall with a log and then push till their chests crack up into brisket dinners.

Numero five-o: There's a bunch of space-laser indoor bull-stuff in this turkey. Herc has to fight these mechanical katydids that look like they came out of Junior Bodine's erector set. Lou don't even use his bare hands. He kills em with a stick. Gimme a break.

Numero six-o: This redhead bimbo named Ingrid Anderson

wears little Chinese hats on her garbonzas. This is the lady the Hulk wants? He cleans up after 10,000 horses for this porkchop?

Numero seven-o: Sybil Danning is the evil queen, but she *can't get the Hulk to drink the spiked wine.* Whenever Big Steve had a mickey in his goblet, he drank that sucker and went around the rest of the day like a loaded pistol. [I need to watch my English, because of the dairy-equipment joke that got jerked last week by the *Times Herald* high sheriffs.] Anyhow, the Hulk kung-fus seven or eight guys *before* he drinks the stuff.

Bottom line on this one: No breasts. Seven beasts, but the only decent ones are these two giant rubber snakes that attack the Herc when he's a baby. Thirty-three dead bodies. No motor vehicle stunts, unless you count this one pathetic chariot scene. One-half pint blood. Six bimbos in training bras. Alleged kung fu. No Steve Reeves. Give it two and a half. Check it out.

Can't even compare to the flick about the bald-headed space babies buried under Hollywood. What happened was the Army found em when they came floating down and decided to put em in sterilized barrels underground. But the space babies start yelling out messages through their brainwaves, and they hook up with the head of this blond fox named Cherie Currie who's hanging around with Robert Carradine

at his place in the Hollywood Hills. Then they go and get Keenan Wynn, who's either the last mining prospector in Hollywood or the only one they ever had, I couldn't tell which one.

Anyhow, Keenan lives up there in a tent, playing Scoutmaster around his campfire, and he helps Carradine and the fox to find out how to get down into the military base. Course, they're all dumb as a box of rocks about it, so they go down there and get bombarded by bald-headed space-baby brainwaves and then get arrested by the Army.

Meantime the bald-headed space babies are killing everbody in sight. So the general of the Army decides the only way to save the world is to bury everbody down there, including his own men. Only Carradine and the fox break open the space-baby incubators, and the space babies pour out of there and start knocking down doors until everbody gets out.

Then they all decide to put the space babies in the back of Keenan Wynn's horse truck and go out to the Mojave Desert for a while with two Indians.

But once they get out there, the whole U.S. Air Force takes off from Edwards and it looks like it's gonna be bombola time, but then the bald-headed space babies get nekkid and go out in the desert and talk to another planet and a lot of weirdness comes down at the end.

Art film. Great space-baby effects. No breasts. One-half pint blood. Fourteen dead bodies, I think. Brainwave kung fu. Goes to No. 4 on the Joe Bob Briggs Best of 83 list. (By popular demand, I'm putting the list in the paper again. You turkeys *cut it out* this time.)

Joe Bob says check it out.

Joe Bob's Best of 83:

1. *Screwballs:* most imaginative use of female breast jokes.

2. *The Concrete Jungle:* best women-in-cages.

3. *Bloodsucking Freaks:* gore and perversion extravaganza.

4. *Wavelength:* bald-headed space babies.

5. *Eagle's Shadow:* Jacky Chan kicking heads in Hong Kong.

6. *Chained Heat:* bimbos-behind-bars.

7. *Losin' It:* Bordertown garbonzas and studs in heat.

8. *1990: The Bronx Warriors:* Vic Morrow's last drive-in flick, about bikers and punkolas who take over the Bronx.

9. *High Test Girls:* all-time garbonza champion.

10. *10 to Midnight:* best Chuck Bronson-sweeps-the-sum-off-the-street flick.

Joe Bob's Mailbag

Joe Bob Baby,
There once was a DI reviewer
Who liked things that crawl from the sewer
Most folks thinks he's mad
But he really ain't bad
Cause he stabs with a pen, not a skewer.
By the way, do you know how to tell if someone's as dumb as a box of rocks? If they don't know the difference between a comma and an apostrophe! Preciate the heck out of your rebarbative comments. As I'm sure Wanda Bodine is fond of saying,
Keep it coming.

Your Fan Jan Winstead, McGuire, Sechrest & Minick Dallas

Dear Jan:
Pretty good pome for a bimbo.
Thank you for your retardative comments, too.

Dear Joe Bob,
I read your reviews faithfully when I was living in Dallas. I have since moved to Emporia, Kansas, but I still read your reviews

thanks to my Granny who sends the paper each Friday. Keep up the good work. You have fans everywhere!

Love ya
Lea Ann
Emporia, Kan.

Dear Lea Ann:

We allow Kansas circulation and the better parts of Nebraska, but please NO SOUTH DAKOTA. When we get up that high, we're talking North.

All letters to Joe Bob should be sent to:
Joe Bob Briggs
Movie Critic of Rockwall, Texas
Living Dept.
Dallas Times Herald
1101 Pacific
Dallas, Texas 75202

Deathstalker—No. 1 on Joe Bob's Hit List

Last week I took Chubb Fricke out to the Grapevine Highway to look at RVs with built-ins, and while we were out there I stopped off at Le Bodine to see why Wanda had a road-grader parked out front of her Porta-Neon sign. What it said on the sign was:

Le Bodine
Continental Cuisine
(American Menu on Request)
Opening November 1983
Aerobic Rockabilly Glamourcize
Fall Classes Forming Now

I went in to see what the hey was going on, but believe me you don't want to know. To make a long story longer, I ended up taking Wanda Bodine to the finest outdoor flick of 1983. We're talking *numero uno*. We're talking top of the Joe Bob Briggs charts.

We're talking *Deathstalker.*

I was totally disgusted. This flick has bimbos in chains, arms ripped out of their sockets, heads hacked off with pickaxes, little blond porkchops getting raped by gorillas with leprosy, sumo wrestler pig-heads that pummel skulls with sledgehammers, a lot of spears through the kidneys, house pets that eat human fingers, and a guy who gets hooked up to two horses while everbody makes a wish.

You're probly wondering what I was disgusted about.

I was disgusted because Wanda was in the car. At least she kept her clothes on this time, so I didn't have to worry about *that,* but she puked up a Cheese Whopper all over the styrene seat covers that Bubba Barclay traded me almost new for five bucks and a radio that had the FM dial broke off. The Stalker woulda known what to do. If the Deathstalker was in the car, he woulda pinned Wanda's wrists together with one hand, ripped off her blouse with the other hand, looked her over and said, "Take a hike, you're disgusting."

Believe me, I know.

All I did was tell her to either clean it up or go ride home with Bo Riggins. Give you some idea, Bo Riggins works at Yello Belly Dragstrip selling Co-Cola.

Anyhow, here's the deal on the Stalker. He looks like Miles O'Keeffe, only his stomach isn't caved in like Miles's was in *Ator the Fighting Eagle*. But the Stalker definitely puts in time on the Nautilus equipment, and actually he would look a lot like my ownself, if he didn't have blond wimpola surfer hair blowing around his face like he's just been aerosoled at Vidal Sassoon's. This is totally beside the point, and I don't want to have to mention it again.

We start off with a leprosy-face old man raping this bimbo who's chained to a tree, but before he can get the job done, the Stalker shows up and spears him through the neck and runs a couple of his buddies through the ribs with a sword. One guy's about to get away, so the Stalker has to throw his dagger forty feet through the turkey's heart. The Stalker cuts the chains off the girl, yanks her blouse off—and then *he* starts to rape her. The Stalker can tell he's doing the right thing, if you know what I mean and I think you do. Only he gets distracted and she escapes.

Next thing, the Stalker goes to see the king who's living in a tent because Munkar the Magician stole his castle and his daughter. The king wants his castle back.

The Stalker says, "You talking to me?"

The king says he wants the Stalker to go rescue his castle, and if he wants to he can bring back the girl too.

The Stalker says no way, José. "I'm an outlaw," he tells the old geezer. "I steal and kill to stay alive."

Next thing, the Stalker goes to the old prophet woman, because we all know in this kind of flick you have to talk to the old prophet woman before you get to go kung-fu everbody in sight. The prophet woman says the Stalker needs three things to get control of the world. One of the things is the sword of justice. The other two things are the amulet of life and the chalice of magic, but let's face it, who the hell cares? The old prophet woman says she can help out with the sword, but Munkar has the other merchandise.

One more thing before we paint the screen red. The harem. Course, we're talkin the evil magician's harem, this place where all the bimbos in chains get auctioned off to wrestlers, geeks, half-human pig-face weirdos that smell funny

—basically your Confetti's dance floor on the weekend. We've got some ancient female mud wrestling. Munkar's there, but he don't even get in the whirlpool. Munkar is this bald-headed space cadet with a spider painted on his head, and he likes to *watch*. We're talking some nice rape-and-pillage party scenes, but here's the topper: Barbi Benton is Munkar's prize prisoner. Munkar buys her a see-through nightie, chains her arms and legs to a post, and tells all these extras from *Planet of the Apes* that they can fight over the right to "stand in" for Munkar.

What I'm leading up to is, the Stalker decides he wants to rescue the king's daughter *after all*. Even though the Stalker picked up a blond nympho on the road into town, he decides to go for the groceries.

Munkar's p.o.ed.

Munkar decides to kill the Stalker, but he can't jack with him because the Stalker has the magic sword. So what he does is he tells one of his old ugly warriors that he's gonna turn him into a Barbi Benton lookalike, and then the Stalker'll toss his sword down.

Let's talk transformation scenes. I know, I know. I said there would *never* be a transformation scene to compare to the kid who got changed into a giant katydid in *The Beast Within*.

I was wrong.

This transformation is so painful that the guy has to grab his chest and start screaming when the garbonzas start to pop out, and then he grabs a place

which the *Times Herald* high sheriffs asked me not to put in the newspaper, and when you think about it, this whole scene is very necessary to the story, because what the hey, can *you* imagine what it would be like to change into Barbi Benton in two minutes?

So the Barbi Benton lookalike takes his dagger and goes to the Stalker's bedroom, and the Stalker throws her on the bed and gets ready for business, but *something* tells him all the *equipment* is not working properly, and he gets rid of the fake bimbo before something happens that could make you vomit.

Then we got about a full hour of nonstop death and violence till it's time for the Stalker to meet Munkar. Great Saturday Night Wrestling moves in the tournament arena. The Stalker likes to stick his sword through a guy, then *twist* it, then jerk it out and wipe off the blood on the dead body. The Stalker is not a nice guy.

Okay, we're talking thirty breasts. Full exposure on Barbi Benton. Twenty-two corpses. Kung fu, sumo wrestling, and Saturday Night Wrestling. No motor vehicle chases. Six quarts of blood, most of it okay, some of it a little thin like they made it up with watercolors. Several excellent beasts, including Little Howard, Munkar's household pet in a basket that will only eat human eyes and fingers. Not one, not two, but *three* heads roll. No bimbo skin defects. Great sledgehammer scene—has to be seen to be believed. Best of all, no words actually spoken by Barbi Benton at any time.

No. 1 on the Joe Bob Briggs Best of 83 Drive-In Movie list, re-placing *Screwballs,* which stayed up there for six months.

We're talking four stars.

Joe Bob commands you to check it out. ∎

Hells Angels Forever —It's Really Nasty

Ever so often I come across a flick that has something to say. Like *Door to Door Maniac.* Remember that outdoor classic? I think it was 74. It pretty much said it all on the subject of mental health in America. Did for me, anyway.

Anyhow, last week I told Wanda Bodine that it was time to go to the Joe Bob Briggs Documentary of the Year. It was time to get *serious* and *learn something* instead of just sitting in the trailer house all day watching her toenails grow. It was time to see the first flick that goes into the correct role of women in American society today. Course, you probly guessed it by now.

We're talking *Hells Angels Forever.*

Wanda wanted to know did it have any dancing in it. Ever since Wanda saw some indoor bullstuff called *Flashdance,* she thinks she's gonna be the first beauty-parlor owner to dance in the ballet. I've seen Wanda throwing her equipment around in Rockabilly Glamourcize class, and let me tell you,

this bimbo couldn't dance her way out of a Styrofoam Del Taco carton. When they handed out legs, Wanda put hers on upside down. I've seen fallen arches, but when this porkchop walks, her heels don't touch the ground.

You're probly still wondering just how bad a dancer Wanda is.

If dancing talent made your insides hot, we'd have to thaw Wanda out ever night for dinner.

Course it has dancing, I said to Wanda. *Hells Angels Forever* has *everything* in it—dancing, singing, gratuitous violence and nudity that is absolutely necessary to the story, and a lot of big hairy guys with tattoos.

Wanda immediately said she'd go, but then she said, "Only if I don't have to watch the Hells Angels drive their bicycles through their neighbors' yards and mean things like that."

Wanda may be dumb as a box of rocks, but she's not afraid to advertise. That's why I told her she *needed* to see this movie. That way she could see it's *natural* for her to be empty as a pine box. She could discover something about her role in life.

This flick was made for people just like Wanda. It's the educational film put out by the Hells Angels their ownself. They started in on it in 1972 and this year they finished it, so you can see this is no Hollywood bullstuff deal where they churn those suckers out ever year. This is the drive-in *Gandhi*. We're talking eleven years dedication, plus they had to figure out how to punch those little holes on the edge of the film.

Okay, we all know the great biker flicks, right, starting in 54 with *The Wild One* and moving on up to the granddaddy of em all, *The Wild Angels* in 66, with Bruce Dern sleazing around with a bunch of original Southern Cal Angels. *Hells Angels '69* wasn't too bad, and *Hell's Angels on Wheels* was one I kinda like because it didn't have any plot to get in the way of the orgies and busting-of-heads scenes, and it was one of Jack Nicholson's best flicks before he started making indoor bullstuff.

Anyhow, the Angels finally said, what the hey, we'll make our own flick. And like I say, they worked eleven years on this sucker, so they could get rid of a lot of the *myths* about the Angels. Like here's a few things I learned in the flick:

Numero uno: The Angels don't go looking for violence. They're not like that. They will *not* hit you in the head with a ball peen hammer (like one guy in the flick) unless you do something like touch their jackets, or say, "Excuse me, Mr. Hell's Angel, sir, but that's a very interesting pile of crap you're driving."

Numero two-o: The Angels are good to their women. Like one of the ladies says, "I been around here four years and I only been hit once. And I deserved all seven of those stitches." The reason the Angels are so understanding is because of what this Angel said: "They're all sleazes, but we got the best-looking sleazes." There's this one great scene of a Hells Angels wedding, where they're reading the vows, and one of em for the lady is "I will honor and obey him, unquestioning his every move, and I will not inherit any rank or title that belongs to him."

Numero three-o: The reason Sonny Barger spent five, six years in jail was all these federal agents got together and framed the Hells Angels about two hundred times for drugs, weapons, stuff like that.

Numero four-o: All their neighbors like the Angels. When you see the New York chapter out on the sidewalk, with guys walking around carrying knives, ball peen hammers, chains, gunning their engines, yelling stuff at each other, beating each other up for funsies, setting up a B-B-Q pit in the open, watching this 300-pound Angel with tattoos on every inch of his body while he crunches things between his pinkies—*nobody ever complains*. This proves that the Angels are pretty good guys.

Numero five-o: Whenever the Angels get hauled into court,

there's always somebody on the jury that don't want to put em in jail.

Numero six-o: That time they had a riot in Cleveland, it was about 130 members of The Breed against twenty-four Angels. The Angels put twenty-nine in the hospital and killed four of em. Only one Angel got killed. But the Angels didn't have anything to do with it. It was the other guys— *they started it.*

Numero seven-o: Willie Nelson, Jerry Garcia, and Bo Diddley write songs about the Angels and help get Sonny Barger out of jail whenever the cops put him in. That's because they understand why people are *harassing* the Angels all the time—because they're a *little* different.

So what the hey, this is America, right, and you couldn't even *have* the Hells Angels in a place like Communist Russia. So what we got here is obviously an educational flick, and all the violence is in there for good reasons, like, "If you don't want your face to look like this guy's, don't pass forty Angel Harleys on the shoulder of the highway or say stuff like 'Hey, what kind of chicken head is that on the back of your jacket?' "

We're talking three and a half here. If any member of the Angels is reading this, I'd like to say, what the hey, it *might* be four if you want it to be, but why do you always turn off the camera just before somebody gets his head turned into a pepperoni pizza? Four breasts. Three excellent motor vehicle scenes (Angels cruisin their Harleys). One quart blood. No beasts, except the ones in the cast. Three orgies. Two bars busted up. One scene of the Angels practicing with their *legal, registered, unconcealed* firearms, which they use for sports purposes only. Fifteen great tunes, including Willie doin "Angel Flying Too Close to the Ground," Johnny Paycheck doin "Angel of the Highway," Elephant's Memory doin "Angels Forever."

We're talking something really *nasty* here. Wanda han't said a word to me since we saw the flick, which proves how effective it is. I'm moving it to No. 3 on the Best of '83 Drive-In Movie list.

Joe Bob says *definitely* check this baby out. ■

Commie Russia Sending Aerobic Dance Spies to Infiltrate U.S.

First they tore down the screens at Texas Stadium. Then it was the D.I. in Haltom City (they even trashed the super-buffalo screen). But now I'm afraid we're talking the No. 1 Yankee jerkola crime of 1983.

We're talking Invasion of the Aerobic Dance Instructors.

Last week they ripped down my gym. It was this second-story walkup place on the edge of downtown. It was called "Gym." It was run by a gimp-legged guy named Lester. They didn't even tear it down for a high-rise office building. They tore it down for the *parking garage* of a high-rise *condominium*. We're talking the kind of stuff that goes on in Communist Russia. But that's not the worst part. Once they run us out and closed Lester down, they tried to make everything all right by giving us all tickets to a "spa."

A "fitness spa."

Up by Don Carter's Lanes on Skillman, out where the geeks and weirdos go to diddle around in their Danskins. Pardon me while I puke, but I'm afraid we're talking Wimp City USA.

For the Communists and fe-males in the audience, I'd like to explain the difference between a *gym* and a *spa:*

Numero uno: No bimbos in a gym. Lester wouldn't even let em in to use the Co-Cola machine. At a spa they let em run around un-caged wearing yarn on their ankles.

Numero two-o: A gym does not have "exercise equipment." A gym has *weights.* Period. Okay, a little Nautilus *maybe.* But the only way to tell whether it's real weights or wimpola spa-city North Dallas bullstuff is like this: It ain't a weight if you can lift it more than two times without making a sound like a constipated wild jungle animal.

Numero three-o: A gym does not have a "jogging track" or a "Jacuzzi." A gym has a *boxing ring* and a *steam room.* Now, hold on a minute, I know what you're thinking—no bimbos, steam room, nekkid muscle training— what about "the boys"? Hey, I know all about "the boys" because I was in the army one time for two weeks. And all I got to say is, so what, you turkeys, this is America and as long as they don't tell me how to play "Dance Fever" on the mouth harp, I don't tell them how to butter their toast. You talk about something *dangerous*, put a few bimbos in the steam room and just watch where those hands go.

Numero four-o: A gym does not have any guys named Kevin walking around dressed like ambulance drivers, trying to get people to "tone up." A gym has a guy named Vick walking around handing out jockstraps. The only thing Vick ever says is "Shake it off, you'll be able to breathe again in a minute."

Numero five-o: Gyms do not have a picture of Victoria Principal in her leotards by the door. Gyms have a picture of Floyd Patterson, training for the Liston fight. It's usually hanging over the cigarette machine.

Let's send this Aerobic Dancersize spa-city rip-off business back to Leningrad where it belongs. It's gettin to where you can't find a decent medicine ball in this town.

I know what you're thinking. You're saying to yourself, "Joe Bob, you took Wanda Bodine to see *Mortuary* coupla months ago in Cleburne at the Big Chief D.I."

Wrong, Oklahoma Breath, that was *Mausoleum*. We're talking *entirely* different material this week, because one thing *Mausoleum* didn't have that *Mortuary* does have is *embalming needles.* We are talking grisly.

Mortuary starts off with a guy getting it in the back of the head with a baseball bat and then sailing into ⸱the swimming pool

like Lloyd Bridges looks when somebody cuts off his hoses. Next thing, we see these two wimps messin around in a mortuary, and while one of em's in the next room, the other one gets the embalming needle crammed through his stomach by a guy in a white mask. His friend figures he must've decided to leave, so he goes to the roller rink with his girlfriend Christy, whose daddy it was who got Reggie Jacksoned to death. Christy tells the dude how she's been sleepwalking *in the pool* ever since her daddy died. They're both dumb as a box of milk duds, though, and so they can't figure out who did it even though everybody else can after about fifteen minutes.

What we got here is a wimp mental patient workin in a mortuary where his daddy used to lock him up in a dark room with the dead people when he was little—fairly decent combination, specially since the guy gets all the great lines in the flick, like "I hate being an embalmer; nobody wants to date me." His name's Paul, and his idea of a good time is to take his friends into the room where they drain out all the blood from the bodies. He likes to take women there too. "I'm going to embalm you," he tells them. "It won't hurt."

Too bad that Paul is a one-technique sort of guy. Embalming needle through the stomach and/or chest area. Hardly any variety, except when he goes to work on Linda Day George one night while she's sleeping, but I won't go into that because I have been warned by the high sheriffs this week not to "exceed the bounds of good taste," and I'm getting an extra $2.50 for this column as of last week.

Anyhow, what we got is seven corpses. Three quarts blood. Five breasts. No beasts. One motor vehicle chase. Heads do not roll, but one great hacking death with an ax. Linda Day George keeps her clothes on. Two and a half stars.

Joe Bob says check it out. ∎

Don't Swagger On Down to Commerce Street Until You See *Ninja*

This is the night when the entire population of Oklahoma comes down here to puke on Neiman-Marcus. [Editor's note: Texas-OU weekend for all you foreigners.] I accept that. I understand. People have *needs,* and people from Oklahoma have a need to be geeks, weirdos, and royal jerkolas. I want to request, however, that any of you turkeys from Oklahoma who can read should tell everbody to please barf on the phone company and not on Neiman-Marcus. If the Adolphus Hotel puts a lot of monkey-suits out on the sidewalk to keep everbody out of the lobby, then it's okay to barf on them too. But I like to sit by the window at the Steakhouse Unique, and I *don't* want to see last night's three-two beer all over a Neiman's window full of aerobic Danskins. It's not a pretty sight.

Have I made myself clear? I thought so.

Anyhow, let's talk about kicking heads in.

You might want to go check out *Revenge of the Ninja* tonight before you head over to Commerce Street, because I have a feeling we're going to see some chopsocky this year out front of Sol's Turf Bar. I been practicing all this week with twelve-inch "Game of Death" rosewood-handled, ball-bearing, studded-handle Nunchaku sticks with deadly eight-inch swivel chain.

I would just like to put in right here for anybody who's wondering: I use these novelty items for amusement purposes only. They are *unconcealed* at all times. And I had nothing to do with that little incident with the Marines on the parking lot at the Longhorn Ballroom last week. I'm one of your major supporters of the U.S. Marines.

Like I say, though, *Revenge of the Ninja* is going straight to the top of the charts, because we're talking every form of chopsocky known to man. I'll just give you some idea with this fact: *nineteen* dead in the first five minutes. We're talkin pickaxes, we're talking your flying stars to the eyeball cavity, we're talking swords and arrows through the throat area.

It starts off with Sho Kosugi, who use to be karate champion of Japan, coming home and finding his entire family wasted by Ninjas except for the baby. You know they're Ninjas because they wear black raincoats and Batman masks. Kosugi has to kung-fu five at a time till he's killed all of em, and then this American named Arthur Roberts comes along and says, Hey, you need to haul buns out of here before some more Ninjas start hanging around your neighborhood. And Sho says where will he go? And Roberts says, Where else, Salt Lake City, you can open up a Japanese doll gallery. And Sho says, Why didn't I think of that? And so anyhow, Sho never figures out that Roberts wants to put *heroin* in the dolls.

Okay, enough plot. Six years later Sho's kid, Kane Kosugi, already has his black belt and he's learning samurai Ninjitsu chopsocky kung-fungus, whatever-you-call-this-stuff, so *he* can be a Ninja, but Sho has to tell him, No way, José. Don't touch that stuff. But the kid likes to try his stuff anyway, practicing with this blond bimbo named Ashley Ferrare while his daddy plays with the dolls. Kane gets hassled on the way back from school one day, and there's this Kid Fu five-on-one scene that's fairly decent midget-sized chopsocky.

Next there's this Mafia guy who don't want to pony up for the heroin that Roberts brought over in the dolls. So Roberts has to go put on his Ninja costume and a silver hockey mask and go around acting like a jerk. One Mafia guy gets his head screwed off in a toilet. This old rummy gets a throwing star in the eyeball and it makes him look like a mess, I'm telling you. This next guy gets it with a blow-dart hatpin in the neck while he's diddling around in a hot tub with a bimbo. But finally the turkey goes too far, and the Mafia sends these goons over to clean out the doll gallery, and I'm sorry but Sho is just a *little* p.o.ed. When he sees em getting away in a van with all his dolls, first we got the greatest motor vehicle chase scene in the history of the drive-in (they're driving, Sho is *running)*, and then when he catches up to em, you know what we got.

We're talking Kung Fu City.

While Sho is killin four, five of em with his bare hands, Roberts is back at the doll gallery, spearing Sho's *mother* through the back. You think Sho was p.o.ed before?

We got *Death Wish* with a black belt.

First Sho stops at a public park to kick in the heads of five punkola weirdos that have a bad attitude. He don't know it, but while he's doing that, Roberts is chainin the blond bimbo in a hot tub and has the kid tied up in the next room. When Sho finally finds Roberts, it's time to get *nasty.* It's time to play Spiderman up the side of the tallest building in Salt Lake City so Sho can have a kung-fu party with Roberts on the volleyball court. We're talking hands, legs, feet, sticks and blades, throwing stars and those little pointy things that look like jacks but make your face look like it caught on fire and somebody had to put it out with a meat tenderizer.

We're talking the body-count champion of 1983: forty-four corpses. We're talking four breasts. Excellent kung fu, kid fu, sumo, Ninjitsu, bimbo fu. We're talking the greatest kung-fu motor vehicle chase in history. One beast. Two quarts blood. Drive-In Academy Award nominations for Sho and Roberts and the director, Sam Firstenberg. I know *Deathstalker* is just two weeks on top of the list, but I gotta move it down to make way for *Revenge of the Ninja.*

Yes, we have a *new* Numero Uno.

Joe Bob says check this sucker out. ∎

The Evil Dead:
We're Talking
Red Meat City

I'd like to get disgusting here for just a moment, if you don't mind. I'd like to talk *The Evil Dead.*

Most of you turkeys know by now that I've been waiting *a year and a half* for this flick. I wrote letters. I screamed at the jerkolas in New York who bought the rights to this mother. I told Sam Frogg to get it for the First Annual World Drive-In Movie Festival and Custom Car Rally, but Frogg couldn't deliver the groceries. I called up every meat-packing plant in the Fort Worth Stockyards to see if they'd be interested in sponsoring a screening. I wanted it for "Red Meat Night" at the Highway 183 Drive-In in Irving. I wanted it for the "Too Grisly for Cable" festival at the Godley Drive-In. You know what they all told me? No way, José. Nobody has any respect for the arts in this town.

You're thinking, Hey, what's

the big deal, just another zombie splatter movie, right?

One difference, Oklahoma Breath. In this sucker, there's only *one way* to kill the zombies.

We're talking total dismemberment.

Hands, arms, legs and, yes, of course, what else . . . *heads will roll.*

You thought those were zombies in *Night of the Living Dead?* Excuse me while I go buy you a copy of "Richard Simmons Sings Frank Stallone." Could we have a little wimp music here, please?

You think those were zombies in *Dawn of the Dead?* Would you wait here just a minute while I go check the showtimes for *Flashdance* for you? You might want to look around for some yarn to put on your ankles and a T-shirt with Snoopy on the front.

Now that I've cleared the room, let's take a look at *The Evil Dead* on the old barf meter, and I think you'll agree that this is the paint-the-room-red vomit champion of 1983. Cherry Dilday went along for the ride, lost her lunch in the first half hour, tossed her cookies all over the upholstery, ended up so trashed she forgot to take her clothes off till the second feature. This baby is off the scale. You might want to pack a few Hefty Bags in the trunk, because I'll just say this: It's not a pretty sight.

The Evil Dead is a classic, because it follows the Joe Bob Briggs ultimate test of a splatter flick: *Anybody can die at any time.*

This flick was made for about

three dollars by a guy named Sam Raimi who says he's from Detroit. Sam is probly a psychopath. Remember, when you see this one, that Sam is capable of anything. How about a woman raped by the woods? Not raped *in* the woods, *by* the woods. These vines start snaking around her arms, and her legs, and her neck, and she struggles and the woods throws her down on this wet ground, and then things start to *grow* all over her, and then for the big finish this enormous tree limb comes down and . . . well, it's not something the high sheriffs are gonna let me get away with anyway.

We've got your basic Spam-in-a-Cabin plot. These five teenage porkchops go to a cabin in the woods, like *Friday the 13th,* only it's a better cabin and better woods, and you know from the first five minutes this is gonna be some *weird* bullstuff because of all the *unseen presences* everwhere. You just don't know when it's gonna start. And I'm not gonna tell you.

How about a scene where a zombie with superhuman strength stabs a guy in the ankle with a No. 2 wooden pencil—rams that baby all the way through?

How about a chainsaw scene where this girl has to be sawed up into itty-bitty pieces by her friends because she turned zombie on em?

Now we're getting down to the nitty. They find this book in the basement that's written in human blood and bound in human flesh, and it says that zombieism is *contagious,* and that the bottom line is, they're all goners. Just in case they don't get the message, the unseen zombie presences also leave them a reel-to-reel tape recorder. "You will die," they say. "One by one we will take you."

The movie then starts raising a lot of moral questions, like: If your girlfriend turns zombie on you, what are you supposed to do?

Only one thing you *can* do. Go get a meat cleaver and start making like the butcher at Safeway. This is the first mistake they make, see. When this girl starts spewing white slime out of her mouth and going around breaking people's arms with her bare hands and growing Dracula teeth, instead of everybody just getting together and saying "Hey, hold it a minute, heads have to roll here," they monkey around and try to stuff her in the basement for a while till they figure out what to do.

The star of the flick is this guy named Ash (Bruce Campbell, who gets the 1983 Drive-In Makeup Award for effective use of blood on the body; we're talking gallons on the face alone). And Ash can't get his act together. Like when his girlfriend finally gets stabbed in the back, turning her back into just a normal dead person instead of a zombie woman, Ash *knows* what he has to do. He takes her into the chainsaw room and starts to make her into chicken-fried steak, but then he sees the locket he gave her and he breaks down and decides to just *bury* her instead. You can see in the picture on this page what happens to old Ashley.

I've decided I won't even *try* to tell you about the girl who has to cut off her own hand. Or the scene where the zombies start decaying and aging two thousand years in about two minutes.

I'll give you an idea what I'm talking about: this one may make *Chainsaw* eligible for the Disney Channel.

We're talking nineteen *gallons* of blood. One breast. Four beasts, unless you include the rapist forest. No kung fu. No motor vehicle chases. Drive-In Academy Award nominations for Raimi the psychopath; Bruce Campbell; Ellen Sandweiss as Cheryl, the forest rapee; Sarah York as Shelly, the girl whose hand is on this page. No question about it: grisly, nasty, disgusting . . . four stars. Spam-in-a-Cabin champion of 1983.

One more thing. The flick is not rated. The rating board probly wouldn't look at it.

Joe Bob says check it out.

The Evil Dead flies to the top of the charts, even though this is heavy drive-in season. The 1983 list, for you turkeys who forgot to cut it out last time, goes like this:

1. *The Evil Dead:* Spam in a Cabin

2. *Revenge of the Ninja:* every kind of kung fu known to man

3. *Deathstalker:* starring Barbi Benton's upper torso and a Miles O'Keeffe lookalike who goes around throwing spears through people

4. *Screwballs:* most imaginative use of female breasts; best *Porky's* ripoff

5. *Hell's Angels Forever:* best documentary; best on-camera use of a ball peen hammer

6. *The Concrete Jungle:* best bimbos in cages

7. *Bloodsucking Freaks:* gore and perversion extravaganza

8. *Wavelength:* best bald-headed space-baby flick

9. *Eagle's Shadow:* Jacky Chan kicking heads in Hong Kong

10. *10 to Midnight:* best Chuck Bronson-sweeps-the-scum-off-the-street flick ∎

Joe Bob's Mailbag ——

to Joe Bob Briggs

I would like to tell all those sleeze bags and so called classy upstand citizens of Dallas that your column is the best trash I have read in years; matter of fact its the first thing I grab for when I get my Times Herald.

The citizens of Dallas should appreciate a good critic. Your column has brought depth and meaning to my life.

You have fulfilled my dreams.

KDLH
Dallas
Born and Bread

Dear KDL:

Just exactly what WERE those dreams?

Beer, Patriotism, and Halloween: Communist Victory

God put Irving on the face of the earth for several good reasons, and one of em is so we can have a town that's wet but you can't buy a beer there to save your soul. Some bozos called the Texas Alcoholic Control Board are trying to save my soul and yours too this weekend, because I'm almost ashamed to say this, but the government of this state has told me to take the Second Annual World Drive-In Movie Festival and Custom Car Rally and stick it in Lake Ray Hubbard.

The head alcoholic of the Alcoholic Control Board says, "No beer permits for drive-in use." He says, "*Especially* no beer permits at the Highway 183 Drive-In in Irving." I said, "What if we give all the beer money to poor people?" He said no way, José. I said, "What if we give all the poor people free beers?" He made a noise like a jungle animal.

We're talking a Communist in Austin.

Excuse me if I'm a little p.o.ed.

You're probly wondering what I'm gonna do.

You're probly thinking to yourself, "I guess that's it for Joe Bob. He's history. He's finished. No way he's getting out of this one. Test pattern time. Curtains."

Hold on a minute.

I been discussing this situation with my lawyer, Bubba Barclay. Bubba's in from Bossier City again, because I got him a room in the Alamo Courts on Fort Worth Avenue so he can try to get Rhett Beavers out of Garland Jail. Bubba says he needs an extra fifty and he thinks he can get Rhett released to Palmer Drug Abuse, but only if Rhett swears off Arkansas Polio Weed forever, or until he gets out of Palmer Drug Abuse, whichever comes first.

Anyhow, Bubba says we can go to court and get an injunction. He says the Texas Alcoholic Board is violating the First Amendment. He says it's against the Constitution to stop people from watching *Wanda the Wicked Wardeness* or *Driller Killer* or *Gas Pump Girls,* just to give a few examples, and that it's impossible to watch any of those flicks without *several* Buds first, and so they have ipso defactoed their ownselves. I told Bubba to sue those suckers into Oklahoma. I told him to go wake up Sheriff Byrd and make him aware of the Irving situation only remember not to let Don drive out there by himself.

Meantime, there's a *certain* Dallas radio station that's about to take this matter up, and I'm not allowed to say anything else, but believe me, we're talking some *serious* media lies on our side.

Let's talk *Dead Zone*. It's by Stephen King, and we all know what that means: We *could* have some indoor bullstuff on our hands, like *Ghost Story*.

Nope. This time we have fairly decent material. Christopher Walken is this wimp schoolteacher who runs his VW bug into a milk truck and doesn't wake up for five years. By that time his girlfriend is tired of watching him sleep with a tube up his nose, so she's gone off and married some other turkey. Walken is p.o.ed. But that's not half of it. He starts going to see Inspector Clouseau's boss, who is now a shrink, and finds out that when he grabs somebody's hand, he can see their past and their future. His eyes bug out like a katydid and lightning goes up his arm and pretty soon he's twitching around the room and watching people drown and get killed in the war and girls get hacked into salami sandwiches by a guy who likes to use sewing scissors. Great scene where Walken leads the cops to the psycho killer creep, but before they get to him the dude decides to fasten his scissors to the bathtub fixture and let his face drop straight down on them. He's still twitching around when they get there.

Anyhow, some fairly intense scenes between Walken and Martin Sheen, who's running for senator on the loudmouth ticket and wants to be president. Walken sees Sheen's future, and it says Nuke City U.S.A. Chris knows what he has to do—Lee Harvey Oswald time.

We're talking two breasts. One excellent motor vehicle crash. One quart blood. No beasts. Seven dead bodies. No kung fu. Heads do not roll. Tom Skerritt blows away Colleen Dewhurst in slow motion. Drive-In Academy Award nominations for Walken, as the geek schoolteacher; David Cronenberg, the director who made *The Brood* a long time ago and then started working indoors; and Martin Sheen for acting like a politician. This sucker was produced by Dino de Laurentiis, who remade *King Kong* a few years back, remember? Dino's English was a little better then. He said, "When monkey die, everybody cry."

Three stars.

Joe Bob says check it out. ∎

Ugly on a Stick:
Joe Bob Sets
the Record Straight

Wanda Bodine hired this new shampoo girl that everbody calls Chloris. Everbody except me. I call her Ugly on a Stick.

Chloris weighs about twenty-seven pounds and stands six foot eight. (That's not counting when she has on her platform clog shoes.) She has these little beady eyes like a Pekinese dog that was hit by a bakery truck and still remembers it. Sometimes she'll start whining and carrying on and bothering all the other employees at Le Bodine until Vida Stegall agrees to give her a manicure. It don't help.

One time I went in the trailer house right after Ugly on a Stick started working there, and the first thing happened is Vida pulled me aside and said, "Joe Bob, I just want you to know that there's a new girl in the back."

I said "What?"

Vida said, "She's a very nice person and she's ugly."

I went back to take a look, and Chloris had her head bent over the sink and was mixing up some kind of super industrial-strength hairspray remover, and at the same time she was yelling over at Audrey Tullis that she needed some new seat covers for her Vega, or a new Vega, whichever one she could get out of this guy named Curtis. From what I could tell from the back end, Curtis was a student at Texas School for the Blind. Before I could get away, she turned around and folded her lips together like a piece of cellophane that's been all wadded up for five minutes and then you sit around and watch it pop out full size again—that's what Ugly on a Stick's lips looked like, only they'd been wadded up more than five minutes.

"Hi," she said, "I'm Chloris."

"Rhett Beavers," I said. (What the hey, the man's in jail, he don't give a diddly.)

Chloris said, "I hope you don't mind that I'm ugly."

Now, I would like you to know that I'm not a prejudiced individual. I don't have anything against ugly people. Some of the finest people I know, like Chubb Fricke, practically invented Ugly. In fact, I'd be willing to take up a collection to let ugly people get those Handicapped Parking stickers so they could park by the front door of Kip's Big Boy even when the lot was full, and feed their ugly faces. We could have the Ugly Telethon or something, the Ugly-thon, invite some famous ugly people like Henry Kissinger or the Dallas City Council to make speeches about how someday maybe we can wipe out ugly as we know it. We could set up the Ugly Research Foundation, have a Walk-an-Ugly-Mile Weekend to raise money. On second thought, maybe it'd be easier just to have a haunted house.

Anyhow, I'd like you to know that there's several *unfortunate* myths going around about ugly people. I think it's our responsibility to get rid of them, so that ugly people aren't always getting fired from their jobs or told to move out of their apartments because people think they can catch Ugly from them. So here would be a few of those myths and how we can get rid of em:

Numero uno: Many people like Vida Stegall believe that all ugly people are "really nice" individuals. This is not the case. Many ugly people are jerks. This includes Ugly on a Stick.

Numero two-o: Many people believe that all ugly people wear bad beards. This is not the case. Only ugly people of the male species wear bad beards.

Numero three-o: Many people believe that ugly people can't get jobs because they're bad for business. This is not the case. People like to have ugly people around,

cause then they don't feel so ugly any more. Besides, Wanda Bodine will hire anybody.

Numero four-o: Many people believe that you should fix up ugly people with dates, because everbody feels sorry for them and so it makes people feel better to know they have dates. This is not the case. I don't feel sorry for them.

Numero five-o: Many people think there is no such thing as ugly. Wanda Bodine thinks this. She told me, "Everybody is beautiful to *someone.*" This might be a Dean Martin song, but it is not the case. When you see true Ugly, you know it. If you don't believe me, I'd like to introduce you to Chloris.

Numero six-o: Many people believe that Barbra Streisand is not ugly. This just goes to show you how misinformed the general public can be.

Now that we've cleared up all these myths about Ugly, I know you would appreciate my moving on to another subject. This is not a pretty sight.

Okay, okay, I know, you're probly thinking to yourself, But what gives, Joe Bob? I believe you *have* taken a few bow-wows to the drive-in in your lifetime.

I do admit it. (I would like to point out that I required May Ellen Masters to wear a bag over her head most of the time.)

And you're also thinking, And you wouldn't tell us all this about Ugly on a Stick unless you took *her* to the drive-in too.

And *that's* where you're wrong.

To finish up this story. When she turned around and looked at me and grinned through her snaggle teeth like a hyena, I said, "Nope. You *are* ugly. I do mind that you're ugly. I think you should join Ugly Anonymous and admit you have a problem."

"Thank you," Ugly on a Stick told me. "Do you think I'm ugly in particular places or all over? For example, my upper body."

"Honey," I told her, "if you were in a drive-in movie, the breast count would be in the negative numbers."

It's conversations like that that allow the ugly people of America to face up to their problems and get their acts together. And Chloris, if you're reading this, would you get it together somewhere else?

Speaking of ugly, after I had the heart-to-heart with Chloris, I drove out to West Texas to see Wings Hauser, ugliest movie star alive, in *Deadly Force*. I had to head out I-20 because I'm being barred in Dallas again and they tore down the Belknap on the Grapevine Highway and I just couldn't stay in town anyway what with being turned down for a beer permit in Irving and everything. It was damned humiliating.

Anyhow, *Deadly Force* is this flick about a psycho killer creepola who wastes seventeen girls in L.A. and carves *X*'s in their bodies before this old burglar named Sam calls in Wings to kick some hineys. You remember Wings. He was the gonzo pimp-with-the-pecs in *Vice Squad* who liked to work over his girls with wire coat hangers. Now he's doing a Chuck Bronson number: Wings was kicked off the force for sweeping too much scum off the street. So old Sam goes out to New York to find Wings, and Wings says, "Okay, I'll go look for the creepola but only because he pushed your granddaughter off the balcony of her high-rise apartment." But then Wings says, "Wait just a minute, I'll have to stop off at a warehouse on the way to the airport and talk this extortionist into not blowing himself up and destroying the entire New York shipyards, but that'll only take a few minutes." So after Wings clears that up, he hits LAX and finds some lily-livered cops waitin around to tell him to lay off the psycho creepola case or he's doing some Crossbar Hotel time. Then a Mafia guy tells Wings the mob has a contract out on him.

It's pretty clear by now that Wings is going to have to get out the wire hangers again.

But first Wings goes and finds his ex-wife, this blond bimbo TV reporter, and gets some nookie.

Then Wings gets beat up a lot.

Then Wings keeps finding dead people keeled over on the street.

Then Wings keeps having car chases where he doesn't catch the killer, but they're pretty decent car chases anyway.

Then Wings starts thinking that the killer is sleeping with his ex-wife, and so he goes puttering around this institute where they do Rolfing or Elephant-Man Therapy or something. While he's in there, Wings figures out what's up, and I think you know what comes after that.

We're talking Handgun City.

Wings gets a Drive-In Academy Award nomination just for being so ugly. Seven breasts. Three motor vehicle chases and one excellent crash and explosion. Eleven dead bodies. Six guys get the bejabbers beat out of em. Two quarts blood. No beasts except for Wings. Heads do not roll. Bimbos not allowed to talk too much. Academy Award nomination for Paul Aaron, the director, for keeping things moving.

Three stars.

Joe Bob says check it out. ∎

Ninety-three Dead Establishes New Drive-In Record

I tooled out to Garland Jail on visiting day so I could tell Rhett Beavers how I solved the Kennedy Assassination, but Rhett was Moved, No Forwarding Address, if you know what I mean and I think you do. I knew this would happen soon as deer-huntin season started. I told Bubba Barclay to put a twenty-four-hour watch on the cell, get some gorillas thrown in there with Rhett for his own good, but Bubba's a lawyer, so he acted like he knew what he was doing.

Bubba kept saying "I'm getting Rhett released to Palmer Drug Abuse."

"He won't go."

"It'll get him out of jail."

"Rather be in jail."

"Palmer Drug Abuse is not so awful."

"Let me tell you something, Bubba. *Carol Burnett* gives money to Palmer Drug Abuse."

Bubba said, "What?"

"That's all I got to say."

And meantime Rhett figured out it was deer-huntin season, walked off the job one day during exercise period, and I can tell you exactly where he is: Arkansas. Polio Weed harvest time. Soon as Rhett finds him a place in the Ozarks, settles back long enough to light up, and lets that total dope paralysis set in, we're talking Hibernation City. We'll be lucky to see Rhett back here by May.

Too bad too, cause we're coming up on Drive-In Heaven season. It's gonna be so cold this winter that even the breasts on the screen'll turn blue. Some of our *wimp* drive-in owners have already cut back to weekends only. Some of the Yankee drive-ins are all boarded up. Wanda Bodine has been begging me to go by Western Auto and get one of those super industrial-strength car heaters like they use to put in Hemi Cudas where you twist the knob and it turns everthing inside the car into a charbroiled steak dinner. But I had to tell her: No way, José. *Maybe* we can throw a couple Navajo blankets in the backseat, but otherwise I'm telling you, this is the time when I want to spend my money at the box office.

Now till April we're talking flicks you can see *only* at the drive-in, *only* in the South and Southwest, for *exclusive* one-week runs. Remember *The Grim Reaper,* that flick about the cannibal that eats teen-agers in Europe? Played middle of January, one week only, never been seen again. Remember *Mad Monkey Kung Fu,* the classic? Same deal. Remember *Bloodsucking Freaks,* one of the reddest flicks in ten years? One sucking week. In winter.

Time to separate the indoor crapola from the real movies. Time to get rid of *The Right Bullstuff* and bring back *Night of the Living Dead. (Night of the Living Dead,* which was voted the No. 1 drive-in movie in the history of the world by Joe Bob Briggs readers, is on the comeback trail starting today. Drive-ins only.) Excuse me if I'm a little p.o.ed, but if they make *one more movie* starring Dudley Moore, I just might lose control entirely and take my twelve-gauge out to the North-Park Six or whatever it is and start blowing some screens away.

What I'm trying to say is, time to get back where we belong —in the backseat.

Let's start with *Stryker.*

I'll just say right up front that we may be talking the best *Road Warrior* rip-off ever made. I know, I know, a lot of you turkeys think *Warlords of the 21st Century* was the greatest because it had a maniac housebus that ran up and down the highways in New Zealand, blowing away innocent villages.

Okay, *Stryker* don't have a deranged Winnebago. Mostly it's got a bunch of weird, stripped-down, California flake-o off-road vehicles running around Argentina like some leather gangs were trying to invade the Falklands or something. Gang leader *Numero Uno* is this turkey named Stryker, who looks like Kris Kristofferson after a four-day drunk or one of the Bee Gees who's not Barry Gibb wearing fat leather armbands on his wrists.

In the first scene Stryker sits up on this mountaintop and watches a fairly decent motor vehicle chase where these punkola goons are chasing this bimbo with enormous garbonzas across the desert. They're not trying to get her garbonzas, though, they're trying to get her water, cause we've had this nuclear war and everthing's exterminated and blah

blah blah and, you know, all the stuff in *Road Warrior,* only this time they're fightin over *water* instead of *oil.* (Ordinarily I don't like it when they change the facts too much in rip-offs, but I'm gonna overlook it this one time.) And the bottom line is Stryker comes along and has to waste six of em before the girl jumps in a Mustang that looks like it's been sittin for about three years at Goss-on-Ross Trading Hoss—Se Habla Espanol, and then she makes like a bakery truck and hauls buns out of there. Stryker plays cowboy, stares at her garbonzas a little while, and then he goes off by himself.

Next thing, Stryker meets this midget army, and I have to say we have some of the finest midget acting since *Time Bandits.*

Next thing, the garbonza woman gets chased around the desert by *another* gang. All-Bimbo motorcycle and buggy gang.

Next thing, this bald-headed Fu Manchu hook-arm turkey takes a hostage and tries to get him to tell where the water is, but he won't talk, and so Fu Manchu sticks a gun in the turkey's mouth and pulls the trigger and watches the back of his head turn into Niagara Falls.

What all this comes down to is the garbonza woman knows where a secret water supply is, and all the gangs want her to fess up, so they all start trying to find her and wasting each other while they're at it. There's this sniper who blows up a jeep and turns it into a D-minus project in metal shop. Then the same dude chases a humongous water truck in their jeep and kills about four guys and then the last one gets run over and smashed by a Mustang.

Then garbonza woman gets tortured, chained up, and gang-raped, until Stryker comes along and throws a knife through one of em and kung-fus the other two. As you all know, I am not in favor of gratuitous violence unless it is necessary to the story. This particular gang-rape triple-murder scene is necessary to the plot.

Then a guy gets buried up to his neck and sand kicked in his teeth, and Fu Manchu's men use his head for a Sani-Can. Then we have a little midget torture, then Stryker has to spear a few guys and do some grenade work, and there's a little knife-throwing demonstration, and then all the bimbos get out their bows and arrows and make long-distance voodoo dolls out of Fu Manchu's men. Then they all go out to the Bimbo Fortress, where the water is, and get ready for the final attack, but before they do the blond bimbo takes Stryker into her cave, if you know what I mean and I think you do.

Before she does it, the bimbo says, "People don't communicate any more," which is about all she says the whole flick but she says it real good.

Then we have some midget blowgun scenes, then Fu Manchu's men get some old army tanks and start trying to waste the Bimbo Fortress, then they get inside and have this final battle of

Fu Manchu against the bimbo's leader, this turkey who looks like Vidal Sassoon's gay grandpa. I won't give away anything else, cause I don't want to spoil the suspense, except I will say that the guy who dies last gets about fifty rounds through his pathetic body.

We're talking Top Ten material here, strictly on the basis of the death count.

We've got *ninety-three* corpses, which is the all-time drive-in record. (I would like to add that each one of the ninety-three on-camera killings is absolutely necessary to the story.) Six breasts. Twenty midgets. Medium kung fu. Superb bimbo fu. A couple quarts blood (most of these guys don't bleed when they die.) Six motor vehicle chases, one crash-and-burn, one exploding vehicle. Some great Mohawk haircuts. Drive-In Academy Award nominations for Steve Sandor (Bee Gee lookalike), Monique St. Pierre (garbonza woman), Cirio H. Santiago (the director may be from Argentina, but he knows his drive-ins): Number six on the Best of '83 list, right behind *Hell's Angels Forever.*

Three and a half stars. Joe Bob says check it out. ∎

Pieces: Care for a Few Spare Body Parts?

A lot of the ugly people of this country have been writing in and saying that I'm prejudiced against ugly people. This is completely untrue. I'm only prejudiced against the ugly people that I personally have to look at every day. The rest of you turkeys I don't care diddly about.

I'm gonna answer each and every one of these ugly letters just to *prove* I can communicate with a person of the ugly persuasion. And I would like to also point out that Ugly on a Stick, the shampoo girl at Le Bodine that I told you about week before last, is a personal friend of mine, and when I was over at the trailer house this week I went back to say hi to her.

"Hi, Rhett," she said. "I'm still ugly." (Okay, okay, I han't told her my name yet.)

"Chloris," I told her, "I know you're ugly, but I'd like to point out to you that you'll probly never in your life be attacked by a maniac with a chain saw."

Ugly on a Stick said, "What?"

"Chain saws are never used on ugly people."

"What?"

"Never been an ugly girl yet that was killed with a chain saw, unless you count the bimbo at the beginning of *The Evil Dead,* and she don't really count because she'd already turned zombie when Ash took the Black-and-Decker to her."

"What about Marilyn Burns?"

"Okay, okay, I admit she was no Barbi Benton, but what the hey, she *escaped* at the end and anyhow Leatherface didn't really try to get her with the chain saw. He was just tryin to scare her back to the house so his grandpa could take a sledgehammer to her head."

"Oh."

So see, sometimes ugly people surprise you. Like I didn't realize Ugly on a Stick had ever seen *Texas Chainsaw.*

"When'd you see *Saw?*" I asked her.

"See *Saw?*"

"When?"

"Saw *Saw* in Sausalito."

"You from Flako Land?"

"What?"

"You come from drugola coke-head aerobic danceland and surferville?"

"Yeah, I come from California."

"Chloris?"

"Yeah?"

"You are still ugly."

So as you can see, many of my close personal friends are ugly, including Chubb Fricke. In fact, Chubb is so ugly you might say Ugly is his chosen profession in life. Chubb han't spoke to me ever since we had the fight at Bronco Bowl over whether the Diving Pig at Aquarena Springs was still alive or not. Chubb said the pig drownded in the San Marcos River, and I told him it was impossible for the pig to drownd in the San Marcos River because the pig was a trained Diving Pig, and that if something drownded in the San Marcos River it was probly a horse or a dog or maybe just a big old ugly person, but it damn sure wasn't the Diving Pig, because I've seen the Diving Pig and that sucker can flat swim. And I won't tell you what Chubb said about the Diving Pig, because I don't have time to tell you every little thing said by a ugly person in this world, and so I'll just get to the point and say the reason I was over at Le Bodine talking to Ugly on a Stick is so I could take Wanda Bodine to the drive-in to see *Pieces.*

I think you know what's coming here. You probly already realize we're talking Top Ten material. It's that time again.

Time to set up the Home Craftsman workbench, dust off the Poulan, paint the room red.

We're talking Splatter City.

You won't believe it, but this is the best chain-saw flick since the original *Saw.* I'll just put it this way: Heads roll before the titles roll. A little wimp kid decides to hack his mother in the head with an axe so she'll let him have his porno puzzle back. Then he decides to saw her head off and put it in the closet so the police will find it and think a degenerate did it. The cops find the kid in *another* closet, with blood all over him, whimpering and saying "Where's my mommy?"

Anyhow, next thing it's forty years later, and there's a gonzo geek pervert maniac going around a college campus and cutting up coeds into little bitty pieces and then he gets a Hefty Bag and takes home the parts he wants and he leaves the rest of em for the cops to find. Only thing is, the cops can't figure out why he only takes certain parts—like sometimes it's white meat, sometimes it's dark meat, this one girl he just wants the head, the next one he wants a couple arms. And ever time he turns a coed into a lambchop, the geek goes back to his apartment and sticks some more pieces into the nudie porno puzzle his mama took away from him just before he turned her skull into a piece of squashed cabbage.

So they keep finding all these partial dead bodies lying around on the campus, but the dean of the college decides to keep the news away from the media. They even think they have things all wrapped up when they find this gorilla heavy-breather gardener with a bad beard who likes to walk around carryin his chain saw, revving it up like a cycle and squinting out of one eye. But when they put this ugly geek in the jail, they still keep finding red coed meat on the college Astroturf and so they start looking real hard at this homosexual "professor of anatomy" who keeps a human skull on his desk. "It was a present from one of the students," he tells everbody.

Next thing, this blonde in a black bikini drops her top and dives into the pool all by herself, and the creepola maniac fishes her out with a net and cranks up the chain saw and takes home a Baggie of spare parts. Give you an idea what I'm talking about: The cops have to *stack* her on the stretcher.

Then the maniac goes to aerobic dance class and decides he wants this blonde in a Danskin wearing yarn on her ankles, and he follows her into the elevator and stops it between floors and hacks off her arm on camera.

Then we have some gratuitous kung fu, when Linda Day George shows up to be the undercover cop who's gonna be the bait for the goon. (How come Linda Day George stars in thirty drive-in movies ever year and I never can remember one single thing she says?)

While Linda Day George is playing kung fu with this kickbox professor, our friend Mr. Black-and-Decker is going after a bimbo on a waterbed, but he doesn't want any electrocutions or anything so he has to use a butcher knife that goes through the back of the head and comes out of her mouth.

I'm not gonna go through ever single saw scene, but I would like to mention the one where a brunette gets it through the stomach, on camera, in closeup, and it's not one of those quickie deals where the camera cuts away just when the blood starts to spurt like

Niagara Falls. You see the *whole deal.*

That's what I like about this flick. Honesty. All on-camera chain-saw deaths are absolutely necessary to the plot. Heads roll twice. Arms roll. Legs roll. (In the last scene, something rolls that the *Times Herald* high sheriffs won't let me put in the paper, but I'll just put it this way: I can still feel it. If you know what I mean and I think you do.) Nine living breasts, two dead breasts. No motor vehicle chases. Good kung fu. Eight corpses. One beast with a chain saw. Four gallons blood. Not much talking. Drive-In Academy Award nominations for Paul Smith, as the ugly gardener who likes to diddle around with a chain saw; Dick Randall and John Shadow, who wrote this sucker and didn't put a lot of talking in it; and J. Piquer Simon, the director, who keeps things moving. Straight to number five on the Best of '83 Drive-in Movie list, right behind *Screwballs.*

Splatter City.

Four stars.

Joe Bob says check it out. ∎

The Mystery of the Diving Pig

Ipreciate the heck out of you turkeys who don't have anything better to do than write letters to Joe Bob's Mailbag about the Diving Pig.

I don't have time to go down to San Marcos and check this situation out. Evidently the Diving Pig *has* been seen *alive* within the past year. Chubb Fricke still says the pig drownded in the San Marcos River, but Chubb han't been two miles from the Bronco Bowl in the last thirty years.

Okay, I have a few questions about the Diving Pig.

Numero uno: This guy in East Texas says there's a bimbo who goes up on the high board with the pig and beats him with a stick till he goes off the end. If this is the case, then this would *not* qualify as a Diving Pig. This would be a Falling Pig. This is *not* the same Diving Pig I saw at Aquarena Springs, because that pig should've been called Pig Luganis.

Numero two-o: A few of you guys claim the Diving Pig is worth the money but you don't say how much money that is, 50 cents or five bucks or 50 pesos, so how can anybody decide unless we have the true facts here?

Numero three-o: What *kind* of dive can the pig do? Barb from Waco says the Diving Pig has been diving ever day for twelve years and the pig knows how to do a can-opener. I might've believed this one if she'd said it was a cannonball, but from what I can tell, this alleged pig can only do belly busters and half twists. I'm still checking this out, though.

Numero four-o: Do people swim in the pool after the pig goes in there? What does the water look like?

Numero five-o: Why don't you geeks in San Marcos write in? Are you ashamed of the Diving Pig? Is the pig dead or alive? Is the pig a professor at Southwest Texas State?

These are just a *few* of the questions I had about the Diving Pig. I'm trying to decide whether it's worth a trip down there. I can watch Ugly on a Stick go off the high board anytime I want. ■

There's No Escape from Cherry Dilday, Except *Escape 2000*

They were gonna auction off Cherry Dilday last weekend up on LBJ Freeway, but they never could get an opening bid. I ain't lying. I told Cherry to be there to raise some money for crippled kids, but the way the thing came out I think maybe we should've auctioned off a crippled kid to raise some money for Cherry Dilday. I'm talking pathetic. I'm talking a room full of empty chairs. Even the twenty-eight guys who entered the Joe Bob Briggs Lookalike Contest couldn't manage to throw any pennies up onstage. If Cherry'd been a stripper, she would've had to stuff dollar bills in the customer's pants. I'm talking audience in the negative numbers.

Okay, I know *some* of you turkeys think that was funny as heck. I know you were all sittin around the lobby of the Sheraton, checking out Cherry's dilday and saying "Hey, what would you pay for *that?*" And then when somebody give their honest answer, you yukked it up and decided you wouldn't *even* pay that much. Well, I want to tell you guys something. Girls who're dumb as a box of bacon bits have feelings too. You don't know what you were missing. I'm here to tell you that Cherry Dilday *does* have a financial value, because I threw a little jack in the kitty myself just to try to get the bidding started, and so I can tell you exactly how much she's worth.

She's worth 35 cents.

I tossed 35 cents in there, and

soon as I did they grabbed me and said I won Cherry Dilday for the night. I said, "Couldn't I just have her for the daylight hours?" And they said no way, José. So then I said I would like to donate Cherry to a poor person. And they said, no, we don't have people that poor in Dallas, and besides Cherry Dilday was nontransferable. And so I said, Well, at least can you put some more clothes on her and maybe put a bag over her head for the duration of the evening? And they said basically it was a question of how much you could do with 35 cents, because if they went to 7-Eleven and asked for a paper bag, some guy from Vietnam would want to charge em a dime for it and so they would be out some profit, plus that wasn't even counting gas, and besides all 35 cents was going to crippled kids and so the bottom line was that I grabbed Cherry, unbagged, and hauled her out to the Toronado and told her that it was just this one time and she'd better forget it if she expected any decent place like Steakhouse Unique, because it was just two or three times around the block and if she didn't like it she could hitch her way down the Grapevine Highway, which is exactly where I would be leaving her.

That's when it started. You turkeys don't *realize* what a nice guy like me has to go through just because you dimwit creepolas decided to *have a little fun at the Cherry Dilday Auction.* Cherry started moaning like a wounded buffalo. She was Basket Case City.

She wanted to know if her thighs were too fat, or if she was getting zits on her head, and whether she needed to have surgery on her garbonzas like Mariel Hemingway, and what did I think about her mild case of Pimiento Cheese–colored skin rash. And I had to tell her not to worry about all those things, because it was really her face and her face alone that people couldn't stand. This made her feel much better.

But the reason I'm still so p.o.ed after all this time is that she roped me into laying out some more cash after I asked her how much she would take to stop sniveling around all over my upholstery.

And she said, "Well, you could buy me a stimulated diamond necklace."

"What's a stimulated diamond necklace?"

"You know, it *looks* like a diamond but it's stimulated."

"Where do you get one of them suckers?"

That's where I made my mistake, because she started rattling off some fairly dangerous names, like Zale's, Corrigan's, Adelstein's, and so I had to recover pretty fast and say, "No, Cherry, I know the place for the best stimulated diamonds in town."

I took the bimbo to Pawn Tex Jewelry and Loan out on Kiest.

They know me at Pawn Tex because I've traded wedding rings three times, engagement rings only two times because of that May Ellen Masters incident on the day Woolco went out of business. I went in and asked if they had any stimulated diamonds, and they said, for you, Joe Bob, we can stimulate all of these rocks you want stimulated. And I was fairly pleased with the way things were shaping up, until Cherry pointed her finger at this little number in the shape of a katydid with Super Glitter where the eyes were supposed to be.

"What's all that Super Glitter on there for?" I asked her.

"That's the stimulated diamonds."

So I asked the guy at Pawn Tex how much for the katydid necklace and he said, "Is that with or without the stimulated diamonds?"

I said, "Have they already been stimulated or will we have to wait?"

"They're stimulated," he told me, "about as much as they're gonna be stimulated."

So then he told me the price and I was a little p.o.ed I asked Cherry why in heck she had to have *two* stimulated diamonds, and she said because katydids have two eyes, and I told her I would gladly punch the eye out on a katydid so she could see how they look and then it'd only be half the price. She was startin to tell me how she needed both eyes and about that time I saw some of the boys from the Bronco Bowl, including Bobo and Rhett, coming in through the front and I didn't want them getting any ideas about why I was in Pawn Tex buying a stimulated diamond katydid for

Cherry Dilday, and so I said, what the hey, I'll spring for the full double-eye deal. Cherry made a noise like a guinea-pig farm at sunrise.

I forked over four bucks and we left.

I told Cherry that was it, then, now, and forever, and if she wanted to see *Escape 2000* that night, she could either wear a head bag or sit alone in the backseat or go hang around the video games in the concession stand until she got picked up by a drunk. She took the second choice so she could keep mooning over her two-eyed katydid.

It was a fairly decent flick. First thing, all these people get sent to concentration camp because they're "deviates." It's a place like in Communist Russia where they train you how to think, and as we all know, one of the first things that happens under any Communist regime is that all drive-ins are closed, so I think we all realize just how vicious they can get. In this case, all the guards watch the bimbos gettin off the bus and yell stuff at em like "Hey, fresh meat!" One of the bimbos is Olivia Hussey, and the sergeant's idea of a good time with her is to knock her down, put this rope around her neck, and make her do something that the *Times Herald* high sheriffs wouldn't like. Then they take this midget woman out of the line and make her perform her reeducation speech, which goes "I am a deviate, the lowest form of life on earth." She has to keep saying it over and over, and when she messes up, this Nazi Cochise starts kicking her into a little pile of mincemeat.

Next thing, we get nineteen consecutive breasts in a shower scene. Modern single-scene drive-in record.

Next thing, they put Steve Railsback in a cage and torture him.

Next thing, they burn this guy alive and try to gang-rape Olivia Hussey, but she gets away by zipping up a guy's pants before he's ready to be zipped, if you know what I mean and I think you do.

By the way, Olivia does a shower scene, but I'm fairly sure she uses stunt garbonzas. They're huge mothers, though, whoever they belong to.

Finally all the guards decide to let five prisoners go so they can hunt em down. We got Olivia. We got Steve. We got a foxy blond bimbo. We got a weirdo jerkola redhead freak. We got a guy who acts like Bruce Dern all the time.

They start tracking em down, and we got quite a few well-acted scenes. The redhead freak gets his little toe ripped off by this green-eyed werewolf in a dune buggy. There's a Joan Collins lookalike who's ridin around on a horse and shootin exploding arrows at people. A lot of the guys get kicked in the groceries. The werewolf gets his eye gouged out and his body sliced in half in a beautiful scene with an exotic motor vehicle. Then the Nazi Cochise gets his hands chopped off with a machete. Then Railsback goes nuts with a recreational vehicle and fights the whole Communist Air Force.

We're talking exploding heads. We're talking recreational vehicle crash-and-burns. We're talking bimbo meat factories. Twenty-one breasts, including two stunt breasts. Thirty-four dead bodies. Six pints blood. One beast (gonzo werewolf). Four motor vehicle chases, two crash-and-burns. Heads roll. Hands roll. Stomachs roll. Little toe rolls. Three stars. Joe Bob says check this baby out. ■

Joe Bob Narrowly Escapes Grisly Fingernail Death

I had to haul Ugly on a Stick over to Eckerd's to buy some new fingernails. (Last week U.O.A.S. said to me, "Joe Bob, I'm still ugly. But I've decided I want to be called by my proper Christian name of Chloris." I said, "Sure thing, Ugly.") Last time this came up, Chloris got one of those acrylic jobs from Vida Stegall, but Vida had to put so much glopola on the cuticles that Chloris looked like she was balancing hood ornaments on her fingers for the next three weeks. This time I was anxious to get the job done right, because Chloris said if this worked out she was gonna quit as Wanda Bodine's shampoo girl and get a new job.

"Chloris," I told her, "you're too ugly to get a new job."

"Every individual has one beautiful feature, and if you'll notice, mine happens to be my hands."

I looked at Ugly's hands. They looked like the rest of her body, like a Mr. Potato Head set without a potato.

"I'm gonna be a hand model."

"What?"

"I'm gonna go down to Kim Dawson's and get me a job being a hand model."

"What's a hand model?"

"You know, like this . . ."

Ugly on a Stick held her hands up about shoulder high, flipped em upside down, and then she pointed both of em to the right.

"What was that?"

"Hand model on *Price Is Right.*"

Next thing Ugly rubbed her hands together like she was cold and held her palms straight out.

"What was that?"

"Hand model on Ivory Liquid."

"Ugly, I don't think there's such a job as hand model."

"You don't know everything. I took the Dedra Langhorne Eight-Week Hand-Model Home Study Course, and just the course alone took $250, so you can see what kind of money I'm talking about."

But then Chloris said, before she went down for her audition at Kim Dawson's, she needed me to drop her by Eckerd's for some new fingernails. I said okay I would, because I'd kind of like to help U.O.A.S. get a job somewhere else besides Le Bodine where I have to look at her two, three times a week. But I made Ugly give me a dollar for gas.

When we got to Eckerd's, Chloris told the bimbo at the cosmetics counter she wanted to try on some fingernails, but this gal said no way, José, you buy or you fly, and so Chloris had to pick out a set of claws by sight. We got some airplane glue and went out to the car to see how they fit.

I squirted on the cement and Chloris stuck those suckers on. All except the ring finger on her right hand. That one kept popping up like a scab on a goose.

"That's my double-jointed finger," she said.

"It looks plain old crooked to me," I said.

"It is *not*," Chloris told me, and she had me keep putting more cement on there until after a while it was all bubbling up around the edges and dripping all over her knuckles.

"There," she said. "That's about right."

Ugly's fingers were approximately fourteen inches long. You could eat at Hunan's with these babies and leave the chopsticks in the wrapper. Soon as we got the final one stuck on, Ugly started waving em around in the car, doing some of her aerobic hand-model exercises, and I had to tell her to knock it off before she put somebody's eye out.

The only thing was, Ugly had three of her fingers glued together.

I'd just like to say right now, this was *not* my fault. If Chloris wasn't so dad-burned anxious to put one of those plastic swords on the end of her trick finger, this wouldn't never happened. But I told her, "Ugly, there's only one way to take care of this situation, and that's for me to rip those sumbitches right off your fingers before you get a fungus growth like last time when Vida did your nails."

Chloris said, "What?"

I said, "It's like a Band-Aid. You got to yank that sucker like you're firing up a Lawn Boy. You cain't even think about it. It's gotta happen so fast you don't know what's coming or going. You got to . . ."

By this time I thought, what the hey, what am I waiting for, and so I reached over and grabbed one of those plastic punji sticks and basically pulled it from here to Odessa.

Chloris made a noise that sounded sort of like a Maytag that gets stuck in the spin cycle and starts throwing out dirty underwear all over the floor right before it breaks down. It's not a nice noise that Chloris made. When she made it, she grabbed the seat with her left hand, clenched it in a fist, and stuck a hole in my upholstery so deep that when she brought those nails up where I could see em, she had a handful of car-seat stuffing that looked like what's left over after you crunch up a box of Wheat Chex.

I have to admit, there was a

little bit of blood, but it was only on three fingers.

It took me a half hour to calm her down. She was hysterical. She jumped out of the car and took her good hand and put it on the side of the car and scratched four lines in my paint job about five foot long. Then she started screaming some stuff at me that was way past Ugly. Finally I tried to say something that would help, like "Come on, does it really hurt that much?"

"Who's talking about hurt when you've ended my modeling career?"

I told her, no, that wasn't true, because those fingers would scab over after a few weeks and she'd be good as new.

"What about my 250 bucks?"

I told her it was the kind of a talent that once you learned it you never forgot it, and Dedra Langhorne herself would tell her that. After that she sort of calmed down and I started to feel sorry for her, and I have to admit, I started wanting her to get that Kim Dawson's job more than ever, and so I thought before she went back to Le Bodine and started her rehabilitation period, I would try to help out with some free advice.

"Chloris?"

"What?"

"When you go to that audition . . ."

"Yeah?"

"Just to make sure the Kim Dawson people aren't prejudiced . . ."

"Yeah?"

"It might be a good idea to wear a big old brown paper sack over your head."

"What?"

"A paper bag. Get a double-strength Safeway No. 12."

"You think?"

"Yeah, because you know what, Chloris?"

"What?"

"You're still ugly." ∎

Dirty Harry Here Just in Time for Best of 83 List

Some news poured in this week about Rhett Beavers. Friend of mine named Hank Sturgeon ripped it out of the paper and sent it in:

PEMBROKE PINES, Fla. (AP)—A $1,000 reward has been offered for information leading to the capture of a man who stalks a quiet neighborhood wearing noth-

ing but sneakers on his feet and a paper bag over his head.

Police said the man has surprised at least three women in their homes, slapping, pushing, choking, or punching them. One victim reportedly cut the man with a knife two weeks ago. None of the women has been raped.

Police Chief John H. Tighe said the man also may have committed six burglaries. . . .

A citizens group called Race Against Crime has offered $1,000 for information leading to the man's arrest.

"It's kind of uncanny that a guy could come out naked and disappear so fast," said Capt. John Lombardo. "There's no pattern."

Looks like Rhett went home for Christmas again this year.

The only thing that don't fit is the choking and punching. Slapping, probly. Pushing, okay, they might deserve it. But if I know Rhett, we're talking a man all stoked up on Arkansas Polio Weed for the past fourteen weeks (ever since he walked off from the Garland jail), and I just don't believe Rhett has the upper body strength to light the end of an illegal controlled substance, much less assault a full-grown woman. With APW, we're talking *total paralysis.*

Speaking of crime in America, I did my patriotic duty this week and fishtailed the Toronado out to Grand Prairie to see *Sudden Impact* while most of you turkeys were sittin around in your quonset huts watching small-

screen indoor bullstuff and calling in sick. I'm claimin the modern drive-in endurance record of *eight degrees* on the outside of the car (two degrees inside because Wanda Bodine was with me), and I would just like to point out that while I was toughing it out, proving I'm a drive-in kind of guy, they closed the concession stand on me. They claim the Co-Cola machine quit on em and then all their buns froze up, if you know what I mean and I think you do. So we're also talking three hours *without food and drink* (except for the Cheese Whopper that Chubb Fricke left in the backseat last week, which I'm not counting because Wanda Bodine threatened to put her fingernails through my eyeballs if I went for it).

Fortunately it was worth it.

It was worth it because of Dirty Harry.

Dirty Harry has this problem. He keeps finding these male bodies with their main equipment blown away. (We have a temporary absence of high sheriffs at the *Times Herald* because they're all gone back north to their Communist Yankee homes so they can eat cranberry sauce. I'm tempted to take advantage of this. I'm tempted to say "There were all these guys with their gazebos blown off." I'm tempted to, but I won't, because I'm not that kind of guy, and because the high sheriffs have told me three times now that I can't use the word gazebos in the newspaper *unless* I say that a gazebo is an outdoor bandshell. So I would like to say, in all fairness, that what I mean is that these guys got their outdoor bandshells blown off.)

Dirty Harry is p.o.ed. There's a gazebo mangler out there, and that bothers him. Dirty Harry's in a bad mood anyway. First this lady bimbo judge tells Dirty Harry he "conducted an illegal search" and so these goon jerkolas he picked up can go free. (Dirty Harry doesn't call them goons. He calls them a name sometimes used for human waste.) Next thing, Dirty Harry's cop boss tells him he didn't have probable cause to pick the goons up, even though he found stolen goods in their car.

"Psychic don't count," he tells Harry.

I think we all know what time it is. I think we all know it's .44 Magnum time. I think we all know it's time for Harry to say "Go ahead. Make my day."

So Dirty Harry goes to a diner for coffee, and while he's there he blows away four black guys in the middle of a robbery, and then he feels a *lot* better.

Then the police commissioner calls Dirty Harry in and says, "What the *hell* did you think you were doing?"

And Dirty Harry looks at him and moves his sunglasses a little bit and just says, "My job."

And the commissioner says, "You're a dinosaur, Callahan. Don't you know who I am?"

And Harry says, "Yeah, you're a legend in your own mind."

We're talking some serious heavy load that Dirty Harry is carrying around now. We're talking a man who's getting *concerned* about the state of the world. We're talking a guy who's *sick and tired* of "a society where teachers are being thrown out of fourth-floor windows because they don't give As."

We're talking the scene where Harry gets out his .44 Magnum Automag.

Now you remember Harry's plain old .44 Magnum, right? Most powerful handgun in the world. Well, he's got a new one, only there's this one difference. It still blows anybody's head off that Harry *wants* to blow off, but it does something else too. Harry clips on that Automag sucker, and the thing shoots *forever*.

Next thing, time out for some plot. This blond bimbo named Jennifer is leaving town, but before she does, she goes by the hospital to see her zombie sister who hasn't talked for the past ten years because of what "they" did to her. Jennifer tells her, "I saw one of them, and I killed him." The sister still looks like a zombie.

Some hitmen try to kill Harry by firing about nine thousand rounds at him. Harry blows em away with three shots.

Then the goons follow Harry's car and throw a fire bomb into the back of it, and Harry has to play hit-and-run in this monster car chase where he runs the guys into the San Francisco Bay and they drownd, and now Harry's in *big trouble*. The commissioner's had it. He's sending Harry to a little boonie town called San Paulo to investigate the gazebo murders. San Paulo is where a guy just got his outdoor bandshells blown off on the beach.

So Harry goes there, but first he has to steal a van from a nursing home so he can chase this bank robber through the streets and knock him off his motorcycle. Then somebody gives Harry a bulldog called Meathead. Then Harry goes into a bar looking for information on the gazebo murders, and this sleaze lesbo woman starts to get *familiar* and so he has to deck her with a right cross.

Then Meathead saves Harry's life.

Then Harry has to go rough up a couple guys at the fish market to get information.

Another guy gets his gazebos taken care of.

Dirty Harry is making lots of friends in San Paulo by now, be-cause he has great opening lines like "Tell me, how's your slut sister?"

I don't want to give away the ending, but I'll just say that Harry gets to say "Go ahead, make my day" two more times, and he puts the .44 Magnum Automag to good use.

We're talking five breasts. We're talking one beast named Mick the Spic. We're talking two pints blood. Three motor vehicle chases, one motor vehicle explosion, one motor vehicle dumped into the bay. Gazebos roll. Body count: twenty-one. Some kung fu. Better than *The Enforcer,* not as good as *Dirty Harry.* Drive-In Academy Award nominations for Clint, Sondra Locke as the bimbo gazebo killer, Paul Drake as Mick the Spic. *Sudden Impact* makes it just in time for the Final Best of '83 Drive-In Movie list, going straight to No. 9. ∎

Joe Bob Briggs
Looks Back at 1983
and Gets All Choked Up

Time for the Joe Bob Briggs annual report on world drive-in censorship, and let's face it, it's been a damn poor year. One of our fellow drive-in lovers down in Australia sent in this article last week:

The British Parliament is planning to bar violent and gory video cassettes. The government also plans, according to United Press International, to make all video cassettes sold in Britain subject to classification. Fines of up to

$15,000 and/or jail terms will be meted out for selling unclassified material.

Scotland Yard's obscene publications squad showed more than 70 members of the House of Commons a sampling of violent cassettes and reportedly, "Several members of parliament had to leave the room."

"The theme of violence running through these films includes hangings, castrations, disembowelings, severing of hands, arms and legs, drillings of the chest, back and forehead," said Commons member Gareth Wardell during the debate on the proposed Video Recordings bill, which if approved will become law next year.

I never have trusted those English guys, because as we all know, there's *not a single drive-in in England.* These people are some of the most disgusting drive-in-haters in the world. That's why normal working people have to go out and buy those cheap little Yokohama plastic cartridges so they can go home and shove em in their small-screen indoor-bullstuff imported TV sets, because if they didn't do that, they'd never get to see *Please Don't Eat My Mother* or *Spasmo* at all.

So I'm not really surprised that the poor little babies had to leave the room. They always have to leave the room anyhow, because they drink tea all day long and they eat stuff called kidney pie. Now *there's* something that's disgusting enough to ban from the public.

I think we should all take a moment and give thanks for all the rights we have in America that sometimes we take for granted. Then, after we do that, let's go kick some behinds over there.

Okay, okay, I know, we can't go all the way to London, England, to tell these people what royal jerkolas they are. Kung Fu City is out of the question. So instead of that I'm gonna get on the case and fire off a letter to Scotland Yard and get the names of all seventy movies that they showed to Parliament, and then we're gonna show those suckers to an impartial research audience of red-blooded non-Communist pure-dee American drive-in-goers who are fortunate enough to live in a place where they can watch flicks from the comfort of their own motor vehicles. And then I'm gonna personally drive to England and let those turkeys see the scientific evidence.

And I'll promise you one thing: Heads are gonna roll.

If you would like to be present at the Too Grisly for Parliament Film Festival, let me know and I'll put you down for a few spare body parts.

Everybody has their favorite drive-in memories from the last year, I guess. Maybe it was Jim Brown saying "I may not know kung fu, but I'm an expert in *gun fu*," and then blowing away fourteen white guys in *One Down Two to Go.*

Maybe it was the incest, cannibalism, caged women, and devil worship of *Midnight,* one of the better *Texas Chainsaw Massacre* rip-offs in my memory.

Maybe it was *Timerider,* best biker Western sci-fi comedy of the year.

Maybe it was all the baby-killing and village massacres in *Ator the Fighting Eagle,* starring Miles O'Keeffe in his first talking part.

Maybe it was the scene in *Bloodsucking Freaks* where the midget makes love to a head.

Maybe it was the magician with orange fingernails in *The Sword and the Sorcerer* who cuts the girl's tongue out.

Maybe it was when Madman Marz put Dave's head between the carburetor and the fan belt of Betsy's truck in *Madman.*

Maybe it was the scene in *High Test Girls* where they get twelve complete bouncing breasts in one single shot.

Maybe it was the scene where all the bimbos-in-cages get *hosed down* in *The Concrete Jungle.*

Maybe it was the time the entire cast of *Spring Break* gets drunk on Miller.

Maybe it was when Chuck Bronson goes to the hospital cafeteria where the psycho has been making like Richard Speck in *10 to Midnight,* and Chuck says, "I *hate* quiche!"

Maybe it was the little head-in-the-toilet joke in The *House on Sorority Row.*

Maybe it was the Boys Town scene, featuring prefab breasts, in *Losin' It.*

Maybe it was when Ward and June are having trouble in the bedroom in *Screwballs,* and so June says, "Ward, I'm worried about the Beaver."

Maybe it was when the army arrests the bald-headed space babies in *Wavelength* because they're living underneath Hollywood.

Maybe it was the transvestite wrestling scene in *Chained Heat.*

Maybe it was the big hairy hippie in a Viking costume who goes running around turning teenagers into meat salad in *Don't Go in the Woods.*

Maybe it was when Fred Williamson kung fus eight orange-haired punk rockers at one time in *1990: The Bronx Warriors.*

Maybe it was the scene where Dr. John Cassavetes finds all this *weird sperm* when he examines the mangled bodies of all these tortured bimbos in *Incubus.*

Maybe it was when Jacky Chan, the new kung-fu champ, grabs his opponent in the place we can't talk about in the newspaper and yanks upward and the guy *dies,* in *The Eagle's Shadow.*

Maybe it was the scene where Burt Reynolds's daddy makes jewelry out of doo-doo in *Stroker Ace.*

Maybe it was the giant whale attack in *Yor.*

Maybe it was the Attack of the Itty Bitty Breastlings in *Getting It On.*

Maybe it was the mechanical Erector-Set katydids in *Hercules,* starring the Hulk.

Maybe it was the scene where the ugly warrior has to grab his chest in pain because he's being transformed into a Barbi Benton lookalike by the evil magician in *Deathstalker.*

Maybe it was the ball peen–hammer scene in *Hell's Angels Forever,* documentary of the year.

Maybe it was the embalming-needle murder in *Mortuary.*

Maybe it was when the old rummy gets a throwing star in the eyeball in *Revenge of the Ninja.*

Maybe it was the scene where Ash has to take a chain saw to his girlfriend because she's turned zombie on him in *The Evil Dead.*

Maybe it was the all-time drive-in record of ninety-three dead bodies in *Stryker,* which was also the best *Road Warrior* rip-off of the year.

Or maybe it was something real simple, an old story like the one about the gonzo geek pervert maniac who goes around a college campus cutting up coeds into little bitty pieces and getting a Hefty Bag and taking home the parts he wants and leaving the rest of em for the cops to find. Of course, I'm talking *Pieces.*

Remember, it's almost 1984 and you already can't see *Pieces* in England.

It's a sick world.

Joe Bob says check out 1984 anyhow. ∎

Joe Bob Assaulted: Feminists Want Him Canned

I'm spraying on some quiche repellent and heading out to L.A. this week to talk to Chuck Bronson about being the honored guest at the Second Annual World Drive-In Movie Festival and Custom Car Rally, and so I won't be here to check out *Gates of Hell* and I also won't be here to protect myself from attacks by Billy Murchison or by the gang of females who are sending in these postcards to the *Times Herald* high sheriffs asking those guys to fire my buns. Here's one of em that poured in yesterday from Charlotte Taft, President of the National Organization for Women.

To the editor:
I am personally offended by the space your paper gives to Joe Bob Briggs' column which glorifies violence and brutality to people in general and women in specific. There is nothing witty or amusing about this viciousness, either in fiction or in fact. Women will no longer be victims of an adolescent

cruelty which has the power of the media.

We got about fourteen of these babies in one day, and the high sheriffs tell me they're still coming in.

I think you know what we're talking about here.

We're talking Attack of the Mushmouth French-Fry Heads.

Now, I don't have time to answer every bimbo with 13 cents for a postcard, so I'd like to take just a minute and state the Joe Bob Briggs position on violence against women.

Numero uno: I have enormous respect for women. Especially when they have garbonzas the size of Cleveland.

Numero two-o: I am violently opposed to the use of chain saws, power drills, tire tools, rubber hoses, brass knuckles, bob wire, hypodermics, embalming needles, or poleaxes against women, unless it is *necessary* to the plot.

Numero three-o: I don't believe in slapping women around, unless they beg for it.

Numero four-o: I would like to settle this matter in the easiest way possible, so I hereby challenge Charlotte Taft to a nude mud-wrestling match. She can pick the time and place.

Numero five-o: I'm gonna need some female reader support when I get back, and since Wanda Bodine and Cherry Dilday couldn't write their way out of a paper bag, I want the Real Women of Joe Bob's audience to give me some letter support. As usual, we're going to do this the non-Communist drive-in-going red-blooded democratic American way, which means we're gonna take a vote.

Send em to Joe Bob "Nothing Witty or Amusing About This Viciousness" Briggs, The Cruel Adolescent. ■

The Power Makes People Look Like Ugly on a Stick

When I got back from L.A. last week, I had to go help Wanda Bodine find Ugly on a Stick because we heard from Wanda's little brother Junior Bodine that they were gonna put Ugly in a rubber room at Timberlawn. What Junior actually said was "That gal has some keys missing on the accordion."

I knew this was gonna happen ever since Ugly on a Stick fell in love with Dumptruck Lewis.

We finally found her. What happened was Ugly on a Stick was standing around on the traffic island up at Central and Fitzhugh and when the cars stopped for a light, she pressed her face up against their windows and screamed out that she was collecting money for a "beautification campaign." I told Ugly not to do this. I *told* her that you can only act crazy on a traffic island when you're collecting for orphans or Jerry Lewis or flowers. I guess I shoulda paid a little bit more attention, but I have to admit, sometimes I'll leave the room while Ugly's talking just so I can rest my eyes.

By the time I got there, there was already several accidents in progress.

"Chloris," I said. I decided to use her Christian name because of her delicate mental condition.

"Hi, Joe Bob," she told me. "I'm still ugly."

I asked her if she was doing what I thought she was doing.

"I just need $413 more."

"How much money you taken away from folks?"

"Eighty-three dollars today, but one guy told me he'd pony up a hundred if I wouldn't stand here any more."

This whole thing started when Ugly had that date with Dumptruck Lewis. Dumptruck pulled four years in Nam, and when he come back he never was the same. Rhett Beavers was the only guy who could talk to him. Dumptruck and Rhett used to go out to DFW Airport and smoke Arkansas Polio Weed together and then come back home and everybody would say, "Where *you* been?" and they'd say they went out to "fly Braniff." That's the kind of guy Dumptruck was. He used to trade guns over at Pawn Tex Jewelry and Loan until they made him stop because of something they forgot to take out of his head in Danang.

What I'm trying to say is, Dumptruck was a real nice guy until Ugly on a Stick got ahold of him with her fourteen-inch lacquered fingernails.

First Ugly told Dumptruck that she was going to the plastic surgeon to get an estimate on what the charge would be for a new face. She was gonna do it all for Dumptruck, she told him.

But when Ugly got to the doctor's he told her he couldn't give out an estimate because her face was totaled.

That's when Ugly on a Stick decided to settle for a garbonza job. She called this toll-free number she got out of the back of *Cosmopolitan* magazine that said you could get a completely new pair of hooters for about $5,000. Ugly figured she'd need a couple thou more, because she told Dumptruck, "I want those suckers out to *here.*"

Next thing, Ugly went down to Pawn Tex and tried to get a thirty-year breast improvement loan, but this guy that works there named Rollo said he thought it would be hard to repossess and anyway he didn't know if he wanted to. (I probly don't have to point this out, but Ugly didn't have anything to trade in, if you know what I mean and I think you do.)

Finally, Ugly found this doctor in Matamoros who said he'd do the whole job for $1,000 American. His name was Paco, and he was the only licensed vet in the entire state of Tamaulipas. But Ugly still couldn't raise that kind of jack, so she told Dumptruck she was gonna split the difference. She could raise $500 and get one garbonza this year, then save up the money she gets from doing shampoos at Le Bodine until she can afford the other one. Dumptruck said that sounded fine to him, but what about inflation. Ugly said she didn't think inflation would work unless they figured out some way to plug up her pores.

That's how Ugly ended up standing on the traffic island, collecting for a "beautification campaign."

I told Ugly to get her buns in the backseat of the Toronado and keep her face visible at all times so we wouldn't get arrested for carrying a concealed weapon. Then I hauled her over to Dumptruck's house and told him to keep her locked up until I could get some cashola for her trip to see Dr. Paco.

Next thing, I needed to relax, so I went to see this flick about Aztec demons that rip people's faces open. It's called *The Power.* It starts off with this professor who loves this little clay buddha from Mexico so much that he can make his students' noses start spouting blood if he wants to, only the little booger gets to him and he can't control the Power and he starts floating in midair and screaming, and then the whatever-it-is shishkebabs him on the class flagpole. He wiggles like an oyster for a minute and then it's Red Meat City. Get the idea? This Meskin buddha creates some serious *turista.*

Then this fat guy goes down to the Mexican desert and roots around until he finds the owner of the little clay buddha, but he has to kill two people to get it away.

Then these three high school kids go play with a weejee board in a mausoleum, and they stir up some Power and after they leave the security guard gets his head turned into a piece of wax paper when a three-ton cement block falls on it.

Then the Power starts levitatin stuff like crazy in one of the kids' rooms, and the kid gets panicked and buries the little buddha, and then they decide to go to the media with their story. The bimbo reporter for the media thinks they're Looney Tunes, but her messed-up geek boyfriend buys the story and falls in love with the buddha and pretty soon people start gettin knives stuck through their eyeballs and their faces start turning into silly putty.

I won't give away the plot because there's not any, but there's an *outstanding* scene where the geek boyfriend grabs this blond bimbo and grinds up her hand in the garbage disposal. I wanted to point this out because some people say they never do anything new and different in drive-in movies. This was totally original. A touching scene.

We're talking seven dead bodies. No breasts. No motor vehicle chases. Two pints blood. Minimum kung fu. Good flagpole-through-the-heart scene. Hands roll. Heads flatten. Excellent scene where a demon with twenty hands gropes this girl in her bed. Two okay transformation scenes, where people turn into pasty geeks. Drive-In Academy Award nominations for Susan Stokey, the chief bimbo, and J. Dinan Myrtetus, first nominee for the Chubb Fricke Memorial Award given to fat actors. J. Di is the guy in the desert. Three stars.

Joe Bob says check it out.

Joe Bob's News Desk: A lot of Joe Bob's distinguished big-mouth slopehead critics, like the feminist I challenged to a nude mud-wrestling match, don't think there's any connection between the plots of drive-in movies and real human life, and they also think people only make up drive-in movie plots for kinko geek degenerates like myself.

Fortunately, I keep the non-Communist public of this great country informed.

DELAVAN, Kan. (AP)—Julia H. Stoddard, who lived near Delavan, Kansas, was known in Delavan as the "Dog Lady," and was last seen more than a week ago. She may have been eaten by some of her more than 100 dogs, authorities said.

I just want you people to consider one thing. If Julia had gone to *Cujo,* she might be alive today.

But not now. Now it's too late.

I don't know about you, but I think real human life is disgusting. ∎

Joe Bob Absconds Without Leaving Forwarding Address

❝ ❞ **I**'ve had it. Too many high sheriffs. Too many members of the National Organization for Bimbos. Too many guys named Todd living in Dallas. Too many of my fellow Babtists on my case. Life is a fern bar and I'm out of here. I'm history." ◼

Joe Bob Still Gone but Inspired by *The Being*

[Editor's note: Joe Bob Briggs remained partially missing this week. We say "partially" because we received the following review. On the back of the envelope Joe Bob had written "Still p.o.ed." Under that he wrote "I didn't do it."]

The Being is a flick with a plot. Dorothy Malone has a five-year-old son who falls into the local nuclear-waste dump, turns into a glopola monster, and eats half of Idaho. I'm telling you this upfront so you'll know what's going on when this giant bloody animal hand comes through a car roof and rips a teen-ager's head off in the first scene.

(Message for the National Organization of Bimbos: The teen-ager is of the male persuasion, and so is every single creepola except one who gets offed in this movie, and the one female is Ruth Buzzi which don't really count, and so get off my back.)

Next thing, Martin Landau is a scientist on TV explaining how, just because there's a *little* nuclear waste in the town water supply, that don't *necessarily* mean anything is wrong with the water.

Next thing, we got a great drive-in scene where these two

kids start pawing each other in the front seat, and a giant green brain moseys over by the car to watch, and then blood starts oozing out of the car radio and the glove compartment *and* the air conditioner, which makes you pretty sick considering it's three, four hundred to get one of those suckers fixed, and then the giant brain starts going around the drive-in jerking turkeys out of the windows of their cars and digesting them. A cop goes over there to investigate, but when he gets in the cars he sits in this green slime glopola, and then he goes home and finds some weird Jell-O in his bed and has to run in front of a train to escape.

Then some kids throw some slime on Dorothy Malone's house.

Then a hand comes up through the stomach of this cop while he's sitting in his car. He pretty much gets his intestines ripped out while he watches. The man looks like a Jimmy Dean Sausage factory.

You probly know what happens next. Time for the slime glopola monster to go to the salad bar.

First time we get a look at him, he's going after these three old boys who decide to burn down the massage parlor. Looks just like the mutant in *Forbidden*

World, only bigger. Genetic DNA city. Cyclops. Hamburger Helper with teeth. Plus he has this octopus tongue that can roll out of his head like a lasso and pretty much rip the bejabbers out of anything it touches. Like one old boy gets his hand scissored into a piece of lunchmeat, and another one gets yanked through a plate-glass window, and then the slime glopola monster decides to go over to Ruth Buzzi's house and do some tongue exercises on her neck.

Finally, the creature starts drop-kicking Martin Landau around a warehouse until he gets so mad about being Dorothy Malone's son that he decides to just slime everybody to death. Then the cop figures out that the creature is indestructible except when you shine a flashlight in his eye.

We're talking some serious slimework here. Body count: Twelve. Five breasts. One and one-half gallons blood. Two motor vehicle chases. One crash-and-burn van scene. Excellent slime glopola monster with moving mouth. Drive-In Academy Award nomination for Jackie Kong, the *bimbo* director of *The Being.* Hands roll, arms roll, legs roll, and, of course, heads roll. Three stars.

Joe Bob says check it out. ■

Joe Bob Recognizes Himself Just in Time After Tussle with the Law —

Editor's note: Joe Bob Briggs, still missing after three weeks, was reportedly seen in New Orleans by his friend Rhett Beavers. Rhett called to say that Joe Bob apparently had a religious experience on Bourbon Street and stayed awhile to preach on the streets, but he would be back next week because he wasn't getting too many conversions and also because nobody knew what he was talking about. Rhett also said Joe Bob got into "a minor tussle" with the authorities but not to be concerned because they released him on his "personal recognition" after he recognized himself.

Joe Bob Can't Hack Transvestites, Turns to Preachin' Instead

I'd like to explain about this little *misunderstanding* down in Norleans. I was minding my own business. I was hanging out on Bourbon Street for the same reason everbody hangs out on Bourbon Street—to see garbonzas the size of Costa Rica. They said I was drunk, but I only had four Hurricanes and a few Jaxes. I *was* a little p.o.ed by the jerkolas standing around playing saxophone music on the street, mainly because saxophone music sounds like a Hereford bull gettin his gazebos chopped off. But I'm not a violent kind of guy, so I never even considered grabbing one of those guys by his Brillo beard and turning him into a wind instrument. Now, maybe I *was* a little depressed by the meaning of life, but I got over that by going to see *Scream of the Demon Lover* on Canal Street and then thinking about how true that movie still is after all these years.

No, I'll tell you what it was started it all. It was one of those hatchet-faces dressed up like a bimbo.

I'm talking "female impersonators." Excuse me just a moment while I puke.

You probly don't realize this if you han't been down there in a while, but Norleans has gone all to hell. It's Geek City U.S.A. I can't hardly believe it, because Norleans used to be the greatest border town in America and it wasn't even on a border. Remember the Cat Woman? Only professional bimbo in the U.S.A. that could do more with her hindquarters than Heaven Lee. Heaven Lee used to work out of Printers Alley in Nashville, but ever once in a while she'd go on the road and hit Dallas, maybe the Wild Hare or someplace like that. *Even the Wild Hare is all closed up.* You see where this kind of thinking can lead you. I think you can see why I was gettin depressed down there. I musta walked five, six blocks and all I see is "female impersonators," transvestites, vestransites, reverse-trans-uptights, weirdos-in-tights, people who got all their body equipment put on wrong and they're getting *money* for sticking on some Mary Kay cosmetics and packing their legs into a set of Ultra-Sheers.

I don't know what you would've done in my position. Call it my Babtist upbringing. Call it Fate. Call it three-two beer. I started to preach. Right there on Bourbon Street. I started talking about right and wrong. I said, "You can put breasts on a male individual, but that don't make em garbonzas." I started talking about what the Good Lord intended. I said, "Give Norleans back to the righteous." I started talking about Evil and Sin and a guy I knew once named Ugh Barclay. I said, "What do you mean, two bucks cover charge?" I said a lot of stuff I don't remember. Oh, yeah—I said, "You people all go back to Tulsa where you belong."

I don't remember when it was they cuffed me. The cops tell me I was blindsided by a bunch of geeks in spiked high heels, which would explain the puncture wounds on my upper thighs. They took me to a place called the Hotel Dieu Hospital and put this armed guard outside the room, I guess so none of those transvex-fly-by-nights could get at me with their lacquer fingernails.

Next morning they said I could go on my personal recognition, so I told em I recognized myself and they let me go.

I'd just like to mention one more thing that happened. You probly know that Norleans is gonna have a world's fair this year, which I hope to hell is better than the Knoxville World's Fair, which was the most pitiful excuse for a world's fair ever invented. But anyhoo, while I was down there they put this picture in the paper of a couple mermaid sculptures they're gonna use at the entrance to the world's fair, only now they might not be gonna use em because everyone is mad because the mermaids have huge garbonzas. According to the paper, the garbonzas on those suckers are "four feet wide with nipples the size of dinner plates."

We're talking Costa Rica.

But Norleans *don't want garbonzas.* There's a group I call the

Boob Brigade that's tryin to get those breasts put in halter tops or something.

That's it for Norleans. That's the last disgusting straw. If you can't see giant garbonzas in Norleans, where *can* you see em? This country's getting more like Communist Russia ever day.

Coming back the Toronado broke down in Lake Charles and I had to put it up on blocks a couple days while Rhett Beavers brought down some parts from Grand Prairie. So I dropped in at the New Moon D.I. just about ever night and that's where I caught this flick called *Weekend Pass.* It automatically goes on the 1984 Top Ten list because it has absolutely no plot to get in the way of the story.

It's about these four sailors from San Diego who go up to Hollywood for the weekend. First they watch some strippers. Then they go to the beach and watch some bimbos. Then they go to aerobics dancing class and watch some more bimbos. Then three of em hire this Chinese-lady masseuse named Chop Suzi to get "the nerd" overhauled, if you know what I mean and I think you do. Great high-heels-on-the-spine scene. Then they decide to go get some soul food in Watts, and the Negro sailor has to kung-fu one of his old creepola punk buddies. Then one of the sailors goes off with this Hollywood bimbo in a black leather miniskirt, and she tries to get him to use a device called the Space Shuttle on her, only he can't figure out how to operate it, so he goes to this comedy club to watch one of the other sailors make a horse's behind of himself, and then the four of em go off and watch some more bimbos and then they take the bimbos home with em and then they go back to the navy.

Okay, let's talk nitty: Twelve breasts. Some kung fu. One-half pint blood. No motor vehicle chases. One beast: the punkola gang leader, one of those guys with muscles that look like horseshoes are growing on the outside of his body. No plot. Heads do not roll. Drive-In Academy Award nominations for Cindy Hazard, the "Space Shuttle" girl; Chip McAllister, the dude from Watts; and Grand L. Bush, the beast.

Three stars. Joe Bob says check it out. ■

Joe Bob's Mailbag ——

Joe Bob—

Whats all this phoney baloney bullstuff about you hiding from the National Organization of Bimbos (NOBS)? It don't seem like you to run away from NOBS.

And even if you are why did you pick Mississippi? I thought Oklahoma was the only place where they didnt have NOBS.

Sounds like a Commanist

conspera connspir plot to me.

"Trash" Baggs
Tyler

Dear Trash:
Oklahoma has some bimbos, but under state law, they're officially classified as taxable livestock.

Joe Bob in Moral Dilemma over "Dangerous" Sell-out to Pack of Foreign Papers

Wanda Bodine went stark raving crazy last week when she found out the Dallas Cowboys cheerleaders are gonna have a *written* test this year. Wanda's been giving Dallas Cowboys cheerleaders try-out seminars and selling aerobic-dancing routines for 25 bucks apiece. Last week she sold "Steam Heat" to thirty-seven bimbos, and the week before that she gave out about eighty different versions of "I'm Gonna Wash That Man Right Out of My Hair." So when I found out about it I had to tell her that, basically, she was a jerk and she didn't realize that this wasn't no Miss Texas bullstuff, we're talking Dallas Cowboys here, she needed a decent topless-bar routine only she had to sew those garbonzas *inside* the costume and zip em up tight so they look like somebody took a couple watermelons and wrapped an Ace bandage around em. Then these girls would have a

running chance at the Dallas Cowboys cheerleaders written test.

Wanda said, "What?"

Also, Wanda forgot to notice when the deadline was for the Dallas Cowboys cheerleader letter where you explain "Why I want to become a Cowboys cheerleader." Those suckers are due next Wednesday, and let's face it, most of these girls haven't even decided on their topic yet.

Course, I told Wanda I would help out if there was some cold cash on the line, and so I'm heading out to Le Bodine this weekend to do some *rewrites.* Give you some idea what I'm talking about, here's one of em Wanda sent over to me:

WHY I WANT TO BE A DALLAS COWBOYS CHEERLEADER

Because I want to meet Bob Hope and have a recording con-

tract. And maybe sleep with Merv Griffin.

And also I want to be in a TV movie maybe called The Cowboys Cheerleaders Go to Hong Kong and Get Fondled by Some Funny-Looking Short Guys.

Thanks you for your consideration and when do I find out?

I told Wanda this just wasn't gonna cut it, and besides that, these girls needed some cramming for the written test, and so I told her that for an extra fifty American I'd do some tough sample questions, multiple choice only, like the ones they were gonna have to know in that big S.A.T. at Texas Stadium.

Stuff like:

What does "first-and-ten" mean?

a. When the guy don't have enough money for Around-the World.

b. The number of yards needed for another first down.

c. The number of dollars needed to file a paternity suit against a Dallas Cowboy offensive lineman.

d. A song by Lionel Richie.

The correct answer, of course, is "a." You'd be surprised how many people don't know this one.

You're probly thinking, Hey, Joe Bob, why are you telling us about the danged Dallas Cowboys cheerleaders auditions when *Sexpot* is at the drive-in tonight?

I know, I know, I shoulda been out there checking it out. The correct title, by the way, is *Women Like This Were Meant to Be Handled,* but that was too big to get on the marquee. I shoulda been handling the breast-count duties on that one. But I been pretty depressed this week, and I guess I better just spit it out and fess up and tell you what happened.

I was minding my own binness, being a good Babtist, keeping my private parts clean, writing up "Joe Bob Goes to the Drive-In," collecting my forty a week, hanging out at Deke's, getting a little nookie on the side here and there but nothing to write home about, and then the high sheriffs go and sell off my column. No sweat, right? Who gives one? But then this week the list come in of what papers are gonna be printing this sucker starting next week, and I guess I might as well come right out and admit it.

We're talking some Cleveland. (I know what you're thinking: *Joe Bob, does this mean no more Cleveland jokes?* But wait a minute, I'm not through.)

We're talking some Denver. (I know, I know, I can't breathe up there either.)

We're talking some Enid, Oklahoma. (Yeah, that's right— Oklahoma. But wait, because this next one's gonna be the toughest one of all.)

We're talking some San Francisco.

That's right. I admit it. "Joe Bob Goes to the Drive-In" in

Geek City U.S.A. Home of wimp drive-in-hating movie critic Peter Stack. I don't know about you, but I've got some serious *moral* problems with that. So I went to the high sheriffs last week and I said, "Hey, jerkola french-fry heads, I don't think I can do it."

They said they thought I could.

I said, "It goes against my principles to write a column for Communist-speaking cities."

They said they didn't believe it did.

I said, "You guys are trying to make me part of the *media.*"

They said they didn't give a flying frijole.

I said, "How much cold cash do I get for this?"

They told me.

I said, "Never mind."

Then I went back out to the trailer house and I prayed about this for a long time and I said to myself, "Can I do this? Can I stop dumping on San Francisco? These people are from out of state so what difference does it make? Can I be *objective* on Texas-OU Weekend? Can I stop comparing Cleveland to Ugly on a Stick's chest? Can I buy a gas mask and go out to Colorado and talk to some people wearing orange backpacks?"

I talked to The Big Guy about this. I waited for an answer. I got it.

It was "No way, José."

The Big Guy says I don't have to be nice, but I'm counting on my buddies in Texas to keep me in line. If you *ever* see some Communist crapola seeping into this column when I'm not looking, you zap off a letter to the Mailbag and nip that bullstuff in the bud. I preciate the heck out of it. And the high sheriffs won't.

Let's make America safe for Texas. ∎

Gary Hart Is Strange, and So Is This Movie About Cornflake Kids

Last week I drove out the Grapevine Highway to take Wanda Bodine to see this flick called *Children of the Corn,* about these kids in Nebraska that like to carve up their parents and make gasohol, but then Wanda made some remark about how cute Gary Hart is and I'm sorry but I had to stop the Toronado in the middle of I-35 North and tell her that the drive-in was a family place, and if she started mentioning members of Congress again I was gonna have to do a little elective neurosurgery, if you know what I mean and I think you do.

But while I'm thinking about it, let's get this out of the way right now. How many people are sick of Gary Hart? Could we have a show of hands, please? I thought so.

Nice hair, though, Gary.

Before I tell you about the giant groundhog mushroom cloud in *Children of the Corn,* I need to get down to the nitty here. A lot of you turkeys are reading this column for the first time this week, and you're probly thinking, Who is this guy? What is this? Why am I reading this? Where can I get a good massage?

There's a few things you need to know.

Numero uno: I review DRIVE-IN movies. For you people in San Francisco, that means OUTDOORS. In Communist Russia, you can't do this. Drive-ins are illegal in Communist Russia. But we are privileged to watch movies the way God intended us to see em, in the personal privacy of our own automobiles. I don't want to have to say this again. Understand?

Numero two-o: If you like indoor bullstuff like *E.T.,* please go get in your Toyota and fold your body into a balloon animal and drive to the mall.

Numero three-o: Maybe you're like my friend Chubb Fricke, who played two weeks on the PBA tour in 1948 and never has quit talking about it ever since. Chubb is what's known as an old fat guy. Old fat guys are

easily offended. Old fat guys shouldn't read this column. All of the old fat guys should turn directly to the fishing report so they can go down to the Legion Hall and tell somebody about all the crappie that's biting on Lake Tawakoni.

Numero four-o: Or maybe you're a member of the National Organization of Bimbos. The National Organization of Bimbos says I don't respect women. The National Organization of Bimbos says I "endorse violence against women." I've said it before but I'm gonna say it right here again: I am violently opposed to rape, brutalization, beheadings, disembowelings, arms and legs hacked off with chain saws, hypodermics through the eyeball, power drills through the stomach, those scenes in the movies where the monster squeezes girls until their eyes pop out and they explode, butcher knives across the knees, and spears through the ear, unless it's necessary to the plot.

Okay, now that we've weeded out all the wimps and been canceled in seventeen cities, I feel much better about myself.

Let's talk Big Steve King.

Steve's a pretty scary guy. Wanda Bodine went under the seat three times on this one. Better than *Cujo,* not quite *Dead Zone,* but what the hey? Steve delivers, right?

Children of the Corn starts off one day when the Babtist church in Gatlin, Nebraska, is letting out and everbody is headed over to the coffee shop to eat something greasy and disgusting like meat loaf. Only once they try the coffee they start grabbing their throats like somebody just forced em to watch a Bob Hope special, and then they start making noises like a major Maytag appliance starting to break down, and then their kids come in the restaurant and start mowing them down with meat cleavers and sickles and pickaxes. One guy gets held down while they stick his hand in the automatic roast beef slicer. It's okay, though, because nobody was ordering.

Now it's three years later, and this little kid is running through the cornfields with a suitcase, trying to make it to the highway, but a man with a butcher knife in his holster turns the kid into shishkebab meat and then puts him out on the road so some tourists will run him down like a potato pancake.

Then this movie starts to get grisly.

I don't want to go into all the plot here, because it's boring, but basically what we got is a bunch of little brats that killed all the grownups in town and now they make gasohol all day and murder tourists and worship this kid named Isaac who has a Buster Brown haircut and stands about two foot six and looks like Charlie Brown with a piece of goat meat lodged in his throat. There's also a kid named Malachai who looks like Alfalfa with his hair grown out like a hippie, and Malachai likes to kill little dogs and old-coot gas-station owners. I call em the Cornflake Kids.

Anyhow, these two tourists come along and figure out something's wrong when the streets of the town are deserted and rotten cornstalks are sticking out everywhere. This doctor and his blond girlfriend go walking through all these buildings full of cornstalks and after about fifteen minutes they say, "There's something strange about this town." The Rhodes scholar who says this gets hung up on a cornstalk cross so they can sacrifice her to He Who Walks Behind The Rows. But first they have to wait for Amos. Amos is the nineteen-year-old wimp who likes to carve on his chest with a farm implement and drain his blood into a cup so everbody can drink it. Amos wants to "go to Him" by strapping himself up there on a cross while the Cornflake Kids crowd around him and do a Vienna Boys Choir number. Amos and the blond bimbo are gonna "go to Him" together, because the bimbo's husband is hiding out over in the atomic-bomb shelter with a couple little kids who have been hiding out from Isaac and playing Monopoly for the last three years.

A little too much plot getting in the way of the movie, but a decent drive-in flick anyhow. Ten dead bodies. One dead dog. No breasts. One motor vehicle chase. About two pints blood. Heads do not roll. Hands roll. Excellent groundhog - mushroom - cloud monster. Great scene where Peter Horton, the tourist with an IQ of

24, gets strangled by a demon cornstalk. Drive-In Academy Award nominations for Courtney Gains as the hippie Alfalfa, John Franklin as Charlie Brown, Fritz Kiersch, the guy who made this sucker, and Big Steve, who made it all possible. Three and a half stars.

Joe Bob says check it out. ∎

Joe Bob's Mailbag ———

Dear Joe Bob

My friends, Peggy & John, and I are wildly curious about your physical appearance. Please put an end to our seemingly endless speculations by sending us a picture.

Many thanks,
Sylvia Warmbrodt
Dallas

Dear Sylvia:

What are the THREE of you going to do with my picture?

I'm sorry, but that's just too disgusting.

Stuck On You Competes with Cowboy Cheerleaders for Nothing-to-it IQ Award

Excuse me if I'm a little ticked off this week, but some jerkola Aggie bought the Dallas Cowboys and when they held the press conference about it he refused to comment on the main question of the day. I think you know what I'm talking about, Mr. Bum Bright. I think you realize what we all want to know. I don't think you'd like us to have to repeat that scene in *Two Thousand Maniacs* where the good old boys start playing mumbledy-peg on a guy's face because he's from out of state. So I'll just spit this one out:

Are you or are you not going to eliminate the Dallas Cowboys Cheerleaders written test?

I brought this up two weeks ago while the Bimbettes were in Lebanon doing some Vic Damone specials or something and I had to launch the "Cowboys Cheerleaders Out of Middle East Now" campaign. (If you'll notice, Reagan brought our girls home as soon as "Joe Bob Goes to the Drive-In" came out.) But let's face it. The Cowboys cheerleaders aren't what they used to be. We gotta go all the way back to the '77 Super Bowl team to find the kind of class airhead bimbo that made this city great. We all know what happened after that. They started personality interviews and accepted a few college graduates and agreed to consider girls even when their first name didn't end in the letter "i" and before you know it the squad got Miss American-ized and turned into a bunch of Barbie Doll California surfer-girl bullstuff.

The reason I know so much about this is because Wanda Bodine has seventeen girls entered in the cheerleaders tryouts this year who all came out of her Rockabilly Glamourcize class at Le Bodine. Wanda worked up so many "Flashdance What a Feeling" routines that they ran out of Danskins and ankle yarn at Irving Mall. I talked to Wanda last week, though, and she says half of these sisters won't make it past the written test and the other half don't know where Texas Stadium is. I want to give you an idea of how tough the academic requirements are getting. Here's a sample question from the Dallas Cowboys Cheerleaders written test:

Q. What is halftime?

a. What the waiter says ten minutes before Happy Hour's over.

b. The signal that the music already stopped and so you can quit kicking your white vinyl boots into the ABC cameraman's field

of vision and start bending over so your cowgirl vest flies open like a piece of Kleenex that's been soaked with a fire hose.

c. Walter Mondale speed-reading.

The correct answer, of course, is "b," even though most people say "c" because it's a trick question: They stick current events in there to try and trip you up.

I think it's crystal clear what's going on here, though, and I'm asking Bum Bright to stop it pronto. We want some girls named Buffi this year. We want some biographical data sheets that say "Staci is a Libra who enjoys working with mentally handicapped deaf children and playing the home version of *Family Feud*." We want some serious cleavage. And I *don't* want to have to repeat myself again.

Speaking of academic requirements, I know a lot of you turkeys have been writing in to Joe Bob's Mailbag to ask "When are we going to get to see Professor Irwin Corey in a serious dramatic role?"

I promised it would happen. I never had a doubt that the man could handle it. You know what I'm talking about. Maybe you were there at the triple-screen Gemini Drive-In last week for the premiere. It's here. It's real.

I'm talking *Stuck On You.*

Stuck On You goes straight to No. 2 on the Joe Bob Briggs Best of '84 Drive-In Movie list, as the first flick of the year that has absolutely no plot to get in the way of the story. It starts out with Professor Irwin Corey belching seven or eight times. The prof is a divorce-court judge who's trying to straighten out these two french-fry heads who got married even though they like each other.

Then Professor Irwin Corey makes a banana daiquiri and smears it on his chin.

Then there's the zoo-animal disco scene.

Then Professor Irwin belches.

Then there's the hippie body-painting scene and the scene with the singing jive rabbis.

Then Professor Irwin Corey cuts the cheese.

I forgot to mention the beach stampede scene.

Then Christopher Columbus comes to America in a Pinto and explores Pocahontas.

Then the two french-fry heads tell Professor Irwin Corey a flashback about the time they had to get a block and tackle to force this bimbo into her designer jeans.

Next we go back to medieval times and see how women were tied to sapling branches and catapulted over fortress walls.

And then the wimp husband named Bill tells everbody how he used to work in a chicken factory until he figured out a way to increase egg production by showing the chickens a film called *Deep Cluck*.

Then Bill dresses up like a clown and chases a car.

Then Professor Irwin Corey staples a Barbie Doll to death and says, "I know what's wrong with you people. You hate each other."

I'm not about to give away the ending of this mother. We're talking nine breasts. One pint blood. Twelve wild beasts. One motor vehicle chase, with crash and explosion. Excellent midget performance in the Spanish-maid-costume scene. One gross-out food eating scene not quite up to the standard set by *Surf 2*. Heads do not roll. Hands do roll. Very funny "Black Plague" scene. Yellow-water-in-the-pool scene tells us a lot about the modern world and the way we live today. Drive-In Academy Award nominations for Professor Irwin Corey, the one and only, and Lloyd Kaufman and Michael Herz, the boys who made this sucker as well as drive-in classics like *Waitress*. Lloyd and Mike specialize in movies with no plots, and let's face it, there aren't many of those guys left. What I'm trying to say is:

Three stars. Joe Bob says check it out. ■

Joe Bob's Mailbag ——

Dear Mr. Briggs,

I recently read some of your articles and realize that you may have inadvertently succumbed to the grasp of the devil. I hope this letter arrives in time to appeal to what remaining spark of decency there may remain in your body. I suspect I'm too late.

There are so many perversions in your writings that I cannot possibly address them all. I suggest that you concentrate on cleaning up one perversion at a time.

Start off by omitting using the word 'b----t.' Instead of 'b----t,' why not write 'bosom,' or, even better, use 'b---m'? I prefer the term 'upper frontal parts' myself.

By using this gradual cleaning-up approach, maybe you will eventually even cease recommending that our young folks attend such dens of iniquity as those found at drive-ins.

Yours truly,
Buford B. Beane
Prosper

Dear Buf:

How about hooters, ta-tas, garbonzas, and cruise missiles? I wouldn't want to offend anybody.

Foreign Readers Get Mad at Joe Bob

The United States Supreme Court has ruled that every week something in "Joe Bob Goes to the Drive-In" has to have socially redeeming value or else the FBI sends a guy out to the Highway 183 D.I. to bash my head in with a stick. I think this is fair. That's why it's time to review the Joe Bob Briggs Drive-In Foreign Film of the Year. Call it Outdoor Culture Week. Call it my way of educating the public. Call it an excuse to get this dang column finished. But we got everything in this one. We got a little Marcello Mastroianni. We got a little Sophia Loren. (On second thought, we got more than a little Sophia Loren, if you know what I mean and I think you do.) Of course, you know what I'm talking about by now.

I'm talking *Sex Pot.*

Some of you turkeys probly saw this flick under its original indoor bullstuff title, *Oopsie Poopsie.* ("The Picture That's Good Enough to Eat!") And if you did you already know it's one of Sophia's most dramatic roles since *Cinderella Italian Style* in 67. Sophia's looking more voluminous than ever since she got out of jail over in Italy for not paying her income tax. She used to have to do all those degrading sex-object roles just to make a buck, but now her husband Carlo Ponti is taking care of business and getting her back into the classics like *Sex Pot.*

We've all heard this story before. Marcello is this Mafia guy who makes Sophia dress up like Rita Hayworth so he can slap her around. So Sophia starts thinking how life was a whole lot better when she was a hooker picking up perverts on the interstate, and she thinks she might go back to that, but then she says, what the hey, these hooters are not getting any younger, and so she decides to put on a Vegas show with three other bimbos while she still has all the equipment in working order.

Then Sophia changes her lingerie.

Then she gets kidnapped by some wimps that work for Marcello, and she has to punch one out. Marcello finds out about it and slaps her around again. In fact, Marcello slaps her around ever time she asks a question. Sophia never figures out that this is for her own good. One time Marcello is trying to have a *private* conversation and so he tells Sophia to go in the other room and gargle so she can't hear what the heck is going on, and every time she stops gargling he has to throw something at her head to get her started again. I understand that if you try this out on women, they figure it out after three, four times and do it without asking.

Then Sophia changes her lingerie again.

Next thing, Marcello discovers this little number that looks even more like Rita Hayworth than Sophia, so he dumps his main squeeze. Sophia is bummed out that she don't have anybody to slap her around any more, so she tries to hang herself with a feather boa, but Marcello finds out about it and slaps her around for trying it.

Then Sophia puts on some new lingerie.

Then Sophia decides to sing, and I'm sorry, but I don't want to go into this because it's not a pretty sight.

Then Marcello has to hit her in the head with a shoe because she didn't wash all the dirty clothes, but the reason is, she didn't have time because she was out investigating this murder that Marcello is involved in.

Then Sophia decides she needs some different lingerie, and while she's putting it on she gets kidnapped again, only the cops come after the Mafia wimps this time and we get some pretty decent motor vehicle chases where Sophia hangs out of the car, if you know what I mean and I know you do.

I know what you're wondering: Does Sophia drop her top or what? You know Carlo's position on this issue. You know *exactly* how far that cleavage line can go. So even though we get a lot of jiggle action, I gotta be honest:

No breasts. (Automatic one-star deduction.) Two dead bodies. Minimum blood. Heads do not roll. Kung fu and bimbo fu. Vegas show tune. Sophia slapped around and struck with heavy objects twenty-six times, but only when it's necessary to the plot. Great scene where Sophia imitates Rita Hayworth. Excellent motor vehicle chase and double crash. No beasts except Marcello and his killer wimps. Great dubbed moaning.

Three stars.

Joe Bob says check it out. ∎

Wanda's Talkin' Breach; We're Talkin' Meat Beach in *Where the Boys Are*

Rhett Beavers got back from Florida last week with one of those I-bought-a-flamingo-ashtray grins on his face, and I could already tell he was missing a few face cards. Rhett never did have what you would call a Sears Diehard upstairs, and let's face it, the boy han't been the same ever since that rap for possession of seventy-two pounds of Arkansas Polio Weed for his personal use. Rhett han't been in town more than two, three days before Wanda Bodine was swearing out a warrant again, telling everbody Rhett breached her, when everbody knows Rhett couldn't breach diddly. The boy was paralyzed on that stuff for seven weeks.

Anyhow, all I was able to find out is Rhett made some kinda deal with Vida Stegall and Vida quit her job at Le Bodine right in the middle of a wet-set. Vida said she'd be danged if she was working any more in a trailer house, even if it did pay $2.10 an hour, because Wanda Bodine promised three months ago to put Vida's name on the Porta-Neon sign out front and give her a promotion to aerobic-dance instructor, but that fell through when the Dallas Cowboys cheerleaders announced they were having a written test this year and so Wanda had to devote all her time to giving private lessons to the bimbos who ponied up three hundred cold American apiece for *Footloose* routines.

Then when Rhett got back from jacking around in Florida, he went straight to Vida Stegall and *claimed* he had exclusive North Central Texas rights to Irlene Mandrell's Texersize. (Irlene is Barbara's little sister, one of the finest actresses in the history of *Love Boat*, and looks like she was shot through the back with a couple of meat tenderizers.) Rhett's deal was simple. He would set up Vida in a "permanent structure of some kind" within one-half mile of Six Flags Mall. (It was the mall part that got Vida's attention.) He would also deliver two hundred posters of Irlene wearing a Danskin the size of a washrag, and it would say on there "Everyone will want to take me home and Texersize!" Vida had to provide enough blow-dryers and "ladies' stimulated fingernails" to get in the beauty-parlor bidness, and she had to come up with a name for the place. Vida decided on Vida's House of Shellac.

Soon as Vida was able to rent a Porta-Neon, Wanda said, "We're talking breach."

I don't want to go into all the details, because I'm too lazy, but basically it came down to how Wanda *is already* the exclusive eastern Tarrant County franchisee for Rockabilly Glamourcize, and anybody who teaches Rockabilly Glamourcize has to sign a slave clause that says, according to Wanda, that Wanda can dump Vida into a Commercial Osterizer and turn her into grape syrup. Basically speaking, that's the kind of lawsuit we're talking about. I'm staying out of it, because I think we already got too many lawsuits in America, and we oughta learned by now that the best way to settle our differences is to knock the bejabbers out of one another.

Now. What this is leading up to is, Rhett came back from surfola bimboville, puked all over his floormats on reentry, and started babbling about this flick in Lauderdale called *Where the Boys Are.* I told him I saw the sucker. He said there's another one. I said, yeah I know, it's called *Spring Break,* about all these turkey college kids who go down to Lauderdale and get nekkid and drink Miller Lite and have a wet T-shirt contest. It gets four stars if you're drunk on Miller, two stars sober, three stars drunk on Bud. Rhett said I didn't know what I was talking about, because there was a flick called *Where the Boys Are* at the Century D.I. in Grand Prairie, and I better check it out because it had a pretty active porkchop counter.

I'm here to tell you, this is the best movie about stupid white people since *Summer Lovers.* No plot to get in the way of the story. Total IQ of the cast: 17. Starring these four bimbos whose philosophy of life is "All you need is a bikini and a diaphragm." We've heard this before, of course, but it was the way she said it.

Now. A lot of people wonder why Lorna Luft han't never made it in the movies. She was waiting for the right role, that's all. Lorna is the daughter of Judy Garland and Sid Luft, so you know she's got talent, but also she's got the looks: She looks exactly like Sid Luft. In this flick Lorna plays the boring bimbo with a boyfriend back home. Lisa Hartman is the virgin. Wendy Schaal is the valley girl. And Lynn-Holly Johnson is just horny. She goes around trying to have a religious experience with Conan the Barbarian.

We've got a lot of beach meat on the screen here, some halfway decent drunks, a Hot Bod Contest, some romantic scenes with a rubber blowup dummy, three parties, a woman who walks around with her garbonzas all caged up, and some real bad singing. The turkeys who made this dude didn't even have the decency to go find Connie Francis.

In other words, you people in Lauderdale are sick.

Eleven breasts. No blood. One beast (Conan). Great scene with Rod Stewart's wife trying to go to bed with everything that moves. Two motor vehicle chases, one with crash. Lorna Luft does something pretty amazing with a cucumber. One Aggie joke. Heads do not roll.

Three and a half stars on Bud. Three stars on Miller. Four stars on Arkansas Polio Weed. ▪

Joe Bob Announces 1983 Drive-In Academy Awards

I had to take Rhett Beavers out to the faith healer in Mabank last week or else I woulda had this sooner. A lot of you turkeys been writing in saying "Hey, what the hey, where the hey is the 1983 Drive-In Academy Awards?" and I'd just like to point out that I don't take this responsibility lightly. This is not any Hollywood indoor bullstuff deal, where they wheel em in from Palm Springs every year to cast ballots for people who send out hams in the mail. This is not any teensy-weensy-screen TV jerkola banquet where they listen to Herb Alpert play "Oh what a feeling." This is a legit deal. This is for the non-Communist drive-in-going public of America. You know what I'm talking about. It's that time of year again. It's time to give out the Hubbies. (Junior Bodine's shop out in Mineral Wells did a great job this year engraving the Chevy hubcaps. He only had to cross out letters five or six times.)

Okay, let's get down to the nitty.

BEST ACTOR

• Chuck Bronson *(10 to Midnight),* blowing scum off the streets and saying lines like "I hate quiche"

• Vic Morrow *(1990: The Bronx Warriors):* Remember when he rides in with nine hundred guys carrying industrial-strength blowtorches and orders them to burn the eyes out of everbody they see?

• Bruce Campbell *(The Evil Dead),* who makes the mistake of not chain sawing his girlfriend after she turns zombie on him

• Christopher Walken *(Dead Zone),* the geek schoolteacher who runs his VW bug into a milk truck and don't wake up for five years and then his eyes bug out like a katydid and he starts twitching around the room

• Wings Hauser *(Deadly Force),* kicking hineys all over the Elephant-Man therapy institute

And the winner is:
Big Chuck, of course.

BEST ACTRESS

• Kathryn McNeil *(The House on Sorority Row),* making like Jamie Lee Curtis

• Lynda Speciale *(Screwballs),* for her moving performance as Purity Busch, the ice queen and official school virgin

• Ellen Sandweiss *(The Evil Dead),* the bimbo who gets raped by the forest

• Monique St. Pierre *(Stryker),* the garbonza woman forced to fight it out with the baldheaded Fu Manchu hook-arm turkey

• Corinne Alphen *(Spring Break),* the brunette *Penthouse* Pet of the Year who sings "Do It To You" and makes all the guys smash Miller cans on their heads

And the winner is:
Monique, for her enormous talents.

BEST BEAST

• Miles O'Keeffe *(Ator the Fighting Eagle),* the beefcake Tarzan turned barbarian, trying to keep his breechcloth on

• The 300-pound Baby Huey in *Midnight* who hangs around the graveyard and carves up Babtist preachers

• Lou Ferrigno *(Hercules):* the man has veins like a road map of Louisiana

• Little Howard *(Deathstalker),* the household pet in a basket that only eats human eyes and fingers

• Christine *(Christine):* drop a cigarette on the upholstery and this '58 Plymouth Fury might have to dump your body in a Goodwill box

And the winner is:
Christine, for the best performance by a motor vehicle in history.

BEST KUNG FU

• Jim Kelly *(One Down Two to Go):* shoeleather to the groin on fourteen white guys

• Johnny Yune *(They Call Me Bruce?):* he got his black belt in a state where they just have a written test

• Fred Williamson *(1990: The Bronx Warriors):* Fred against eight punkola freaks on roller skates

• Jacky Chan *(Eagle's*

Shadow), master of the snake style *and* cat's-claw, who thwocks and whooshes his way through fifteen complete fight scenes including everything from one-on-one to eight-on-two, then grabs Old Goat-Hair in the place we can't talk about in the newspaper and watches the turkey die.

• Sho Kosugi *(Revenge of the Ninja),* kicking in the heads of punkola weirdos in the park, Ninja warriors, Mafia guys, using hands, feet, Nunchakus, blades, throwing stars, and those little pointy things that look like jacks but make your face look like it caught on fire and somebody had to put it out with a meat tenderizer

And the winner is:

Sho Kosugi, the only actor ever to win a high-speed chase when he didn't even have a car.

BEST SUPPORTED ACTRESS
(formerly BEST CHEST)

• Sabrina Siani *(Ator the Fighting Eagle):* bleach-blond Amazon bimbo who wins the contest when they tie up Miles O'Keeffe and have a nude mud-wrestling match to see who gets to be his sex object for one night

• *High Test Girls:* the entire cast, eighty-three full exposures from Lisa Robertson, Nancy Patricks, Polly Quigley, Sherri Richards, Kathy Close

• Linda Shayne *(Screwballs):* Bootsie Goodhead herself, who made movie history in the now-famous drive-in scene when the nerd jumps out the back of the van and the door catches on Bootsie's halter top and she has to rub her breasts against the back window for a full minute

• Betsy Russell *(Private School),* the blond witch bimbo who likes aerobic dancing leotards, underwire bras, group showers, and Lady Godiva imitations

• Barbi Benton *(Deathstalker),* chained to the wall in a see-through nightie while extras from *Planet of the Apes* fight over the groceries

• Ashley Ferrare *(Revenge of the Ninja),* the blonde who demonstrates bimbo fu at its finest

And the winner is:

Bootsie Goodhead, the one and only.

BEST SPECIAL EFFECT

• *Midnight:* the women-in-dog-cages scene, where they get fattened up for the Baby Huey blood-drinking scene

• *Timerider:* first moto-cross western, where Lyle Swann gets time-zapped into 1877 by the Reagan administration

• *High Test Girls:* twelve complete bouncing breasts in one shot while the bimbos are running nekkid through the woods; still unknown how they found a camera that could handle it

• *Screwballs:* the famous bowling-alley scene where the ball gets stuck on an important anatomic part of stuntman Alan Daveau, and the explosion that gets it off

• *Wavelength:* when the bald-headed space babies come to life in their sterilized barrels in a secret laboratory underneath Hollywood

• *Deathstalker:* when the magician turns the Stalker into a Barbi Benton lookalike and he nearly dies of chest pains

• *Amityville 3-D:* when Candy Clark burns up on camera

• *Escape 2000:* Oliva Hussey's stunt breasts in the shower scene

And the winner is:
Screwballs, for the bowling-ball levitation scene.

BEST GROSS-OUT SCENE

• *They Call Me Bruce?:* the part about the guy who gets his jollies out of being whipped on the back by Margaux Hemingway; not a pretty sight

• *Ator the Fighting Eagle:* the tarantula torture scene

• *Bloodsucking Freaks:* when the doctor decides to do "a little elective neurosurgery" with a power drill while he's humming "The Marriage of Figaro"

• *Madman:* when Madman puts Dave's head between the carburetor and the fan belt on Betsy's

truck and turns his face into a pizza

• *The House on Sorority Row:* head-in-the-toilet scene

And the winner is:
Madman, for terminal engine trouble.

BEST PICTURE

• *Hell's Angels Forever:* documentary of the year, with a lot to say about the correct role of women in society today; best on-camera use of a ball peen hammer

• *The Evil Dead:* spam in a cabin

• *Revenge of the Ninja:* every kind of kung fu known to man

• *Deathstalker:* starring Barbi Benton's upper torso and a Miles O'Keeffe lookalike who goes around throwing spears through people

• *Screwballs:* most imaginative use of female breasts, best *Porky's* rip-off

And the winner is:
The Evil Dead Was there ever any doubt?

Night of the Zombies is this flick about a SWAT team in Italy that blows away some terrorists and then decides to go to the jungles of New Guinea to find out why everbody down there at the chemical research center is turning into zombies. What the hey, they just had a little genetic DNA accident, and now these rats are eating off people's faces and all the lab assistants are turning zombie and chewing off each other's shoulders. But when the SWAT team gets over there with this blond-bimbo TV reporter, they find out that a lot of the jungle tribes have turned into Buckwheat zombies and started making little boys eat their daddies and stuff like that and the only way to get rid of em is to use a shotgun on their brains until they disappear. Meanwhile all the zombie natives start eating dead people and the bimbo decides she needs to stop this by painting big white circles on her breasts so they'll think she's one of them, but then things get a little too nasty when the zombies want to eat her fingers and so she has to escape with the SWAT team in a four-wheel drive vehicle and then take this Evinrude out to the island where the research center is, and then they all have to fight about nine thousand Buckwheat zombies at once.

We're talking seven breasts. Maggot closeups. Forty-six dead bodies. One motor vehicle chase. Five on-camera vomiting scenes. Heads roll. Hands roll. Fingers roll. Forearms roll. Intestines roll. Seven quarts blood. Two soldiers eaten alive. Two rat dinners. Two and a half stars. Joe Bob says check this sucker out. ∎

Friday the 13th, Part 4
Had Better Be Good—
They've Made It Four Times

Remember when Betsy Palmer got her head sliced off with a machete and movie history was made? Course you do. We all do. I think all our lives were changed on June 13, 1980, the *original Friday the 13th,* the dawn of the eighties, the day red meat came back into the American diet. In Friday *Numero uno* Betsy played "I've Got a Secret" one too many times, and then when she shot Bing Crosby's son through the eye with an arrow, let's face it, it was all over, the woman was setting herself up for the Benihana treatment.

I don't want to get all choked up talking about past history, though. I'm not even gonna mention the ax in the face, the double-reverse blade through the bimbo's throat, the scene where Jason becomes a born-again mongoloid, or the national *Friday the 13th, Part 2* scandal when the Motion Picture Airhead Association told everybody they were gonna X-rate the sucker unless the spear-through-the-twin-humps scene came out. We all have our personal favorite *Friday the 13th* highlight scenes. Mine is the one in *Numero two-o* where Jason sticks Betsy Palmer's mummified head in Alice's icebox. That scene always said a lot to me personally. In my book, it pretty much stated the final word on the subject of personal grooming in America.

I've said it before, but I've got to give credit where it's due. Some people know how to make sequels and some people don't. Like *Halloween III,* the one that didn't have Jamie Lee Curtis, we all *know* that was a joke. But these *Friday the 13th* people know their sequels. These people don't just make up a new story. These people made the *exact same movie* four times in a row.

I guess you know what I'm leading up to. I guess you know what day it was last week.

It's time again.

Friday the 13th, Part 4 starts with Jason the Mongolard getting crated up and put in the ambulance and took off to the morgue so they can put him in the deep freeze. We all know this don't mean diddly to Jason, specially since he already spent twenty-two years growing moss on his arms at the bottom of Crystal Lake, and while he was down there he had time to find a hockey-goalie mask to wear over his lizard face.

First thing off the bat, this nerd working at the morgue is horsing around the utility room trying to get a nurse to get down on the concrete and make like Fritz Von Erich trying to execute a double leg lock. Only all the bimbo will do is toss off lines like "I am *not* going to fake any more orgasms for you," and "You're the Super Bowl of self-abuse," until the guy gives up and goes back to watching TV Aerobicise to get his jollies.

We know what this means. It's biodegradable human garbage time. These two jerkolas didn't even have actual human sex before Jason decided to turn their bodies into grape Jell-O. They just *thought* about it a lot. (One thing I like about these numbers is they have a lot of moral philosophy mixed in.) He gets a hacksaw to the throat with a twist. She gets sliced open like a fried catfish. And then a few minutes after that this fat girl is sitting by the road eating a banana and trying to hitch, and somebody comes along and shoves a knife through the back of her throat so it comes out the front, and I know, you probly have problems with this one.

You're thinking, Is the fat-girl throat-gouging necessary to the plot? After all, she didn't have sex. She didn't screw around with anybody. She didn't even get a ride. But you have to remember, she was FAT.

As you all know, I don't approve of gratuitous violence unless it's necessary to the plot. That's why I had to explain about the fat girl being fat.

Okay, who can tell me what

happens next? That's right. The kids go back in the woods.

Why do they go back in the woods? Because they think Jason's dead? Because they're horny? Because they like to drink Coors and play Def Leppard on their Sony Walkmans and make like fruitcakes?

Nope. Basically, it's because they're all dumb as a box of Ritz crackers. This, of course, is why they all deserve to die.

Down to the nitty. First this brunette sex machine (Judie Aranson) decides to take off all her clothes in the middle of the night and go down to Crystal Lake and swim around and lie in the life raft. It's not so bad when Judie gets a metal underwater surprise, but when her boyfriend (Alan Hayes) swims out there to find her, we're talking shishkebab action right through the lower privates. Then Jason puts his hockey mask back on and starts breathing around the screen and we get some more plot development: corkscrew through the hand, butcher knife in the forehead, bimbo - through - a - plate - glass - window, a particularly nice scene where a guy is stabbed through the stag-movie screen, a guy who gets his skull mashed into the bathroom tiles and his eyes gouged out with Jason's thumbs, a little nympho who gets an ax through her terry-cloth jumpsuit, another guy who gets his hands nailed to the door, the big paint-the-house-red finale, and some stuff that the high sheriffs won't let me put in the newspaper. There's also some grisly scenes.

They're calling this sucker "The Final Chapter," maybe because Jason's head gets turned into a box of melted Milk Duds at the end, but I wouldn't worry about it. The mongo's died four times now.

We're talking thirteen bodies, as usual. Sixteen breasts. Ted White does a hell of a Jason. Two gallons blood. No motor vehicle chases. No kung fu. Heads roll. Hands roll. Academy Award nominations for Kimberly Beck, the blond fox Jamie Lee Curtis screamer role; Corey Feldman, this creepy kid who hangs around making slime glopola masks; and Camilla and Carey More, as identical porkchops who ride around on their bikes trying to have mindless sex in Jason's woods. Joseph Zito, the director, gets one-half star off for cutting away too quick, especially on the butcher knife to the forehead scene. It's Joe's first time out, so I'm letting him off with a warning, but I want to tell you this one more time, Joe, if you're gonna make a sequel, *make a sequel.*

Three and a half stars. Red Meat Champion of 1984.

Joe Bob says check it out. ∎

Joe Bob's Mailbag

To Editor (San Francisco Chronicle):

One cannot help wonder that if children were being stripped naked, or stabbed with butcher knives repeatedly, or blown to pieces by a sawed-off shotgun, what kind of person "Joe Bob" would be considered then. If homosexuals were disemboweled with power drills or blacks hacked with an ax, what type of public outrage this would cause? And yet, in film after film, women are subjected to this treatment and nothing is thought to be wrong.

Women are not products, we are human beings. We are like you. We get angry, cry, meet disappointments, get bored, frustrated. We get up in the morning, go to work, pay bills, clean sinks.

This attitude indulged in by "Joe Bob" can only be inspired by hatred and fear. This sort of thing is not funny; it is only hurtful and degrading. Please stop.

Cheryl Cain
San Francisco

Dear Cheryl:

I hear you, babe. But what about a nekkid black homosexual child that attacks ladies and squeezes their eyeballs out while they're cleaning the sink? Are you gonna tell me THAT's not funny?

Brod Crawford Puts Away a Few Lobster Dinners for *Dark Forces* Role

I know a lot of you girls were boning up for the Dallas Cowboys Cheerleaders written test last weekend and so you didn't have time to hang around Kip's Big Boy acting like you didn't know your Danskin straps were hanging halfway down your arms. Frankly, I needed the time off, because I was sick of hearing about how goldanged frigging *terrific* Vida Stegall's tryout routine is. It's this Interpretive Aerobicize number called "Mr. Landry, Let's Boogie," and it has a lot of Fellowship of Christian Athletes theme songs in it and backup vocals going:

> Get down, Tom, get down
> Gonna get down, Tom, get down

And ever time they say "get down" Vida does a double overhead leg kick and lands upside down on her hands and comes about a half inch from knocking her teeth out, if you know what I mean and I think you do.

I'm sure it's truly amazing and all that, but my personal opinion is Vida don't have the chance of a mangy scrap dog when it comes to the Texas Stadium finals on May the fifth. I *told* Vida last year she was gonna have to change her name. I *told* her she needed something like Buffi or Teri or Sandi, or *maybe* she could even risk it on a "y" name like Vikky, or your "ie" like Melodie, but "a" names weren't gonna cut it. Especially not Vida. Tisha maybe, but not Vida. If Vida was black, she could go for something African like Lola Falana, but Vida's as white as the little box by John Glenn's name on the ballot.

Now it's too late and there's not a durn thing Vida can do. About all that can happen is she can try to score a hundred on the written test. And even though I'm violently opposed to the Cowboys Cheerleaders written test, because I think it's watered down the quality of the stock the past couple years, and even though I've lodged a formal protest with Tom Landry and Bum Bright on this

issue, I'm such a nice guy that I'm gonna print a few more sample questions this week so that Vida can have a fighting chance.

Numero uno: What is a quarter?

a. 20 cents

b. 15 minutes

c. Something the fans throw on the field when the cheerleaders bend over

Numero two-o: What are the Cowboys' colors?

a. Blue

b. Silver

c. Black, white and Rafael Septien

Numero three-o: What does Roger Staubach do?

a. Sells Rolaids

b. Takes Rolaids

c. Talks through his nose

d. Stands around saying "Gee whiz, it sure was nice to get kicked in the hiney by Tom Landry all those years"

Numero four-o: What is meant by the term "pigskin"?

a. Too Tall Jones's nickname

b. A team in Washington

c. A rubber object carried by the Cowboys Cheerleaders when they go to crippled children's hospitals and Bob Hope specials and Japanese talk shows in order to discuss the importance of human feelings in the world today

Now, before you girls go home and start working on these answers, I want you to remember that there are *only* thirty-six places on the team and there are about 17,824 bimbos trying out, and the difference between making it and falling on your sleek and firm haunches, the difference between putting on that Cowboys Cheerleaders two-inch fringe vest and tying on that halter top and sticking your toes in those white vinyl boots, the difference between becoming a Network TV Bimbo and just going back to hanging around the bus station—the difference, I'm telling you, amounts to one word.

Breasts.

That's all I'm gonna say on the subject. I think you know what needs to be done. Go for it.

I got so carried away there I almost forgot about the flick. I mainly went to check out *Dark Forces* because of Broderick Crawford being in it. Brod, baby, where you been? Haven't seen you in a few thousand years. (Can we have a little *Highway Patrol* music here?) Brod's been putting away a few lobster dinners, judging by his physique, so most of this movie he just sits around frowning at people and talking without opening his mouth, like he usually does, but finally he has to start moving around a little bit because the flick has a plot and so everthing gets *real slow.*

Dark Forces starts out with this little bald-headed boy having a birthday party, and you find out the reason he's bald-headed is he's been puking up blood and having chemotherapy and it's about time to take him to Disneyland, if you know what I mean. I thought no way, José, I'm not watching this sucker, I don't want to see a whole movie about cancer babies. But *no problema,* because this clown that comes to his party turns out to be Jesus Christ. I'm talking Robert Powell, who was the Big Guy on that *Jesus of Nazareth* TV series, only now he's got a Mac Davis haircut and he's started wearing Neil Diamond shirts and painting his fingernails black so he looks like Bert Convy with a demon inside him. I never did figure out what this Powell guy is, but he comes by the house one day and the kid gets better and grows hair and starts talking again, and then Powell teaches him to make the marbles on his Chinese checkers set pop around the board without human hands, and he teaches him to concentrate real hard and when he does the windshield on the car will bust out, and when all this bullstuff starts happening the kid's father gets freaked and starts campaigning for office.

I forgot to mention one other thing about the demon guy. Everwhere he goes women want to hike up their skirts and say stuff like "Anyone for strip poker?" and when that happens Powell has to teach the bimbos how to control themselves and keep their clothes on. Then other times he likes to rape em. I think the devil is making him do it, but I can't swear by it because this flick has a bunch of plot getting in the way of the story.

Okay, so what happens is Powell starts staying over in the kid's mother's bedroom, if you know what I mean, and I can't rightly blame him because the woman wears her dresses down to about here and she is what you might call *hot*. But then the kid's daddy gets p.o.ed, and the kid's daddy is David Hemmings, and you probly know what that means: Blow-up.

You may be wondering what Big Brod has to do with all this. I'll tell you. Big Brod is David Hemmings's political advisor and Mafia hitman. Big Brod's line is "We put you in the computer and the computer said you'll do." Big Brod calls the shots. When Big Brod sees the Mac Davis Demon levitating pianos and cutting off old ladies' fingers at a party, he thinks maybe something's wrong. So he decides to put the guy in jail and then blow him away before he can screw up the campaign. Before this dude is over, we're talking some serious chopsocky.

Four breasts. Three dead bodies. Three quarts blood. No motor vehicle chases. Minimal kung fu. One beast, not counting Big Brod. Excellent Chinese-checkers special effects. Drive-In Academy Award nominations for Robert Powell as the clown in a Neil Diamond zoot suit; Carmen Duncan, the hot housewife, a talent of enormous proportions; and, of course, Big Brod, who turns in

a huge performance. The best demon flick of '84.

Three stars. Joe Bob says check it out. ∎

Joe Bob's Mailbag

faculty, UC School of Social Work
Kurt Schlesinger, M.D., psychoanalyst
Sheryl Ruzek, Ph.D., MPH, faculty, UC Department of Sociology
Barbara Artson, Ph.D., psychologist
William Goldman, M.D., psychiatrist
Burton Wise, M.D., neurosurgeon
Myra Wise, Ph.D., psychologist
Gloria Sparrow, J.D., attorney
Laurel Samuels, Ph.D., psychologist
Ruth Goldman, Ph.D., professor, San Francisco State
Ellen Lewin, Ph.D., anthropologist
Ann Merrill, Ph.D., anthropologist

Rachel Kahn-Hut, Ph.D., sociologist, San Francisco State
Rachelle Goodfriend, M.A., counselor
Richard Snowdon, Child Assault Prevention Project
Diana Russell, Ph.D., professor of sociology, Mills College
Muriel Brotsky, L.C.S.W., assistant director, Jewish Family Services
Velia Frost, L.C.S.W.
Philip Frost, M.D.

Dear gang:

You people would feel a whole lot better if you shortened your names and made a big dogpile and had sex together.

Mary Crosby Tries to Remember Her Lines in *Ice Pirates* Epic

Remember when the first *Billy Jack* came out? Remember what happened? *KAPLOOEY:* Bombola City. Lasted five minutes. But then some jerk in Duluth, Minnesota, got some of his buddies together and watched it 17,000 times in a row to try to jack up the box-office numbers, and it worked. Hippie kung fu. Couldn't get enough of it.

Nobody even minded that Tom Laughlin's wife was ugly as a piece of oatmeal cookie left up on the dashboard for three weeks. Everybody and his bird dog wanted to beat up some New Meskins for Peace. I have to admit I got into it myself and twisted the arms off several New Meskins over by Roswell. Course, I didn't give a hang about Peace, I just didn't like New Meskins.

Next thing that happens, *Chainsaw*. Remember?

About as popular as a fat kid doing can-openers in the pool.

Then some mass murderers over in Tupelo started watching it, and the entire state of New Jersey went to see it, and pretty soon *Texas Chainsaw Massacre* was the best teen-age cannibal flick in the history of barbecue.

Listen up now, because I'm about to make a fairly heavy point.

It took the drive-ins to make America sit up and say, "Billy who?"

It took the drive-ins to make America sit up and say, "Chain what?"

It took the drive-ins to make America sit up and say, "What the hell's a drive-in?"

And it's happening again. It's happening right now. There's a flick that's in the drive-ins now because it made about 20 cents in the hard tops. Some of the perverts and missing links in the audience already know what I'm talking about.

I'm talking *Ice Pirates*.

Now before I go into this, I need to point out that I'm on triple extended probation because of some *misunderstandings* we had

the last two weeks which I can't talk about because if I do then my fellow Babtists will sue us for about seven billion dollars and I wouldn't like that because the Babtists have already built enough giant Kleenex boxes with steeples and I don't want to be financing any more of those. But I'll say this. Because of various kinds of Communist pressure, the high sheriffs took a Weed Eater to my column again last week. Some people just have *filthy* minds. I'm so disgusted I'm not even gonna mention what the high sheriffs threatened to do to my gazebos if I try to sneak *Crotch Shots on Parade* back into the newspaper. They think I made that up. They don't believe it's a gay musical comedy in New York City. I had to promise I wouldn't bring it up again. *Crotch Shots on Parade,* that is. And I probly won't.

Where do you start with an epic like *Ice Pirates?* How about a little robot kung fu? How about some *Babes of Bagdad* roller derby? (Remember when Paulette Goddard put on a steel-reinforced Maidenform and nineteen pieces of costume jewelry and made like Colonel Khadafy's dancing girl? That was *Babes of Bagdad.*) How about Mary Crosby acting like she's trying to remember her lines from the last episode of *Starsky and Hutch?* As you can see, when you've got *Ice Pirates,* you've got it all.

Okay, here goes. *Ice Pirates* is about a bunch of guys in "Captain from Tortuga" costumes who go bouncing around the universe trying to find ice cubes so they can carry em back to their high-and-dry galaxy, only it's not that easy because some meanies called the Templars own all the fresh-water supplies and the Templars have a robot army that wants to put Robert Urich in jail because they hate the way he grins through the side of his mouth on *Vegas*. Anyhow, the Templars capture Robert Urich, the head beefcake pirate, and Mary Crosby, the princess who likes to shop at Frederick's of Hollywood, and a bunch of their friends, and they all go to the Water Planet and get put on the human-body assembly line where they're tied on a conveyor belt and all these gears start carving their clothes off and then old coots with razor blades start shaving off their whiskers and then this enormous bear-claw steel trap gets em between the legs and turns em into white-haired gay hairdressers in spaghetti-strap T-shirts who work in the Water Planet sewerage plant. I was personally looking forward to Robert Urich losing his gazebos and turning into a white-haired gay hairdresser in a spaghetti-strap T-shirt, but at the last minute the horny evil Water Planet queen saves him and his sidekick and lets the two of em go to a punk-rock party where they escape after they program this robot to speak jive and then swipe some giant Big Wheels and start popping wheelies.

Next thing, John Carradine stands inside something that looks like the *Barbarella* love tube and says evil stuff. Big John is the Head Templar.

Next thing, Robert Urich discovers a space herpy on his ship, and it looks pretty disgusting, but he chooses not to tell anyone about it, which is his right as a human being.

Then the thirsty pirates go to a planet called Sweetwater, which is inhabited by midgets and bikers who haven't taken a shower since 1936. One of the bikers makes the mistake of talking to Anjelica Huston while she's dressed up like Mick Jagger and she has to slash his head off with a bull-whip and then put another guy's eye out because he doesn't sound "sincere." I know the feeling.

Then the pirates go to Prairie Dog Town and get chased around by the world's largest four-wheel-drive vehicle while it crushes a bunch of pet burros and baby javelinas, and then they go back to the spaceship and get grossed out because the space herpy jumps out of their Thanksgiving turkey, and then they're attacked by bikini-clad Samurai women on horseback, and then a Negro Tarzan swoops down and cuts a king's head off, and then Mary Crosby and Robert Urich go into the bedroom and big Bob says, "I think I should take my saber out," and then there's a robot gang fight and Mary Crosby gets pregnant and I guess that's enough plot because I don't want to give away the story.

We're talking the most underrated and unappreciated Outer Space Bestiality and Mindless Violence Flick of the last two months. Four complete breasts and quite a few see-throughs. One gallon blood. Four motor vehicle chases. Human kung fu, robot fu, bimbo fu. Seven beasts, including Drive-In Academy Award nominations for the space herpy and the frog lady. Fourteen dead bodies. Three heads roll. Eye rolls. Four stars.

Joe Bob says check it out.

Joe Bob's Mailbag ———

Dear Joe Bob:

As a woman of many hyphens, I am disgusted by your use of subliminal suggestion in your name as an insult to all womankind. As any bright young pearl-of-the-party is sure to pick up on, your name conjures the most tasteless perversion when the "J" and "B" are transposed. Please don't print this letter as I do not wish to call undue attention to your subtle derogatory hint. As for telling any of my fellow sisters about it, my lips are sealed.

Lucy Hopgood-Hilary-
Surnan
Moody, Calif.

Dear Luce:

I obviously have no idea what you're talking about, cause what does Boe Bob Jriggs mean?

Please be more specific about your perversions in the future no matter whether you deliver them in writing or orally.

Burned-up NOW Bimbos Can't Hold a Candle to *Firestarter*

I didn't want to have to do this. I'm not the kind of guy who looks for trouble. I never like to cram huge farm implements down the throats of people and watch them come out the other end, because that's a durn nasty business. In fact, I was really counting on a quiet weekend at home. I thought maybe I'd buy a *Penthouse* and read the up-close-and-personal interview with Wayne Newton, where he explains why he's not in the Mafia, and then I was gonna help Rhett Beavers install his earth-station TV dish 'cause he claims he can pick up educational flicks from Denmark, and then I probly would have gone out to the Century Drive-In in Grand Prairie to catch *Please Don't Eat My Mother,* which I learn something new from every time I watch it and, let's face it, we can all stand to learn something new once in a while.

Like I say, I didn't want to have to do this. But I'm afraid I don't have any choice. I'm afraid I'm gonna have to make like Chuck Bronson and start wiping some scum off the sidewalk. I'm afraid it's time to name names. I'm afraid I'm being attacked again by the you-know-what. Yes, they're on the rag again.

I'm talking Invasion of the Ladies with Excessive Facial Hair.

Last week, in the drive-in-hating city of San Francisco, California, the National Organization of Bimbos started passing out Communist manifestos at something called the End of the World Fair, one of those stop-the-nukes deals, to try to get "Joe Bob Goes to the Drive-In" forcibly removed from the pages of American newspapers. On the front of these suckers it said *"CANCEL JOE BOB,"* and on the back it said "Violence against women will not be tolerated in the world or in the media —Cancel Joe Bob Briggs!" and then it had room on there for a message to the San Francisco *Chronicle,* where all the editors were so scared of getting beat over the head with purses that they had to get on the horn to Clint Eastwood and try to get him to come

downtown with his Smith and Wesson .44 Automag and hope some bimbos would go ahead and make his day.

Most of you turkeys know this ain't the first time the National Organization of Bimbos tried to scissor off my gazebos. In fact, I admire their spunk. They write more letters to Joe Bob's Mailbag than the Babtists, the gays, Donnie Wildmon's Legion of Decency, the french-fry head mayor of Irving, Texas, and the employees of Jimmy Dean's Pork Sausage plant combined. I don't have time to read all these suckers anymore, and they're starting to clutter up the backseat of the Toronado, so let's get it over with. Let's get to the bottom of this thing.

Okay, gals, what's wrong?

Was it something I said?

Maybe there's a reasonable explanation. Did you all get bumped from the Dallas Cowboys cheerleaders finals? Did you break a fingernail?

Is it that time of the month again?

Whatever it is, you gals do *not* have a positive mental attitude and I want to help out because I have enormous respect for women, and I especially have enormous respect for enormous women. Come on, let's see a little smile. That's better. Now. Here's a few tips you might use to get this *anger* out of your system:

Numero uno: Buy a new dress and put it on your VISA card.

Numero two-o: Go down to a

mall that has a Frederick's and try on some sexy underwear.

Numero three-o: Better yet, go down to Georgette Klinger's and for a hundred bucks they'll give you a makeover and some fingernail wraps and fix your hair like Susan Anton's.

Numero four-o: Stop off at Häagen-Dazs and treat yourself to a couple scoops double chocolate. You can start your diet again tomorrow.

Now, if you do one of these things you'll probly feel better instantly and you won't have to go around passing out leaflets and raising your blood pressure and making your mascara run. But in case it doesn't work—in case you still feel like lighting aerosol cans of Breck Creme Rinse and throwing em through the windows of the *Chronicle*—then I have one more solution.

I personally challenge the Communist premier of the San Francisco National Organization of Bimbos to a nude mud-wrestling match. Three falls. No holds barred. Kung fu allowed. Bimbo fu also allowed. We can hold it at Berkeley and charge admission. Winner take all.

Sorry to get carried away with that, but sometimes I feel like a United Way agency and I just *really* want to help those ladies deal with their aggression. Meantime, Big Steve King has a new flick out called *Firestarter*. (This is only Steve's second movie in two months and the fourth or fifth one in the last year. What's wrong, big guy, you send the type-writer out for repairs?) What we got here is a little girl who when she gets mad she can stare at your shirt and turn your body into Bananas Foster.

It's the same little girl from *E.T.*, the indoor-bullstuff flick that gave monsters from outer space a bad name, and the way you know she's about to turn somebody into a Roman candle is she stares real hard and her hair flies out sideways like a birddog that's backed into an electric fence. The CIA is trying to catch the little girl so they can strap her on a B-52 and nuke Russia.

David Keith is her daddy, and she and him are running around accidentally setting people's shoes on fire because the CIA killed the little girl's mommy and stuffed her in the ironing closet so she wouldn't talk about the LSD experiment that turned em all into psychic cherry bombs. David Keith was so p.o.ed about that that he made two G-men into blind zombies just by scrunching his hands up through his hair and staring at em like they just totaled his Camaro. That little stunt got em in so much trouble that they had to go hide out at Art Carney's house.

Then the CIA tries to kidnap the little girl, only when they get there she goes out on the front porch and lasers about sixteen government agents and turns their cars into Tinker-Toy sets and makes Art Carney's farm look like Miami Beach after the frat boys from Georgia get through with it.

Anyhow, the CIA holds the

two of em prisoner so they can study the little girl and watch her turn wood chips into Boy Scout campfires and make cinder-block walls into a gravel parking lot, and George C. Scott acts like he's the janitor so he can get the little girl to be his friend and do whatever it is that Martin Sheen wants her to do. Martin Sheen is the boss of the CIA, and one time he says to George C. Scott, "You know, if she ever figures this thing out, you're gonna know what a steak feels like inside a microwave oven."

But he's wrong. It's better than that. By the final scene we got enough quick-fried FBI agents for a fire-juggling act on *Star Search*. These guys look like somebody just poured lighter fluid on Richard Pryor.

Hot stuff. Forty-five dead bodies, a new 1984 record. Nine motor vehicle explosions, including a copter. One gallon blood. No breasts. (The only choices were the little girl and Louise Fletcher, so, hey, what can I say?) One beast (George C. Scott as a cigar-store Indian). Extra points for the exploding-golf-cart scene. Great kung fu scene (Big George kills a guy with a single chop on the nose). Exploding heads. Drive-In Academy Award nomination for Drew Barrymore, the little girl, and Mark Lester, the director who never lets the plot get in the way of the special effects.

Three and a half stars for the body count alone.

Joe Bob says check it out. ∎

Joe Bob Warns You: This Wimpy Spielberg Stuff Isn't Fit for Outdoor People

Steven Spielberg is a wimp. I'm sorry, I had to get that out of my system. I don't normally like to use strong language in the newspaper, but let's face it, the man is a walking can of Chef Boyardee noodles.

Now, I know about all you punkola drughead orange-hair geeks. I know you been camping out at the Monkeyplex 8 so you can fork over 5 bucks, plus 17 more for popcorn, to watch Harrison Ford swing on ropes and smash balsa wood with his bare hands.

I know about all you weasel-face jackleg nerds that drive Caprices and work at IBM. You guys been waiting all *year* for this, han't you? You stayed straight up to now, you made everybody think you knew what you were talking about, you avoided the indoor bullstuff and watched flicks the way our American God meant for em to be watched.

But what happens when Steve Spielberg comes along with another wimp picture?

You say, "Maybe Steve's not a wimp anymore. Maybe this one's a winner."

And then you go watch the sucker and what do you have?

You want your mind to turn to Jell-O?

You want me to have to report you to the national wimp patrol?

You want to have forced sex with E.T.?

I'm trying to say this in a nice way, because this double-life, indoor-outdoor business has a way of eating you up inside. You may think, Just this once, but pretty soon you're sneaking in to see Dustin the Midget Hoffman in *Tootsie,* and then it's on to the hard stuff: Meryl Streep.

Now I ask you, Do you or do you not want to go to bed at night with Meryl Streep on your conscience?

I didn't think so.

Pretty nasty thought, isn't it?

Okay then, just remember last year, when little Stevie Spielberg got ahold of one of the greatest drive-in directors in the history of the world, Tobe Hooper, and Stevie said to him, "Tobe, I want you to make a picture for me." And Tobe's from Austin and

so he don't always know which end of the camera to look in, and he needed a little spare jack at the time, so he says, "What?" And so what happens? The guy who gave the world *Texas Chainsaw Massacre* turns out a piece of pure-dee Southern California crapola called *Poltergeist,* about a TV set that sucks up little girls.

So when you start thinking about this Indiana Jones dealie, just think of it this way: This year it's just Harrison Ford. Next year it might be something completely off the deep end, like Goldie Hawn.

Let's talk snakes just for a minute, just to give you one example what I'm talking about. Little Stevie supposedly did this big-deal snake scene in *Raiders Numero Uno.* But remember in '82 when *Venom* came out with the black mamba that crawled up Alan Bates's pants leg? Let's see Stevie match that one with his indoor bullstuff. Remember the black mamba camera that went all over the house at snake-eye level, so we could see the whites of their eyes just before they bought the farm with *repeated* black mamba strikes at stomach level, causing quick, extremely painful death, followed by more repeated strikes at the face? Best of all, remember *Black Cobra,* the all-time great drive-in movie that asked the eternal question, How much snake can one woman take?

Now *that* was a snake flick.

So this week we got another one. While everybody else was folding theirselves into balloon animals so they could squeeze through the doors to watch the itsy-bitsy screen at the mall, I stretched out in the Toronado to see *Conquest.* That's the title, and it's pretty much the title of my own life, but the main reason I'm bringing it up is this: Sabrina is back.

We all remember Sabrina. Sabrina Siani. She was the bimbo in *Ator the Fighting Eagle* who had to kung-fu a tribe of Amazons for the honor of giving her body to Miles O'Keeffe, only Miles O'Keeffe didn't want her, which shows you where *his* career's going these days. But anyhow, Sabrina is trying to pass herself off in *Conquest* as Sabrina *Sellers,* but don't worry, it's the same gal, I'd recognize those talents anywhere.

Sabrina's got a bigger role this time. She's a bloodsucking cannibal queen who likes to get nekkid and let long, thick snakes slide all over her body while she wiggles her thighs like a Calvin Klein commercial. Ever once in a while she'll send out one of her soldiers, these apeman guys dressed up in Wily Coyote faces, to bring her back the head of a virgin. She likes to let all the Missing Links rip the virgin's clothes off and spread their legs apart so that Sabrina can come along and hack off the top of their skulls like a coconut and then suck the good stuff out of a straw.

I know, I know, you've seen it all before, but here's the good part: whenever Sabrina has snake sex, she always sees George Rivero come running up with a bow and arrow and shoot a laser through her body. Well, we all know that George han't done diddly since the Duke died, and if you see this movie you'll know why: George let his hair grow out like he's Cochise the Hippie, and so it's not hard to believe he'd go around shooting laser arrows through Sabrina.

But before you can figure out how George got the laser bow, you got to go through a whole lot of plot where you see this kid named Ilias shooting Planet of the Apes people through the gazebos. Then George tells the kid that if he'll show him how to use the bow, George'll tell the kid how to talk to the animals, and so they go off to a whorehouse and have a pretty good time till somebody sets their cave on fire and one of the bimbos gets her face cut off and before it's all over George has to take a slingshot to seven or eight Wily Coyotes and pretty much soak the desert with Heinz 57.

Sabrina is a little p.o.ed, so she burns up one of the Ape People and then tells this Erector Set warlord that if he'll go kill the bow-and-arrow man, then she will "offer you my body and my soul forever."

Miles O'Keeffe didn't want it, but this dude says okay.

Meanwhile, George and the kid are walking around in West Texas or somewhere and talking to the birds and dodging some poison darts that fly out of the scrubgrass. Then the kid gets shot in the leg with one of em, and these giant sores start erupting all over his body, and this purple airplane glue starts coming out of em, and pretty soon we're talking AIDS. George has to go get some Tyler roses or something to rub on the kid's leg, and while he's doing that we get a fairly decent zombie attack with about twelve zombies rising up out of a lagoon, and then we get some kung fu with George Rivero fighting a George Rivero lookalike with ten-inch double Nunchaku sticks made out of tree limbs and rope. Then the two of em go fight some Mummy Men who wear fishnet hose over their face, and then George has to kung-fu some killer bats, and pretty soon we're ready for the paint-the-cave-red finale, where George faces off with Sabrina and they both try to chop off anything with skin on it.

Best sword-and-sorcery since *Deathstalker.* Three heads roll. Arms roll. Legs roll. Top of skull rolls. Twenty-five breasts. Five gallons blood. At least sixty beasts. No motor vehicle chases. Excellent kung fu. Beast fu. Snakes in every major scene. Drive-In Academy Award nominations for Sabrina, for two obvious reasons; George Rivero, for his performance in *Rio Lobo;* Andrew Occhipinti, the Kid, for be-

ing the guy who has X-rated sex with Bo Derek in *Bolero;* and Lucio Fulci, the director best remembered for *Zombie II,* who turns out the best American drive-in flicks Italy has to offer.

Call it three stars.

Joe Bob says check it out. ∎

Joe Bob's Mailbag ──

Dear Briggs,

You blew it again, Briggs. All you had to do was have "The Bounty" shown at a Drive-in Theater, and you could of reviewed it. Imagine, "Three hundred bouncing breasts, one bucket of blood, one head crushed, lots of flogging, lots of sex, no beasts."

Also, G.C. Scott is a bad choice for "Fire Starter". Should of used you instead.

Sincerely,
Donald N. Wright
Garland, Tex.

Dear Don:
Those were foreign breasts.

Our Ronnie Reagan: He's a Drive-In Kinda Guy, If You Know What We Mean

Dear Ronnie,

I realize you're not gonna have anywhere to hang out when you come to Dallas this summer to get crowned king of America. The Dallas high sheriffs are doing everthing they can to make sure it's the most boring convention in the history of the world, including making all the Communist protesters go fifteen miles out to a campground so they won't mess up the valet parking. We called up John Hinckley's dad the other day to see if they're gonna let the boy come home anytime soon for a visit, but the doctors said no way, José, even though he han't said anything about Jodie Foster's thighs in several weeks. The only thing else that might happen is we could have some folks coming down from the hippie camps in Tennessee where they've been smoking Arkansas Polio Weed ever since 1967 and waiting for the end of the world. So those people might have group sex out in front of Neiman-Marcus, but other than that there won't be anything to look at.

That's why I'm writing to you, Big Fella.

A few of us were out at the Gemini Drive-In committing Class C misdemeanors the other night, and somebody mentioned that we would either have to bus in some guys from Houston so we could beat the stuffings out of em or else we would need some other form of entertainment during the G.O.P. Toga Party.

Then somebody said that we already *got* everthing we need in the drive-in archives.

We got *Girls on Probation,* that law-and-order classic.

We got *Cowboy from Brooklyn.* (Love your Texas accent, Ron.)

We got *Naughty but Nice.* Of course you were naughty.

Of *course* we got *An Angel from Texas.* (Starring you and the ex.)

We got *Juke Girl.* (Nice vigilante stuff.)

We got *The Girl from Jones Beach,* the flick based completely on the shape of Virginia Mayo's body.

We got *Tugboat Annie Sails Again,* where you worked for The Skipper, a/k/a Alan Hale.

In other words, we've decided you're really a drive-in kind of guy. You were making drive-in movies before there was hardly any drive-ins. Now a lot of in-door-bullstuff people han't seen all these flicks and so they wondered what the big deal was about your acting, and I had to tell em, "Ron was the guy that, five minutes after you saw the movie, you never could remember he was in it."

And you and I both know, every movie *needs* a guy like that to do a little plot in the middle of the story, like the time when you made the speech about academic freedom right in the middle of *She's Working Her Way Through College,* and the entire cast had to act like they were listening to you. I don't have to remind *you,* Ron, that it's durn thankless work to always be walking around behind Errol Flynn holding his sword and being a wimp for Barbara Stanwyck to step on.

But what I'm trying to say is, since you don't have anything to do here for the whole week, we'd preciate the heck out of it if you'd make like a baker's truck and haul buns out to the Lewisville Drive-In or the Kaufman Pike or any other drive-in site of your choosing and prove to America that you *are* a drive-in kinda guy and we'll put a mike up top the concession stand so you can address the non-Communist drive-in-going public

of America and then we'll show *Hong Kong* where you star as a guy who opens his own Army Surplus Store, and after that if we have time we'll watch *That Hagen Girl,* where you fall for Shirley Temple even though she's jailbait.

Also, maybe the hippies will put up a picket line and we'll have to bring in the Dallas S.W.A.T. team and billy-club em into submission.

Or if you don't like that idea, we can tool over to Fort Worth and get sloshed.

Either way, lemme know in the next week or so which flicks you want us to put up on the big screen. Just between you and me, dude, this could be extremely important in the white-trash precincts, including my own trailer park, if you know what I mean and I believe you do.

We're already chalking you up for the "W" column, Ronnieboy, mainly because Walter Mondale is a box of rocks and Gary Hart is so pink that you have to stick his head in a vat of Johnson's Baby Powder ever morning just to get him ready for TV.

And, Ron, one more thing. When you get out to the drive-in that night, try to keep it clean. I don't want to have to mention that again. ∎

If You're Lookin' for *Bad Manners,* You've Come to the Right Place

Wanda Bodine kept having these people come in the beauty shop and say "Can you make my hairdo look like a frozen catcher's mitt that got stuck on my head, only when you shake it the light goes through it like a kaleidoscope and sometimes pieces of it fall off and you can play Pick-Up Sticks on the floor?"

Wanda's usual answer to this request was "What?"

And then they'd have to say "You know, I want my hair to look like Sarah Purcell's on *Real People.*"

And Wanda'd say, "Not everyone can wear a Sarah Purcell, you know."

And maybe they'd say forget it and maybe they'd say, "I feel like carrying around an extra thirty, forty pounds on my head," and so Wanda would go ahead and give 'em the Purcell Treatment.

Anyhow, Wanda Bodine's registered trademark on the Purcell Treatment came through last week and so we went over to the grand premiere on the Grapevine Highway to watch seventy or eighty bimbos do some serious ozone damage with aerosol cans. Do you remember that time on *Real People* when the two homosexual midgets taught a flock of penguins how to play rugby? That's basically what we're talking here. They had these giant pictures of Sarah hung up everwhere so the shampoo ladies would get inspiration, and then they would take each individual bimbo and string her up by her heels and blindfold her and walk around her in a circle with industrial-strength cans of Aqua Net aimed at her head. You had your choice of the three-can treatment or the five-can treatment, but State Farm was refusing fire insurance on the five-can.

Once they were soaked to the gills with Aqua Net, the bimbos were returned to upright positions and then Wanda passed out ball peen hammers so the hairdressers could pound every head into Purcell perfection, so the hair sticks out exactly eight inches from the side of the head and can be used as an umbrella for up to three people. You may recall the episode of *Real People* when this African tribe sewed elephant ears on the shoulders of a sacred pit bulldog. This is basically what the thing looks like when you get through with it.

Unfortunately, we had one little accident when Chloris, the shampoo girl affectionately known as Ugly on a Stick, dropped a Bic lighter on Fran Stuble's forehead and started a two-alarm brushfire that caused Richard Pryor to send Fran a telegram a couple days later. Wanda was gonna fire Chloris until they found out Fran liked her face better *after* the surgery. So Wanda just decided to take $29.95 off Ugly on a Stick's salary, the cost of one Purcell, cause the brain doctors had to cut off Fran's Purcell in Parkland Emergency Room.

Also, now Fran talks with a Vietnamese accent. The doctors said this was impossible, but Fran goes to the Holy Interstate Pentecostal Church and I happen to know that on Sunday morning when they get down on all fours and lick the carpet and start yelling for Jesus, there's this one old guy that starts doing a Ho Chi Minh voice like he's been watching too much kung fu and then everbody starts hallucinating about being Boat People getting skishkabobbed by Satan and dumped in the Chinese Ocean. I just wanted to point this out so you wouldn't think Fran was crazy or something.

This reminds me how a lot of you people in North Carolina been writing in to say "Joe Bob Goes to the Drive-In" is satanic.

So I'd like to state my official position on Satan one more time:

Numero uno: I'm opposed to Satan.

Numero two-o: I'm a Babtist once-saved-always-saved sinner, and so Satan stays way the hell off in Communist places like Massachusetts.

Numero three-o: I only heard of one place in North Carolina where they got Satan, and that's in the big-deal eastern wimpola snob capital of french-fry-head intellectuals: Chapel Hill.

Okay, I'm leaving you doubters in the hands of the Lord and going on to *Bad Manners,* which is this nerds-in-prison flick I saw last week. Take five or six fourteen-year-old Southern California surf-brain punks, stick em in reform school, zap em two or three times with electric cattle prods, and pretty soon you got a fairly decent drive-in movie. We're talking the San Quentin of orphan homes, where they got this psychiatrist who goes around asking questions like "How did you relate to your mother?"

And this kid says, "I love my mother."

And the shrink says, "Yeah, you and the Los Angeles Dodgers."

Most of the time these punks just walk around having mashed-potato fights and sticking things down their pants, but ever once in a while they do something gross. Like the time when five of em get together and cut the bejabbers out of their fingers so they can be bloody brothers. This makes the warden a little p.o.ed. So when they're about to get turned into chicken-fried steak by this principal who has glasses made out of Co-Cola bottles, they decide to make a run for it and head for Santa Barbara.

They wanna go find their buddy, a little blond punk called the Mouse, because Martin Mull and Karen Black went to the orphanage and bought him for a pet. But once they got the kid home, he started breaking into daddy's computer and giving away all the family money, and then he started hassling Garth, their son the Samurai Hare-Krishna Buddha who likes to chew the heads off smallmouth bass. Then he started hiding in the shower so he could flash Instamatics of his stepsister's itty-bitty breasts. Then he started eating the dinner bell. Then he started jumping up and down on the roof of daddy's Ferrari Roadster. Other than this, he was a pretty good kid.

Anyhow, the guys from reform school hit the road while the nun is off in the chapel getting her jollies, only they get lost up by Bakersfield and have to go in the bus station and steal wallets and start a brawl and set off the indoor sprinkler system and try to con Richard Deacon out of some Greyhound tickets. They steal enough jack to take a taxi with a drunk driver who feeds em Budweiser all the way to Santa Barbara.

I'd just like to point out right here that drunk driving is no laughing matter, and the driver shoulda limited his consumption to Miller Lite, Coors, or Löwenbräu only.

Then they throw up in the cab.

Finally it's time to trash Martin Mull's house, drive a motorcycle into the swimming pool, set the pool on fire, shoot up Karen Black's sculpture gallery with a pistol, attack Garth with whipped cream, get in a fistfight with Mouse's parents, steal a Triumph, and do some other things that I won't mention because in my opinion they are irresponsible and destructive acts of vandalism.

Best nerds-in-cages of 1984. We're talking two dead bodies. Six breasts. One gallon blood. Great who-cut-the-cheese scene. Three motor vehicle chases, including one crash-and-burn. One wheelchair crash. Superb cattle-prod effects. Three food fights. One shower scene. Mad dogs. One face-eating rat. Best *Born to Be Wild* biker rip-off scene of the year. One transvestite. Terrific Valium pancake scene. Drive-In Academy Award nominations for Karen Black, for getting thrown through a plate-glass window; Michael Hentz, El Nerdo; and Martin Mull, for getting paid for this flick.

We're talking three stars. Joe Bob says check it out. ■

You Know What We're Talkin About in *Breakin'* —a Whole Lot of Dance Fu

There used to be some racists in my neighborhood, so ever once in a while me and Bobo Rodriguez would go over and beat the tar out of em. Normally I'm not a violent kind of guy, specially when it means I might get my face mashed into a potato pancake, but one thing I learned from *Billy Jack* is there's times when you just have to let a 32-ounce Louisville Slugger do the talking or else the violent bigots and intolerant people will take over your city.

I never did ask Bobo what race he was, but I'm pretty sure he was a Negro. His skin was the color of Taster's Choice Decaffeinated, which means he could go either way, but one time he tried to change his name to Bobo al-Salaam, and when he did that everybody started calling him "Al" because they thought he was saying "Al Sloan," and he kept trying to pronounce it for three, four weeks but finally he gave it up and went back to Bobo Rodriguez. The only thing I ever heard Bobo say about his roots is his family come from somewhere in Norway.

Anyhow, Bobo's the guy that first taught me about racism. Bobo's the guy that showed me it's not the color of a man's skin that matters, it's how much money he's got. Bobo used to say "Hey, look at Sammy Davis Jr. He's black, he's Jewish, he's short, he wears too much jewelry. But let's face it, he did it his way."

I used to be a racist. When I was growing up out in Lamb County, Texas, it was against the law not to be a racist. Even the black people were racists. They had to walk ten, fifteen miles out of their way to find a Meskin farmworker they could refuse to talk to. And the Meskins were just waiting around for the Vietnamese to show up so they could make boat people jokes. That's what happens when you lose a war. Pretty soon you can't go in 7-Eleven without wondering whether those guys are putting dog meat in the frozen burritos.

I got over that pretty quick, though. Racism is a nasty beast. It makes you stereotype people. I first realized this when Bobo introduced me to that enormous contribution of the black-skinned peoples of the earth to this great country of ours. You know what I'm talking about.

I'm talking Negro Dancing.

Rhymin and climbin, boppin and hoppin, glidin and slidin, jukin and pukin—whatever you wanta call it, we're talking a whole lot of *g*'s missing out of their words.

Bobo Rodriguez was a great Negro Dancer his ownself. Back in the sixties, he was one of those guys who would do splits out in front of the high school marching band and lean back so far he could turn his body into a piece of human salt-water taffy and touch the Astroturf with his forehead between his ankles and keep on stridin till he did a 360 flip and wrapped his ankles around his neck and spun a baton around his wrists like a piece of Jimmy Dean Sausage. It was too bad Bobo wasn't *in* the marching band and so he got kicked out of school for doing that.

Anyhow, I was thinking of Bobo last week when I headed out to the Century D.I. in Grand Prairie to check *Breakin'*, starring Shabba-Doo and Boogaloo Shrimp. (It's fairly obvious to me that these Muslim names are catching on.) We got some of the finest Negro Dancing since the time I saw the halftime show between Grambling State and Texas Southern in the Cotton Bowl. And those guys didn't even know how to dance on their heads. To me there's basically three kinds of break-dance head spins:

1. Basic Skull Fracture: at least three times all the way around, with major hair loss.

2. The Suicide: arms straight, legs straight, ready to use your face for a Dr. Scholl's arch support.

3. Permanent Brain Damage.

Breakin' shoulda been called *How to Teach Stupid Honkies How to Rip Up Their Danskins and Thrive on Jive.* It starts off with this *Flashdance* lookalike bimbo named Kelly doing a *Staying Alive* dance-class routine where the object is to see how much of your jumpsuit you can get bunched up around your rear end before you lose your PG. Kelly is one of those Rhodes scholars whose idea of a good time is to go sit on the beach with guys from the chorus line and talk about their Liberace record collections, if you know what I mean and I think you do. So Kelly meets this gay Negro who takes her over to Venice Beach so she can watch people do some pretzel-sandwich moves, and pretty soon a couple brain-damaged jukers named Shabba-Doo and Boogaloo are on their way over to the Arthur Murray Studios to hassle Kelly's extremely *white* teacher. He kicks em out for dancing like black people.

Next thing, a couple bad dudes from Watts show up and call the two jukers "chicken." I guess you know what that means.

Dance fu.

But Shabba-Doo and Boogaloo blow it when the big Friday-night rumble dance comes along. The guys from Watts wipe em off the floor because they have a hot bimbo and Our Team don't. So what do they do? They decide they're gonna teach a *white person* to dance. So they start practicing in the garage where Shabba-Doo and Boogaloo live, only when it's time to break for lunch they go down to the nearest country-western redneck bar for a bite, cause, what the hey, there won't be anybody in there that cares about two black dudes walking around with a white girl. I think you might be starting to see what we're dealing with here: IQs in the single digits.

Anyhow, there's a lot more plot in there, specially after they get a Tony Franciosa lookalike to be their agent and he gets em booked in the big dance contest where everbody does ballet except for these three geeks in tennis shoes. But at the last minute Shabba-Doo decides he don't want to show for the contest and Kelly keeps trying to tell him he's just acting black, but he says, "No way, José, I'm not going unless you see something first." And so he takes her out to where this crippled kid with no legs is break-dancing on his crutches and she thinks, hey, if I think black maybe I can be black, and pretty soon they're on their way to the big production number, which I won't reveal except I'll say, we're talking serious brain damage.

No blood, no breasts, no beasts, but a whole lot of killer dancing. Kung fu. Dance fu. Great broom-dance scene. Heads spin. Legless break-dancing. Drive-In Academy Award nominations for Lucinda Dickey, as the white guinea pig; Shabba-Doo; Boogaloo; and Bobo al-Salaam, who made it all possible. Three and a half stars.

Joe Bob says check it out. ■

We Talkin' Cherry Dilday for Vice President to Get That Pervert Vote

I think you know what you got to do, Fritz. I think you know what time it is. I think you know why the Democrats are meeting in San Francisco, the only city in America where you can buy any disgusting thing you want for 20 bucks. Let's face it, you guys are looking at Desperation City and the only thing that's gonna help is a direct appeal to the Pervert Vote. Of course you know what I'm talking about.

I'm talking Cherry Dilday for Vice President.

We don't have much time, Fritz, so quick let's look at the facts.

Numero uno: The National Organization of Bimbos says you either put a porkchop on the ticket or else they take their hairy underarms to the North Pole.

Numero two-o: Cherry Dilday don't have a job. You get the Unemployment Vote.

Numero three-o: There's never been a bimbo in the White House.

Numero four-o: Those marks on Cherry Dilday's neck can be cleared up with a little Nair creme.

Numero five-o: You gotta take Texas away from Big Ron. You got two choices: Lloyd "I'm Old and I Look Like It" Bentsen, the only man in history to ever put an entire American Legion Hall to sleep, or Cherry Dilday, who would be the first vice-presidential candidate with extensive beauty-salon experience. She knows how to do Marcels the hard way, and she can whip out a wet-set ever ten minutes.

Numero six-o: Cherry Dilday can blow-dry your hair without the aid of an electrical appliance.

Numero seven-o: I been watching all the bimbos you talked to so far, Fritz, and I just got two words to say. Oink, oink.

Now, I know what you're thinking, big fella. You're thinking, Okay, okay, she's got all the right equipment. She can even run for office with a bag over her head

if necessary. But what about her background? What happens if we get three, four weeks down the pike and Cherry Dilday comes in and says, "Oh yeah, I forgot. I been treated for vee-dee 192 times at Parkland Emergency. But I'm *completely* cured." I'm with you on this one, Fritz. The last thing we need is another Eagleton deal.

Here's what we do. We announce *up front* that we're going after the vee-dee vote. Studies indicate that 97 percent of the American people have had, do have, or will have vee-dee at some time in their life. But what is this country doing about it? Do you see Jerry Lewis holding telethons for vee-dee victims? Is there anybody taking the AIDS people to Disneyland before they check in upstairs? Do you know how many people, at this very moment, are clutching their privates in agony, begging for political relief?

Fritz, this woman can help America. The people she's slept with in Texas alone can deliver the South. And history will remember. Someday they'll say in the schoolbooks that Fritz Mondale, the first Charlie McCarthy dummy to run for national office, was also the guy that had the first Escort Service running mate.

One more thing, Fritz. This girl will do *anything.*

Of course, the drive-in moviemakers of this great country are always out there dealing with the great political and social movements of our time. And this week we got a flick that I think pretty much sums it up for all of us on the matter of how men and women need to put aside their petty differences and learn to live together in peace and harmony. The flick is called *Caged Women.*

I'm trying to remember the last time we had a bimbos-in-chains flick come through town, and I believe it goes all the way back to *Chained Heat* a year ago. Course, it's been ten years now since *The Big Doll House,* the all-time greatest jailmeat movie, but I think with the growing awareness of the importance of bimbos in this society, people are getting nostalgic for the old standards about women chained up like zoo animals.

Okay, *Caged Women* starts off with the black-haired virgin checking into the Crossbar Hotel and finding out what a toilet it is. The guards eat her food and rough her up a little bit, and then she gets introduced to the lesbos with knives. Then the male prisoners, who live next door to the bimbos, start a riot in the exercise yard and beat the bejabbers out of a homosexual, and while they're doing that one of the female guards takes a bimbo prisoner into her cell and they start sharing some Vick's Nasal Spray and rubbing each other's groceries while the warden watches. The warden looks like Cinderella's mother after a three-day drunk. Then the warden gets out a whip and plays a Michael Jackson medley on the prisoner's milky white flesh while the bimbo is doing some excellent dubbed moaning. The virgin gets all bent out of shape, cause she's trying to sleep.

I forgot to mention that this is one of those Italian deals where everbody looks like they take a shower about once ever nine days.

Then one of the wise old bimbos says, "We're just numbers, not human beans."

Then this old lady decides to help the virgin out, but it's too late cause the virgin throws a bedpan all over two guards and gives a new meaning to the words "Paint the town brown." We're talking female mud-wrestling without benefit of mud. Then the warden beats her up a little bit and throws her in The Hole and about two hundred rats eat her face. While this is going on, the warden is playing around with her male slave, then after they're finished they call in these two geek janitors who rip off this blond prisoner's clothes and start making Def Leppard noises.

Then there's some plot, but after that's over the virgin and the doctor who treated her rat-riddled body decide to escape. She takes pity on the doctor cause he's in for killing his wife because she had cancer. Then there's a homosexual gang-rape in the exercise yard. Then the warden blackmails the doctor into being her personal stud. Then a bunch of people get killed and the warden has to start beating up the virgin again until she fesses up to being a reporter for Amnesty International. Then she gets raped a couple times and gets her ears cleaned out by a bellringer and finally we get the big bust-out scene.

Classic bimbos-in-cages. Not much plot to get in the way of the story. Twenty-one breasts, including a couple that should count twice. Two quarts blood. One beast (Godzilla the Warden). Five dead bodies. Five brawls. Four rapes. Two gang rapes. On-camera vomit. Some kung fu. Nightstick fondling. Whips, chains, and toilet seats. Excellent rat attack. Great scene where they put a steel drum around the virgin's head and start pounding on it with clubs. On-camera vomit. Directed by the Italian master Vincent Dawn.

Two and a half stars.

Joe Bob says check it out. ∎

Joe Bob's Mailbag ——

Dear Dr. Joe Bob Briggs,

I'm inevitably in love with your wright ups about movies! Don't *ever* listen to the Bimbos who say otherwise!!! Also—RU a Christian? Do you beleive in Christ as your savior? Well I hope so! Cuz if you ever have a problem—just turn to the Lord! He really loves you! Please—I hope you are a Christian—cuz even though Ive never seen you—I hope someday we shall meet in Glory!!

Love—
Helena
Dallas

Dear Helena:

If He really loves me, why can't He ever make the payments on my pickup on time?

Are you talking about the Glory out by Sweetwater, or the roadhouse across from Golden Triangle Bowl? Either way, I'll meet you there, honey.

McNeil-Liar Misquote Ruffles Joe Bob's Feathers; *Cemetery* Flick Discovered

Everbody thinks it was my fault about the international incident on the pinko Eastern Establishment socialist TV channel last week when the plug got pulled on *McNeil-Liar Report.* I was misquoted, AS USUAL. This bimbo reporter from Austin goes on there to talk about Geraldine Ferraro, and what happens? Communist censorship. I've said it once and I'm gonna say it again, cause you turkeys never seem to learn, but *do not trust* ANYTHING *you hear in the media.* The PBS network is some kind of conspiracy deal, cause if you notice, they don't have commercials on there *and* they show Gene Kelly movies in prime time. We're talking some sick people.

Now I'm gonna tell you what happened.

Last week Fritz ignored my advice on putting Cherry Dilday on the ticket and went for the kinky kompromise. So, of course, I was besieged by reporters asking for my reaction to the obvious betrayal of the Texas vote and the thousands of men who have slept with Cherry on a personal basis. So one of these hacks was named

Molly Ivins and they had her on *McNeil/Liar* being interviewed by this *other* bimbo named Charlayne Hunter-Gault who, if you've seen her, looks like she has to strap on her face with a piece of baling wire so there won't be any creases in it. Charlayne asks questions in a way that kind of reminds you of Vincent Price after he's been smoking Arkansas Polio Weed for three days.

Anyhow, Charlayne had pretty much committed mass murder by putting the western third of the United States into a deep coma, when this Ivins woman says, "I called up Joe Bob Briggs to find out what he thought about Geraldine Ferraro," and Charlayne says who the heck is Joe Bob Briggs, and Molly says who Joe Bob is, and Charlayne says that's interesting and what did he say, and Molly says, "Well, Joe Bob said he really liked Geraldine's garbonzas."

That's when the turkeys pulled the plug.

Now, I'd just like to clear the air here and say two things about these PBS monkeys:

Numero uno: Molly Ivins

should definitely get credit for being the first human bean to use the word "garbonzas" on network teevee, but she got it wrong. I would never speak that way about a public official. What I actually said was "Geraldine Ferraro has at least two enormous talents." I think you can see the way the media's trying to twist my words around here.

Numero two-o: If PBS would *check their facts* once in a while, they'd find out that I can personally verify my remarks. The election of a vice president is no laughing matter, and I'm putting my career on the line here. Now, I think if they'd get their reporters in gear, they'd also find out that Geraldine has a voice that sounds a little bit like a big fingernail scratch across a 45-record of the Stones doing "Gimme Shelter." This is probly not a big problem for Fritz, so long as Geraldine'll agree to go through the entire campaign with a bag over her head. I know it would be uncomfortable, but let's face it, Geraldine, you're doing it for women all over America. It's the symbolism of the thing that matters.

Speaking of symbolism, our old friend Lucio Fulci, Big Lucy, the main man in Italy, just came out with a new flick called *House by the Cemetery.* As we all know, Big Lucy has been doing the best Italian rip-offs since *Hercules,* stuff like *Gates of Hell* last year and *Suspiria* and, well, you know, the classics. This one starts off with some fairly heavy symbolism. A teen-age kid gets some scissors

rammed through his heart and then his girlfriend has a knife stuck through the back of her head so it comes out her mouth. I know, I know, you've seen it before, but Big Lucy likes to hold that camera steady for a *long time* while the knife goes through and run up that vomit meter rating. I think Big Lucy is really trying to tell us something about teen-age violence in America, and I would encourage you to take the kids to this one.

House by the Cemetery is about this typical American family that is real happy except they can't understand why they look like Italians. They don't worry about it, though; they just pack up and move to New England and buy the house where the teenagers just got shishkabobbed. Soon as they get there, their little blond-headed kid starts seeing visions of this spooky little Sissy Spacek girl who tells him to not go in the durn house. She makes her point by cutting the heads off her dolls and making blood pour out, but the symbolism is too heavy for the kid, he can't figure out what the heck she means by that.

So then the father goes off to study about this Dr. Freudstein character who used to live in the house, and while he's gone the babysitter comes over and hears a baby crying down in the cellar and she goes down there to check it out and gets attacked by a bat. Now, maybe you don't think that sounds very disgusting. You han't seen this bat. We're talking a huge bloodsucker that keeps comin back and spewin slime all over the room and diving straight at the bimbo's face. The father has to gore the bat to death with a big ole set of scissors.

Next thing, the mother of the family is dusting and cleaning and she notices that in one of the rooms there's a grave in the floor. Course, she don't think anything about it. But then she starts hearing these noises down there.

When her husband Norman gets home, he has to give her a bunch of Valium. "It's bad enough living next to a cemetery," she says, "but do we have to live with a tomb in our hallway?"

He tells her yes they do and to get ahold of herself.

Then this zombie realtor comes by to check on the family and nobody's home, so she starts walking around in the house and the tomb cracks open and swallows up her leg and something with scales on it comes up out of the basement and goes to work with a crowbar: stomach first, then the chest, then the jugular, and I believe we may be talking more actual blood here than we've seen since *Nightmare*.

Then there's some plot about Dr. Freudstein. And what ends up happening is this little spook girl keeps saying "Go away, do not go in," and the Family Stupid keeps saying "Hey, how about we go down in the cellar and see if there's any more bats down there." And what we end up with is a new record: enough liquid to open a plasma center.

One throat-cutting, slow motion, ear to ear, *three times* on the same lady. Two heads roll. One head rolls down the stairs. Underground meatlocker scene, if you know what I mean and I think you do. Maggots in the throat. Great slime glopola lizard-face genetic-DNA creature attack. Nine dead bodies. An eighty-two on the vomit meter. Twelve gallons blood. One beast. Two breasts. No kung fu. No motor vehicle chases. One of Big Lucy's best. Three and a half stars.

Joe Bob says check it out. ■

Joe Bob's Mailbag ━━━

Joe Bob Briggs—
What sort of man reads Joe Bob Briggs?

Men who watch Joe Bob Briggs' kind of movies. Joe Bob Briggs' kind of movies are visual Muzak for the frontally lobotomized. Joe Bob Briggs' kind of movies are lava lamps for the search and maim set. Joe Bob Briggs' kind of movies are soundtracks for the 'Beat my girlfriend silly over the head with a Lone Star longneck for goin' out with that country singer, and then dumping her over a cliff at Eagle Mountain Lake and partyin' til dawn with my buddies' kind of man.

Joe Bob Briggs is the Dr.

Gene Scott of Rank, if you know what I mean and I think you do.

Craig Whatley
formerly of Denton & Ft. Worthless, TX
San Rafael, Calif.

Dear Craig:
What?
I've told you guys before and I don't want to have to repeat it, but lay off that prescription stuff that comes up from Mexico.

Joe Bob Defends Miss America 1984 and *Cannonball II*

Why are we discriminating against this woman just because she's black, female, nekkid, AC-DC, and Miss America? I want you people to *back off* and give Vanessa a break so she can get her head together and maybe go do some boat shows or something. I'm sick of this kind of racism in America and I don't want to have to tell you again.

Vanessa's tough, though. She can handle the p.r. She can handle a lot of things. She can handle slimeballs like Bob Guccione. She can handle handles. She can handle photographers who don't know how to focus the dang thing. She can handle millions of Americans making fun of her garbonzas. Vanessa can handle it all.

Vanessa took a licking and came back ticking.

Out at the Century Drive-In in Grand Prairie the other night, we all took a poll on Vanessa:

1. Is she or isn't she?

2. Does she or doesn't she?

3. Would she if you gave her a hundred bucks?

Vanessa got extremely high marks on all three questions. That's the kind of healthy American female we're talking about. Besides, the people that run that contest in Atlantic City should of known something was wrong in the first place. I didn't know the bimbo was black until they put it in the paper. I thought she just had a great tan. When she meets people, they probly say, "Funny, you don't *look* black." Vanessa's the whitest black person since the *Amos and Andy Show,* and so my guess is the Miss America people didn't know what they had till the morning after the pageant was all over and they woke up and said, *"Oh my God we elected a Negro!"* and somebody said, "I *told* you that would happen if we kept putting one in the finals," and then ever since then they been trying to get the goods on the woman. I mean, what if they looked at the private pictures of ever bimbo elected to be Miss America? They'd probly find doggies and elephant harnesses and all kinds of stuff. But that's what happens when you're black and nekkid in America.

Speaking of famous black people, Sammy (I Did It My Way) Davis is one of the 17,000 stars in *Cannonball II,* and the reason I bring it up is I notice Sammy han't been on the Carson show for several days now and so I wondered what happened? *Sammy, baby,* slap that knee and let us know you're around, how bout it? Now I figured it out, though. Sammy was busy making *Cannonball,* which is one of the best sequels since *Death Wish II.* Remember how the first *Cannonball Run* was *already* a sequel since it ripped off *Cannonball,* one of the all-time great cross-country road-race flicks? Remember how *Cannonball Run* didn't make any sense cause you couldn't tell who was winning the dang race until the end? Well, it's hard to believe, but in *Cannonball II* you cain't even tell at the end. They made the exact same movie, except they told Farrah Fawcett to take a hike because she was zero in the first

one and she refused to pop her top for Burt Reynolds, and then they forgot to put the ending on it.

Cannonball II stars ever guest on the *Tonight Show* for the past twenty years, plus some porkchops who were hanging around Hollywood in halter tops when they started the camera, plus a whole lot of twisted metal. We start off with a few crash-and-burns, then Dom DeLuise comes on so Burt can twist his nose and insult him and pretty much say "Dom, if it wasn't for me you couldn't get a job, could you?" I think this is unfair, though, because I remember one time when Dom was funny. It was on the *Dean Martin Show.*

Speaking of Dean Martin, I forget what he does in this flick except I remember he checks into the Dunes and Sammy hangs outside Dean's eighteenth-story hotel window in one of those hilarious Rat Pack scenes. Then Dean does a great joke about his drinking: "My liver died last year." (While I'm thinking of it, where the heck is Joey Bishop? If you're gonna do *Cannonball,* let's get the *entire* Rat Pack and *do Cannonball.)*

Let's see, who else we got? Oh, yeah, how could I forget? Telly! The *original* Mr. T. Kojak gets to slap Charles Nelson Reilly's glasses off. Then there's Susan Anton and Catherine Bach, who oil up their skin and go around stealing cars by exposing parts of their jumpsuits. And, of course, we got Sid Caesar and Tim Conway and Don Knotts. How about Arte Johnson? George "Goober"

Lindsey? You want to talk acting? What do the words Joe Theismann mean to you? I'm talking Mel Tillis. I'm talking Ricardo Montalban. I'm talking Jim Nabors and Shirley MacLaine and Louis Nye. Excuse me, I'm getting carried away.

Finally, we're talking two of the biggest stars in drive-in history. Big Frank, who looks like he was so excited about being in *Cannonball II* that he put on an extra forty, fifty pounds to get ready for the performance. And . . . hold your breath . . .

Jacky Chan. Mr. Kung Fu 1982. The new Bruce Lee. The only thing better than Jacky Chan's kung fu in this flick is the scene where Goober fights with a monkey. Well, I take that back. There *is* one scene where a pickup drives over a Firebird that's pretty good too, and then there's the scene where the Racing Nuns buy a six-pack and some chili dogs, and I almost forgot the one where Sammy, Dom, and Burt all dress up like women and dance to a Supremes song, but for my money the best scene in the flick is where Jacky Chan kung-fus twelve Hell's Angels for no apparent reason.

Absolutely no plot to get in the way of the story. Two breasts. Half pint blood. One beast (Telly Savalas). Two solid hours of motor vehicle chases. Five automobile crashes. One Marlon Brando imitation. One levitating car. One underwater car. Every guest on the Carson show for the past twenty years except David Brenner. Great kung fu. Monkey fu. Some bimbo fu. Monkey driving a limo. Four brawls. One little old lady thrown through a plate-glass window. One trailer-house crash. Arab jokes. Jap jokes. Sammy wears *all* his jewelry. Three stars.

Joe Bob says check it out. ∎

Joe Bob's Mailbag ——

Dear Joe Bob,

What about the religious implications of the drive-in? Do you perceive any theology—either latent or up front—in any of these outdoor epics you write so stirringly about?

Maybe during one or more of your drive-in evenings you've run across a movie that my readers should know about. Perhaps a possession/ exorcism / demon - worship story along the lines of "Amityville Horror," or "Children of the Corn."

Is God at the drive-in? Please advise.

Cordially,
John Justice
Raleigh, N.C.

Dear fellow Babtist:
Yes I do perceive some latex theology at the drive-in, but you'll have to read about

*it in my book in the chapter
"Where Are You Parking in
the Drive-In of Life?" about
the night I walked that drive-
in aisle and got saved.
Course, the most religious
double feature ever made was*

*that Roman Catholic twin-
bill:* I Drink Your Blood *and*
I Eat Your Skin.

Joe Bob Praises Lawmen for Arresting Morganna; *Meatballs* Star Makes It Big

You're probly expecting me to make some cheap jokes about Morganna getting busted last week. You probly think I saw the article in the paper:

Morganna Roberts, known as "Morganna, the Kissing Bandit," was arrested Thursday night at a Dallas nightclub on a public lewdness complaint. Police said Ms. Roberts, thirty-three, of Columbus, Ohio, was arrested after allegedly beating a customer over the head with her breasts during a strip tease performance at 10's for Gentlemen at 9410 Marsh Lane at about 11:30 P.M. The customer, Kenneth Crowder, was arrested on the same complaint for allegedly cooperating with the stunt.

You probly think I'm gonna say something like how we've had enough breast-beating in Dallas

and now it's time for action. You probly want me to say something about how Morganna busted out of jail. You might even think I'd be sick enough to talk about how there's not a jail big enough for Morganna's two enormous talents. But I got to tell you, I was in the audience that night, I was a personal witness to the crime, and I've got to get serious here for a moment: This is *no laughing matter.* I got a look at these nuclear garbonzas, and we're talking deadly weapons.

I know it's not a popular stand to take, but I want to commend the Dallas police for doing what had to be done. If they didn't take the action they did, *when* they did it, those bazookas might of got out of control and then who knows how many people could of been seriously injured or, let's face it, boobed to death.

Not many people know it,

but more Americans die ever year from breast attacks than get killed in their bathtubs. It's one of those facts we don't like to think about. But let's take a look at the numbers in this case:

60.

23.

39.

That's right. I didn't believe it myself. I didn't know it was legal to have hooters that size unless you mount yellow warning flags on both sides for oncoming traffic. Also, I know for a fact that if you pull in at a weigh station on the interstate and you're hauling 60s without a license, they'll write you a 90-buck citation for the structural damage you're doing to the asphalt. These were *unlicensed* atomic duffel bags, unleashed on an unsuspecting public. I'm sorry, but Morganna has got to learn to either find a leash big enough for those B-52s, or else get a safety deposit box at Fort Knox and keep em under armed guard at all times. We don't want another Three Mile Island.

I'd like to mention that there's two sides to ever story, though, and in Morganna's case there's more than two sides, cause if Morganna turns sideways the world disappears. And so what you *can* say for Morganna is, she did *not* hit that turkey on the top of the head. She had the guy's head down there in the valley of the shadow of flesh and she was whacking him directly on the ears. So let's not exaggerate about what was going on here. Morganna certainly knows better than to hit

anybody directly on the soft part of the skull, where she can cause permanent brain damage and possible orgasm. Unfortunately, the guy did have temporary hearing loss and possible eardrum damage, which means Morganna got carried away and should be held fully responsible for all hospital costs. She's got to learn not to point those things at somebody unless she intends to use em. But this is not the time for cheap jokes.

If you write in, though, I'll sell you some for a dollar.

Speaking of human basketballs, Misty Rowe wins the annual Joe Bob Briggs Jiggle Award for her enormous performance in *Meatballs, Part II,* which has some of the greatest acting she's done since the last time she worked with Junior on *Hee Haw.* Misty's job in this flick is to keep trying to do it with a wimp named Jamie, only wherever they go to be alone, the John Philip Sousa Marching Band shows up.

Meatballs, Part II has a lot in common with the original *Meatballs* starring Bill Murray. The main thing they have in common is they have the same name. But *numero two-o* has a lot of stuff missing from the first one, like the race between the school bus and the paraplegic kid in a motorized wheelchair. Like the seven-year-old kids having bayonet practice at Camp Patton. But the best thing is the alien "E.T." kid who comes to camp from a Jewish planet in outer space and wears a yellow raincoat all the time and lives in the outhouse. His name is Meathead, and all he likes to do is eat Big Macs and smoke Arkansas Polio Weed and levitate people.

There's some plot in there, but I forgot what it was. *Extremely* disappointing breast count: zero. One motor vehicle chase, including paraplegic. Four brawls. Half pint blood. One flasher. One armed conflict. One wild bear. One guy dressed up in ladies clothes, including black lace panties. Three Jewish aliens. Minimum kung fu. One guy blown away in the hilarious hand-grenade scene. One beast, a guy named Mad Dog, who likes to eat dog biscuits, beat up little kids, and marry his ancestors. Drive-In Academy Award nomination for Joaquin Martinez, for doing the best Indian chief with a Meskin accent of the year. Misty Rowe keeps her top on, so it's only . . .

Two and a half stars. ∎

Joe Bob Offers GOP Dating Service Plus *Joy of Sex* Deal

Rhett Beavers came by the house to tell me there's a convention in town and he wanted me to help him work a Monte Carlo Night over by the Sportatorium, but I had to tell him to stow it. It's illegal in the state of Texas to rake 18 percent off the top from drunks who wear pillbox hats and hang around Neiman-Marcus at night going "Hey, baby, wanna see my Olds Cutlass?" But Rhett said no, I didn't understand him, it wasn't that kind of convention, it was a convention of Big Ron's friends, and they were all gonna be plenty p.o.ed when they find out the Dallas police is running all the decent hookers out of town.

That's why I started the Republican Dating Service. Rhett never would of thought of it on his own, cause he watches so much Empty-V his brains are scrambled, but I recognize a needed social service when I see it. Here's the deal. What does a Republican want in a dating service? (We'll get to the Republican Nude Modeling studio concept in a minute, but let's keep it simple right now.) *Numero uno,* he wants to use his American Express gold card. *Numero two-o,* he wants the bimbo to be on time and prepared to humiliate him if necessary. *Numero three-o,* he wants a receipt for $24.99 or less so he won't have to itemize on his Form 1040.

No problema! I know where to find the last remaining 20-dollar hookers in America, as long as you don't mind how some of em rate on the ugly meter. I can also offer a special discount deal for the handicapped, specially any blind Republicans in town, cause Ugly on a Stick will provide all services, pay *you* three bucks, and write it off on *her* Form 1040. For those Republicans that might be having trouble with this, think of it as the national budget. We're talking negative digits here. The only thing you got to worry about is hiring Ugly on a Stick so many times she puts you in a higher tax bracket.

Any military men at the convention? Meet Cherry Dilday. She'll do anything if you let her touch your M-16 rifle.

Guys from New York? Vida Stegall knows how to make screaming sounds exactly like the traffic at 42nd Street and Fifth Avenue, but you have to pay the full $24.99 for that and you might have to fork over some subway tokens.

Guys from Cleveland? You probly never had the Guadalajara Treatment. Ask for Margarita and she'll wrap your tacos in a serape.

Guys from San Francisco? Oh yeah, I forgot.

Guys from Saginaw that wanna see where Kennedy got killed? You can spring for the Assassination Special, which includes a forty-five-minute stopoff at Dealey Plaza (we provide the Kodak, no charge), one complimentary "Three-Shot" cocktail, express elevator tokens for the ride to the sixth floor of the School Book Depository, and a leisurely ride through all three streets of the Triple Underpass. Southfork Ranch optional. Ask for May Ellen Masters, but please, no kinky stuff.

For an extra $24.99, we'll haul you over to Fort Worth in the Republican Limo for a look at people who do it with cows. After that, hey, it's a free country, you're on your own.

Finally, ask for the $24.99 Party Bottle and we'll take you to the Century Drive-In in Grand Prairie for the late showing of *Joy of Sex,* followed by personal introductions to some of the filthiest bimbos since God created Bulgaria. You might get lucky and see Tanya Sandage twist her body into every sign of the zodiac, in order.

One thing about this *Joy of Sex* flick, though, I read the original book it's based on and I just don't get it. The book had a whole heck of a lot better story to it. Remember the giant gila-monster position, with illustrations? Not in the flick. Remember the *menage à quadriplegic?* No way, José. Remember "Greco-Roman wrestling with midgets"? Doesn't exist. Remember how it teaches you to attain sexual gratification with the aid of a Slinky? *Censored from the film version.*

Nobody likes this kind of Communist mangling, specially when they turn a perfectly good story into Attack of the Stupid White People. This is one of those

California drugola surfer high-school Valley Person flicks about a guy who can't realize his sexual potential (he's a wimp loser).

While the kid is trying to score some action, Colleen Camp shows up at school advertising pumpkins under her sweater. Colleen has been off making indoor bullstuff and han't really been around the drive-in since *The Cheerleaders*, but what the hey, her talents aren't sagging yet. Colleen is the narc who's trying to bust up all the Arkansas Polio Weed rings, but what happens is she falls in love with the wimp and tries to pummel him into orgasm at the drive-in. It don't work.

One more question. Where's the underwater side-saddle scene where the guy turns into a human blender? They cut that one out too.

Disgusting two stars. One measly breast. No dead bodies. Minimum blood. One beast (Christopher Lloyd as the coach). Drive-In Academy Award nominations for Danton Stone as Farouk and Colleen Camp as the narc with a large heart, if you know what I mean and I think you do. Kung fu. No motor vehicle chases. *Uno* fistfight. It's no *Valley Girl*, but it's better than *Meatballs, Part II*.

Joe Bob says check it out. ■

Bim Bo Shows Off Bo-dacious Ta-tas in *Bo Lero*

Sometimes you go to the drive-in and get so inspired you get those little goose bumps on the backside of your neck. Sometimes you go and get so inspired you get little goose bumps on the inside of your thigh. Sometimes you go and get chiggers on your feet. Sometimes you don't go. What I'm trying to say here is there's only a few times in life when you're watching the flick and in the middle of it something happens and, *bingo*, you see how a drive-in superstar is born. It happened with Mamie Van Doren in '58, the first year she wore a cashmere sweater four sizes too little. It happened with Peter Fonda in '69, when he did a shaggy-dog imitation and said "I got to do my own thing in my own place and time." And, course, it happened to Jamie Lee Curtis in 78, the first year she got hosed down with watercolors and used for butcher-block practice.

This week is one of those magic moments. It happened. We knew it was possible, we knew she was coming along all these years, we knew it was only a matter of time before the bimbo ripped all her clothes off and ran around acting like a goose that's been wired up for brain research. We knew she could take a bath better than most actresses in the civilized non-Communist world. We knew she could toss her cookies on the big screen.

What we didn't know is she's also the Oral Roberts of the drive-in: She can raise male gazebos from the dead.

I'm talking Bo. Not Bobo. Not Bozo. Not Beauregard. The one and only Bo, the one that's spent half her life saying "Is it time to get nekkid again, John?" Bo Derek, Bimbo Bo. Bim Bo. A woman for the eighties.

Her new flick is *Bo Lero,* and I had to watch it four times before I could completely understand it. Like there's this one scene where she looks at George Kennedy and says, "I have to do something I've been dreaming about for years," and he gets an expression on his face like he just got his foot mashed in by a Caterpillar fork-lift, and then the flick goes into Super Slo-Mo, or Slo-Bo in this case, and she starts running through the grass and tossing her clothes all over creation and playing peek-a-boo with her buns and doing aerobicize with her garbon-zas. But this is the kind of thing you have to wait for in the flick. They build up to it. It's maybe thirty, forty seconds into the movie before she starts jumping out of her jumpsuits.

Okay, here's the plot. Bo's a virgin and she can't find anybody that'll go to bed with her. Hey, we all know the problem, Bo, we're with you. So what does she do? She decides to go to the Sahara Desert. When she gets there, she starts wearing a chandelier on her head so she'll be attractive to the camel jockeys, but the only guy she can find is this wimp sheik who lays around smoking coconut juice out of a hippie pipe. He don't really want to go to bed with a Bim Bo wearing a chandelier either, so Bo has to try to get his attention, so she says, "I've come all this way to give you something you may not even want—my virginity."

The guy decides he'll check it out. So they go out in the desert and Bo watches a belly dancer shake her tummy like a piece of Jimmy Dean Pork Sausage and then Bo imitates her and we find out the gal's got muscles on ever side. Then Bo asks the sheik how to do it, and the camel jockey pulls out a jar of honey and pours it all over her body and tries to lick it off, only he just ends up looking like a guy at the Kiwanis Convention that gets his head stuck in the fruit salad, and I'll tell you what, I don't know much about the sex habits of people of the Arab persuasion, but I think you can see right here why we can't get this Middle East business taken care of. Bo tells the turkey she wants to play around, and he pours *food* on her *stomach*. They don't even do that in Key West.

So Bo decides it's not happening in the Sahara, so she packs up her virginity and goes to Spain to try to force somebody to jump in the sack. Course, now it's twice as hard, cause everbody's heard she's into camels and honey. Anyhow, she goes to a bullfight and watches this guy fight a bull on a horse. The guy never gets down off his horse, and you'd probly think Bo could figure it out and say, hey, wait a minute, I think you need to get down on the ground and put a blanket in front of the bull or something like José Jimenez used to do, but they forget to do that and so Bo dresses up in another chandelier and goes to a goat dinner with the bullfighter and George Kennedy. I never did figure out why George Kennedy was following Bo around all the time, but I'd like to say right here this is Big George's greatest performance since *Chattanooga Choo Choo*.

Then Bo has to bribe this thirteen-year-old gypsy girl to take her to where the matador lives, but when they get there the guy's making the sign of the two-humped whale in a hot tub with a gypsy woman, and everbody is just a little p.o.ed. And then the thirteen-year-old nympho tells Bo the matador is *her* man too, and Bo says no way, José, but the little munchkin pops her top and says, "I am woman, ready, juicy too."

Then there's almost a bull at-

tack and Bo puts Kleenex in her hair and gets high on Turkish farm products with another bimbo and then they go buy the matador's wine company and ride some horses on the beach and then the gypsy woman finds out Bo is hanging around and so she starts screaming "You beech! You beech! You American beech!" until they bag her and toss her into the history books. Then, finally, the turkey agrees to go to bed with Bo, and so to make it sexy, Bo dresses up in a sheet and a spiked helmet and licks the guy's ear and says, "Will you do everything to me and show me everything I can do to you?"

And the guy says okay and pretty soon 27,000 violins start to play and the sound about busts out the windshield. You may think that's it. No more plot. He goes for the groceries and it's all over.

No way, José.

Next scene, the matador gets gored in the gazebos by a bull. Bo starts crying and says she wants to marry him anyhow. But the matador says no way he can do that, because there's not any Valvoline in the crankcase. So Bo runs into his room wearing some German overalls and points at him and says, "That *thing* is going to work, I guarantee you it is." And I don't know about you, but it was just so beautiful the way she said it, I get all choked up just remembering it now.

So Bo is gonna raise the dead gazebos. Course, there's a lot more plot, like this Scotsman guy that comes along and drops his skirt and jumps in bed with Bo's friend and says stuff like "Ay luvv yew, ah rilly dyuh." And then Bo figures out how to do it. First she makes like Lady Godiva, which you can understand if you're reading this in one of the non-Communist papers that didn't censor the *real* picture of Bo on horseback, and then the guy screams, "Make me whole again!" and then Bo shows up in the guy's bedroom and sticks her hair in the water fountain and shakes it on his stomach and throws a cape over his face and says, "Olé!" and then they do a tongue lock and, you maybe aren't gonna believe this, but they go to heaven. We're talking a movie Jerry Falwell should recommend to every member of his congregation. They get holy, and the guy gets the full use of his gazebos back, and we're talking the kind of experience that makes you want to go back to church and say, "No, Oral, make *me* whole again!"

We're talking Bo-dacious tatas. Bo does everthing. Twenty-eight breasts. Two snowcapped peaks. Slo-mo. Slow-Bo. Sex with food. Morocco Polio Weed. One guy in a dress. One wimp sheik. Bo kisses a horse. One thirteen-year-old nympho. Seven grocery-delivery scenes. Bo takes a bath. Bo takes a swim. Bo takes a sauna. Bo takes a ride on a horse. Bo takes a swan dive. Two belly dancers. Three bullfights by guys who won't get off their horses. Two motor vehicle chases. No kung fu. One quart blood. Drive-

In Academy Award nominations for Bo, for George Kennedy, and for the bull. Four stars.

Joe Bob says check it out and see history made. ■

Joe Bob's Mailbag ———

Letters to the Editor
CJ Newspaper
Columbus, Ohio
Re: *CENSORSHIP REARS UGLY HEAD: JOE BOB DECAPITATED*

The unbelievable has happened. The N.O.B. has brought the keesh-eatin' wimps at your paper to their knees, and the red-blooded, true-blue Americans of Columbus have been deprived of our one source for upcoming cultural events, namely Joe Bob's no-holds-barred yet tasteful drive-in flick reviews. We're talkin' el pinko plots here. Like, the gratuitous waste of real Americans havin' to buy the Cleveland Plain Dealer just to read Joe Bob. Like, this weekend I'm gonna have to pay good money before I can find out if "The T & A Team" sucks or what. It stars Lucy Brett, Lola Meyers and Sue Justine but that's no guarantee some dumb plot won't get in the way of the action. Now I gotta mess around checkin' out this movie that for all I know don't even rate a one-jiggle yawn. In case any of you Cleveland ethnic types read the C-J for weird recipes for keesh-shu-bob and funny, un-American stuff like that and happen to read this: Just remember—without eternal vigilance, the National Organization of Bimbos could strike there. Jackie Lee says: check it out.

Jacqueline Lee Brown

Columbus, Ohio
cc: Joe Bob Briggs, Philosopher

Dear Jackie Lee:
    The score is Bimbos 2, Red-blooded Joe Bob Non-Communist American Newspapers 36. I'm counting the Babtists that banned Joe Bob from Fort Smith, Arkansas. Let's face it, there's a Cuba on every continent.

Cowboy Cheerleaders Should Be Ashamed of Humongous Coverup

Nobody got a lick of work done this week cause the new Dallas Cowboys Cheerleaders posters came in the mail. *Could I have a little silence, please?* One more outburst like that and I'll clear this newspaper.

Now, I know we're getting into controversial territory here. I know everbody wants a chance to say their piece. I know you're *all* p.o.ed about this year's blond quotient (46.9 percent). But let's just *remain calm* until I get finished going over the annual Cowboys Cheerleaders Meat Market Report.

As we all know, this is the first year they used the Cowboys Cheerleaders written test. We are all against it. We all knew it was gonna damage the crop. But that's past history and we have to live with it now. *However,* I do think some of the questions were a little tough, and I think we could work on loosening up the academic requirement for 1985. Like one of the questions on this year's test was "What city do the Denver Broncos come from?" See? Trick question. Also, they asked em this one:

Q. What does the term "pigskin" mean?

a. A girl that's got fungus growing on her thighs.

b. What they wrote the Declaration of Independence on.

c. People that are related to pigs.

d. A football.

Next year I think we need to agree: no "opinion" questions like that. And I want to prove my point by the first shocking Dallas Cowboys Cheerleaders Fact: The 1984 crop has only *five* bimbos with first names ending in the letter "i." Of course, this is the lowest number in history. One Vicki, one Vikki (extra credit for the double-k), two Lori's, and a Kelli. And I'm afraid that's it. Now I'm gonna be a nice guy this year and count some close ones. The Julee goes in. Eydie is a borderline call, but I'll put it through. Still, that's just seven cheerleaders that don't know how to spell their names, for a 21.9 Education Quotient.

Course, that's nothing compared to the second shocking Cowboy Cheerleader Fact: They only got one aerobic dancing instructor. Sure, they got nine secretaries. Sure they got nine college students. But gimme a break. One? *U no?* Excuse me while I barf on a dirty leotard. What have you girls been *doing* with your lives? Aerobic Quotient: 3.1. You oughta be ashamed of yourselves.

Finally, I'm almost embarrassed to tell this one. I think it must be a mistake and they left some information off the 84 poster. I searched through the whole deal, read *all* the parts about how the cheerleaders went

to Ko Rea last year and oiled up some M-16 assault rifles. But I couldn't find *nothing* in there about dedicating their life to teaching handicapped kids how to say the Lord's Prayer. Handicapped Quotient: zero. *Nada.* No way, José Jimenez. We had some years where the entire squad was dedicating theirselves to starting handicapped schools. I shot myself in the foot one year just so I'd be handicapped. Now look at it. It's pathetic.

I think it shows up in obvious ways, too. Check the cleavage on the uniforms this year. Up there on the fringe vest they got this *humongous* blue bandanna hanging down the middle. And let's face it, when you start covering up, it's cause you don't have nothing to hide. If you know what I mean, and I think you do. It was the written test that did it. 1984 USDA Rating: Grade B.

I'm ashamed of you gals.

Speaking of people that can't talk, Arnold the Barbarian is back again this week. Arnold Schwarzenegger, the A-Man, the wildman that put the beef in the beefcake, drops buck-nekkid out of the sky and walks around sticking his arm through the stomachs of punk rockers. Arnold is *The Terminator,* and I'm gonna say it right now, we're talking drive-in heaven. A cross between *The Road Warrior* and *Halloween,* with some *Zombie* tossed in to make it disgusting. Straight to No. 1 on the Joe Bob Briggs Best of 84 list.

The A-Man is this "cyborg"

(half man and half Robotronic City) who gets zapped into El Lay from the future. His mission: to wipe out Linda Hamilton so she can't give birth to the guy who's gonna kill him in the year 2029. So the A-Man gets him some Hell's Angels threads and walks into a gun store and tells Dick Miller that he wants a 12-gauge auto-loader shotgun, a .45 long-slide heavy-duty handgun with laser sighting, a 9-millimeter pistol, and a Plasma rifle with a 40-watt range-finder, and then Dick Miller says, "Will there be anything else?" and the A-Man blows Dick away in slow motion and walks out of the store like a National Guard Armory with legs.

In Arnold's last *Conan* movie, you remember he got to say about fifteen words. In this one they whittled him on down to ten words, probly because he's learning how to do it all with his bod. The man's pure poetry. The A-Man can steal a Dempster Dumpster truck as easy as most people steal a Honda Civic. So strap some firepower on each arm and what do you got?

You got more twitching dead bodies than any flick since *Revenge of the Ninja*.

First Arnold sticks his hand through a car window, steals a station wagon, drives to the suburbs, runs over some kid's playtoys, rings the doorbell, and pumps six shotgun blasts into a thirty-five-year-old woman. Then he looks in the phone book and finds out he killed the *wrong one*. Uh oh. So he goes and does the same thing to *another* bimbo, but after he does it he checks her I.D. and finds out it was her *roommate* he wanted. What are we gonna do with you, Arnold?

But now it's too late, because the target bimbo knows the A-Man is breathing heavy. And she's found this *other* guy (100 percent pure-dee human) who's been zapped from the future to kill Arnold. This guy's nekkid too, because the zap machine won't work if you got clothes on. So he lands in the alley and has to run through a K-Mart with cops chasing him before he gets dressed and steals a shotgun and starts hanging around Linda Hamilton's apartment like those guys that go to the movies in their raincoats. This dude's name is Michael Biehn, and he's having flashbacks like he's been in Nam, and it's making him pretty durn irritated. Especially when Arnold goes in a disco and the guy at the door says, "Hey, buddy, you didn't pay," and Arnold has to blow away twenty or thirty Empty-V fans who could of tried out for *Soul Train* if they lived long enough. Michael shows up before he can dynamite the bejabbers out of Linda Hamilton, but twelve shotgun holes through Arnold's body don't seem to bother him.

The only thing is, the A-Man has to go back to his motel room and carve up his arm to fix it and then stick a knife directly in his eyeball and pull out the eye and throw it in the sink. It's okay, though, cause Arnold remembers to buy some sunglasses and we only have to look at it five or six more times the rest of the flick.

Then there's a lot of plot about where Arnold came from, and the nuclear war they had in the future, and blah blah blah, and then there's a couple *great* motor vehicle chases where they almost catch Arnold, and then Arnold drives his car *through* the police station and kills about thirty cops, and then Arnold shoots up a motel room, and then there's some more chases where Arnold's on a cycle, and then a Mack Truck runs over Arnold and bloodies him up.

Finally Arnold gets p.o.ed.

I'll just say one more thing. When you think he's dead . . . he's not. Even when you think he's dead and he's not, and then you think he's dead again and he's not, and then you think he's dead *again* . . . he's not.

Four breasts. Thirty-seven dead bodies. One beast (the A-Man). Dempster Dumpster truck destructo scene. Arnold and Mike both get nekkid. Intestines roll. Forearms roll. Eyes roll. One pet iguana. One El Lay jerkola disco destroyed. Four motor vehicle chases. One crash-and-burn. Rat-eating refugees who set fires in their TV sets. Seven quarts blood. A seventy-seven on the vomit meter. Drive-In Academy Award nominations for the A-Man; for Linda Hamilton, best screamer of the year; and for James Cameron, who wrote and directed this sucker.

Four stars.

Joe Bob says check it out twice. ∎

Joe Bob's Mailbag ──

Dear Joe-Bob,

As I wrote to your publicity lady, I'll be there. Looking forward to it. Gonna drink some beers and check out the locals and keep doing it until we get it right. Besides, I've been looking for something like this to kinda enhance my literary reputation, if you know what I mean and I think you do. Seems to me like *The Paris Review* and *The New York Quarterly*, which have pretty much ignored me so far, will have to sit up and take notice when they hear about *this* happy crappy.

Well, you wanted me to list my five favorite drive-in flicks, so here goes:

Numero Uno: *Evil Dead*. Spam in a cabin.

Numero Two-O: *The Texas Chainsaw Massacre*. Ain't *nothin'* as good as *Saw*.

Numero Three-O: *Zombie*. The spaghetti western version of *Night of the Living Dead*. Chick with great garbonzas battles killer shark. Dead zombies come up from deeper down and eat the shark. Also a great eyeball-squishing scene. Make sure

Wanda's not in the car when this happens or you're gonna have to get new seat-covers.

Numero Four-O: *Night Warning*. Two very good garbonzas. Several slashings. And a spectacular head-removal. Also a very good picture to go to the head, buy popcorn, do the horizontal bop, etc.

Numero Five-O: *Blood Feast*. This is an oldie and not exactly a goodie, but it is to the drive-in horror picture as we now know it as the Neanderthal Man was to the Cro-Magnon. Shot in four days. Main set is a Florida motel room. The main character, a mad Egyptian named Fuad Ramses who runs a catering service, carves up a lot of girls. Best exchange:

DETECTIVE: To your knowledge, did the dead girl have any friends?

LANDLADY: No. She only belonged to a book-club.

Not bad, huh? See you at the drive-in

Best wishes,
Big Steve
Stephen King
Bangor, Maine

Dear Big Steve:

You're the king, big guy, but NIGHT WARNING?!

Anything you say, Stevie boy.

You aren't gonna believe what we got waiting for you. Even after you get it, you aren't gonna believe it.

Night Patrol—
The New Champion in Midget Pooting

Rhett Beavers got me booked into the Texarkana Airport Holiday Inn East lounge for New Year's Eve this year, so I'll be slacking off on the flicks between now and then. Rhett says ever since I punched his head in like a cheese ball at a fat people's convention, he's developed a new respect for my singing career. We tore up the first 954 pages of the Rhett Beavers Personal Management Contract, so now all it says is "Rhett Beavers agrees to get some money for Joe Bob Briggs or else his face will look like Roy Acuff used it to play Dueling Banjos." A lot of people were shooting for the Texarkana gig this year. Jackie Mason begged for it. Jack Carter said he wasn't doing the Poconos unless he could play Texarkana first. Sergio Franchi, Mel Torme, Charo—they were all on the horn to Vinnie Cordova, the booker for Club Stiletto. Peggy Lee wanted to use the club to premiere her new show: "Peggy: The Obese Years." But Vinnie said no way, José Dimaggio. Vinnie wanted a new sound, a new style, a new way of bringing in the New Year.

Really what Vinnie said was "Gimme some a that pickup-truck music," but we all knew what Vinnie meant.

Vinnie was talking Western Wave. It's sort of like taking Duran Duran and sticking three pounds of horse manure in their britches. Or you could imagine it maybe if I said it's a cross between early Ernest Tubb and late Eydie Gorme (the oh-shut-up years), with a lot of drum solos from old Perry Como songs tossed in. It's the most original sound since Chubb Fricke ate six bowls of jalapeno chili at the Elks Lodge.

Vinnie says Frank might be there for the late show.

We're shooting a live Empty-V video, with lots of close-ups of my teeth and smoke spewing out of a garden hose.

We're opening with "Donka Shane."

We're closing with "You Were a Ten When I Found You, But Inflation Has Made You the One."

And my encore: "God Wouldn't Of Made Linoleum, If He Knew Your Heart Was That Flat."

Western Wave. All new stuff. Rhett takes four percent, so buy a couple extra Harvey Wallbangers to take home to the kids.

Speaking of gaseous fumes, *Night Patrol* is the second best flick in drive-in history about the subject of uncontrollable pooting. Of course, the all-time pooting champion is *King Frat*, where the entire plot is based on the ability to poot. *Night Patrol* can't compete with that one, because *Night Patrol* doesn't *have* any plot, but *Night Patrol* is the new champion in the midget-pooting category.

Billy Barty, one of the finest midgets in midget history, is the captain of the police force in El Lay, and he stands up on top of his desk so he can stare Pat Paulsen in the belly button and order him to go out on night patrol. Only you can't hear him because of all the little poots in the background.

Course, I've seen ever Pat Paulsen movie ever made, I'll go see anything the man makes, but I'll say it here like I always say it:

Hey, Pat, get some sleep.

Pat stars in this one along with Linda (the Vomit Queen) Blair, who started her comeback last year as a piece of tenderized goat meat in *Chained Heat*. I forget what she does in this one. Mostly she sits around the police station making announcements over the radio like "Victim shot fifteen times in head, says he needs help." She's really in love with Pat Paulsen, but nobody believes it because, let's face it, Pat could have his way with any woman he wants.

I happen to know a lot about the making of this flick, because of my close personal friend the director, Jackie Kong (no relation to King). Jackie came all the way to Texas to thank me for being the only critic in America who didn't throw pig doo-doo on her last movie, *The Being*. (Remember the one where Dorothy Malone's son eats half of Idaho?) Me and Jackie are on a first-name basis now, so I asked her straight out, "Okay now, honey, how'd you make those pooter noises?"

And she said, "I held auditions."

"I don't believe it."

"No, it's true. We had *volunteers*. But I was tough. I knew exactly the sound I wanted. Finally one of my editors went home and came back with a tape full of the precise sounds I wanted."

"We're talking Billy Barty midget poots, right?"

"That's right."

"What was it like working with Big Pat the first time?"

"Great. What an actor."

"Jackie, you're a heck of an artist."

"Thank you."

"Especially when you work with midgets."

What we got here is one of those *Airplane II* deals where everybody runs around doing Woody Woodpecker imitations and crashing cars and shooting pigeons with .44 Magnums and doing mouth-to-mouth resuscitation on dead drunks and doing a bunch of jokes about cockfights and sperm banks, if you know what I mean and I hope the high sheriffs don't.

In other words, art film. They do a lot with the camera, like this guy says, "I know she loves Melvin, it's written all over her face," and the camera moves over to the bimbo and it says "I Love Melvin" on her face. That kind of stuff. Then these two gay guys come into the station and start talking about how this robber "gave us the slip," and then they show us a slip. Hilarious stuff. Like the time the cops have this maniac surrounded and they pelt him with about nine thousand rounds of gunfire and then they call for a "backup unit," and this police car drives up going backward and the cops jump out of it and run backward over to the building.

Excuse me if I take a moment here to laugh my guts out.

Okay, then there's Jaye P. Morgan, who goes around kicking men in the gazebos and managing this stand-up comedian's career, the one that only works with a bag over his head. Then some guy with a paper bag over his head holds up a leather lesbo bar called the Meat Market Saloon, and, uh-oh, I'm afraid to tell you this, but it looks like plot ahead.

I'm telling you, though, *don't*

worry about it. It goes away pronto and then all we got left is this joke about the *Dyke Van Dick Show,* and another one about how "This lesbian bar is so tough that the pool table has no balls."

No, no, I'm giving it away—sorry, I can't help myself—you got to see this one, first of the big Christmas flicks. One old rummy that gets raped by three women. One armed robber that steals people's arms. Transvestite dancing. Bag woman dancing. French subtitles for no reason. One guy in a straitjacket driving a car. Kung fu. "Cream of Washroom Soup" gross-out scene. Great sex-pervert jail scene. Six breasts. Heads do not roll. Three dead bodies. Three brawls. Two thousand poots (approximate). One sperm-bank gross-out scene. Drive-In Academy Award nominations for Pat Paulsen, Billy Barty, Jackie (no relation to King) Kong, Linda Blair. Three and a half stars (low blood count).

Joe Bob says check it out. ∎

Big Chuck Masters Helicopter Fu in *Missing In Action*

Ever year this happens to me. Ever year I get my act booked for New Year's Eve, buy four bottles of complimentary pink near-champagne, put money down on a rhythm box, spring for the plastic glasses, and then what happens? Some *sleazeball promoter* tries to capitalize on my talent. He turns it into a *commercial* operation instead of just giving me the $9,000 I deserve. He sells me down the old Porta-Toilet.

Rhett Beavers left town last week. Right before he left he called me up and said, "Joe Bob, we may have some *contract* problems out at the Texarkana Airport Holiday Inn East lounge."

"You mean Club Stiletto? Whattaya mean contract problems?"

"They're talking breach."

"Okay, okay, I'll *pay* for the gold-sequin tux, but they still gotta come up with cash for the complimentary snow-scene paperweights."

"No, no, it's even worse than that. Vinnie says he's invoking the Buddy Hackett Clause."

"Not the Buddy Hackett Clause!"

"Yeah, I know, it's rough."

"I don't believe it."

"It's true. I reread the contract. It says 'All agreements may be nullified at any time in the event that Buddy Hackett agrees to perform in the Twin Cities for the holidays.'"

"Twin Cities?"

"Texarkana, Arkansas, and Texarkana, Texas."

"I thought Buddy was working the Poconos."

"Changed his mind, I guess. I been trying to get him on the horn, but he's basking in Palm Springs and I can't get through."

"Isn't there anything in the contract that says he has to make up a new joke or something before he comes?"

"Nope. Something like that we could win easy, but it's clean as a whistle."

"Why'd we agree to the Buddy Hackett Clause in the first place?"

"It's standard in the industry, Joe Bob. When you start talking New Year's Eve, you gotta take Buddy into account. It could happen to anybody."

"So what else can you get me?"

"On this short notice? Ashdown, Arkansas, maybe. Chillicothe . . ."

"I'll *never* play Chillicothe again after what they did to the truck."

"Joe Bob, let me give you some personal advice. Calm down. Get over this. Sleep on it. Don't let it get to you. I'll be back next week, we can chew it down to size and spray it all over East Dallas."

"What?"

"Industry talk."

"Right."

So Rhett Beavers left town and I thought everthing was sliced-and-diced, and then this letter poured in from Ken Perry, the country-western music critic for the Texarkana *Gazette.* You got to understand, if Ken Perry dumps dead lizard meat on your show, you're finished in Texarkana. I'm telling you, the guy can break you. So he writes in:

Dear Mr. Briggs:

I just got word of your planned New Year's Eve Extravaganza, and let me tell you that Texarkana is ready. We've had a pretty good year entertainment wise. Ray Charles played here Thanksgiving. And Jerry Lee Lewis is playing tonight. And, of course, we're really excited about Bette Perot (Ross' sister) who will be making a homecoming speech at tomorrow night's Pioneer Descendents Association Gala. Your show, though, should be the biggest thing yet.

The only problem as I can see it, is that there is no Airport Holiday Inn East. The Twilight Motel is available then, however, and it's just down the street from the Naughty Night Lounge, a real Joe Bob Briggs Bar if there ever was one . . .

Now I would *never* accuse my personal management agent, Rhett "Swifty" Beavers, of telling me a fib. But, believe me, *somebody*—either Rhett or Buddy

Hackett—is lying on this deal, and I'm gonna get to the bottom of it.

Speaking of people *Missing In Action,* Big Chuck Norris is out there swingin his hairy underarms through the jungles in the best exploding-bamboo flick of 1984. As we all know by now, there's about three million American citizens that are still in secret prisons in Nam. So far, we've busted loose a thousand of em in *Uncommon Valor,* the first exploding-bamboo epic, and about three other Nuke-the-Gookers. We're all waiting to see what Sly Stallone does next summer in *Rambo: First Blood, Part 2,* but till then we gotta just stick with the Twin Chucks, Norris and Bronson, while they buy up all the handheld rocket launchers in Bangkok and point em at little bald-headed guys with yellow fingernails.

Ever since *Forced Vengeance,* Chuck's been working on his expression. Chuck is the only actor in the non-Communist world who can do a whole movie with the same expression. To take advantage of this, the writers keep giving him less and less words. He's still not in the Arnold the Barbarian class, with Lou Ferrigno and the big boys, where the dialogue is down to six, seven words a movie, but he's getting there. Chuck does the first twenty minutes of *Missing In Action* without saying nothing —just bombs-over-Nam, Bayonet City, kamikaze-grenade, arms-flying-through-space flashbacks. Finally Chuck can't take it any more so he kicks in his TV set and we know it's time. Time to go back to Nam and get his buddies out.

Chuck goes back to Saigon with a senator and a bimbo on a diplomatic mission, but Chuck's not very diplomatic. Like he keeps calling it Saigon even when they tell him it's Ho Chi Minh City. And like he refuses to shake hands with the president. And like he sneaks into the president's house and throws a knife through his stomach. Stuff like that. Then Chuck kung-fus a few gook soldiers and they run him out of Nam, and he goes off to Bangkok to buy enough ammo to blow up Argentina, and while he's there he picks up M. Emmet Walsh, the famous drive-in drunk villain, and takes him back to Nam for a two-man assault against about 27,000 Vietnamese troops guarding the secret jungle prison.

Also, ever time Chuck opens his closet or gets in his car, some Bruce Lee imitator jumps on him and tries to kill him.

We got everthing. We got 102 dead bodies, the 1984 drive-in record. We got Bayonet City, Grenade City, Machine Gun City, Rocket-Launcher City. We got POW wrist-hanging chest torture. About a thirty-seven on the kung fu meter, far below Chuck's usual standard. Helicopter fu. Raft fu. Two breasts. Great Bangkok topless-bar meat market scene. Two brawls. One exploding building. Two exploding gook boats. Four exploding bamboo huts. One exploding M. Emmet Walsh. Three motor vehicle chases, including one between a car, a truck, and a boat, and one between a big boat, a little boat, and a copter. Two crash-and-burns. Three crash-and-drowns. One ax in the stomach. Drive-In Academy Award nominations for Big Chuck, for mastering the single-expression movie; M. Emmet Walsh, for wearing a lot of bad Hawaiian shirts; Lenore Kasdorf, for being a gratuitous bimbo fox; and Joseph Zito, the master, the same guy who made *Friday the 13th: The Final Chapter*. Joe directed this sucker in the Philippines.

Three and a half stars.

Joe Bob says check it out. ∎

Joe Bob Hit Hard by the Meaning of Christmas

Excuse me for getting a little sentimental this time of year, but you know how I start to get all choked up when I see people making fools of themselves at the mall. You know how I love it when they put the fuzzy dice on sale. You know how it makes me cry to see the Andy Williams Christmas special. But don't get me wrong. I'm not crying because I'm sad. I'm crying because I'm p.o.ed. When are they gonna get that turkey off the air?

Anyhow, it's that time again. It's time for the annual Joe Bob Briggs Christmas story.

This year I want to tell you about my little nephew Wilbur and what the spirit of Christmas means to him.

Little Wilbur lives in a cardboard box down on Elm Street. He crawls around in an alley behind the Cattleman's Restaurant and sniffs the bacon drippings. Sometimes a maniac who smells bad will give little Wilbur a nickel, but then Wilbur will lose it because he can only count up to four. Wilbur is so poor that sometimes he rents himself out as a doorstop.

A lot of people would say little Wilbur has a sad life. But not little Wilbur. Wilbur doesn't say that. Wilbur doesn't say anything, because he has a harelip and people can't understand him. But if we *could* understand him, he's probly saying he has a sad life.

Sometimes we say, "Wilbur, why do you live in a cardboard box?"

And Wilbur will raise up his little pig face and wave the little fingers on his filthy hand and a tear will roll down his snout. And then he'll say, "Blurghl fliml."

But I can understand Wilbur, even if nobody else can. I've decided it's my gift from Santa Claus this Christmas, like a tongue-talkin holy-roller that's been turned into a human satellite receiving dish. What Wilbur said was "Do you have change for a nickel?"

I guess one of the hardest things I ever had to do was tell little Wilbur about how it's not gonna be a very merry Christmas around the trailer park this year. He said, "Flotsatch herkerelly?"

And I said, "Because we can't go to the Christmas movie this year, little w-man."

"Flotsatch Pia Zadora?"

"No, it was called *Silent Night, Deadly Night,* but some bad people came and they took it away from us."

"Zimmelbo?"

"You see, what happened, Wilbur, is it all started in Milwaukee. You're not old enough to know this yet, but everthing starts in Milwaukee until we wise up and take it away from em. Anyhow, the flick was called *Slayride,* and we been waiting all year for it, but then the movie company, they changed the title to *Silent Night, Deadly Night,* and as soon as they put it up on the screen the ladies with pink hair started writing their congressman and appearing in public with harlequin glasses. They got it banned in Milwaukee, then they went to Jersey, Chicago, Peoria, and Fort Worth, even though it never did play in Fort

Worth, but that'll give you some idea of who we're dealing with here."

"Zimmelbo Derek?"

"Right. These people are missing a few face cards."

"Fraz tindle."

"It has *everthing,* little Wilbur. In the very first scene we get to see Santa Claus get grumpy and rob a store. Then Santa stops a car, murders Daddy, rapes and murders Mommy, and makes little Billy go to a Catholic orphanage where the nuns tell him if he's not a good boy, Santa will be mean to him. Course, little Billy gets a Santa phobia and pretty soon he makes like a G.I. Joe and starts turning people into Tinker Toys. Axes, knives, one nekkid lady gets impaled on some deer antlers, Billy screws one guy into the electric-light sockets on his tree, we got a bow and arrow through the garbonzas, heads roll, and there's a great scene with a cardboard-box opener."

"Clissterama!"

"I knew you'd like that one. But there's only one problem, Willy."

"Bodiddly?"

"We aren't allowed to see the flick. The movie company cratered. It's history. It's out of here. They said no way, José Garagiola. And what that means is that this Christmas we'll just have to do without."

And little Wilbur started to cry, and I thought my heart was gonna break, and then he looked straight at me and said, "They're all a bunch of slopehead mushmouth jerks, aren't they, Uncle Joe Bob?"

"*Hallelujah!*" I shouted. "The boy is *healed!* The boy can *speak!*"

So I put little Wilbur back in his cardboard box and I gave him all the candy that was melted on the dashboard of the Toronado and I felt like I finally knew what the meaning of Christmas really is. It's that we only have to talk to Wilbur once a year. ∎

Joe Bob Needs Your Drive-In Academy Awards Vote

There's been a little confusion about just *who* is eligible to vote for the Drive-In Academy Awards. In past years a lot of sick and disturbed individuals have called up the paper or come by the trailer park, expecting they could cast a vote for the Hubbies, and so I had to make a list of eligibility rules. Here's how to tell whether you can vote or not.

Do any of the following statements apply to you?

1. I have been a permanent resident of a home for the feeble-minded for at least eight of the past ten years.

2. I am in favor of the Handguns-for-People-on-Welfare Act.

3. I live in a stolen portable toilet.

4. When I watch a Jerry Lewis movie, I completely identify with Jerry when he dances like a duck and hits himself in the head with a broom-handle.

5. I like to hang around the Greyhound station and make new friends.

If the answer to any one of the above questions was yes, you are definitely eligible to vote.

Now answer these.

1. I own a Police album.

2. I watch Empty-V until "Like a Virgin" comes on, then I get up and dance on my thumbs.

3. I can name every cereal manufactured by Kellogg's.

4. I drive a Z.

5. I refer to my car as a Z.

You people are Communist agents and I don't want you sending in any letters to Joe Bob's Mailbag.

Okay, may I have the envelope, please? (Winners will be announced at gala ceremonies in El Lay this year, on the same night as the fake Academy Awards.)

Send in your ballots and I might even open some of em.

Joe Bob's Mailbag ———

Dear Mr. Briggs:

We regret to inform you that we are considering dropping your column. The language and content just isn't on par with the readership of FOCUS.

When the Mayor told us that your column was also running in the Raleigh N&O, I was ready to dump it right then and there . . . not wanting to be associated with the likes of THAT bunch. After much pleading and sniveling from the editorial staff that assured me that they could get the Raleigh rag to drop your column, I decided to give you another chance.

If you could try to loosen up a little in the next few weeks, we might keep your column. Try not to be so high-class. If you would just be half-class like the rest of our editorial staff, your column might fit in fine.

Enclosed is a copy of last weeks paper. If we're going to give you page one headlines, we expect some SERI-OUS sleeze. After all, we're paying the big bucks for this stuff.

Sincerely,
John Tucker
Publisher
FOCUS
Hickory, N.C.

P.S. You tend to glorify Bimbos too much. Here in the Tar-Heel State, we tend to place women BENEATH a pedestal.

Dear John:

Tar Heel?

You know, I've heard of foot fetishes, but some people are just so disgusting they oughta be crated up and shipped C.O.D. to El Salvador.

I resent the remark about my "half-class." That was something that happened when I was a very small child. I got kicked in the class so many times it made my whole life "half-classed."

You keep hassling me and it's gonna cost you TWO bucks a week.

Joe Bob Wakes up Half of Texas to Get a "Thought for Today"

Last week me and Rhett Beavers got trashed on Shiner Beer and didn't get home till three, four in the A.M. It wouldn't mean diddly to me, except I missed the *Thought for the Day* on Channel 5. Flipped the set on, and all they had was some commercials about Marines lying around the beach and playing with their Seiko watches.

I *never* miss the *Thought for the Day*. I make it a part of my daily spiritual life. Like you probly remember the thought for the day of April 28, 1984, which went like this: "A teacher asked a little girl in her class, 'Would you rather be called black, or Negro?' And the little girl answered, 'I'd rather be called Carrie.'" So for two, three weeks after that I tried it. I said stuff like "Do you realize the NBA is 85 percent Carrie?" And, "Please use the Carrie drinking fountain." And I was a better person because of it.

So anyhow, last weekend I come home one night and they already played the thought for the day. So I panicked. I called up the station, but they didn't know what the thought for the day was. I woke up half Texas trying to find somebody that remembered the thought for the day. I called the cops, I called the Babtist church, I called Suicide Hot Line. I figured they're required by law to know the thought for the day, but no way, José Garagiola. I knew I was just putting it off. I was gonna have to face it.

I was heading for a whole day without a thought.

I'm not gonna sugar-coat it. It was rough. All day people looked at me and said, "Joe Bob, what do you think?" And I'd have to say, "I can't today." And they'd say, "Penny for your thoughts," and I'd say, "Hey, just be happy that you still *have* thoughts. Some people aren't so fortunate. If you thought about people besides yourself ever once in a while"—and then I realized what I was saying. "If you *thought* about people." He could think about people. I couldn't. I started crying inside.

I didn't know what to do, so

I started trying to remember some of the great thoughts of *other* days, the classics from the past. Like the one for September 12, 1974: "It only takes a second to show how much you don't care, but it takes a whole day to get out of jail." I think that was it. Something like that. Then I remembered the one from October 2, 1969: "We may all look different on the outside, but on the inside we all look disgusting." I was really surprised they put that one on TV.

But it wasn't working. They were thoughts for the *wrong day*. They were *old* thoughts. I'd already used em up. I needed the thought for *today*. So I toughed it out all day. I waited up late. I had Channel 5 turned on at 8 o'clock the next night, and I kept watching that sucker until the *Thought for the Day* finally did come on, and here's what it was: "I saw a bumper sticker the other day and all it said was 'U R NEAT.' That's what God is saying to us. We *are* neat." It was a *great* thought, better than any of the thoughts I've had since 1968. I figured out that anything you see on a bumper sticker is just God talking, like when he says, "I Brake For Born-Again Christians."

But it didn't last. Five minutes after I got the thought, I needed a new one. It was wearing off. And then I realized what was happening: I was one day behind on my thoughts and I always would be. There was no way to make up the thought that was already gone. The only thing I can think of is to have people in other cities send me in their thoughts for the day, but from the *same day* when I missed the thought for the day—February 12, 1985—or else I could be a vegetable for the rest of my life. Please take pity on me so I can stop saying "I never thought of that."

Speaking of people with a lot of empty space between their ears, *Avenging Angel* came out a couple weeks ago and I been too embarrassed to review it up to now. You remember *Angel* from last year? The three-star classic about the fifteen-year-old lambchop who goes to high school in the daytime and then goes down to Hollywood Boulevard at night and stands on the corner until some guy gives her fifty bucks if she'll go off-camera with him? Remember? Well, they messed it up.

I don't know how many times I have to say this, but if you turkeys are gonna make a sequel, *make a sequel*. Bring the dead people back to life and *do it all over again*. Go watch *Friday the 13th* one through four. But don't change up the plot on us. I shoulda known something was wrong when they didn't call it *Angel II*.

Here's what we got. It's four years later. Angel decides to hang up her crotchless panties and become a lawyer, so she's in college. But then some gorilla face mutants machine-gun a bunch of cops, including Cliff Gorman, the cop who rescued Angel from the streets after she blew away the psycho creep hooker killer into seventeen pieces. That makes Angel wanna go back to Hollywood Boulevard and find the killers and turn their heads into Rice-a-Roni too.

Okay, so what's wrong with that? I'll tell you. Because *it's not really Cliff Gorman.* It's some impostor named Robert S. Lyons, trying to pass himself off as Cliff Gorman, and Angel don't even notice. Course, that's not too surprising, because *it's not really Angel.* The jerks who made this so-called sequel *fired Donna Wilkes.* It took me about half the movie to figure it out, but it's not Donna Wilkes up there. It's some bimbo named Betsy Russell. Remember how Donna Wilkes looked like she was about twelve years old and she put on that little miniskirt and rubbed on some lipstick and had nice little transvestite friends in Hollywood and it was so cute? Well, Betsy Russell looks like she just had a head-on collision with a Max Factor truck.

Of course, Betsy did attend the Chuck Norris School of Drive-In Acting, which means she does the entire movie with one facial expression, but other than that, she just goes around saying stuff like "I'm gonna get those bastards, so help me God," and hanging around with Rory Calhoun and some street freaks, and going to the law library to help her cute hooker friends get out of jail, and talking to Ossie Davis, who's the police chief, and killing gangsters with the fumes from her makeup kit. At least in *Private School* she whipped her blouse off.

All Betsy does in this one is attack a cop with a sack of groceries.

I can't even go on with this review, I'm so disgusted. Five breasts. Nineteen dead bodies. Kung fu. Bagel fu. Female impersonator fu. Stunt baby. Two motor vehicle chases, one with pet-cemetery hearse. Drive-In Academy Award nomination for Rory Calhoun, who gouged some more money out of New World Pictures for shooting off his six-guns and yahooing around. Two stars.

Joe Bob says—nope, I can't even say it. ■

Joe Bob's Mailbag ——

Dear Joe Bob,

I don't think I ever wrote to you and told you what a good time I had in Dallas. Hope you'll give me about five years to build up a suitably disreputable stock of drive-in schlock and then invite me again. In the meantime, I was wondering if it might not be possible to kinda bridge the gap between drive-in movies and your standard indoor bull stuff art-house flick. For instance, what would you think about *Ghidra the Three-headed Monster Meets Citizen Kane?* Or what about *Night of the Living Women in the Dunes?* Or maybe the *Ingmar Bergman Chainsaw Massacre.*

Could be something in it. Give me your thinking on this.

Best wishes,
Big Steve King
Bangor, Maine

Dear Big Steve:

Okay, you're invited for the 11th annual World Drive-In Movie Festival, which we'll hold in 1992 if we don't forget, but this time you got to drive YOURSELF down here. I know it's tough on your $72 million annual income, but the Toronado can't handle another trip all the way up there to the end of the world, also known as Bangor.

By the way, Big Steve, I noticed where you wimped out on the Blood Feast screening. I don't forget these things.

Joe Bob Exposes His Real Feelings About Feminism

Some twin sisters from Memphis came out to the trailer house last week and said they were gonna raise my conscience, and I had to tell em I liked my conscience down in the dirt where it belongs. But they said, no way, José Bob Briggs, they were gonna teach me some principles of feminism, and so I said what anybody'd say under those circumstances: "Only if you take a shower first."

It took about six, seven hours for em to show me the difference between boys and girls, but they kept raising my conscience all night long. When they finally untied me, my conscience was raised so much you could of used it for a color weather map. Then Shirley, the sister that still had all her teeth, told me they were gonna go ahead and make me "vulnerable" for no extra charge. That only took about a half hour. Then, after they relieved me of my vulnerables, they started working on my "feelings." One of the sisters kept exposing my feelings with the back of her hand while the other one caressed my vulnerables. As you probly know, this is illegal in the state of Texas except when you have a health inspection license. It's okay, though, cause Rhonda, the sister with hair on both sides of her head, showed me her license. In fact, she kept showing me her license over and over again, until I had to tell her to stop it or else she could of been mistaken for a javelina hog on the first day of huntin' season.

What I'm getting at here is, I'm a new man. I learned my lesson. I learned how to stop treating women like old pieces of dirty laundry and start treating em like pieces of beat-up Woolco lawn furniture.

No, really, let's get cereal here for a minute.

Here it is. Here's what happened to me:

I've used the word "bimbo" for the last time.

I know, I know, it's not gonna be a popular stand, but I'm not a popular kind of guy. There'll probly be 27,000 letters to Joe Bob's Mailbag, demanding bimbo rights. You know what I say to that? Eight zero. The big eight-oh. It's the eighties, guys. We got to get in touch with our true feelings and then lie about em.

You probly don't even think I can do it. Ordinarily I use the word "b----" an average of 92,000 times a week. So go ahead and scoff. Try to *make* me say it. You can't do it. I'm immune. I've finally seen women for what they really are, and believe me, it's not a pretty sight.

Shirley and Rhonda are coming over again Tuesday night to raise my conscience eight or nine more times. That's how committed I am. I even painted a sign for Rhonda and Shirley and put it up

in the bathroom at the Debonair Danceland for the benefit of those who want to get their vulnerables altered. I even sent a letter to Geraldine Ferraro telling her how I'm sorry I made fun of her two enormous talents.

They aren't really that enormous, are they? It's the kind of distortion we're all guilty of when we look at the world through plastic glasses with a fake mustache on the bottom.

Speaking of nekkid women that need to be chained up all the time, Leslie Wing is the star of *The Dungeonmaster,* and it's one of the finest performances by a whining, nagging woman since the kinky star of *Human Animals,* the ultimate dog movie.

No plot to get in the way of the story. Fifteen beasts. Sixteen dead bodies. No breasts. Two quarts blood. Kung fu. Guitar fu. Devil fu. Wax statue fu. Two motor vehicle chases, with head-on crash-and-burn. Dueling cartoon firedragons. Gratuitous aerobic dancing. A forty-seven on the vomit meter. Drive-In Academy Award nominations for Leslie Wing, the woman in chains, and Richard Moll, the devil that likes to burn up cats. Special drive-in AA citation for being the first movie in history to have seven directors. They kept firing em till they got it right.

Two and a half stars. Joe Bob says check it out. ∎

Joe Bob's Mailbag ———

Dear Joe Bob:

Could you please tell me, what is it that women want?

Yrs., etc.
John McLean
Dallas

Dear John:

You think we put garbage like that in a newspaper?

Dear Joe Bob:

I am sure that you have heard, but I wanted to let you know that the Seattle Times has seen fit to drop your excellent column of movie reviews out of its Tempo section.

Needless to say, this decision has caused a great deal of consternation among hard-core Joe Bob fans in the Tri-Cities of Richland, Kennewick and Pasco, Washington.

Four of us have gotten together to write a letter to the editor of the Time's Arts and Entertainment section. Check it out!

Meanwhile, we will have to try to locate another newspaper with the journalistic integrity to carry your writing.

Cheers!
Steve Irish
Richland, Wash.

Dear guys:

I hope you realize "Tempo" is a foreign Eyetalian word.

Joe Bob Makes Do with Warped Brain He Got from Evolution

One time when I was in Nashville they took me over to the hospital where all the Grand Ole Opry stars go to get their brain surgery, and I said, "Hey, can anybody walk in here and get a free brain examination," and they said, "Everbody except people with harelips," and so I let em take a look inside my skull to find out the answer to the question, What made me turn out like this anyhow?

What they found out was, I wouldn't of been this way except for the school I went to in Hooks,

Texas, where they deformed my brain without my permission. J. Finley Epps Junior High School was one of the very first places in America to start teaching evolution instead of the truth. They taught me that I'm descended from Darwinian monkeys, which is the kind they have in places like Boston, when we all know what the truth is: It was *God* that made us look like monkeys.

Course, as soon as the doctors found out what was wrong, they said, "Joe Bob, we're sorry to have to break this to you, but we're gonna have to go inside your head with a drill and try to laser out some of that evolution teaching that's in there or else you'll just keep getting weaker and weaker until you start eating banana pudding all the time and begging to go on the *Donahue Show.*"

And I asked em if there wasn't any other treatment for it, and they said, "We could try chemotherapy, but we'd have to take you to Disneyland first."

And finally I said, "Oh hell, just leave it."

And they didn't wanna do it at first, but I figure, if that's the kind of brain they gave me in junior high, I'll just stick with it till I get ready to go back and finish eighth grade. But that means I got to explain some things about my personal beliefs that were caused by gettin taught so much evolution:

Like I used to believe that, In the beginning God looked like a monkey and He created the heav-

ens and the earth and He created man in His own image and He called him ugly. And then a lot of time passed and we evolved into human beans. Course, now I know from personal experience with people like Chubb Fricke and Ugly on a Stick that we're still as ugly as we ever were.

And I used to think the preacher at Antioch Babtist Church looked like a gorilla with a blow-dry pompadour haircut, but now I know that God kicked him out of the Garden of Eden like everbody else and forced him to wear a plaid sport coat.

And I used to think it was natural for people to go around groping each other like bunny rabbits and shooting each other's ears off in beer joints and stealing each other's wives and putting down your brother man like he was a piece of rotten goat meat. But now I know it's God that wants all those things.

So you can see I don't need the surgery anyhow. I already know how to comb my face.

Speaking of intestine-eating cannibals, *Make Them Die Slowly* is getting censored and banned all over the United States and thirty-one foreign countries, and I think we all know why. Umberto Lenzi, also known as the Italian Lee Harvey Oswald, made this one, and, okay, Umberto is a *little different* from you and me. But just because we don't agree with somebody's opinions is no reason to start Communist censorship all over the lot. Okay, okay, so Umberto did put quite a few scenes in of anacondas eatin little furry animals and tigers chewin up monkeys in the jungle. And, all right, he did get a little carried away with the punji-stick impalements. But when Umberto did that scene with the three-inch-long bloodsuckers, where the cannibals tie the American drug dealer to the stake and gouge out his eyeball with a machete and hack off his privates, I have to say, I really *felt* something. It was like in *National Geographic* or something.

What we got here is a bunch of stupid white people from New York University who go down to the Amazon Jungle to prove cannibalism don't exist, but on the way they have to keep stopping so this blonde named Myrna can have sex with anything that moves. Then they meet up with these two coke-head drug dealers that are down there using the natives to make bean-bag chairs and pretty soon everbody's getting turned into a Swanson TV dinner. There's a great educational scene where the cannibals put Aunt Jemima flour all over their faces and eat scrambled Joe. But I guess my favorite part is when they start cutting off different parts of Mike's body, like they were ordering out from Colonel Sanders, and while they're doing that they do the female version of *A Man Called Horse* on Myrna and then they put the top of Mike's head up through a hole in a wooden table so they can make cheese dip.

We're talking world drive-in record material here: a ninety-eight on the vomit meter. Fourteen dead bodies. Eight breasts. Squished-bird eating. Caterpillar eating. Cannibal torture. Leech sucking. Caged humans. Stupid white people torture. Pig torture (don't tell Ralph). Blow-dart fu. Eyeball rolls. Arm rolls. Gazebos roll. Half a head rolls. Two gratuitous furry-animal murders. Great slime-eating tribe of extras. (Hope you guys got the full 20 cents a day for your work.) Turtle hacking. Hooks through the—no, I can't say it, I have too much respect for women. Drive-In Academy Award nomination for Umberto Lenzi, for escaping from the asylum long enough to write lines like "What a waste of vacation!" and "No, don't eat that! It might be Rudy!"

Four stars. Joe Bob says scream like hell till your neighborhood drive-in lets you check this sucker out. ∎

Joe Bob Resorts to Ad to Find the Right Woman for Falling in Love

This week I decided to fall in love. I never have done it before and I think it might be kind of kinky.

It's about time anyhow. It's been two weeks now since the twin sisters from Memphis came down here, raised my conscience eight or nine times one night, taught me to be vulnerable, and then untied me. I been a new man ever since. I decided right then and there what I needed was a woman, and I was willing to pay good money for one. So I started looking through my mailbag under "Virgins Seeking Fulfillment," and so far this is all I come up with:

Numero uno: Two extremely nasty females in Denver that sent in some pictures of theirselves, goosing each other in a K-Mart photo booth. It looks like they're offering some kind of Mormon package. No neck-down information. A five on the Purina Dog Chow meter. Acceptable at 2 A.M. on a Tuesday night.

Numero two-o: A blond fox in Sarasota that sent in a bunch of astrology bullstuff, wanting to know my sign. (The bull, of course.) Blurry Polaroid of her and her weasel-dog. She says she needs somebody to "make me laugh." She looks like she laughed once back in 1954. Got some mileage on her, and evidently she stuffs money down the front of her dress. I could probly marry this one for three, four weeks.

Numero three-o: Punk-rock groupie in North Hollywood that asked me a bunch of questions about Empty-V. Didn't send a picture but describes herself as a weirdo. Probly my kind of girl, unless her hair looks like a map of Uganda.

Numero four-o: Girl in North Richfield, O., that writes on bunny-rabbit stationery and puts little hearts over her i's and wants me to come take her away to some exciting place like Toledo. We're talking statutory.

Numero five-o: Married lady in Akron that can bench-press a Chrysler and got a jail sentence for beating her husband to a mushy pulp that looked like a roll of Charmin tissue that got dropped in the toilet bowl. Wants to crush me with her thighs. I referred her to Chubb Fricke, the horniest ex-professional bowler in Texas.

I could go on with this list, but I think you can see what we're looking at here: a cross-section of American femalehood. Too hard to choose. So I decided to throw all of em out and go directly for the groceries. So I wrote up a "Personal" ad for the lonely-hearts column, only then I thought, What the hey? Why not just abuse my position as an American journalist and put the sucker in my column and then I won't have to pony up to a buck fifty a line. So here's what I come up with:

Mostly white male, over 19, drive-in movie critic, shy, drunk, wants to meet sensitive, caring slut. Prefers to fall in love, unless you have huge garbonzas, which I'll handle on a breast-by-breast basis. Do you like long walks in the park? Then take a hike. Under 75 years old desired. Experienced virgin preferred. Send photo so I can do an ugly check. This is serious. I am NOT jacking you around. *We're talking death-do-us-part, unless we get a divorce. Love, Joe Bob Briggs, P.O. Box 33, Dallas, TX 75221.*

My heart is pounding wildly.

I can't wait. I'm gonna make the big step. I'm gonna keep looking until I find the meat of my dreams. ∎

Joe Bob's Mailbag ——

Dear Joe Bob,
  I have been reading your column for a while, and I don't understand what is going on. What are "garbonzas"? What does the suffix "fu" mean? What are "groceries"? When you say, "if you know what I mean, and I think you do," what do you mean? Are you communicating in some kind of code?

Ever questioning,
Juris Odins
Denver, Colo.

Dear Juris:
  Okay, "garbonzas" are a type of pea grown in California. The suffix "fu" refers to people who fail to take showers. "If you know what I mean and I think you do" means "Don't tell Juris Odins what this means."

Joe Bob Denies He Killed Chernenko, Wants to Meet New Honcho

Just when I was learning how to pronounce Konstantin Chickenski. All I got to say about it is, I was nowhere close to Moscow when the death occurred. I have no knowledge of any circumstances surrounding the man's trip to Commonist Heaven. (I understand he rode up on a tractor.) I will have no further comment.

All I got to say is, death does not make me happy. The fact that the guy's lying there cold as a mackerel with his face all puffed up from all the drugs they pumped in him—this does not make me want to laugh. But I'm *not* gonna talk about it. I don't want to dwell on it.

I'll tell you one goldurn thing, though. The man was not happy. He was all screwed up from working in the KGB and sneaking around Bloomingdale's spying on the Russians that were trying to buy crotchless panties and take em back to the wife in Vladivostok. They say Chickenski was so good he could disguise hisself as a Ford Fairlane and cause internal revenue agents to sit on his stomach while he was working. But that's enough of that. The man is dead. He's outta here. He's history. They're working overtime this week, ripping up the Commonist Encyclopedia and puttin in that embarrassing incident with the Siberian huskie when Chickenski had to be excused from the table.

Okay, let's see who's next in line to keel over like a goldfish that had Amoco 10-W-40 poured in his tank.

Grabachek. Mikhail Grabachek. Take a good look at him. Remember that face. Remember how he looks like a deer on the first day of season. Remember that shiny head with the tattoo on it. They say he got that tattoo when he was in the navy. He got drunk one night in San Diego, went over to Tijuana, and told em to write "Mother Russia" on his bald spot, only he forgot how to spell it so he told em to erase it and do it in French. That's the kind of guy he is. Tattooed.

So let's all be nice to the guy by sending him the following letter:

Dear Grabachek:

We don't want you to nuke us, and we don't wanna have to nuke you for being a Commonist, so we'd like to invite you over to agree to act peaceable except when we get mad at one another.

We're getting a keg and everthing.

Do you know how to play Vodka Chugalug?

Want us to line up some dates for you, and if so, do you like em nasty, fat, or what? I probly have a few close personal friends I could line up to remind you of the five-year plan for Soviet agriculture. We can also provide farm animals, but only if you give us twenty-four-hour notice.

We'll slip you a few Playboys *on the side.*

No hugging, though.

What I'm trying to say is, let's gets drunk and talk world extermination. Detente City.

Later gator,
Joe Bob Briggs
Drive-In Ambassador

As you can see, I'm all for talking to the Russians, at least till we get more nukes than them.

Speaking of ugly, *Ghoulies* opened last week and I got to say it's the best *Gremlins* rip-off in the last month.

What we got here is the finest midget actress working today. Tamara de Treaux. People talk about Drew Barrymore being in *E.T.* Tamara de Treaux *was* E.T. She was inside the guy, turning him into a star, but does Spielberg the wimp give her any credit? She

had to go get drive-in work before they'd even let us see her face, and she's *great* in a leading role as a Satanic midget.

Here's the deal. This college-student couple inherits a haunted mansion, only they don't know it's haunted cause they're so stupid they both look about thirty-five years old and they still han't graduated. Little does Jonathan know that it's the same house where his daddy ripped out his mama's heart and let her get eat up by rat-monsters. But now Jonathan starts reading the magic books in the basement and dressing up like a Ku Klux Klan member and holding a spear up and saying "Gitchee Goomee Gomer Pyle," until his eyes turn green and his robes starting flying in the wind and these little yellow-intestine creatures show up and then two midgets get zapped into the room so they can say, "We are here to serve you, Master."

Then Jonathan throws a party, but his wife gets suspicious, freaks out, and ruins the scrambled eggs when the ghoulies start playing in the food and jumping around on the Greek statues, and especially after Jonathan's father jumps out of the grave and comes back after twenty-five years, looking like Professor Irwin Corey with face herpes. So Jonathan zaps his wife into a trance and wraps up all his dinner guests in Ku Klux Klan sheets and the slime starts to spew.

We got nine dead bodies. Two breasts. Midget fu. Tongue fu. Devil fu. Two beasts. Tongue-talkin. Whining. Wailing. Screaming. Face-eating. Rat attack. Spear-chucking. Exploding heart. Laser-eye special effects. Academy Award nominations for Keith Joe ("They call me") Dick, as a stoned geek; Peter Liapis, as Jonathan, who says things like "I've got an idea! Let's do a ritual!"; Lisa Pelikan, as his wife, for saying stuff like "You bastard! You didn't tell me you were into magic!"; Luca Bercovici, the star of *Parasite,* who directed this sucker; Tamara de Treaux, the *real* E.T.; and Peter Risch, for best performance by a male midget dressed up like a clump of moss. With the one-star deduction, we're talking two and a half stars.

Joe Bob says check it out. ■

Joe Bob's Mailbag ——

Dear Joe Bob,

You are a disgusting, chauvanistic, redneck, racist, sexist, etc, etc—and I think I love you! Here in the home for the mentally troubled you are hot stuff! Could you print a picture of yourself? All of us girls would like to pin you up. We have to have your column smuggled in— "they" seem to feel it caused those last two riots—and maybe a food fight.

Love (or lust),
Lili M.
County Mental Health
San Diego, Calif.

Dear Lili:

The last time I sent a picture of myself you people acted normal for three weeks and seventeen people lost their jobs. I'm not gonna be responsible for that ever again. Do you understand me? Now act crazy like you're supposed to.

Joe Bob Announces
Annual Academy Awards
for Best Drive-In Bullstuff

Okay, let's get right to it before all the nominees start taking their clothes off like they did last year, in a shameless attempt to influence the members of the Academy, if you know what I mean and I think you do. The drive-in Academy Awards are not the time for immature attempts at humor, specially since some of you gals have such small breasts.

I'd like to lead us in a moment of silent prayer at this time, for the late, great drive-in star Vic Morrow, who was chopped into smithereens by a helicopter being used to make indoor bullstuff. As you know, the Hubby Awards always begin with the Vic Morrow minute of silence, which will start right now.

Amen.

The Drive-In Academy is now in session. Would everyone in the reading audience please raise his or her right hand or hands and repeat the Drive-In Oath after me. Big Steven King will be leading the oath from his home in Bangor, Maine. All right, Steve, you may begin:

We are drive-in mutants.
We are not like other people.
We are sick.
We are disgusting.
We believe in blood,
In breasts,
And in beasts.
We believe in Kung Fu City.
If life had a Vomit Meter,
We'd be off the scale.
As long as one single drive-in
Remains on the planet
Earth,
We will party like jungle animals,
We will boogie till we puke.
Heads will roll.
The drive-in will never die.
Amen.

Okay, dry your eyes immediately and pass me the first envelope. We have a special award this year. We've never offered it before, but it's the Chubb Fricke Memorial Award for Fat Actors. The nominees are:

J. Dinan Myrtetus (for *The Power),* the Chubb Fricke lookalike in *Surf 2;* Broderick Crawford in *Dark Forces;* Michael Rapport in *Hardbodies;* Powers Boothe in *Red Dawn;* William

Marin in *The Warrior and the Sorceress.*

And the winner is: Broderick Crawford, who put away eighty-four lobster dinners just to train for his role in *Dark Forces,* the movie where the devil tries to break Broderick's neck but he can't because *Broderick doesn't have a neck.*

We will now proceed to the traditional Drive-In Academy Award categories. All winners will receive an engraved Chevy Hubcap whenever I get around to sending em out. We'll begin with:

BEST DIRECTOR

Lucio Fulci, the Italian Stallion, working with killer snakes on *Conquest* and zombie realtors on *House by the Cemetery,* the best dubbing in Rome, and sets that make Italy look exactly like Paramus, N.J. It's about time we recognize these foreign directors for the contribution they're making to the drive-in experience worldwide.

BEST GROSS-OUT SCENE

And the winners are:

Sammy Davis Jr., Burt Reynolds, and Dom Deluise, dressing up in ladies' clothes and singing Broadway show tunes in *Cannonball II.*

BEST ATTACK-OF-THE-STUPID-WHITE-PEOPLE FLICK

Sheena, Queen of the Jungle, for the killer-flamingo attack and the scene where the wimp says "How much I love you, Sheena, so much it busts my heart."

BEST BEAST

The space herpy in *Ice Pirates,* the only sci-fi monster ever to spread a veneral disease by jumping out of a Thanksgiving turkey.

BEST EXPLODING BAMBOO FLICK

Missing In Action, with Big Chuck Norris liberating seven million of the American prisoners still being held in Southeast Asian prisons by turning the gooks into rice-paddy manure.

BEST KUNG FU

Grace Jones, wild woman in a burr haircut, breaking male spears and poling guys in their privates in *Conan the Destroyer.*

BEST NUCLEAR-WASTE DISPOSAL FLICK

The Being, where Dorothy Malone's kid falls into the nuclear dump, turns into a glopola monster, and eats half of Idaho.

BEST PSYCHO

John Diehl, hooker killer in *Angel* who likes to make love to dead bodies and twist knives in bimbo stomachs and suck the yolk out of the bottom of eggs while he's looking at a picture of his mama and scrub himself raw with a brush and drool a lot and dress up like a Hare Krishna. He also does some weird stuff.

BEST ACTOR

Arnold the Barbarian, now doing ever picture he makes with less than ten words of dialogue, and continuing to wear all his muscles on the outside of his body.

BEST ACTRESS

Lucinda Dickey, the dark-horse candidate, overcoming 30-million-dollar Tanya and Bo budgets to prove that white people can dance like Negroes, in *Breakin';* little girls can break all bimbo-fu records, in *Ninja III: The Domination;* and one actress can make three movies for the extra-low-budget Cannon Group in a single year.

BREAST ACTRESS

Maria Socas (of course), for her four-garbonza witch-lady Argentine belly dance in *The Warrior and the Sorceress.*

BEST FLICK

Finally, the moment we've all been waiting for.

And the winner is:

The Terminator! Was there ever any doubt? Arnold, come on down here and don't say a few words. Once again, in 1984, a bleak year for the outdoor cinema, drive-in history was made.

Finally, I'd like to say a few words to you people who didn't win Hubbies this year:

You didn't *deserve* to win. Check you in 86. ■

Joe Bob's Mailbag ——

Dear Mr. Comrade Briggs,

I just want to tell you how futile is your fight to save drive-ins of U.S. I and other tireless workers for Soviet supremacy are ever plotting to tear down the American outdoor big-screen movie places. We know that the less violence, blood, and ammunition Americans are viewing, the weaker is their will to combat aggression. The less firm female flesh they are seeing, the less stiff is their resistance to certainty of Soviet world domination. As we destroy militaristic U.S. drive-in industry we are ever building the Soviet drive-in propaganda machine which we invented first anyway. Right now, both of the drive-ins in Soviet Union are booked with highly popular films on tractor repair, but soon all five of our beautiful Soviet actresses will star in different adventure films that will be shown.

While American citizens fall asleep in too-warm indoor movie boxes during three-hour pictures about Soviet satellite country of India, stout communist people honk their horns with happiness as they watch the west get beat-up again on bigger-than-yours Soviet cold outdoor-air movie screen. Ha!

A. Soviet Spy
working to close all the
American drive-ins
Mesa, Ariz.

Dear Russian Spyski:

Ever since we let Jimmy Carter negotiate, we been giving away all our drive-in technology. And what do we get in return? Nada.

But just wait till we send Lee Iacocca over there to dance around the table with Grabachek. The man's an animal.

Joe Bob Fumes over Easter Egg Censorship

Okay, there's no need to get hysterical here. Calm down. I han't decided yet whether I'm gonna round up eighteen thousand extremely stupid drunk wranglers and take em down to the Galleria shopping center and start kicking in the windows at Tiffany's and Marshall Field's, because I'm not that type of person and I wouldn't want anybody to get hurt and I specially wouldn't want the old ladies with big ole diamonds on their neck wrinkles to get scared out of their orthopedic underwear and start shopping at Neiman's. We wouldn't want *that* now, would we?

Course, putting my left boot upside the head of a wimp jewelry-store salesman is not my favorite thing in the world to be doing. It's probly about my third favorite thing in the world to be doing. But these people leave me no other choice except to disregard my personal feelings and start drop-kicking some personnel.

They censored me off the face of the known human globe again.

About two months back they called me up and said they wanted me to be in the annual celebrity Easter egg contest where they get famous people like Morey Amsterdam to paint stuff on ostrich eggs and then they put em on display and then they have an auction at the World Championship Tennis fat-ladies ball and stick it to a bunch of oilmen for the big bucks. It's basically a Vegas scam they run ever year for illiterate people that got more money than God.

I agreed to do this for one reason and one reason only: I wanted to raise some money for *little helpless crippled children.*

I have an extremely personal reason for doing this. I refuse to say what it is, but it has something to do with the long-term effects of Arkansas Polio Weed use. I'm sorry, that's all I'm gonna say. It's too personal. I'd tell Jerry at the telethon, but that's it. Anyhow, like I say, I wanted to help some little pathetic crippled children.

So I got a team of big-deal fancy designer artist guys in Dallas to work for *878 hours* painting my big ole ostrich egg. I'm not gonna tell you which fancy designer artist guys it was, cause they say they're too modest and also their wives'll kill em and also they'll never work again. But I told em *exactly* what to do with the egg. I wanted it to be a patri-

otic theme, the most beautiful thing we have here in America, All-American, enormous, but something the ordinary guy can own. Almost ever household has at least two, and there are more than 200 million of em in the United States alone. So anyhow, I spent all my time for two months directing the work on this egg, and two weeks ago I take it over there to the 95-billion-dollar bigwhiz shopping center where they wanted to put it out in front of Tiffany's—and what you think happens?

They put a big black box over it. I called up a wimp named George and said, "Why's there a big black box on my egg for the little crippled children?" And he said, "We can't put it out in public." And I said, "You know, I could of made this egg for my personal favorite charity, the United Negro College Fund, but I gave it to you so we could get some heavy jack for the little gimps." And he said, "It's a very accurate representation of what it's supposed to be. What can I say?"

And I said did you cover up Goldie Hawn's egg? She han't made a decent flick since *Private Benjamin,* she *deserves* to get hassled a little bit. And he said, no way, José.

And I said did you put a whammy on Lee Iacocca's egg? That man could stand to be stuffed in a black box. And he said nosirooney.

And I said what about Liberace, Bill Blass, Linda Gray, Peter Max, Phyllis Diller, Greer Garson, George Burns, and all the *other* Johnny Carson guest hosts that hang around the post office all day collecting million-dollar checks for saying "Gee, I love to work New York"? Nope. Nope. Nope. Nope. And nope.

Only *one* egg got censored. And I think we all know what that means. First I want signs put up at ever drive-in and Western Auto in town, saying "Boycott Tiffany's." Do *not* buy any stimulated diamonds at that place, just tell her to wait till you get to Vegas. And then I want you to go find ever crippled kid you can and say, "Hey! You! Kid! Wouldn't you like to see Joe Bob's censored drive-in Easter egg? The one they say is too graphic for children?" And then let's *see* how committed these people are to the crippled kids of America. But if that don't work, we only got one choice. I'm sorry, I hate to do it, but we may have to resort to:

Egg Fu Yung.

Speaking of people that look like a plate full of scrambled eggs, *Friday the 13th, Part 5: A New Beginning* is the best Spam-in-a-cabin flick since *Friday the 13th, Part 2*. I don't wanna put down Three and Four, but, let's face it, after fifty-two kids die in the same cabin, it's time to try something new.

They got a new cabin.

I'll just run over the plot real quick: machine in stomach, ice pick in neck, fat kid axed in the back for being fat, Meskin blowtorched through the face for wearing a slick black jacket, another Meskin's throat slit for driving a bad car, coke-head in a Charger axed in the head, hot-to-trot waitress axed in stomach, tummy machete for a redneck that smells bad, garden shears in the eyeballs for two nekkid dopers making the sign of the two-humped whale in the woods, steel pipe through the back for a black dude with gold chains and a Michael Jackson haircut, head sliced off a guy named Junior for being named Junior, cleaver in an old hag's head while she's making slop stew, a cleaver in the head for a guy cause he stutters, a cleaver through the back for the girl who laughs at the guy that stutters, and a cleaver through the muscle shirt for a punker girl that practices Negro dancing all the time. I think we can see why all these people had to die.

Satisfies the first Joe Bob rule of horror: Anybody can die at any moment. Best *Part 5* sequel in movie history. Six breasts. Twenty-one dead bodies. Eight kitchen implements. Six lawn-and-garden implements. Four farm implements. Three auto-body-shop implements. Two martial-arts devices. Three quarts blood. Heads roll. Eyeballs roll. Hand rolls. Kung fu. Bulldozer fu. Chainsaw fu. Outhouse fu. Golden Hockey Mask Award for Dick Wieand, only the fifth Jason in history. Chubb Fricke Memorial Award for Humongous Actors: Dominic Brascia, as the obnoxious chocolate-eating Joey. Drive-In Academy Award nominations for John Shepherd, as

Tommy, so disturbed by the death of Jason that he beats the crap out of everbody he meets; Carol Lacatell and Ron Sloan, as Ma and Pa Geek; and Melanie Kinnaman, for doing the Jamie Lee Curtis screaming crawl through the muck. Four stars.

Joe Bob says check it out. ▪

Joe Bob, Drive-In Artists, Join Forces for Minorities with "We Are the Weird"

This is the day you all been waiting for. I realize a lot of the radio stations in the country decided to exploit this thing commercially and not take it in the spirit it was intended, but this is the first *official* day of the drive-in song, "We Are the Weird," written and performed by all the drive-in artists of the world, for the benefit of minority groups in Africa and the United Negro College Fund in the United States, cause I think we should be sending as many Negroes to college as we can, specially the stupid Negroes. We cut the record last week, and everybody was there, and it was the emotional experience of my life. Leatherface showed up, Jason was there, Mamie Van Doren, Jamie Lee Curtis, the Swamp Thing, Pia Zadora, Big Chuck Bronson, and they all stood there, swaying from side to side, arms linked (except for the Mutant, who don't have arms) and singin their little hearts out.

I'd like to point out how I don't get a penny out of this, except 35 percent raked off the top for use of my personal production facilities out at Lake Grapevine. Other than that, I don't get nothin. Lyrics by Joe Bob Briggs, music by Smokey Robinson and the Everyday Occurrences. Here goes, world premiere, Empty-V video comin later, you were there, attention please ladies and gentlemen, could we have ladies and gentlemen, could we have a drum roll please, here it is, b/f/d for charity, thank you, could we have a little silence in the room *por favor?*

(First verse boys only:)
There comes a time
When we need a piece of meat
When the world
Must scrape together some grub
There are Negroes dying
And it's time to make em eat
They don't really need no Nutra-
Sweet.

(Take it, girls:)
We can't go on
Pretending day by day
That someone else
Will build the cafeterias . . .
We all need chow to stuff our faces
with
And the truth, you know, goat
meat
Is all we need.

(Everbody now, make it wail, sing out:)
We are the weird,
We are the starvin,
We are the scum of the filthy earth,
So let's start scarfin . . .
There's a goat-head bakin
We're callin it their food,
If the Meskins can eat it,
They can eat it too.

(Okay, bring it down, Stevie and Willie only:)
Send em a heart so they'll know
that someone cares
And a lung, and an elbow, and
three big toes,
As the Big Guy told us, we should
always clean our plate,
Cause then all the Africans' stom-
achs won't look gross.

(Backup singers, chorus, Lionel Richie groupies, everbody:)
We are the weird,
We are the starvin,
We are the scum of the filthy earth,
So let's start scarfin . . .
There's a burger bakin
We're callin it Big Mac
But all it really has inside
Is a roach's back.

(Down again, Diana, Michael and all sissies:)
When you're down and out,

And there seems no slop at all.
Cause they took it for the tourists
at the Hilton Hotel,
Let us realize that they need it just
the same
Cause they don't know how to eat a
beetle shell.

(Big finish, drive it home, Hallelu-jah!:)
We are the weird,
We are the starvin,
We are the scum of the filthy
earth,
So let's start scarfin . . .
There's a Moon Pie waitin
And a Dr. Pepper too
And we'll send out for Shakey's
pizza,
Me and you.

I don't know about you, but I'm too choked up to play it again. All I can say is, by buying this song ($19.95, payable to Joe Bob Briggs Records), you are playing an important part in the fight to perpetuate a tragedy. I thank you, the Africans thank you, and Leatherface thanks you.

It's too bad "We Are the Weird" previewed in the same week as my review of *The Last Dragon,* cause the movie's just gonna get swept under the carpet in all the excitement and we're talkin about the best Negro kung-fu musical of 85. The star is a guy named Leroy, also known as Bruce Leeroy, who lives in Harlem above the family binness, the only Negro pizza joint in New York ("Justa directa yo feetsa to Daddy Green's Pizza"). All Leroy does is watch Bruce Lee movies, go to kung-fu class, wear a little Chinaman's hat, say stuff like "I am confused, Master," and take guff off a dude named Sho Nuff, the Shogun of Harlem, who dresses like the heavyweight pimp of the world. What we got here is black guys acting like Chinamen, and Chinamen trying to jive, and stupid white people all over the lot, trying to cheat the Negroes out of their Empty-V record money. We got kung-fu dancing. We got a gang fight in front of a moviehouse screen where Bruce Lee is kick-boxing in *Enter the Dragon.* We got piranha tanks. We got throwing stars, Nunchucks, and Chinese break-dancing to the song "Suki Yaki Hot Saki Sue." We got punks and geeks and professional killer wrestlers. We got something out of the mind of Berry Gordy, king of Motown Records, master of jive music.

No breasts. One quart blood. Eighteen beasts. Ten kung-fu scenes. Disco fu. Kid fu. Lightning-fist Negro fu. Seven brawls. Face-beating. Ankle-biting. Great "Kiss My Converse" scene. Four dead bodies. Drive-In Academy Award nominations for Taimak, as Bruce Leeroy, for being named Taimak; Vanity, as the Empty-V fox hostess, for being named Vanity; Julius J. Carry III as Sho Nuff, the Shogun of Harlem; Leo O'Brien, Leeroy's kid brother, who says affectionate brother stuff like "You chocolate-covered yellow peril ping-pong-playing chow-mein-for-brains kung-fu-head"; Christopher Murney, as one of the best stupid white people gangsters of the year; and a bunch of other Negroes and Chinamen that all look alike. Four stars.

Joe Bob says twist and shout, check it out. ∎

November 22, 1963. April 16, 1985. They said it couldn't happen again.

I guess I'll always remember where I was when they killed me on national TV, right after the Maybelline commercial. I guess we all will. Who couldn't remember the look on the high sher-iff's face when he said, "Joe Bob's dead!" I know a lot of people ran through the streets of downtown Dallas, screaming hysterically:

"The drive-in critic's dead!"

"Oh, my God, Joe Bob is history!"

"He's outta here!"

"He owed me twenty bucks!"

Stuff like that. Even though the high sheriff was arrested at the scene by TV reporters with bad hair, there were immediate rumors of an international Communist conspiracy, the "three-gun theory," the "act of God theory," the bizarre "one-garbonza theory," and the "What would happen if you dropped Joe Bob Briggs off a seven-story building and watched him splatter all over the pavement?" theory.

Course, I immediately called my personal lawyer, Bubba Barclay, and I said, "Bubba, how dead am I?"

And Bubba said, "I don't know, let's go over to Parkland Emergency and find out."

So me and Bubba fired up the Toronado and hauled it up Stemmons Freeway, topped out at a good thirty-five, forty miles an hour, and, course, when we got there it was pandemonium. The first thing I did, I jumped out of the car and grabbed this old crippled guy with IVs hangin out of his arms, and I blinked back tears, and I said to him, "How do you spell pandemonium?"

And he told me and I went on inside and tried to revive me.

It was not a pretty sight. The whole right side of my face was ripped off and sewed on my stomach. My eyeballs were stuck on the back of my knees. All the interns were standin around saying "Hey! You! Want a hit of this stuff?" There were guys with walkie-talkies running all over the hospital, screaming *"We have to find somebody that knows the Drive-In Oath. We have to find somebody before this gets to Moscow."*

Course, it was already too late. I guess the saddest story, the kind of thing that just makes you sick, is when they announced the news to an elementary school class in the little Communist Russia town of Vladi-tube-sock. Hearing that Joe Bob was dead, six- and seven-year-olds cheered.

All over eastern Mesquite, children were sent home from school. In Fort Worth, junior high school students were asked to write essays on the topic "Joe Bob Briggs: Who Gets All His Money?"

Out here at the trailer park, we had candlelight vigils till 2 A.M., which is the time we burned down three mobile homes from letting drunks carry the candles.

Pope John Paul II was so grief-stricken that he refused to comment.

All over the world people were asking the question, "Why? Why this senseless tragedy? Who's next? Wayne Newton?" Other people were asking the question, "Huh?"

How did it happen? people been asking me. What the heck, who the heck, and heck.

It was all for one simple reason: *I wanted to do something for poor little starving nekkid African kids.*

I know it's not a popular

cause. I coulda picked something easy, like starting a cable-TV network for the Ayatollah. But that's just the kinda guy I am. Yes, it's true. I wrote "We Are the Weird." I didn't even want credit for it. I'd be just as happy if I never saw a penny from it and all the money went straight to my four ex-wives. It was just something I wanted to do. Most of the money was gonna go to building a chain of Wyatt's Cafeterias in ever nation of Africa. The rest was gonna be spent on buying basketball scholarships to the University of Houston for every Ethiopian child that wanted one.

Hey, call me sentimental, call me hokey, call me a guy that sleeps in his underwear. You know, in this Easter season of ours, I like to reflect on the meaning of life, which is "43."

But the times we're living in, you can't try to help people anymore. First the National Organization of Bimbos tries to wipe Joe Bob off the face of the earth for saying I'm opposed to slapping women around like dead mackerels, unless it's necessary to the plot. Then ever Pentecostal preacher in Mississippi and all my fellow Babtists give me a "F" for writing the Gospel According to Joe Bob ("Life is a fern bar, let's get outta here"). All my Meskin friends in Corpus Christi turn against me, even though I love the Meskin people, specially the ones that sneak in. The Catholics write in about how my head should be blown off in a Christian manner. Lester Dimskim writes in cause I

called him "the stupidest Lester I ever met."

But I guess what hurts the most is when the Brothers turned against me. Me, the first guy to write about the Negro-dancing spin-on-your-head permanent-brain-damage musical. Me, the guy who watched *Roots* three times and learned to pronounce the ancient African term "colored people." Me, the guy who wrote a song for poor starving helpless nekkid black kids.

When 250 individuals of the black persuasion came down to the Dallas *Slimes Herald* and said, "No, we don't wanna go to the Fairmont Hotel where we can all see, we wanna do it the stupid way and crowd everbody in a little room where they explain the *Slimes Herald* dental insurance plan," which by the way is a pretty decent plan, I knew I was probly gonna die. Here are the protesters' demands:

Numero uno: "We want Joe Bob Briggs to become a black person."

Yea, they got me on that one. I never have done that.

Numero two-o: "Joe Bob Briggs wrote 'stupid Negroes' once and 'stupid white people' only TWICE in that column. We insist this inequality be corrected."

Hey, fair's fair.

Numero three-o: "We are not satisfied with the Slimes Herald *putting a notice on page one that said 'Joe Bob Briggs is the scum of the earth and we the high sheriffs want him turned into a Sunkist*

Tuna.' The Slimes Herald *needs to make him dead."*

You know, "dead" is one of those words that makes you stop and think. It made me stop and think, specially after I was dead.

Numero four-o: "We resent Joe Bob Briggs dedicating the proceeds from 'We Are the Weird' to the United Negro College Fund."

Okay, but a Negro mind is a terrible thing to waste.

Numero five-o: "Joe Bob Briggs has cooties."

Hey, I don't have to take that kind of remark.

In fact, there *is* something that makes me p.o.ed about all this. There's one thing the *Slimes Herald* did that is absolutely unforgivable. I'm sorry, I'm trying to forget it, but I just can't.

On Tuesday and Wednesday, when the *Slimes Herald* put me on the front page as an official racist and bigot, they put Henry Lee Lucas at the top of the page and *me* at the bottom. All Henry Lee did is say he's a mass murderer, *so what the heck is the explanation?*

I'm sorry, it bothers me. Sure, I can find other papers to print "Joe Bob Goes to the Drive-In." They *love* me in Grambling, Louisiana. But it won't be the same.

I wanna leave you with a few "miracle" facts of world history:

1. Lincoln and Kennedy were both assassinated on a Friday. Joe Bob was assassinated on a Tuesday. Makes you think.

2. Lincoln and Kennedy were both succeeded by a man named "Johnson." Joe Bob was killed by a high sheriff named Tom Johnson.

3. Lincoln and Kennedy put their pants on one leg at a time. Joe Bob puts his on two legs at a time.

4. Lincoln and Kennedy never could get a laugh either.

You know, there *was* other news in the world this week besides my death, so I'm gonna get on to more important stuff, like *Lust in the Dust,* the drive-in flick I *would* review except for I don't have no space left and I don't have no job. So let's just put it this way:

Four breasts. Fifteen dead bodies. One riot. One brawl. One gang-rape, with midget. Two quarts blood. One beast (Divine). Thigh crushing. Bullwhip fu. Nekkid bimbo-wrestling. Drive-In Academy Award nominations for Lainie Kazan, as a singing balloon, doing the hit song "Let Me Take You South of My Border"; Tab Hunter, for breathing; Paul Bartel, "Mr. Eating Raoul," who directed this baby; and, of course, Divine, the best 300-pound transvestite actor in Baltimore. Best nudie western since *Linda and Abilene.* Three stars. Joe Bob says check it out. So there. ■

Author's Bio Fu

Joe Bob Briggs was born in a place called Frontage Road, Texas, which sits somewhere in Krankaway County. He is America's foremost expert on drive-in movies—living *or* dead. Joe Bob rose from the dead and is currently syndicated through Universal Press Syndicate to dozens of diseased and deserving American communities, and he says that you'll have to pay for anything else you want to know about him.

Joe Bob is currently compiling the first complete and official history of the American drive-in. If you know of a dead drive-in, a drive-in about to die, or just wanna waste some time telling him about the drive-in of your dreams, or if you wanna discuss the meaning of life, or if you wanna send some disgusting stuff through the mail, or if you wanna be Joe Bob's fifth wife, you can write to:

> Joe Bob Briggs
> P.O. Box 33
> Dallas, TX 75221

You should also write Joe Bob at that address if you just want him to come to your town and be obnoxious there. It's what he does best.